THE PROFESSIONAL BARTENDER'S HANDBOOK

A Recipe for Every Drink Known— Including Tricks & Games To Impress Your Guests

Valerie Mellema

THE PROFESSIONAL BARTENDER'S HANDBOOK

A Recipe for Every Drink Known—Including Tricks & Games To Impress Your Guests

Copyright © 2007 by Atlantic Publishing Group, Inc.
1405 SW 6th Ave • Ocala, Florida 34471 • 800-814-1132 • 352-622-1875–Fax
Web site: www.atlantic-pub.com • E-mail: sales@atlantic-pub.com
SAN Number: 268-1250

ISBN-13: 978-0-910627-95-5   ISBN-10: 0-910627-95-9

Library of Congress Cataloging-in-Publication Data

Mellema, Valerie.
  The professional bartenders handbook : a recipe for every drink known - including tricks and games to impress your guests / By Valerie Mellema.

      p. cm.
  Includes bibliographical references and index.
  ISBN-13: 978-0-910627-95-5 (alk. paper)
  ISBN-10: 0-910627-95-9 (alk. paper)
  1. Bartending--Handbooks, manuals, etc. 2. Cocktails--Handbooks, manuals, etc. I. Title.

TX951.M3739 2007
641.8'74--dc22
                            2007016027

EDITOR: Tracie Kendziora • tkendziora@atlantic-pub.com
INTERIOR LAYOUT DESIGN: Vickie Taylor • vtaylor@atlantic-pub.com
COVER DESIGN: Angela C. Adams • aadams@atlantic-pub.com

Printed in the United States

Printed on Recycled Paper

We recently lost our beloved pet "Bear," who was not only our best and dearest friend but also the "Vice President of Sunshine" here at Atlantic Publishing. He did not receive a salary but worked tirelessly 24 hours a day to please his parents. Bear was a rescue dog that turned around and showered myself, my wife Sherri, his grandparents Jean, Bob and Nancy and every person and animal he met (maybe not rabbits) with friendship and love. He made a lot of people smile every day.

We wanted you to know that a portion of the profits of this book will be donated to The Humane Society of the United States.

–Douglas & Sherri Brown

THE HUMANE SOCIETY
OF THE UNITED STATES ©

The human-animal bond is as old as human history. We cherish our animal companions for their unconditional affection and acceptance. We feel a thrill when we glimpse wild creatures in their natural habitat or in our own backyard.

Unfortunately, the human-animal bond has at times been weakened. Humans have exploited some animal species to the point of extinction.

The Humane Society of the United States makes a difference in the lives of animals here at home and worldwide. The HSUS is dedicated to creating a world where our relationship with animals is guided by compassion. We seek a truly humane society in which animals are respected for their intrinsic value, and where the human-animal bond is strong.

Want to help animals? We have plenty of suggestions. Adopt a pet from a local shelter, join The Humane Society and be a part of our work to help companion animals and wildlife. You will be funding our educational, legislative, investigative and outreach projects in the U.S. and across the globe.

Or perhaps you'd like to make a memorial donation in honor of a pet, friend or relative? You can through our Kindred Spirits program. And if you'd like to contribute in a more structured way, our Planned Giving Office has suggestions about estate planning, annuities, and even gifts of stock that avoid capital gains taxes.

Maybe you have land that you would like to preserve as a lasting habitat for wildlife. Our Wildlife Land Trust can help you. Perhaps the land you want to share is a backyard—that's enough. Our Urban Wildlife Sanctuary Program will show you how to create a habitat for your wild neighbors.

So you see, it's easy to help animals. And The HSUS is here to help.

The Humane Society of the United States
2100 L Street NW
Washington, DC 20037
202-452-1100
www.hsus.org

CONTENTS

FOREWORD

By Dan Mackey
Director of The Pacific Bartending School

As a professional bartender and the owner of a bartending school, I have seen and tasted my share of poorly mixed drinks. For those experimenting in mixology in their own homes, this does not pose as much of a problem as it does for those tending bar in restaurants, nightclubs, and hotels.

Customers have little patience for a drink that is too weak, too strong, or improperly mixed. With this new addition to the bartending handbook genre, there is no longer an excuse for amateur mistakes.

The Professional Bartender's Handbook not only shares proper techniques for mixing and pouring, it also includes nearly 1,500 recipes, from the popular to the zany. The next time a customer orders a Biscuit Neck, you will be prepared!

The information in this book makes it an invaluable team member of any establishment that serves alcohol. Valerie Mellema has done an excellent job of explaining the different drinks, terminology, and service standards while also giving tips, measurements, and relevant insight that will prove helpful to any new or experienced bartender. I cannot wait to incorporate this book into my classes because of the abundant information it provides on a wide range of topics from serving to measuring to toasting. Without a doubt, this book will be a staple in my curriculum for years to come.

DAN MACKEY

The Pacific Bartending School
18010 Crenshaw Blvd.
Torrance, CA 90504
310-515-9002
http://www.pacificbartending.com

Dan Mackey grew up in a restaurant family and started tending bar at the age of 21. After finishing a course at a "national chain" bartending school, he soon discovered that he was completely unprepared for the real world. That is why Mackey opened The Pacific Bartending School in 2005. In addition, Mackey has served as a consultant for Skyy Vodka, House of Blues, and many TV & film production companies and has been featured in the L.A. Times and the San Francisco Chronicle. He has trained staff from a wide range of establishments, including the Four Seasons Hotels, Continental Airlines, Embassy Suites, Marriot, Hyatt, and Hilton Hotels.

INTRODUCTION

Bartenders are an American icon. Stereotypically, they will take their customer's side against the world or host the party for a celebration. An outstanding bartender can be his customer's psychologist, best friend, adviser, and concierge. The bartender knows the best places to eat and can prescribe the perfect drink to make any occasion better.

Bartenders are there for their customers. They want to provide the best service possible, and they strive to remember the names of the regulars.

Bartenders are expected to meld with patrons' ambience requirements: contagious fun, a delightful atmosphere "where everybody knows your name," quiet reflection, romance, "after work" cool down, or dance floor conviviality.

While being everything to everyone, bartenders these days are also held responsible for the behavior of their patrons once they leave the bar. This means preventing patrons from drinking so much that they injure someone or damage property, which can result in a lawsuit for the bar. One bartender said that the job of being a bartender means being able to tell who is drunk from who is stupid.

Aside from having the right personality, the best bartender is knowledgeable about the stock. This means being able to discuss whiskey, bourbon, and Scotch, for example, and knowing how to make drinks that taste good. Being a master mixologist means constantly changing and improving manner and drinks. Customers' preferences can help bartenders discover new ways of creating the same drink. Being a good bartender means learning the intricacies of bartending and what patrons prefer. That is where this book comes in, as it provides the best of the classic drinks and the best of the newest drinks.

CHAPTER 1:
ALL ABOUT LIQUOR, BEER, AND WINE

LIQUORS

Liquors come in a wide variety of flavors and styles. They are the basis for most cocktails and, if not measured properly, can make or break a good cocktail.

BOURBON

Bourbon is one of the most popular requests in a bar. Offering several different varieties and brands is beneficial, as people will order them by name. Bourbon is officially known as "America's Native Spirit," because of its origination in the Appalachian Mountains. The main ingredient is corn, at least 51 percent by law. Corn and the charred oak casks used for aging give this liquor its distinct flavor, bold but not mediciney, smooth and lingering.

Bourbons are available in a variety of ages. Distilleries age their bourbon on a range of timescales, using three to four years as a minimum and 20 years as a maximum. The longer the bourbon is aged the more complex the flavor will be and the more expensive the price.

POPULAR BOURBONS

There are numerous bourbons on the market today. Bourbon is available from several brands, including Jim Beam and Wild Turkey, that are easily found in many bars, restaurants, and liquor stores around the country.

STORAGE

Bourbon should be stored at room temperature and has a shelf life of about two years.

WHISKEY

Whiskey is available in several varieties, including Canadian, American, and Irish. A favorite of many, whiskey is produced in a similar manner to that of bourbon. The liquor gains its variety of flavors from the different types and quantities of grains used in its production. Whiskey is not regulated in the same manner as bourbon, nor are there requirements for its production. This allows whiskey to take on more complex flavors. Typically, whiskey is produced from wheat, rye, corn, malt, and rye malt. A sour mash is the most common mash used, although a sweet mash may be used as well. The distillation process is very much the same as that of bourbon and results in a very similar beverage.

AMERICAN WHISKEY

American whiskey is believed to have first been produced during the Revolutionary war. American whiskey was often made from rye and barley, as these were abundant during this era. As people began moving west, they began using corn to make whiskey. American whiskey is usually aged in charred oak barrels.

STRAIGHT WHISKEY

Straight whiskey is distilled from 51 percent of one type of grain. These grains include rye, corn, malt, malted rye, and wheat.

BLENDED WHISKEY

Forty-seven percent of whiskeys are blended and incorporate various types of grain with 47 percent being a single type of grain. Blended whiskey may also be blended with prune or peach juice, and even sherry. The blend often includes a grain spirit that has been aged in oak barrels. Popular brands include Barton Reserve and Imperial.

LIGHT WHISKEY

Light whiskey is made from a high percentage of corn. This whiskey is not aged in charred or previously used casks.

RYE WHISKEY

Rye whiskey is 51 percent rye. There are also blended ryes that contain neutral grain spirit or other types of whiskeys. Popular brands include Old Overholt, Jim Beam Rye, and Wild Turkey Rye.

TENNESSEE WHISKEY

Tennessee whiskey is made in Tennessee. This whiskey is also made from at least 51 percent of a single grain. Corn is the most common grain used. Popular brands include George Dickel of Tennessee Whiskey and Jack Daniel's Tennessee Sour Mash Whiskey.

CORN WHISKEY

Corn whiskey must be made from at least 80 percent corn and is aged in used or charred oak casks.

WHEAT, MALT, AND MALTED RYE WHISKEY

All of these whiskeys must contain at least 51 percent of wheat, barley malt, malt, or malted rye.

CANADIAN WHISKEY

Canadian whiskey is produced from the cereal grains of corn, wheat, rye, or barley. The percentages of grain used vary according to different distillers. All imported Canadian whiskeys are marked as blended in the United States because the Canadian government does not mandate specific percentages of grain. Popular brands include Black Velvet, Crown Royal, and Seagram's V.O.

IRISH WHISKEY

Irish whiskey is blended in a similar fashion to Scotch. The main difference in Irish whiskey is that the whiskey is distilled three times in a pot still. The whiskey becomes sweeter than Scotch and it is usually blended with whiskey from a continuous still as well. Single-malt Irish whiskey is made from malted barley; however, the whiskey that is blended with Irish whiskey can be made from unmalted barley, rye, corn, wheat, or oats. Irish whiskey is aged in used sherry casks for a minimum of five years. Popular brands include Bushmills, Connemara, and Kilbeggan.

STORAGE

Whiskey should be stored at room temperature and has a shelf life of about two years.

GIN

Gin was developed in the 17th century. The word gin comes from the Dutch word for juniper, which is also what gin smells like. A Dutch doctor blended alcohol with the juniper berries and prescribed the concoction to his patients with kidney ailments; however, it has been shown that gin does nothing for the kidneys.

DRY GIN

The majority of gin is dry gin, as it contains coriander seed. Several other flavorings may be used as well, including fennel, calamus root, orris root, angelica root, almond, cardamom, cassia, ginger, cinnamon, caraway seeds, licorice, orange peels, and lemon peels.

Botanicals are also used in the distillation process, giving the gin its smell and refreshing taste. These botanicals are suspended at the top of the still and the liquor is redistilled to absorb the flavors. Because dry gin is distilled twice, the gin requires more botanicals for the highly flavored liquor that is produced.

DUTCH GIN

Dutch gin is also known as "Holland's Gin" or "Genever Gin." Malt wine infused with juniper berry is the basis for this gin. The malt wine is made from malted barley, corn, and rye. The grains are boiled to produce wort. The wort is then fermented for a few days and then distilled in a pot still. The liquor is often distilled twice with botanicals in a different still. Some Dutch gins also have a coloring that is added to them at the end of the distillation process.

OLD TOM

Old Tom is native to England and is believed to be the gin used to make the original Tom Collins. Although rarely produced anymore, Old Tom was first distilled in the 18th century. Pubs used a sign with a carving of a tomcat and buyers would place their money in the cat's mouth. Customers would then hold their bottle under the leg and the bartender would dispense the appropriate amount of gin into their bottle.

PLYMOUTH GIN

Plymouth gin is produced by only one distiller, the Blackfriars Distillery, and is considered the traditional gin of the British Navy. The gin is completely unsweetened.

FLAVORED GIN

Flavored gins are relatively new products. Natural flavorings such as lime, lemon, or orange are added to them. The bottles are clearly marked as to what flavor the gin is.

POPULAR GINS

Gin is a staple in every bar; however, there are several popular gins, including Beefeater, Bombay, Gordon's, and Tanqueray.

STORAGE

Store unopened bottles in cool and dry places. After being opened, the bottle should have a shelf life of two years.

RUM

Rum is distilled from sugar cane and can be bought in the light and dark varieties. The liquor has been exported out of the Caribbean for hundreds of years. The islands became the main producers of sugar cane and began producing rum, which would eventually play an important factor in global economics.

Rum is distilled from molasses, a syrup that is produced by boiling sugar cane. Crude rum is around 130 to 180 proof. Aged two to 10 years, the aging process determines the type of rum produced. The dark variety is aged in charred oak casks, and caramel is often added to change the color. Rum that is aged in stainless steel casks remains colorless and clear. The majority of dark rum is produced in Jamaica, Haiti, and Martinique.

Rum that is aged for a year produces a light-bodied and dry variety. Amber and golden varieties are aged for at least three years and have caramel added to them for color. Rum that is aged over six years is called vieux or liqueur.

VIRGIN ISLANDS RUM

The Virgin Islands produces dry, light bodied rum.

DEMERARAN RUM

Demeraran Rum is produced in Guyana and features a very dark color with a medium body. This rum is bottled at a very high alcohol content — 151 proof — and is traditionally used in a Zombie.

JAMAICAN RUM

This rum is produced from molasses and is generally full-bodied. The rum ferments for three weeks, is distilled in pot stills, and is then aged in oak casks for at least five years. The color is produced by the addition of caramel.

MARTINIQUE AND HAITIAN RUM

Distilled from the juice of sugar cane, this rum is aged in oak casks, which provides its color.

BATAVIA ARAK

This rum is aromatic and is produced on the island of Java. Molasses is placed in Javanese red rice and allowed to ferment. The rum is aged for three years in Java and is then shipped to Holland, where the rum is aged for up to six years.

AGUARDIENTE DE CANA

This is the name of most South American rums.

POPULAR BRANDS

Many individuals enjoy classic rum cocktails, making a popular rum a staple in any bar. With so many varieties available, there are often several types of rum kept behind the bar, including Angostura, Bacardi, Captain Morgan, and Royal Oak.

POPULAR FLAVORED RUMS

Popular flavored rums include Bacardi, Whaler's, and Malibu.

STORAGE

Store unopened bottles in cool and dry places. After being opened, the bottle should have a shelf life of two years.

SCOTCH WHISKEY

Scotch must be distilled in Scotland to be considered Scotch; however, it may be bottled in other countries. There are two types of Scotch: malt whiskey, which is made from barley, or grain whiskey, which is made from cereal grains. Malt whiskies are divided into four categories depending on where they are distilled.

Blended Scotch is made with both a malt whiskey and a grain whiskey. These liquors account for 95 percent of Scotch sales. Single malt Scotch whiskey is made from one type of malt and is not blended with other malts or grains. There are now about 50 different types of blended Scotch whiskies.

POPULAR BLENDED SCOTCH WHISKIES

Most bars have at least a couple bottles of Scotch on hand. The liquor has seen a resurgence and those who love Scotch will find a wide variety available in most bars, including Ballantine, Cutty Sark, and Johnny Walker.

POPULAR SINGLE-MALT SCOTCH

A bar without a single-malt Scotch just is not a complete bar. A good bar will have at least one single-malt Scotch on hand. Glenlivet is perhaps the most common; however, there are several popular brands available, including Aberlour, Glenfiddich, and Macallan.

STORAGE

Store unopened bottles in cool and dry places. After being opened, the bottle should have a shelf life of two years.

TEQUILA & MEZCAL

The origins of tequila can be attributed to the Aztecs as early as 1000 A.D. This culture produced a milky drink called pulque, produced from the agave plant.

POPULAR TYPES OF TEQUILA

When the shots start, tequila is bound to make an appearance. Tequila is used in a wide assortment of cocktails as well and a well-stocked bar should have at least one gold and one white to suit the tastes of their patrons. Popular brands include Jose Cuervo and Patron.

MEZCAL

Mezcal is also made from the agave plant, but with a different process than tequila. Mezcal is made exclusively in Oaxaca, and features a high potency and smoky flavor. Many believe that the drink also has medicinal purposes. Tribal women drink mezcal to help withstand the pain of childbirth, as the drink is much stronger than Tequila. Laborers and workers drink mezcal, believing it will give them strength.

Worms live in the agave plant, which is harvested during the rainy summers in Tequila. The worms are often stored in the mezcal, then drained, sorted, and placed in the bottles. The worm is a symbol of the agave plant and there are many legends that state that the worm gives strength to the brave soul that gulps it down. Legend also states that the worm is an aphrodisiac. It must be noted, however, that the drink and the worm are an acquired taste.

POPULAR BRANDS OF MEZCAL

Mezcal is rarely found in bars, but there are several popular brands to choose from when adding to one's home bar, including Gusano Rojo Mezcal and Monte Alban.

STORAGE

Store unopened bottles in cool and dry places. Even after being opened, the bottles of both tequila and mezcal will last for many years.

VODKA

Vodka is the national liquor of Russia and other Slavic countries. Vodka is a clear and flavorless liquor, which has been produced in these countries for over 600 years. The drink is easily recognized because of its lack of smell, color, and taste.

GOLD VODKA

Starka is a gold vodka that is aged in wine casks for about ten years.

PEPPER VODKA

This drink is known as Pertsovka and is infused with cubeb, cayenne, and capsicum. This vodka was invented by Peter the Great, who greatly enjoyed pepper in his vodka.

YUBILEYNEYA OSOBAYA

This is another classic flavored vodka, but it has honey and brandy added for a unique flavor.

OKHOTNICHYA

These vodkas are infused with a collection of herbs.

FLAVORED VODKAS

Flavored vodkas are becoming increasingly popular. They are made with a variety of natural flavorings. Approximately 30 different flavors of vodka are currently on the market and more are introduced every year.

More and more bars are featuring flavored vodkas. They allow more room for creativity when putting a twist on old cocktail favorites, such as vanilla vodka and Coke. Popular brands include Absolut, SKYY, Smirnoff, and Stoli.

POPULAR VODKA BRANDS

Most bars carry a wide variety of different vodkas, and well-stocked bars have about three or four different vodkas, including Absolut, Belvedere, Grey Goose, and Ketal One.

STORAGE

Vodka should be stored in either the freezer or refrigerator. Because of its high alcohol content, vodka will not freeze. A refrigerated bottle of vodka or one that is stored in a cool, dry place will have a shelf life of at least three years.

BRANDY

Many countries that produce wine also produce brandy. The liquor is made by distilling wine or fruit, then allowing it to age in oak barrels. Brandies tend to differ from country to country and their flavors and style will vary depending on the soil, the climate, the grapes, the distillation process, and the blending.

AMERICAN BRANDY

Spanish missionaries brought brandy to California over 200 years ago. The climate, soil, and water in California were perfect for making brandy, especially in the San Joaquin Valley. This area produces the largest amount of American Brandy. California Brandy is aged at least two years.

POPULAR AMERICAN BRANDIES

Different bars will offer varying types of brandy. Many bars may only carry one or two brandies, but they tend to be of the popular variety, such as Christian Brothers and Korbel.

FRUIT BRANDY

There are several fruit flavored brandies that are classified as cordials. These are normally over 70 proof. Sugar, natural colorings, and other flavors are added. Flavors include apricots, bananas, coffee, and peaches. Popular brands include Calvados and Kirsche.

STORAGE

Unopened bottles should be stored away from sunlight. Opened bottles can last up to three years and does not age in the bottle.

COGNAC AND ARMAGNAC

Cognac and Armagnac are both types of brandies that are named after their regions of production, much like the wines of France.

Cognac labels have many different designations. These designations refer to the age of the Cognac. Every major brand produces Cognacs that have been aged for different amounts of time. The age marked on the labels is the age of the youngest cognac that was blended in the mix.

- **V.S. (Very Superior) or Three Stars:** aged less than four and a half years
- **V.S.O.P. (Very Special Old Pale):** aged between four and a half and six and a half years.
- **X.O. (Extremely Old), Napoleon, Hors d'age, V.S.S.O.P.,**

Cordon Bleu, Grand Reserve and Royal: aged five and a half years and up to 40 years.

- **Grand Fine Champagne or Grande Champagne:** Identifies cognacs made exclusively from grapes grown in the Grande Champagne region of Cognac, France.

- **Petite Fine Champagne or Petite Champagne:** Identifies cognacs made from grapes grown in the Grande Champagne and Petite Champagne regions of Cognac, France.

POPULAR BRANDS OF COGNAC

Cognacs are not common in all bars. If a bar does carry Cognac, it will most likely be a popular brand, such as Courvoisier, Hennessy, or Remy Martin.

ARMAGNAC

Armagnac is not as well known as Cognac, but it is actually France's oldest brandy. Armagnac has been produced continuously since the 15th century, distilled from white wine grown in the Armagnac region of France.

Like Cognac, Armagnac labels are also regulated by French laws:

- **V.S. or Three Stars:** Youngest brandy in blend is two years old

- **V.O. (Very Old), V.S.O.P. (Very Special Old Pale), and Reserve:** Youngest brandy is four and a half years old

- **Extra, Napoleon, X.O., Vieille Reserve:** Youngest brandy is five and a half years old.

Popular brands include Sempe, Janneau, and Armagnac Lapostelle X.O.

STORAGE

If stored in a cool, dry place, the open bottle should last for two years.

APERITIFS, CORDIALS, AND LIQUEURS

Aperitifs, cordials, and liqueurs have a variety of uses. They can be used as mixers, after dinner drinks, floaters, or aperitifs. The aperitif is the "appetizer" of liquors; they are often enjoyed prior to the meal as a starter drink. Low in alcohol content, they may have a mild to sweet flavor. Many cordials and liqueurs are versatile and fall into the aperitif category as well.

POPULAR APERITIFS

Part of the regular stock of a bar, aperitifs allow bartenders to add fruitful flavors without losing the strength of the cocktail itself. Many aperitifs are consumed straight or as mixers. Popular brands include Dubonnet, Pernod, and Jaegermeister.

Cordials and liqueurs are essentially the same. The names are used interchangeably depending on the country. Those that are sold in the United States are 35 percent sugar. Crèmes and fruit flavored brandies are also available. The high sugar content is what makes these creamy. Many cordials exist and it is impossible to list them all. Popular brands include Absinthe, Amaretto, Anisette, Blue Curacao, Cointreau, Galliano, Goldschlager, Kahlua, Midori, Sambuca, Southern Comfort, and Triple Sec.

STORAGE

Store unopened bottles in a cool, dry place and out of direct sunlight. Many are best if they are kept chilled. An opened bottle should have a shelf life of three years.

BEER

Beer is fermented and brewed from rice, barley, corn, hops, water, and yeast. This popular beverage began in Egypt and has remained popular for thousands of years. There are thousands of different brews available throughout the world; the United States alone is home to over 900 microbrews that are made by small and independent brewers, as well as large breweries. Germany, a country of beer lovers, has over 1,200 breweries.

There are several different types of beers to choose from, with many sounding familiar, although the differences between them may not be easily discernible. Many people prefer one type of beer. Some may like a dark bock while others prefer the flavor of ale. The following list will help to differentiate among the choices.

- **Ale**
  - Top fermented beer
  - Higher alcohol content with the flavor of hops; slightly bitter
- **Bitter**
  - Strong ale
  - Usually an English beer
  - Normal alcohol content with a bittersweet taste
- **Bock**
  - Dark, strong, and slightly sweet
  - Brewed from caramelized malt
- **Ice**
  - Brewed at colder than normal temperatures
  - Chilled below freezing until ice crystals form
  - The crystals are filtered and leave a smoother tasting beer with a slightly higher alcohol content
- **Lager**
  - Bottom fermented beer
  - Stored at very cold temperatures for several months
  - Lager is German for "to store"
- **Lambic**
  - Belgium brewed beer
  - Ingredients include peaches, raspberries, cherries, and wheat
- **Light**
  - Fewer calories and less alcohol
- **Malt Liquor**
  - Fermented at high temperatures
  - Higher alcohol content
  - Pilsner
  - Light, hoppy, and dry lager
- **Sake**
  - Brewed from rice
  - Served warm or at room temperature
- **Stout**
  - Ale that is produced from heavily roasted barley
  - Darker in color and slightly bitter

- **Trappist**
  - Belgium or The Netherlands by Trappist Monks
  - High alcohol content
  - Dark in color

- **Wheat**
  - Wheat
  - Garnished with a lemon and sometimes raspberry syrup

STORAGE

In the U.S., beer is served at 40 degrees Fahrenheit. Beer should be stored away from sunlight and most beers now have dated labels listing the date they were brewed, as well as their expiration. Skunked beer results from direct sunlight exposure and ruins the beer. Storing beer below 40 degrees will cause the beer to have a dull taste.

WINE

For some bartenders, wine can be quite mysterious. Not many bartenders are familiar with the technicalities of wine, such as its production, storage, and proper serving procedure. All bars should have a decent wine selection, even if it means ordering only the most common and affordable wines. Avoid serving box wine because it not only looks tacky behind the bar, but shortcuts are taken during its production. A bartender that is able to provide customers with good, basic information on wine will soon earn respect.

WINE STORAGE

There are several methods to keeping wine fresh. Storing the wine properly prevents it from becoming oxidized and acquiring a vinegar taste. Throw out the wine after four days because it will not have the same taste and great flavor that it had when first opened.

The best place to store wine is in a dark area away from natural and constant, artificial light. The area should also be slightly damp, as the corks may become dry and ruin. The storage area should be well ventilated, free of vibrations, and kept at a constant temperature. Many bars and restaurants may not be able to achieve this if they do not have their own cellar or storage area. They may also store their open bottles in refrigerators at night. While this procedure is suitable for white wines and some hardier wines such as Chiantis, it will greatly reduce the quality of Cabernet Sauvignon.

The best temperature for red wine is 50 to 55 degrees Fahrenheit. The wine can get a little cooler or warmer, but it is important that the temperature remains consistent. Most wines are also stored horizontally; Port, sherry, Madeira, Marsala, Vermouth, Dubbonet, and Byrrh are not.

To store open bottles, it may be wise to invest in a vacuum system, gas system, or gas/temperature system. A vacuum system is the most affordable, costing between $15 and $25, and may keep wine up to three days. Gas systems are a little higher priced and may keep the wine good for six days. After day four, however, the wine may begin to decline. Gas/temperature systems may keep the bottle up to two weeks. These systems reseal the bottle with gas and offer climate control for each individual bottle. These units cost around $200, but the gas will need to be replaced, adding to the expense. Restaurant owners might consider giving wine that is three or four days old to the kitchen where it can be used to cook for up to two weeks.

FRENCH WINE

France divides its wines into four different categories. There are two table wine categories called Vin de Table, and Vin de Pays. A Vin de Table wine label shows only the producer and French designation. The Vin de Pays wine label shows the specific region of France in which the wine was produced. The Quality Wine Produced in a Specific Region (QWPSR) wines are divided into two categories called Vin Delimite de Qualite Superieure (VDQS) and Appellation d'Origne Controlee (AOC). The AOC category demands many restrictions on the grape varieties and winemaking methods, while the VDQS category is not as strict and is rarely used. French law also prohibits wines being labeled according to grape type, which may make it difficult for American wine consumers who generally know wines by their grape type and not by their region. This puts French wine producers at a disadvantage in foreign markets unless the consumer is knowledgeable about French regions and production locations.

There are several popular wine regions in France, each known for its own varietals These include Alsace, Beaujolais, Bergerac, Bordeaux, Bourgogne, Loire Valley, Rhone Valley, Languedoc, and Roussillon.

WINE PRESENTATION

Wine presentation may vary from restaurant to restaurant and from bar to bar. For those people who are new to wine and dining, there is a simple presentation that works for casual and formal events.

When serving a party, present the chosen bottle to the host. Ask the host to verify the bottle and ensure that the correct wine has been received. Use a wine key or foil remover to remove the foil. Take care to remove the foil from the table. Carefully cut the foil around the lip of the bottle, removing only the cap of the foil. Make sure that there are not any pieces that may fall into the bottle.

Place the tip of the corkscrew in the middle of the cork and twist the corkscrew in until there is only one turn of the corkscrew left. Move the wine key so that the metal part is placed firmly on the lip of the bottle. Support this part of the wine key with the thumb. Push the lever up and the cork will come out. Near the end of the cork, work the cork out of the bottle so that they cork does not pop; the bottle should only sigh as it releases the air.

Next, pour approximately one ounce into the host's glass. The host may swirl, sniff, and sip. When pouring the wine, end the pour in a twisting motion to avoid any spilling. Once the host verifies that the wine is good, proceed to fill the glasses of the guests at the table. Moving from the host in a clockwise fashion, pour approximately three ounces of wine in the glasses of the women at the table. After this is done, fill the glasses of the men at the table in a counterclockwise fashion.

Place the bottle in front of the host with the label facing the host. Refill glasses as the party progresses unless otherwise requested. A casual party may refill their own glasses.

Many bars and restaurants also serve wine by the glass, which can come in a variety of sizes. Taster boards are also very popular and allow customers to sample five different wines which will amount to about two and a half glasses.

WINE AND FOOD PAIRINGS

Wine can be more enjoyable when consumed with a meal. Most people are familiar with the old adage "red wine goes with red meat, white wine goes with white meat." This is a good guideline for beginning wine drinkers and servers. Red wines, however, may go great with certain types of fish and white meat that are prepared in different ways. Personal preference is also important when pairing wine with food. If a customer likes Merlot, sell them a nice Merlot regardless of whether or not they are eating chicken or shrimp.

A beginning wine server may choose to examine the backs of the wine bottles. Useful information can be found here, especially what the vintner recommends eating with the wine. Another good guideline is to match the quality of wine with the quality of food.

WINE	PAIRINGS
Cabernet Franc	Steak, poultry, desserts, pasta
Cabernet Sauvignon	Steak, poultry, pork, and pasta
Chianti	Almost anything
Merlot	Almost anything, except seafood
Pinot Noir	Steak, pasta, and lamb
Sangiovese	Steak and poultry
Zinfandel	Steak, poultry, and pasta

Most red wines will pair well with steak; however, certain red wines will complement steaks in their own way.

WINE	PAIRINGS
Chardonnay	Seafood, poultry, pork, and pasta
Gewurztraminer	Steak, poultry, pork, and pasta
Pinot Blanc	Steak, poultry, pork, desserts
Pinot Gris (Pinot Grigio)	Steak, fish, and desserts
Rieslings	Steak, fish, pork, poultry, pasta, desserts
Sauvignon Blanc	Fish, poultry, pork, and veal

White wines pair well with most white meats; however, Chardonnay may also go well with red meats. Remember that personal preference is a good way to pair wine with meals.

WINE	PAIRINGS
Champagne, Sparklings	Fish, desserts, and pasta
Port	Desserts
Sherry	Desserts, Steak, Lamb

WINE AND CHEESE PAIRINGS

Pairing wine and cheese is a long standing French tradition. While wine is almost always better with food, not all circumstances will allow for this; for example, a party or a small get-together. A good idea is to prepare several different cheeses that guests can enjoy with their wine. Matching the right cheeses to the wine will complement the wine. These pairings, like food pairings, are also personal preference.

WINE	PAIRINGS
Cabernet Franc	Sharp Cheddars
Cabernet Sauvignon	Sharp Cheddar, Parmesan
Chiantis	Hard Cheeses (Parmesan)
Merlots	Sharp Cheddars
Pinot Noirs	White Cheeses (Swiss)
Sangiovese	Creamy Cheeses (Brie)
Zinfandels	Blue Cheese or Gorgonzola
Chardonnay	Creamy Cheeses
Pinot Blanc	Creamy Cheeses

WINE	PAIRINGS
Sauvignon Blanc	Creamy Cheeses, Mozzarella, Goat
Rieslings	White Cheeses
Gewurztraminer	White Cheeses
Pinot Gris (Pinot Grigio)	Cheddars (Not Sharp)
Champagne, Sparklings	Creamy Cheeses
Ports	Blue Cheese
Sherry	Blue Cheese

Most of these red wines will pair well with sharp cheddars as well. Red wines are very versatile when it comes to pairing with cheeses, so feel free to experiment. Personal preference on cheeses definitely will influence decisions as it does not make sense to serve what will not be enjoyed.

HOW TO TASTE WINE

Most bartenders have seen the "swirl, sip, and sniff" routine. But many bartenders do not actually know what these wine connoisseurs are doing.

Tasting wine requires many senses. Begin by examining the wine. Look at the wine and notice its color, texture, and clarity. Swirl the glass to see how the wine clings to the glass. If the wine is a blush, it is most likely light-bodied and will not cling to the sides of the glass. On the other hand, a Merlot may cling and come down in stripes or "legs." This means that the wine is medium-bodied. A nice full-bodied Cabernet Sauvignon will cling to the glass and come down the sides in a full sheet.

Next, smell the wine. Take a deep breath. Swirl the glass again and smell once more. New aromas may arise after swirling the wine. This is called the wine's bouquet.

Finally, taste the wine. Take a mouthful and swirl the wine around in the mouth. Allow the wine to coat the tongue and palate. Take note of the texture, flavor, and acidity. Swallow the wine and consider the taste or the after taste. Think about whether the taste lingers or has an effect on the throat. If the wine left a dry taste, almost like tea or walnut, the wine is dry. Experienced wine tasters may notice interesting flavors; for example, some, may find a hint of chocolate in a Cabernet Sauvignon. It generally takes practice to experience the different flavors; however, inexperienced wine tasters may notice different fruit flavors. The most important question to ask is, "Would you like to drink more of the wine?"

Attending a wine tasting is a great way to learn about the different flavors of wines. The professionals can help customers discern the different flavors that they taste. Bartenders should also hold their own wine tasting with someone who knows wines well, perhaps a local vintner. This will enable bartenders to describe wins to their customers.

WINE GLASSES

The type of glass that wine is served in may have a dramatic effect on the wine's flavor and quality.

Restaurants and bars tend to hurt their wine by using all-purpose glasses that are washed and used over and over again. These glasses may be washed in a high heat dishwasher or hand washed by the bartender. Either way, the glasses will pick up odors that are present in the restaurant. The glasses may contain soapy residues and may have been stored in closed closets or cardboard boxes. All of these factors will have a great impact on the way a wine tastes.

Bars and restaurants need to ensure that glasses are stored properly. Depending on where they are stored, the wine glasses may have absorbed a variety of different kitchen or bar odors that may not be noticed until the wine has already been poured. Be sure to rinse glasses, decanters, and carafes in unchlorinated water or mineral water. Glasses may also contain soap residue and it is important to rinse it away. Exhaling into the glass and fogging it up will help to vaporize any soap or invisible residue that is in the glass.

Each type of wine has a corresponding glass. The bowl and mouth of each type of glass is suited to the type of wine that is to be consumed. For example, glasses for Rieslings have a large bowl and the lip of the glass flares out to allow the nose to enjoy the aromas of the wine. Investing in a specific type of glass should only be done if the intention is to enjoy one particular type of wine on a regular basis. These specific glasses will allow the wines to be enjoyed at their best.

SPARKLING WINES AND CHAMPAGNE

Dom Perignon, located in the Champagne region of France, produced the first sparkling wine in the 1600s. A method of bottling the wine that kept the carbon dioxide in the bottle was developed and the resulting product has bubbles when poured as the bottle is placed under extreme pressure.

Only sparkling wine that is made in Champagne can be called "champagne." The wine is made from a variety of grapes through a special process called method champenoise., which is complicated, costly, and time consuming. The typical champagne grapes are pinot noir, pinot meunier, and chardonnay.

The storage of Champagne and sparkling wines is very important. These wines should be stored in an area away from natural light, constant, artificial light, heat, vibrations, and severe temperature variations. Sparkling wines are ready for consumption as soon as they are purchased; however, many Champagne lovers will cellar their wine for a few years before consuming it.

Before serving Champagne and sparkling wines, chill them thoroughly but do not freeze them. Place them in a bucket filled with ice and water for 30 to 40 minutes before serving. While serving, be sure to place the bottle in a fresh ice bath to maintain its temperature. Bottles can also be chilled for several hours in the refrigerator, but this may cause the flavor to go flat because of the motor vibrations and the excessive cold. Bars and restaurants using walk-in refrigerators may not have to worry about vibrations, but excessive cold may be a factor.

Champagne and sparkling wines are best served in fluted glasses at 42 to 47 degrees Fahrenheit. Pour a small amount and allow the bubbles to settle before filling the glass about two-thirds full. Bubbles will continually rise in the glass.

To properly open a bottle of Champagne perform the following procedure:

1. Remove the foil and pull down the wire loop.
2. Drape a towel over the bottle.
3. Place a hand over the cork.
4. Loosen but do not remove the wire cage.
5. Grasp the cork and cage firmly with a hand and rotate the bottle, rather than the cork. The cork should come out on its own with only a slight sigh.

VERMOUTH

Most bartenders know vermouth as what is used when making a martini. Dry vermouth is used in making the martini, but vermouth has a much longer history.

Vermouth is classified as an aromatized wine, meaning it is flavored by botanicals including herbs, spices, flowers, roots, seeds, and fruit. Italy was the first country to produce vermouth in the late 1700s; this vermouth, red and sweet, was appropriately named "Italian." There are several styles of Vermouth, including Dry Vermouth, Bianco Vermouth, Sweet Vermouth, and Rose Vermouth.

STORAGE

Keep opened vermouth in the refrigerator. Bottles that are six months old should be thrown out and replaced. Like wine, vermouth will oxidize and ruin.

CHAPTER 2:
SETTING UP YOUR BAR

When setting up a bar, be certain that you have all of the bases covered. Public establishments should research what is popular in the area, especially liquor laws, and prepare appropriately. For example, if certain types of beer are popular, be sure to offer these beers by the bottle and on draft. For a large after work martini crowd, stock the bar with a variety of vodkas and gins along with the usual liquors. Talk with different bars in the area to see what they sell the most to gain a better idea of what should be offered.

The location of a bar plays a key role in how long it remains in business. Study other bars in the community to gain a better understanding of what works and what might not work. Once a location has been decided on, the next step is to design the inside of the bar. Design is important as it should not only attract customers, but should also allow bartenders and servers to work with ease. Bartenders will appreciate a large bar area that allows them to move around each other. Displaying the liquors allows guests to see what is carried and order quickly.

Refrigeration is essential for a good bar. Many drinks require refrigerated mixers, garnishes, and even eggs. There are many classic recipes that involve raw eggs and a discussion with a health inspector about regulations is important. Eggs need to be properly refrigerated to keep them from developing salmonella, which causes food poisoning. Fruit garnishes and other mixers will also need to be properly refrigerated, especially milk and many types of liquor and liqueurs.

Making drinks is a much easier task when the essentials are close at hand. Cabinets in a bar should not be too high, which will slow down the staff. There should also be a hand washing sink, a triple sink setup, and an all-purpose sink. Bartenders are generally busy and will sometimes need to dump mixing glasses. Bars that will have daiquiri machines will want to store them off the floor, if possible.

Cleaning supplies are essential and should be placed in a designated cabinet away from the beverages. Extra ashtrays, straws, stirrers, napkins, coasters, and other necessities may also be stored here.

Bars should also have a variety of glassware available. Back-ups of glassware should also be stored somewhere easy to access. Glasses will be dropped from time to time and may even crack, making extra glassware a necessity. Bar mats for jiggers and mixing glasses, as well as a holder for napkins and straws, are essential. Bartenders will appreciate a mixing area with a grate and drain so the excess liquor and mixers will easily drain.

Wells, which allow frequently used liquors and liqueurs to be easily accessed, are a necessity in public bars. These allow bartenders to have everything they need in front of them, making the bar run efficiently.

For those who plan to entertain at home, carefully consider the setup. A good rule of thumb is to keep the bar away from food and snacks to prevent everyone from gathering in one area. To get people to spread out and mingle, place snacks in various areas and locate the bar somewhere in between. Consider placing the cocktail bar in one area and the wine and beer in another. Many people prefer to keep their bar in the kitchen, which can be a good idea if a lot of liquids that require refrigeration are used. Also consider placing a small refrigerator in the bar area just for mixers. The placement of the bar will essentially depend on the setup of the house and how much space is available.

NECESSARY LIQUORS

Small Bar	Basement Bar
	The basics of a small bar plus:
Brandy, Cognac, or Gin	Anejo Rum
1 Light Rum	Armagnac
1 Dark Rum	Canadian Whiskey
Blended Scotch	Citrus Vodka
White Tequila	Gold Tequila
Vodka	Russian Vodka
Whiskey (Blended or Irish)	Single Malt Scotch
Bourbon	Spanish Brandy

LIQUEURS & CORDIALS

Small Bar	
Armaretto	Anisette
Cointreau or Triple Sec	Crème de Cacao (White & Dark)
Crème de Cassis	Crème de Menthe (White & Green)
Grand Marnier	Kahlua
Pernod or Ricard	Sambuca (White)

Basement Bar	
* The basics of a small bar plus:	
Applejack or Calvados	Bailey's Irish Cream
B & B	Benedictine
Chambord	Chartreuse (Green & Yellow)
Crème de Bananas	Crème de Noyaux
Curacao (White & Blue)	Drambuie

Basement Bar	
The basics of a small bar plus:	
Frangelico	Fruit Flavored Brandies
Galliano	Irish Mist
Kirsch	Maraschino Liqueur
Melon Liqueur	Primm's Cup
Rock & Rye	Sake
Sambuca (Opal Nera)	Schnapps (Peach & Peppermint)
Sloe Gin	Southern Comfort
Strega	Tia Maria
Tuaca	Vandermint

BEER

Small Bar	Basement Bar
	The basics of a small bar plus:
Lager	Ale
	Porter
	Stout

Beer taps should be located in an area that allows bartenders to easily access the kegs. These refrigerators are essential for keeping the beer cold. The best setup is either one that allows the kegs to stay in a refrigerated area behind the bar or one that allows the beer taps to sit above the refrigeration units. Kegs are very heavy, but the staff should be able to change them out on their own. Once empty, kegs can usually be returned to the vendor for refilling

WINE AND FORTIFIED WINES

Small Bar	Basement Bar
	The basics of a small bar plus:
Red Wine	Blush Wine
Sherry (Cream & Dry)	Port (Tawny & Ruby)
Vermouth (Sweet & Dry)	Rose Wine

Always try to use popular brand names when setting up a bar, especially a home bar. Guests will request specific liquors and will be impressed if they are available. When purchasing wines, make sure that the bottles will be finished to prevent the wine from going to waste.

MIXERS

- Ginger Ale
- Lemon-Lime soda (7-Up or Sprite)
- Cola or diet cola
- Tonic water
- Seltzer water or club soda
- Tomato juice or Bloody Mary mix or clamato juice
- Orange juice
- Pineapple juice
- Cranberry juice
- Grapefruit juice
- Lime juice (such as Rose's Lime)

- Lemon juice or lemon mix
- Sweet & sour mix (powdered or pre-made)
- Grenadine
- Coconut cream
- Fruit nectars (peach, pear, and apricot)
- Heavy cream
- Milk
- Half & Half
- Beef bouillon
- Mineral water
- Simple syrup

FRUITS AND GARNISHES

- Orange slices
- Cinnamon (sticks & ground)
- Maraschino cherries
- Lemon twists
- Lime and lemon wedges
- Apples

- Olives
- Cocoa powder
- Cocktail onions
- Coffee beans
- Cucumbers• Celery
- Eggs

- Bananas
- Berries
- Candies
- Celery seed
- Grapefruit
- Strawberries
- Cloves
- Fresh mint

OTHER NECESSITIES (MANY ARE OPTIONAL)

- Tabasco sauce
- Worcestershire sauce
- Angostura bitters
- Superfine sugar
- Salt and pepper
- Allspice
- Horseradish
- Nutmeg
- Old Bay seasoning
- Orange bitters
- Orange flower water
- Orange syrup
- Peach bitters
- Granulated sugar
- Peychaud's bitters
- Rose flower water
- Whipped cream
- Orgeat (almond syrup)
- Passion fruit juice

CUTTING FRUIT

Cocktails should have the appropriate garnishes. Most guests look forward to eating the olives in their martinis or the cherries in their Amaretto Sours. Fruit must be properly cut so that it can be used to garnish drinks.

LEMON TWISTS

1. Cut off both ends of the lemon.
2. Insert a sharp knife between the rind and fruit to separate them.
3. Cut the rind into strips.

There are special knives designed to cut twists as well. These knives appear to be a heavily serrated pairing knife, but instead have a small, hook-like indention. This indention will cut the right strip of rind off the whole piece of fruit.

SIMPLE SUGAR RECIPE

Ingredients:

• **3 cups water**   • **3 cups sugar**

Directions:

Heat water in a saucepan over medium to high heat. When water begins to simmer, add the sugar and stir until dissolved. Do not allow the mixture to boil. Remove the pan from the heat and set aside to cool to room temperature. Pour the simple syrup into a clean liquor bottle. Store in the refrigerator. Makes four cups or one quart.

ORANGE SLICES

1. Cut off both ends of the orange.
2. Cut across the orange to make wheels, much like when cutting a tomato.
3. Cut the wheels into fours to create four orange wedges.
4. Cut the orange at different thicknesses to make better garnishes.

LIME SLICES

1. Cut the ends off the lime.
2. Cut the lime in half.
3. Cut each half into half-moon shaped slices.

LEMON AND LIME WEDGES

1. Slice the lemon or lime in half the long way.
2. Cut each half into three wedges the long way.
3. These can be sliced into triangle shaped wedges if preferred.

PINEAPPLE WEDGES

1. Cut off the top and bottom of the pineapple.
2. Cut the pineapple in half from top to bottom.
3. Lay the pineapple down and cut it in half again.
4. Remove the core of the pineapple and cut it into quarters.
5. Cut the quarters into wedges.

Fresh squeezed juices are another way to liven up drinks and improve them. Guests will be impressed by fresh squeezed juices. Squeeze juices prior to opening the bar or prior to the party and store them in containers in the refrigerator.

Fruit trays are another necessity in bars. Various styles are available, but the best are made with stainless steel and allow fruit to stay cold and fresh all day and night. There are plastic variations, but these allow the ice bath to melt too quickly, and require periodic checks to ensure that the fruit is being kept at the appropriate temperature.

WINE

Wine needs to be properly stored in the bar. Reds should not be stored in the refrigerator, even while in storage, nor should they be stored in an area that will expose them to light or vibration. White wine should be stored in a temperature-controlled refrigerator. It is best if white wine is not exposed to vibration, but in some instances, this may be unavoidable. Restaurants and bars that intend to serve a fine line of wines should consider a preservation system that consists of inert gases, as well as a cellar that will create the best storage environment possible.

Bars not intending to sell a large variety of wine should instead stock up on a few good, affordable brands. Establishments keeping a small amount of bottles might consider investing in a hand pump system for the preservation of wines.

I HAVE EVERYTHING I NEED, BUT HOW MUCH LIQUOR DO I NEED TO BUY?

Those with bars in their homes should not be as concerned when it comes to stocking the bar. Simply make trips to the liquor store whenever necessary. Bars and restaurants, however, should set up some vendors. Vendors allow establishments to call in orders and may even offer delivery.

Bars and restaurants might consider setting up service through a local liquor store. Many of these stores will order liquor, which can then be picked up or delivered. Also consider contacting a distributor that carries a variety of different liquors and wines. Simply tell them what is needed and call to place a new order. This works in the same manner as beer. Most beer companies have sales representatives and distribution centers which allow for orders to be placed over the phone. Distributors will also service beer taps. Be aware that beer distributors are very competitive; they will often try to talk bars and restaurants into carrying something that is not necessarily needed.

PARS

To make ordering easy, determine how much of each different type of liquor is sold. These numbers are used so there is not an excess of inventory and everything will be fresh. Always keep at least one back-up bottle of every liquor; depending on location, consider carrying more than one back-up bottle. Talk to other bartenders to determine what they frequently sell to determine what brands to stock up on.

FOR A BASIC BAR

The following lists the essentials for a basic bar. With this layout most guests will be satisfied. Have the bar stocked with these at minimum, and have a back-up bottle of everything in storage.

Amount	Liquor
1-750 ml	Aperitif of your choice (Campari, Dubonnet, Lillet, etc.)
1-750 ml	Sparkling wine or Champagne
4-750 ml	White wine
2-750 ml	Red wine
1-750 ml	Dry vermouth
1-750 ml	Sweet vermouth
1-750 ml	Domestic or imported vodka
1-750 ml	Domestic or imported gin
1-750 ml	Rum
1-750 ml	Scotch
1-750 ml	Domestic or imported whiskey
1-750 ml	Bourbon
1-750 ml	Silver tequila
1-750 ml	Brandy or Cognac
3-750 ml	Cordials: Kahlua, Bailey's Irish Cream, Grand Marnier, Chambord, Triple Sec, Sambuca, Crème de Menthe, Frangelico, Amaretto, etc.
12 12-oz. Bottles	Domestic beers

FOR A MORE COMPLETE BAR

Take the basic bar setup and add the following:

Amount	Liquor
1-750 ml	Russian or imported vodka
1- 750 ml	Flavored vodka
1- 750 ml	Imported bottle of gin
1- 750 ml	Dark rum
1- 750 ml	Coconut-flavored rum
1- 750 ml	12 year old Scotch
1- 750 ml	Single-Malt Scotch

1-750 ml	Irish whiskey
1-750 ml	Canadian whiskey
1-750 ml	Tennessee whiskey
1-750 ml	Gold tequila
1-750 ml	V.S. or V.S.O.P. Cognac
1-750 ml	Imported bottle of Port
1-750 ml	Cream sherry
1-750 ml	Italian red wine
1-750 ml	French Bordeaux
1-750 ml	French Burgundy
1- 750 ml	California white
1-750 ml	French Champagne
2-750 ml	Additional Cordials such as Midori, Schnapps, Sloe Gin, etc
12 12-oz. Bottles	Imported beer

THE ULTIMATELY STOCKED BAR

Add the following to the basic and complete bars:

Amount	Liquor
1-750 ml	Flavored vodka
1-750 ml	Imported or super-premium domestic vodka
1-750 ml	15 year old bottle of single-malt Scotch
1-750 ml	V.S.O.P. Cognac
1-750 ml	Armagnac
1-750 ml	Imported brandy
1-750 ml	Dark rum
1-750 ml	Flavored rum (spiced, for example)
1-750 ml	Premium gold tequila
2-750 ml	Additional cordials
2-750 ml	Vintage imported Champagnes
2-750 ml	Domestic Champagne

2-750 ml	French Bordeaux
2-750 ml	French Burgundy
2-750 ml	Robust Italian red wine
2-750 ml	California white wine
2-750 ml	California red wine
1-750 ml	German white wine
6 12-oz. Bottles	Assorted microbrews

Be certain to have mixers in stock. Have at least one bottle of the following mixers; many bartenders prefer having a back up or two. These will also depend on what is popular in the area. For example, if gin and tonics are popular, be sure to have plenty of tonic water. Tonic and club soda are best if purchased in six-packs of small bottles because these will go flat and lose their carbonation very quickly if not used frequently.

BUYING FOR A PARTY

These charts will help determine how much liquor or wine will be needed for a party. These may also help establish pars, depending on the guest count. Most bars should avoid wine unless wine drinkers frequent the establishment.

Liquor	10-30 Guests	30-40 Guests	40-60 Guests	60-100 Guests
Liquor	10-30 Guests	30-40 Guests	40-60 Guests	60-100 Guests
White wine, domestic	4	4	6	8
White wine, imported	2	2	2	3
Red wine, domestic	1	2	3	3
Red Wine, imported	1	1	2	2

Liquor	10-30 Guests	30-40 Guests	40-60 Guests	60-100 Guests
Blush wine	1	2	2	2
Champagne, domestic	2	3	4	4
Champagne, imported	2	2	2	2
Vermouth, extra dry	1	1	2	2
Vermouth, sweet	1	1	1	1
Vodka	2	3	3	4
Rum	1	2	2	2
Gin	1	2	2	3
Scotch	1	2	2	3
Whiskey, American or Canadian	1	1	2	2
Bourbon	1	1	1	1
Irish whiskey	1	1	1	2
Tequila	2	2	2	3
Brandy/ Cognac	1	2	2	3
Aperitifs (choice)	1	1	2	2
Cordials (choice)	3	3	3	3
Beer (12 oz.)	48	72	72	96
Total Cost	$450-$550	$550-$625	$625-$725	$725-$800

This chart allows for one and three-fourth ounces per drink. When in doubt, consult a local bartender and vendors for popular suggestions.

Product	10-30 Guests	30-40 Guests	40-60 Guests	60-100 Guests
Product	10-30 Guests	30-40 Guests	40-60 Guests	60-100 Guests
Soda (2 liters)				
Club soda	3	3	4	5
Ginger ale	2	2	2	3
Cola	3	3	3	4
Diet cola	3	3	3	4
Lemon-lime soda	2	3	3	4
Tonic water	2	2	3	3
Juices (quarts)				
Tomato	2	2	3	3
Grapefruit	2	2	3	3
Orange	2	2	3	3
Cranberry	2	2	3	3
Miscellaneous Items				
Ice (trays)	10	15	20	30
Napkins (dozen)	4	4	6	8
Stirrers (1,000/box)	1	1	1	1
Angostura bitters (bottles)	1	1	1	2
Cream of coconut (cans)	1	2	2	2
Grenadine (bottles)	1	1	1	2
Horseradish (small jars)	1	1	1	2
Lime juice (bottles)	1	1	1	2
Lemons	3	4	5	6
Limes	2	3	3	4
Maraschino cherries (jars)	1	1	1	1
Olives (jars)	1	1	1	1
Oranges	1	2	2	3
Milk (quarts)	1	1	1	2
Mineral water (1 liter)	2	3	4	5
Superfine sugar (boxes)	1	1	1	1
Tabasco sauce	1	1	1	1

Product	10-30 Guests	30-40 Guests	40-60 Guests	60-100 Guests
Worcestershire sauce (bottles)	1	1	1	1
Total Cost	$45-$50	$50-$60	$60-$70	$70-$80

BEER MEASUREMENTS

Barrel Size	Gallons	Equivalent Measurements
1 barrel of beer	31 gallons	13.8 cases of 12-oz. bottles or cans
½ barrel of beer	15.5 gallons	1 keg
¼ barrel of beer	7.75 gallons	½ keg
$1/_8$ barrel of beer	3.88 gallons	¼ keg

DRINKS PER BOTTLE

Serving Size	750 ml Bottle	1-Liter Bottle	1.75- Liter Bottle
1 oz.	25	33	59
1 ¼ oz.	20	27	47
1 ½ oz.	17	22	39

PORTION CONTROL

FREE POURING

The majority of bars do not allow their bartenders to free pour. If the count is off, then there is a good chance that drinks are being sold with too much liquor. Those interested in learning to free pour at home can use the following method.

Take an empty liquor bottle and fill it with water. Place a speed pourer on the top of the bottle and take a jigger that is equal to one and a half ounces. Begin pouring the water into the jigger and count as this is being done. Find a comfortable pace. Consistency in the count will come with practice. Practice filling the jigger until a comfortable pace and rhythm is found. Next, try filling a glass with one and a half ounces of water. Pour the glass into the jigger to check the accuracy of the pour. Do this until confident with pouring the water consistently.

COUNTING SYSTEMS

There are various counting systems in use in bars. These vary in prices and are great for inventory control. To dispense liquor with these systems, pick up the bottle with its pourer, insert the pourer into the activator ring and pour. The ring recognizes the pourer and dispenses the proper amount of liquor with each tilt of the bottle. The metal rings on the pourers tell the activator which liquor it is, as well as the price and type of liquor. These are great for keeping track of how much liquor is sold and how much liquor was poured. They also help prevent bartenders from giving away free drinks because all liquor is accounted for when this system is used.

BAR ENTERTAINMENT

The setup of the bar extends beyond what is behind the bar. Having an inviting atmosphere that guests will enjoy is important. Many small bars do not look like much, but the servers and bartenders are friendly and are the reason that people visit. The atmosphere and the staff of a bar will essentially make it or break it.

Televisions are a key part of any bar. People love to go to the bar and watch a game. This means that the bar needs to have cable and satellite to guarantee all available games can be viewed. Many bars have multiple televisions with each one featuring a different game or news channel. Televisions give people something to talk about, especially if a big football game, NASCAR race, or baseball game is on.

A jukebox is also essential to a bar and should be stocked with a variety of music from rock to alternative, country, pop, eighties, classic rock, and more. Jukeboxes vary from simple to extravagant and many high-tech varieties are available that feature downloading capabilities, allowing guests to download their favorite songs and music.

There should be plenty of space at the bar top. The bar top should have several bar stools so that individuals can have a seat at the bar and can chat with the bartender or servers. For groups, provide tables of varying sizes where friends can gather and hang out.

Dartboards and pool tables are also very popular. Pool has always been a popular bar game and pool tables are part of the American bar tradition. Other games that people enjoying playing while hanging out and enjoying drinks are cards, poker, and dominoes.

CHAPTER 3:
TOOLS OF THE TRADE

There are various tools that are necessities in a bar, from professional grade blenders to muddles and wine keys. Some tools are necessary for making specific types of drinks, while others are used in many different drink recipes. Having the right tools will make a bartender's job a lot easier.

BAR NECESSITIES

- Long bar spoon
- Can/bottle opener (church key)
- Champagne bucket
- Cocktail napkins
- Cutting board
- Measuring cup
- Muddler

- Corkscrew (your preference, either a waiter's key, winged version, mounted version, or rabbit-ear version)
- Covered cocktail shaker
- Juice extractor
- Toothpicks or plastic swords for garnishes
- Strainer
- Wine chillers

- Professional grade electric blender (worth the money)

- Ice bucket and scoop optional for bars and restaurants)

- Lemon/lime squeezer

- Martini pitcher (optional for bars and restaurants)

- Jiggers/measuring shot glasses

- Measuring spoons

- Pairing knife

- Carafes

- Towels

- Punch bowl and glasses (home bar)

- Lime juice/salt/sugar tray for garnishing glasses

- Seltzer bottle

- Shaker set (metal tumblers and a glass that fits - several will come in handy)

- Speed pourers (necessity for bars and restaurants)

- Straws

- Swizzle sticks

GLASSWARE

Most bars have begun to favor all-purpose glasses. However, guests will be impressed if specialized glasses are used.

DIFFERENT TYPES OF WINE GLASSES

- **Balloon glasses:** These glasses range from nine to 14 ounces and are great for red wines because it allows them to breathe. They are also good as "up-sellers."
- **Red wine:** Not as large as the balloon glass, but wider for red wines. They help the bouquet of the wine meet the nose.
- **Champagne flutes:** A must if Champagne is going to be sold. This is the only type of glass, other than Champagne saucers, in which champagne should be served.
- **Champagne saucers:** Allow bubbles to escape more readily.
- **Tulip-shaped glasses:** These glasses are appropriate for white wines and dessert wines such as Rieslings.

- **Sherry:** These glasses complement sherry wines, but may be used for cordials or liqueurs as well.
- **All-purpose glasses:** Work with both white and red wines. These are appropriate when a limited wine list is offered and wine is not the main focus.
- **Carafes:** Bottles of wine are poured into carafes, allowing them to breathe. These are great if half carafes are offered on the wine list or if magnum-sized bottles are used.

Different types of glasses are intended for specific types of wines. For example, pinot glasses, which help to send the wine to a specific part of the palate and help to increase the bouquet, are available. These glasses allow the wine to breathe in a manner that complements the wine.

BAR GLASSES

Although there are a variety of glasses for use in bars, many establishments tend to stick to the basics and serve the majority of their cocktails in the same types of glasses. Some bars may carry specialty glasses for beers. This is becoming increasingly popular in Europe because the beer distributors and companies want to see their beers sold in the proper glasses. Each type of beer has its own style of glass which is designed to complement the beer.

- **Beer goblet:** Stemmed beer glass that is similar to the balloon wine glasses but larger. These hold about 12 ounces.
- **Beer mug:** Self-explanatory.
- **Pilsner:** These are tall beer glasses. Some people believe that they make the beer go flat quickly, while others like them because they are stylish and make the bubbles visible.
- **Pint glass:** These glasses are very versatile. Not only do they hold a pint of beer, but they can also be used for tall mixed drinks.
- **Cocktail:** Basic glass for "straight-up" drinks. Ranges in size from three to six ounces. The larger sizes can be used for frozen drinks and the four and a half ounce size can be used

for martinis and Manhattans. These are stemmed, which prevent warming of the liquid.

- **Collins:** These glasses are used for Collins drinks, as well as more exotic drinks such as fizzes, Mai Tais, Singapore Slings, and different variations of the Long Island Iced Tea. They are good for drinks that require a little more room than the highball glass.
- **Double rocks:** These are intended for larger drinks that are served "on the rocks"
- **Goblets:** These are great for tropical drinks such as blends, daiquiris, and other frozen drinks. Available in 22-ounce hurricane versions, which are used for large drinks.
- **Highballs:** These are good for standard drinks such as Jack & Coke or screwdrivers.
- **Martini:** Extremely similar to the cocktail glass, but they have more of a "V" shape. They range in sizes.
- **Hot drink mug:** These are stylish glass coffee mugs with a handle. They are great for lattes, and Irish coffees.
- **Parfait:** These are used for drinks that contain ice cream, such as a Mudslide, as well as specialty drinks that contain fruit.
- **Pony (cordial):** These are usually used for liqueurs and brandies.
- **Pousse-Café:** This is a specialty glass designed for drinks that are floated such as the Pousse-Café and the Traffic Light.
- **Rocks:** Rocks glasses are common. They can be used for just about anything from highballs to shots and even as a mixer glass. They may be stemmed and range in size. These glasses may also be called "lowballs" or "old-fashioned" and are commonly used for drinks that are "on the rocks."
- **Shot:** The standard shot is one and a half ounces and can be measured with a jigger. The larger shot glasses allow enough space to mix liquors for different types of shots.
- **Sour:** These glasses are known for their popularity when serving "sour" drinks They can be used for Amaretto Sours and Whiskey Sours as well as other similar drinks.

BAR TOOLS EXAMINED

There are so many bar tools available. People do not realize how necessary some are until they are tending bar or hosting a party and realize that having a tool would make things easier. Here, the bar tools and necessities will be covered.

THE LONG BAR SPOON

Many people do not realize how handy these can be, especially when the daiquiri will not come out of the pitcher. They are great for scraping pitchers of frozen drinks, frozen margaritas, etc. Some bars give these to customers when they order pitchers of frozen margaritas, Bellini, or daiquiris so they can serve themselves.

WINE KEYS

This tool is necessary if any corked wine is being served. The best key is the rabbit-eared version, which insert the corkscrew themselves. With a pull of the lever, the cork pops out. The waiter's wine key is also good for use as a pocket-sized wine opener. Be sure to have one that has a knife or foil cutter on one end and works like a lever.

PROFESSIONAL GRADE BLENDER

These are an absolute for serving any kind of frozen drink. The regular home blender is not intended for chopping ice, and they will overheat and burnout.

COCKTAIL SHAKER

There are two types of shakers used in a bar. The shaker found in most bars and restaurants is the Boston style shaker, which consists of two separate containers, a mixing glass, and a shaker glass. The shaker glass is made of stainless steel and overlaps the mixer glass. The standard shaker consists of a shaker glass and a lid. These are also stainless steel and some may have a built-in strainer.

STRAINERS

The Hawthorn Strainer is very popular. These can be used in conjunction with a shaker glass. Most people associate these with martinis, but the main purpose is keeping ice from getting in the drink. Ice in a martini is taboo and not acceptable. The Hawthorn Strainer is spoon-shaped and has a spring coil around its head. Keep at least two of these in a small bar, more for a large bar.

MUDDLER

A muddler is a small, wooden bat or pestle that is made for crushing fruit and herbs. These are becoming a necessity as the Mint Julep and the Mojito gain popularity.

SPEED POURERS

This is another absolute must for the bar. They are great for storing sweet and sour juices and any other liquids that must be poured quickly.

GOOD, SHARP KNIVES

The importance of a good, sharp knife is indescribable. Knives are used to cut fruit and other things, such as sweet and sour packs or boxes. It is a good idea to have a knife made for twists. This is useful for making a quick lemon or lime twist.

POURING TECHNIQUES

SHAKING A DRINK

The main reason for shaking a cocktail is chilling it without watering it down. This also aids in mixing drinks that consist of creams and other liquids that do not blend easily. As a rule of thumb, shake cream drinks and stir clear drinks. Drinks such as martinis can be shaken or stirred, but ask the guest which they prefer. Do not shake carbonated drinks because they will go flat.

When preparing the drink, put in a few cubes of ice and pour the liquors over them in the mixing glass. Place the metal shaker over the glass and shake. Hold the metal and glass containers together to keep them sealed. If the drink is very cold, the two containers will stick together. Gently tap them to break them apart. Do not tap the glass container, as the cold may cause it to break. Use a strainer on the mixing glass to remove the liquid but not the ice.

LAYERING DRINKS

The classic layered drink is the Pousse-Café, a sweet drink layered with a number of liqueurs. These are layered on each other without mixing. Layer the liquids depending on their densities. The main difficulty with layering liquors is that each brand may have a different density even though it may be the same type of liquor. Those with a higher sugar content, like cordials, will have a higher density.

To layer, pour each liquor over the back of a spoon so that it glides on to the top of the next layer. These are tedious and require practice, but once mastered, will create very imaginative and beautiful bar drinks.

FLOATING

Floating is very similar to layering. Generally, floaters are extra shots that are served on top of a drink or are the last ingredient. High proof rum or a liqueur is usually floated on a drink that has been shaken, stirred, strained, or poured for looks. This ingredient will float alone at the top of the drink. Pour the liquor over the back of a bar spoon gently so that the liquor stays on the top.

FLAMING

There are a few drinks that can be sold on fire. This should be done very carefully and away from hair and other liquor. Sometimes a floated ingredient is ignited because of its high alcohol content. For example, 151 proof rum is popular for igniting. The oil from a citrus peel can be ignited for a burst of flavor as well. Have a saucer or wet bar towel handy just in case.

BLENDING

Frozen drinks can be difficult to measure and it is easy to end up with extra mix left over, which means that the guest is not getting the full amount of liquor for which they are paying. If the amount of ice needed is not stated in the recipe, use the same amount of ice that would be put in the glass that the drink is being made for. Place the ice in the blender and add the ingredients. Cover the blender and turn it on. If the blender freezes up, pulse it. If the mix is too thick, add a small amount of Sprite or sweet and sour to loosen it up. After a few seconds, the sound of the blender should change. Stop the blender and check the consistency. Blend again if necessary. Several professional grade blenders come with a special stirrer used for mashing the ice and ingredients towards the blade without catching the stirrer on the blade.

MUDDLING

Muddling requires a muddler and a sturdy glass. Do not use expensive glassware for these drinks. The ingredients are usually fresh mint or other herbs, as well as fresh fruit. Other ingredients may include bitters, sugar, and water. All ingredients are placed at the bottom of the glass and mashed with the muddler. Muddling will bring out the qualities of the fruit, as well as press the oils from the peels.

BUILDING

Some drinks are built in a specific order to create a specific taste. Highballs generally start with ice, then liquor, then mixer. If there is a citrus garnish, the juice should be squeezed into the drink after the mixer. The bartender should then stir the drink.

STIRRING

Classic martinis are stirred — not shaken, although this largely depends on the guest's personal preference. This technique is used for all clear cocktails. Fill the mixing glass full of ice, pour the ingredients over the ice, and use a bar spoon to stir. Chill the ingredients for 20 to 30 seconds. The amount of water that melts will have an effect on the overall drink. Stirred drinks are then strained into a chilled glass.

CHILLED GLASSES

Martini glasses, beer mugs, pilsners, and other glasses used for cold drinks should be kept in a refrigerator or freezer. Without access to a refrigerator, chill glasses manually. Fill the glass with ice and water, or soda, until the glass is overflowing. Allow the glass to sit while mixing the drink. When the drink preparation is complete, dump the glass out and shake it to remove excess water.

SALTING AND SUGARING GLASSES

Rimming glasses ahead of time will allow the salt or sugar to air-dry on the rim while the drink is being mixed. Using a wedge of fruit or a piece of paper towel dipped in one of the liquid ingredients, moisten the outside of the rim of the serving glass. Holding the glass sideways, pour the salt, sugar, cocoa, etc. over the edge of the glass, rotating along the way. This method will lightly coat the rim of the glass and prevents an excess of salt or sugar from mixing and melting into the drink.

CHAPTER 4:
BAR MANAGEMENT

Opening and owning a bar can be a lucrative business, as well as an enriching experience. Bars not only sell drinks, but they are gathering places for family and friends. Bars provide a great atmosphere for fun and conversation and fulfill needs such as companionship, meeting other people, and sharing views.

There have been many trends in alcohol consumption in the United States. The sale of alcohol in bars and restaurants is a $20 billion business. Every adult in the United States consumes, on average, two alcoholic drinks per day. There have been many trends in the popularity of drinks. While some drinks are trendy, others have withstood the test of time. For example, beer and wine became more popular than distilled liquors in the 1980s. Today, beer and white liquors are increasingly popular in the 21 to 30 age group. Conversely, the population over 30 has begun to consume more wine because of their health consciousness.

Modern families consist of two working individuals with two working incomes, resulting in less time for home cooked meals. Instead, many families eat at local restaurants. This trend accounts for the increase in the number of liquor licenses awarded every year. At dinner, families can enjoy a meal as well as a cocktail, glass of wine, or bottle of beer.

Additionally, the United States is a culturally diverse country. Many cultures include alcohol such as wine or beer in their traditions.

As the desire to enjoy a glass of wine at dinner increases, so does the demand for places to do. Not only do new establishments fulfill this need, but they also help to provide more jobs in the local economy, hiring bartenders, servers, bar backs, and even cooks.

THE BUSINESS PLAN

A successful business starts with a business plan. The business plan involves laying the foundation of the business and making projections as to how much money will be required to start the business, as well as how much money will be made in five or ten years. This is a step that is skipped by many businesses, which is a mistake. More and more banks are making it difficult to get the necessary funding required to start a business without a business plan. They want to view the plan and see how the money will be spent. It is well worth the time to make a business plan if funding from a lender is sought.

The first step in writing and preparing a business plan is developing the legal form of ownership. This determines who owns the business and how it is operated. Consider consulting a lawyer, as he or she can help make decisions regarding the legal entity. The legal entity determines how taxes will be paid, who will be responsible for taxes, and who is responsible for expenses if the business is not a success.

THE SOLE PROPRIETORSHIP

A sole proprietorship is the legal entity that is most commonly used by small establishments. In this scenario, the owner is the boss and sets the rules, making every decision that affects the business.

The profit that made in a sole proprietorship is treated as if the money is personal income. The money is also taxed in the same manner. When trouble paying creditors arises, they can come after personal assets to pay off the debt. Sole proprietor must be extra careful when it comes to making decisions.

Owning a bar is a business and the sole proprietor is responsible for keeping track of expenses, profits, employees, and payrolls. Keep in mind that the staff will need to be managed also and competitors and customers must be taken care of.

PARTNERSHIP

A sole proprietor should consider a partnership if he or she feels as though there are too many responsibilities. Choose another individual who is willing to invest with in the business. The partner may be a friend, family member, or even another individual who will complement the strengths and weaknesses of the existing partner. There are several different types of partnerships with varying degrees of protection when it comes to protecting taxes and debts.

In a general partnership, the individuals are equal and there is no limit to the number of general partners a business can have. Everyone works and everyone shares in the unlimited liabilities.

In a limited partnership, there is no limit to the number of partners, but at least one individual must be a general partner with unlimited liability. The limited partners have limited liabilities and are not required to actively participate in the business. Those partners that do not actively participate are called silent partners. The silent partners make no decisions in the business and typically only have investments in the business. It is not legally required that partners have a partnership agreement, but it is a good idea to have business arrangements and responsibilities recorded on paper and signed by all of those who are participating.

The biggest advantage of a partnership is working with someone who has knowledge of the industry. Assets, credit, and talent can be pooled to make a successful business. Partners are only taxed on the profit that is considered personal income and not the income of the entire business.

CORPORATION

A corporation is a legal entity that is separate from the owners and stockholders. The business pays taxes as if it were a separate taxpayer. A corporation requires three or more persons to obtain a state charter and to elect a Board of Directors to run the corporation. The profits per share are distributed to the shareholders through dividends that are distributed to the shareholders. Salary or dividends are taxed as personal income to those who receive it. Additional funds for corporations are raised by selling shares of stock.

The biggest advantage of a corporation is that there is no liability to the individuals involved in the business. The corporation is considered a "legal person" itself and the liability shifts from the investors to the corporation. There are numerous tax advantages, including deductions and employee benefits; however, some federal and state taxes can be quite arduous for a corporation. Many corporations form a subchapter to gain added tax breaks. The income and dividends received by shareholders are reported as their personal income taxes must be paid on that income.

FRANCHISE

A franchise is a license to sell or service an idea or product in a certain area for a fee. This can also mean acquiring a business and having a relationship with the parent company of the franchise. To buy a franchise, there is a larger on-going fee that must be paid for the percentage of business done. The parent companies will help a new franchise owner by including national or regional advertising, as well as personnel training.

The advantage to a franchise is that knowledge, expertise, and financing are gained through the parent company. Some franchise owners view not being their own boss and being bound by the company's regulations as disadvantages.

TYPES OF BARS

When deciding what type of bar to open, think about the various bars in community that are personally enjoyed. Bars can be located in assorted types of buildings, including old libraries, old fire stations, historic houses, and many other venues. Deciding on a type of bar is the next step in the business plan.

NEIGHBORHOOD BARS

The neighborhood bar is one of the most popular types in a community. These bars are places where friends gather after work for drinks, on birthdays, and for a variety of different celebrations. The neighborhood bar is a place people go on a regular basis.

Neighborhood bars may be open for varying times during the day. The hours that the bar is allowed to be open depends on the neighborhood. Some bars are open from 6 a.m. to 11 a.m. and from 4 p.m. to 2 a.m. Once deciding on hours of operation, keep them consistent. Customers enjoy the neighborhood bar as a convenience, knowing that the hours will be the same and their needs will be met.

There are a variety of neighborhood bars. Some are simple beer and wine establishments or brew pubs. These are popular because there is no restriction on how many beer and wine licenses are allotted to a city, while liquor licenses are restricted by population. To attract more people to your bar, a liquor license is key. Even if the city will not allow a new license to be issued, a license can be purchased from another individual or an existing bar with a license.

Many neighborhood bars also offer food. This is personal preference, and establishments interested in having a small grill and kitchen must acquire a license to serve food. There are many small bars that offer burgers, sandwiches, and appetizers. They may serve food all day or only during lunch and dinner times. These options are completely up the owner, but the decision should remain consistent.

Wine and Champagne bars have also become very popular. These are classy and small, serving several different types of wine and Champagnes, as well as cheese and appetizers.

NIGHTCLUBS

A small nightclub or "cocktail lounge" is another popular type of bar to consider. These bars are seen as "two faced" in that during the day, they are open as a neighborhood bar, but at night they transform into an active bar with dancing and live entertainment.

The large nightclub, only open at night, is another option, although it is the most expensive type to open and operate. The atmosphere is extremely important and a lot of money is spent on the look of the bar. The goal is to keep people dancing so they stay thirsty and buy more drinks. More than one bar is usually needed with several servers and bartenders. These bars require advertising and the knowledge of well-trained managers. Nightclubs work best in locations with large populations, and are known for cover charges and higher drink prices.

DANCE CLUBS

Dancing is the main attraction in these bars and, as with nightclubs, the goal is to keep people dancing and moving so they will drink more. To have a great dance club, consider having music piped in via satellite or hiring DJs. A good DJ can make or break a dance club, making the selection a very important step in having a successful dance club.

Ensure that there is a variety of different music available to choose from. Playing classic dance club music, such as "The Electric Slide," will inevitably get people on the dance floor. Many dance clubs allow guests to make requests.

ENTERTAINMENT CLUBS

Entertainment clubs are usually multiple bars inside one large building. These types of bars are becoming increasingly popular in large cities. Many may have up to nine different nightclubs with various themes in them, but the guests only pay one cover charge. A great staff that will work to keep the bars under control is essential. This business heavily depends on repeat customers bringing their friends who bring their friends, etc. Some of the most successful bars of this variety have a sports bar, a karaoke bar, a Top 40 bar, a country bar, a retro bar, and a salsa bar. These bars may hold concerts, contests, and other events to keep the bar fresh and full of people.

CONSISTENCY IS KEY

Many bars open only to close a few months later with the main reason being a lack of consistency. Every bar, no matter what type it is, needs to have an overall theme and design. For example, a bar might want to be a Tiki hut hideaway in freezing cold Minnesota. The owners must design it in that fashion and keep it that way. It is very important to not change the bar's theme after being opened only a short period of time. This will completely throw off customers and they will wonder if they are even in the right place, especially if they really liked the original theme. If they like the theme, they will keep coming back. The theme is the brand, so keep the theme consistent from the logo design on the sign to the paint on the walls and floors.

Ensure that the staff is well-trained and that they have a great attitude. This attitude will transfer to the customers, which will result in regulars. Get to know these customers as they can be word of mouth advertising.

The size of the bar will determine the budget and the concept. Size, room design, tables, games, and dancing space will all come into play. The placement of entries and exits, as well as the maximum occupancy, are determined by the fire department. Design the bar for optimum occupancy because more people inside means more money.

ESTIMATING BAR VOLUME

How much business a bar anticipates doing will need to be included in the initial concept of the bar, as well as in the business plan. Estimated volume in the bar will vary depending on the size, location, and occupancy rating. Establishments can decide how much money they want to make per day based on the number of people that they can accommodate.

There are two ways to calculate the estimated bar volume. First, there is the entertainment bar. With these bars, the room is cleared before each show and each seat represents a minimum amount of income. This example works for bars that have lounge acts or a comedy club. If there are 100 seats in the bar, for example, a $5 cover charge, a two drink minimum at $3 each, two shows per night, $2200 will be made if every seat is full.

250 customers x $5 cover charge = $1250
250 customers x 4 drinks x $3 per drink = $3000
$1250 + $3000 = $4250

These are just assumptions and should be made for every possible combination. Be sure to include these in the business plan. Project these figures on a daily, weekly, monthly, and yearly basis as well. Some lenders even like to see assumptions for five to ten years in the future.

START FROM SCRATCH OR PURCHASE A BAR?

Those who are new to the industry and have a lot of learning to do will probably benefit from purchasing an already established bar with an established clientele. Purchasing a bar that is already thriving means keeping the same knowledgeable staff, managers, and clientele. This should allow for a profit right away. Become a customer at the bar before making a decision about purchasing it. Meet the staff and check out the customers. Note how the staff works and make any mental notes on things that should be changed. For example, maybe the bathrooms need new tile and the bar top could be refinished. Consider purchasing new tables and chairs if they appear to be used and abused.

When buying an already established business, be sure to include certain stipulations in the purchase agreement. It is especially important to include a paragraph that states that the current owner of the bar cannot open or build a competing bar within a specific distance for a certain period of time. This clause can be very important in ensuring that customers remain at the bar.

Most bars are sold for the price of one year's gross receipts. Consult a qualified individual to determine if the price of the bar is correct and accurate according to reported receipts. Receipts that should be checked include liquor delivery invoices, actual sales, and volume of the bar. Nightclub and bar consultants are available to help determine whether or not the price is accurate.

Another great advantage to buying an existing bar is having a proven location, assuming that the bar was doing adequate business. Before remodeling the bar, be certain to plan it thoroughly and investigate the additional costs and whether or not they will pay for themselves. Remodeling is expensive, but it is even more expensive to start from scratch. Take full possession of all the bar's contents in the purchase agreement, unless refurnishing is intended and the contents are not desired. Discuss any changes to the building with the fire department, health inspector, and building authorities.

Personal finances will also play a large part in the decision. If enough capital is possessed to buy an existing bar and run it as it is for a while, take that option. Make wise decisions in the purchasing of the bar.

LOCATION, LOCATION, LOCATION

As in all types of businesses, location is key. There is a suitable location in every community for a particular type of bar and there are two ways to approach the location of the bar. Develop the bar's theme first and look for a location to match, or open the bar in a particular location for convenience. For example, opening a country bar in downtown New York or a wine bar in a rural area would not be a wise decision. There may be a small group of people that are interested in the bar, but if the bar does not match the area very well, the bar will not be open for long.

Also consider how many cities are trying to revitalize their downtown areas. It may be possible to design a bar that fits the downtown location, playing a part in the economy by attracting people to downtown bars and restaurants. Many cities are working on revitalizing their downtown areas by offering deals and bonuses to those businesses that are interested in opening a location there. Unique buildings and warehouses can often be found in these areas that could easily transform into a bar. Several downtown areas already have a theme and incorporating this into a new bar will make it easier to fit in.

Demographics are very important in setting up a new bar. Study the composition of the people who live in the bar's area. A new bar should fill a void in the marketplace in the community. Demographic information can be obtained from the U.S. Department of Commerce, the Bureau of Census, and even on the Internet. Many local organizations may keep track of census information in the area, which is received every ten years. This information can be obtained from the local chamber of commerce, university or public libraries, large newspapers, television stations, and radio stations. A lot of this information may even be found on the Internet. These departments use this information on a daily basis and will be able to discuss the trends in the area. Find out the following information:

- What is the ratio of males to females?
- Are they married or single?
- What age are they?
- Do they have families?
- What are their jobs?
- What are the income levels and what kind of disposable income do they have?
- How far do people in the area travel to work?
- What level of education do they have?
- Which religions do they practice?
- What are their races and national origins?
- Do they own homes or do they rent?
- How much leisure time do they have? What do most people in the area do for fun?
- Do they travel?
- What types of entertainment are popular?

Finding out this information will help determine a location in which the bar will do well. For example, if there is a large population of single people in your area and they all travel down one main highway, up a good after work crowd can be attracted. However, many bars that are located next to other bars do well because single people like to "bar hop." Many cities have one street with many bars and young people like to hang out on this block on the weekends. Many cities are working on developing areas such as this to attract the locals back to an area that was once a popular hang out spot, as well as any tourists who may be traveling through.

Once a desirous location is picked out, drive around the area to see what is going on there. If the area is industrious, a bar that sells beer and liquor may do very well with the local workers. If there are a lot of office buildings or apartment complexes, bars that offer entertainment and dancing might fare well. For those considering a downtown location, find an area that is well lit and appears safe. Pay attention to any new construction of offices or other restaurants. Note the types of businesses and residential areas that are nearby. Parking will also need to be considered for both day and night.

Bars that are located in central or downtown business areas may have parking problems during the day. Bars that serve lunch, however, may attract a clientele for lunch. Depending on the activity level of the city's downtown area, some of these bars do not stay open very late. Rent also tends to be higher in these areas.

Cocktail lounges and beer bars tend to do very well in areas that are considered secondary business districts, which are near other businesses such as grocery stores, shopping centers, etc. These are the types of stores that people visit after work and a bar located here would be convenient.

Bars located in highway business districts also tend to do well with the after work crowd because they are easily accessible and may be on the way home from work for many commuters. Bars that have themes tend to do well in these locations. A bar that is located off the highway may also attract travelers stopping for the night.

Bars in planned shopping center areas and community shopping centers may or may not do well. Some shopping centers will not allow a bar to open unless it is also a restaurant. Be sure to research whether or not a particular shopping center will allow a bar to be opened. If these shopping centers are in good locations, for example near college campuses and offices, then the bar will probably do well. This type of location may offer rent recapture, which allows the tenant to receive a reduced rent rate for making improvements to the building.

Regional shopping centers can be found in strip mall settings as well as enclosed settings. These shopping centers usually have a large number of department stores and other retail shops. There may also be several different restaurants in addition to the food court. The rents in these areas can be high, but the people who visit shopping malls are there to spend money. Singles bars have done very well in shopping centers like these. Other large bars that have several bars in one will also do well in these types of centers.

Areas near neighborhoods tend to have small clusters of buildings and businesses. For example, on a street corner in a neighborhood there might be a small grocery store, a fast food restaurant, and gas station. Many bars may fit into these areas as well. The rent will vary depending on the surrounding neighborhoods, but locals will frequent the bar. People like to drink at bars that are near their homes, which is safer when it is time to go home. Drink prices are generally lower and there are rarely cover charges. These bars will also do well if they are located in close proximity to professional sports complexes, colleges, universities, and transport hubs.

EVALUATING YOUR LOCATION

The best site for a bar will have everything needed to be successful. It is also important to evaluate what comes with the location. Is the bar visible from the highway? Is there adequate parking? Is the location worth paying higher rent? These are all questions to ask when deciding on a location.

The economy of the area is also important. If there are a lot of closed down restaurants and empty buildings in the area, this should be a warning sign. If the bar is located in an unstable economy, the whole area may shut down one night, putting everyone out of business. This is especially true of mining areas and similar industries, which are made up of migrant workers. If the area is dependent on tourists, what would happen in the event of a natural disaster or an airline strike? How would the bar be affected?

The next factor to consider is labor. Are there many people located in the area, and if so, what types of jobs do they hold? Are there several restaurants and bars? If so, are there enough people to staff the bar? Are there homes and apartments for rent nearby? Will the employees make enough money to live near the location? Are there schools and colleges nearby and can labor be obtained from these sources?

Does the bar's location have drawing power? What type of area is it located in? Do people driving in and around the area on a regular basis? Does the building draw the attention of people? Areas that have drawing power are typically intersections between major roads and highways, near stadiums, and other large city attractions. The larger the area's drawing power, the more likely it is that the bar will succeed.

Does the area or building have potential for growth? Is it an area where many new businesses and residential areas are being built? Are there any factors that will present problems when opening a bar? Some areas may have a ban on bars or new construction. The local planning department will be able to answer any questions about where a bar can be built.

Are there many bars in the area and what level of competition do they offer? What services does the competition's offer? If there are mainly nightclubs and dance clubs in an area, consider offering a more relaxed atmosphere. Perhaps, a piano bar or comedy club would fill a void in the area. If the location is in a strip of bars, does bar hopping work for or against the bar? What types of activities do people partake in before stopping at the bar? Do they go shopping or to a movie? If there are several bars in a location, offer an alternative such as a sports bar in the middle of a bunch of dance clubs or vice versa.

Is the bar highly visible? Will people know that the bar exists or will advertising be necessary? Are there visible obstructions that would keep customers from noticing the bar such as a highway bridge, tall buildings, etc.? What are the sign laws in the area; would the bar be able to have a sign large enough to attract people? Street and corner locations are generally considered the best locations for bars.

Are there traffic patterns that would impede people from visiting? If traffic is particularly bad in a certain intersection, people will avoid stopping in those areas because they do not want to deal with the hassle of getting in and out of the location. How do people get around the area and how much parking must be provided? Do people come in by foot, personal vehicle, bus, train, or subway? Should valet parking be offered?

Are there any accessibility issues with getting in and out of the parking lot? Can people easily turn either left or right? Will they have to go around the block to get to the bar because of a median? Is the driveway easily visible?

Is there enough free parking or will people have to pay? If it is downtown, are people allowed to park for free on the street in the evenings? Will other businesses be able to steal these parking spots, and how will this affect business? Will there be limited parking during the day and adequate parking at night? Consider the clientele and weather. Older clientele will want to park near the building, while younger customers may not mind a short walk. Just about everybody will want to park near the building if it rains or snows frequently. How will the weather affect business?

Does the location justify the cost of rent, utilities, etc.? Is there a trade-off between higher rent and a lot of business? How much renovation and remodeling will the location require? Is there room for expansion? Are the property taxes higher in one location versus another?

All of these factors should be carefully considered before making a decision. Choosing the right location may be the determining factor in the bar's success. Thoroughly research the demographics and surroundings of every potential location. Discuss these locations with contractors, bankers, investors, and other consultants.

ATMOSPHERE

Creating the bar's atmosphere is a project that will continue throughout the life of the bar. The first step is to identify the type of bar, what the theme is, and what the name of the bar is. The bar's name should reflect the theme of the bar, as well as the atmosphere. Most bars are dark on the inside, helping people relax and feel more comfortable, no matter what time of day it is. Most bars do not have any clocks, unless they are incorporated into beer memorabilia.

The outside of the bar should be inviting. Signs should incorporate the theme and people should be tempted to go inside to see what the bar looks like. Make sure the sign is illuminated at night with lights or neon. The sign must conform to state and local zoning laws, but that does not mean it cannot be creative. Awnings can be used to attract people and advertise without breaking any sign regulations. Decorations on the outside should be incorporated inside as well. Consider opening walls and adding on patios, especially if the bar is located in a warm or tropical climate, as people will want to linger outside to enjoy beautiful weather. Consider incorporating outdoor activities such as horseshoes or dart boards into the patio as well.

The exterior of the bar should flow into the interior. The interior should be consistent with the theme and design. The furniture, tables, bar top, and layout should all complement each other.

Lighting should be strategically placed so that the bar area is highlighted without making it too bright. Interior lights might accent certain areas of the bar, drawing people's attention to murals or to the restroom. Consider placing lights along the stairs for safety reasons. Light fixtures should also match the theme and design and may be placed above pool tables and dartboards to aid in the playing of these games. Incorporating neon, fiber optics, and lasers into your dance floor will make it fun and animated.

Light transitions in a bar are also important. People's eyes need time to adjust from an area of brightness to an area of darkness. If the bar area is dimly lit, the lights should gradually brighten as people enter bathrooms, for example.

Music and sound are very important to a bar's atmosphere, but be sure that the volume of the music is loud enough that people can hear each other without having to yell. Think about having a "quiet" room that incorporates lighter or muted music where people can hang out and talk. This quieter area will also allow people to take phone calls if necessary. The foreground sound in a bar is generally that of the DJ, music, televisions, and live entertainment. If the televisions are turned up so that people can hear them, keep any music low or muted. Background sound comes from the environment outside as well as any natural sounds from water or wind. Put these sounds to use as people will find them soothing. Natural sounds such as running water will make for an excellent atmosphere in a quieter room.

The décor should also be memorable. The theme of the bar will determine what type of decorations are used. The most common decorations in neighborhood bars tend to be beer signs, mirrored beer signs, and neon signs. The décor should flow into the restrooms as well.

LAYOUT OF THE BAR

The bar top should be the focus of the bar. People should be able to see all of the liquors and the beers that are offered. This area should be well-lit and should draw a crowd. If the bar includes pool tables, make sure that people have adequate space so that they will not be hitting each other with their pool sticks. Supply bar stools for those players that are waiting for their turn.

There are several different types of bar tops that can be used. Some bars run the length of the wall and dominate one side of the room, but there are also island bars that allow people to gather from all sides. Island bars may have bar stools or stand-up drinking areas. The layout of the bar will depend on personal preference, ability to set it up in the building, and atmosphere.

Servers should have their own nook at the bar top. Often called the service bar, this will be the area where they pick up drinks, make drinks, and drop off glassware. The servers should not have to fight with customers for a spot at the bar. Ice and liquor should be easily accessible. If the bar is very busy, consider hiring bar backs to run for ice, liquor, and beer for the bartenders. Back rooms may be a combination of an office, kitchen, liquor storage, and wine storage. They should be easily accessible by staff but not by guests. Back doors should be locked at all times to keep inventory from slowly disappearing or have a separate liquor room that is locked at all times.

If there is a dance floor, several tables and chairs should be set up around the perimeter. There should also be an area that has easy access to the bar. The DJ should be able to see the dance floor easily. Dance floors may be sunken or elevated for a different look and to add dimension to the space.

Restrooms should be easily accessible and large. Women's restrooms need several stalls, preferably with doors that lock. There should also be more than one sink and a ledge for placing drinks, either in the stall or outside. Many women are unwilling to leave their drink unattended because of the risk of their drink being tampered with. Restrooms should be located in an area that is not congested. Large nightclubs and dance clubs will often have separate entrances and exits to keep the flow moving.

SEATING

There should be various types of seating in the bar. Choose low tables with comfortable chairs or booths for private conversations. Around pool tables, have tall tables with tall chairs. The chairs should not be so close together that people have to fight to get around each other. If someone is sitting on a bar stool, a person should be able to stand by them and have a conversation comfortably.

HOW TO OBTAIN FINANCING

So far the basic foundation of a business plan has been prepared. Now it is time to actually dig in and crunch some numbers. The first step to getting a loan or attracting investors is to have a solid business plan. Learning to project future income and profits is necessary. The business plan will show how and where money will be spent, as well as how profits will be generated. The plan should be typed and include all financial information with charts and graphs. Consider hiring an experienced freelance writer, accountant, or financial services company to draft the business plan.

When looking for start-up capital, begin by writing an executive summary with the amount of money required to get started and the proposed terms. Include a brief summary of the business with its name, location, physical description, and layout. If the bar is being purchased, then include photos of it as is. Include information about the management team's experience, which will make a large impact on the lender's decision. Next, list financial needs and how the funds will be used.

The next step is the market analysis. Explain why the proposed bar will do well in the chosen location. How will the bar succeed and what are the goals? The idea is to show the lenders that the bar is going to be innovative and creatively marketed. Discuss the total market environment in the location, as well as any business trends in the area and population growth potential.

Potential lenders will also want to know the advertising plan. Consider a grand opening and contact local radio stations. These are great ways of getting people to the bar on opening night. Think of many innovative promotions that can be used to attract customers. Explain the pricing concept and any other specials that may be used to attract people.

The next section of the business plan will show how the bar will be run. Describe the type of ownership that will be implemented, as well as management hierarchy and staff responsibilities. Include how these individuals will be paid, hours of operation, and any other factors that will have an affect on the way the bar is operated.

The final part of the business plan will deal with finances. If the bar is being purchased, use the financial information from the last owner to make projections. If these are available, use the earnings from the past three years to determine the bar's financial future. If these are not available, give month-by-month projections including one year, five years, and ten years. These projections should include a profit and loss statement, also known as an income statement. To generate this, take the operating expenses, such as rent, labor, office supplies, bar supplies, etc., plus the cost of beverages and food items sold and subtract that total from the projected gross sales. This will show if there is a profit or loss. Consider requesting additional funds from lenders for renovations and remodeling.

The business plan should include a cash flow chart, which will show the difference between expenditures and income for a given period of time. These will take expenditures for loan principal reduction, owner's withdrawals, and reserves for taxes into account.

Another chart should provide a capital expenditures budget that explains how all the money will be used. Be sure to distinguish personal money from the business' loan money. The lenders will want to see where and how their money will be allocated.

Finally, develop a balance statement for the business. This will help to determine the bar's net worth. All of the property and inventory will be converted into cash in the balance statement. Subtract the liabilities to determine the net worth of the bar. In the left column will be the assets. List everything that the business owns, including items that are still being paid for, as well as their current market value. The liabilities are recorded in the right column. These are the business' debts and this is the amount owed as of the day the balance sheet is written. Take the total of the assets and subtract them from the total liabilities. This will determine the net worth of the business. The two columns should balance the assets so that they are equal to the liabilities plus the net worth.

TECHNICALITIES OF SELLING LIQUOR

Bars must comply with the laws at the federal, state, county, and local levels. The laws cover everything dealing with liquor from the manufacturing of the alcohol to when it is served.

The Federal Alcohol Administration (FAA) Act of 1935 is the basis of all federal liquor laws. According to the act, liquor is defined as any fluid or substance, either distilled or fermented, or a beverage with alcoholic content. The FAA also regulates the transport of and quality of alcoholic products, as well as their taxation. These laws cover the manufacturing of the alcohol, aging, packaging, labeling, adulteration, and advertising. The FAA must approve the contents of all liquor and requires that certain information is available on the labels such as the identity, quality, age, net contents, manufacturer, bottler, importer, and alcohol content. The Internal Revenue Code prevents the beverage from being altered in any way, which is prohibited by law. The Treasury controls the size of bottles, and the states limit which bottle sizes may be sold within their boundaries.

STRIP STAMP OR ALTERNATIVE SEAL

The strip stamp seals a liquor bottle after it has been approved by federal regulations. This is a red and white or green and white paper strip stamp tax that goes over the cap and seals the bottle to ensure that the bottle is not tampered with before it is purchased by the consumer. Once the bottle has been opened, the stamp must remain on the bottle as long as there is alcohol in it. The Bureau of Alcohol, Tobacco, and Firearms (BATF) can confiscate any bottles with altered contents or suspected altered contents or with missing strip stamps or seals. No liquor bottles can be used or refilled in any manner. In some states, there may be laws restricting alcohol from being emptied into mixes for frozen drink machines. Be sure to investigate this before opening a bar.

OBTAINING A RETAIL DEALER LICENSE

A retail dealer is any person who sells alcohol as a beverage for the public. The Internal Revenue Service requires that two dealer forms be filed. An Employer Identification Number (EIN) must be obtained by filing the IRS Form SS-4. File IRS Form 11, Special Tax Return, and Application for Registry also. These must be filed before July of each year and empower the government to levy a special occupational tax. The dealer also receives a Special Tax Stamp as a receipt of payment, which allows the federal government to track retailers. The Special Tax Stamp must be available for inspection at the place of business by any BATF officer during business hours. The Special Tax Stamp is not transferable and a location change requires that a new Form 11 is filed within 30 days. Any change in ownership also requires a new Special Tax Stamp.

A retail liquor dealer sells either distilled spirits or wine and pays a $54 tax every year while a retail beer dealer pays a $24 tax every year. A limited retail dealer can operate on a seasonal or temporary basis. This tax is $2.20 per month. If the dealer is a traveling bar such as on a boat, plane, or train, they must file to become a Dealer at Large and pay $54.

Retail dealers are allowed to purchase distilled spirits from:

- Distilled spirit plants
- Wholesale dealers
- Persons appointed to dispose of bankruptcy assets
- Other retail dealers that are going out of business and selling their entire stock

Retail dealers must keep all invoices and bills for all distilled spirits, wines, and beers that are purchased. BATF officers can inspect a retail dealer's records and liquor stock at any time.

TIED-HOUSE INTERESTS

The FAA regulates tied-house interests between wholesalers, manufacturers, and retail dealers. Tied-house interests occur when industry members influence the market by having an interest in the bar or any furnishings of value, providing free warehousing, display and distribution services, assisting in acquiring a license, paying for advertising, guaranteeing loans, extending credit, or demanding a quota on purchases.

Industry members can, however, provide, sell, or loan a variety of bar supplies including wine racks, barrels, and kegs. These may not exceed $100 per brand at any time in one retail business.

Inside signs, napkins, clocks, and calendars are also allowed. These items are limited to no more than $50 per brand per calendar year per retail establishment. Glassware and table accessories may be sold to retailers at a price less than the cost. Additionally, limited amounts of samples may be given if the retailer has not purchased the brand before.

OSHA

Every bar must comply with OSHA regulations. The Occupational Safety and Health Act of 1970 determines that it is the general duty and responsibility of employers to maintain a place of employment that is safe and healthy for working. Bar owners should consult their state OSHA board or local building inspector to ensure that OSHA regulations are met.

TAXES

Bars must report income to the IRS, just like any other business. They must also collect federal income, social security, unemployment, and disability taxes for each employee.

WAGES

The Fair Labor Standards Act (FLSA) requires that employees be paid at least the minimum wage and that bars follow overtime rates. If the bar has total revenues of more than $362,500 gross annual sales, exclusive of excise taxes at the retail level, the bar must comply with the FLSA. If sales are less than $362,500, state laws prevail. For first year bars, the first quarter's receipts will be used to determine annual volume.

In order to accurately determine how many hours employees have worked, determine what "work time" is. For most establishments, this is the time between clocking in and being relieved of duties, minus any required breaks. If an employee is relieved of their duties during a lunch or dinner break, this is not considered work time. If an employer does not intend to compensate an employee for any work, then the employee must be told ahead of time. It is then the employee's decision whether or not they want to volunteer their time. Employee meetings and training programs that are not voluntary are considered work time and employees must be compensated for this. If an employee is waiting for medical treatment or diagnosis at the employer's request, this is considered work time. A "workweek" is defined as a regularly occurring period of 168 consecutive hours and this week may start on any day of the week. The workweek must be fixed and employees must understand what the workweek is. Workweeks are separate from pay periods, which may combine workweeks in different ways.

OVERTIME

An overtime rate of one and a half times the employee's regular hourly rate is required by the federal minimum wage law if the employee has worked over 40 hours in a workweek. If an employee works 40 ¾ hours in a week at a rate of $6 per hour, the three-quarters of the hour is paid at $9 to compensate for the overtime.

To determine overtime for salaried employees, an hourly rate must be calculated first. The rate is figured out by dividing the rate of salary by the amount of hours expected to be worked by the employee. For example, a weekly salary of $500 per week is divided by 50 hours to give the rate of $10 per hour. After working the 50-hour workweek, the overtime hours are paid at $15 per hour. If salaried employees are paid monthly, multiply the amount by 12 months and divide by 52 weeks to arrive at a weekly salary.

TIP CREDITS

A tip is any money given to a bartender or server that is in excess of the bill owed by the customer at his or her discretion. The majority of bar and wait staff receive tips as a form of compensation. Because of this, these hourly employees may be paid a lower hourly rate. A tip credit is the amount of this reduction.

Under FLSA, the employer can take up to 40 percent tip credit provided that the employee's wage is at least the minimum. For example, if the minimum wage is $4.25 per hour, the wage becomes $2.55 paid by the employer and $1.70 credited as tips received. The following must be met in order for the employer to use tip credits:

- Employees must make at least $30 in tips per month on a regular basis.

- The employer must be able to prove the amount of tips earned by the employee; employees must report their tips to the employer.
- Tip credit must not exceed the 40 percent that is allowed.
- The employer must inform employees of tip credit laws and provide records showing the amount of tips claimed.
- Employees must be able to keep all of their tips if the employer uses tip credits against their wages.

UNIFORMS

The Department of Labor allows employers to require employees to wear a specific uniform other than their street clothes. If the employer provides the uniform, they are allowed to deduct this from the employee's check if they are paid more than the minimum wage. This deduction cannot, however, bring their pay below the minimum wage. No deductions may be made if the employee is paid only minimum wage. An employee must be reimbursed for the maintenance of the uniform when paid minimum wage, unless the uniform may be washed at the employee's home.

CIVIL RIGHTS

The federal Civil Rights Act of 1964, Title II, provides that all persons, regardless of race, color, religion, or national origin cannot be discriminated or segregated against. Individuals must be able to enjoy all the goods, services, advantages, and accommodations of any public place. Employers cannot exclude any individuals when setting policies and standards of conduct without any just cause. House rules and policies must be posted to ensure that they are enforced in a fair and consistent manner.

STATE LAWS

Although the federal government regulates a large part of the alcohol industry, the states are also given a certain amount of control. Some states are sole distributors of products and are known as control states. In these states, the retailer buys their product directly from the state. Other states are known as license states and they impose heavy regulations and licensing requirements on manufacturers, distributors, and retailers. This prohibits illegal activities and tied-house interests. States are granted this type of control through the Tenth Amendment of the Constitution.

Various states control their alcohol in different ways. Some states regulate the types of alcohol sold, as well as the bottle sizes in which they can be sold. Other states restrict the days and hours of operation and set limitations on the times and delivery of alcohol, while some control liquor and wine but allow the counties to control the beer and malt liquor. In states such as Texas, there are dry counties, which originated because each county or municipality was allowed to decide whether or not liquor would be sold and consumed in the area. This is often decided by a local vote in the community. Those counties that allow it are deemed a wet county. In contrast to a wet county, a dry county is only able to sell alcohol in private clubs. These private clubs either have free memberships or sell memberships. These work differently in each county, but most dry counties require that customers have a Unicard to prove their membership.

State laws vary from location to location. In researching state laws, find the answers to these questions:

- What is the minimum drinking age? Are minors allowed to drink in the presence of their parents or spouse?
- What type of identifications are acceptable and can more than one ID be asked for?
- Are double or triple shot drinks allowed to be served in one glass? Are happy hours or discount nights allowed?
- What would happen in the event that a person who was drinking left the bar and was involved in an accident that hurt him or others? Is the bar responsible? The employees?

- What is the minimum age someone can work in a bar and serve alcohol? Does serving food change the minimum age requirement?
- Do employees have to pass any health or drug tests?
- Are there any restrictions on the advertisement of the bar?
- Do servers and bartenders have to be state certified before they are allowed to serve alcohol?

OBTAINING A LIQUOR LICENSE

There are two types of liquor licenses: an on-premise license, which regulates a bar by only allowing the liquor to be sold and consumed on premises, and an on and off premise license, which allows liquor to be sold and consumed on the premises and taken off the premises in a package. Licenses will specify what types of alcohol can be served.

The easiest way to purchase a liquor license is from an existing license owner. The owner of an existing bar can sell the establishment with or without a liquor license or buy the license only and transfer it to the new location. Licenses for sale can be found in various places such as newspaper ads, trade publications, or business listings. Prices for licenses fluctuate depending on supply and demand in an area due to the fact that many cities and counties regulate the issuance of liquor licenses depending on population. In some areas, all available licenses may already be issued, requiring the purchase from another individual. As the population in an area grows, the state may issue new licenses, which are then sold to qualified buyers or through a lottery.

To apply for a liquor license, consult the local or state alcohol control board. They will explain how to register with the local city clerk. It is possible that the bar must already be owned or leased before applying. They may also request a copy of the floor plan to determine areas of liquor sales and consumption. Licenses that are issued to partnerships, corporations, and franchises must also submit information on stockholders, corporate seals, articles of incorporation, recorded partnership agreements, and certification of any tied-house interests.

Various states may also require that an escrow, a third party company with no interest in the deal that holds all money until both parties agree upon the deal, is set up prior to transferring liquor licenses. Financial statements may also be required as a part of the application. They may also require proof of tax permits, business licenses from different federal, state or local agencies, copies of the escrow instructions and verification of consideration. Consider posting a sign that states the establishment's intention to transfer or operate a liquor license at the location. Some states may require the obtainment of a list of all schools, churches, hospitals, public playgrounds, libraries, courts, parks, youth facilities, military bases, and private residences nearby because these are areas that the city does not want bar establishments near. States may also require sending out a mailing to nearby residences to alert them that a bar will be opening. After receiving the license, put it into operation with a specified amount of time or it may be forfeited.

There is usually a 30 day waiting period to allow the county or city board to investigate. This is also to allow time for any protests to surface. A temporary license may be granted in some states, which allows the bar to begin selling alcohol right away. There are several reasons that applications may be denied. Neighbors may complain because the bar may create a nuisance in the community or there may be a law enforcement problem. The number of existing licenses is also considered. If the applicant is not the true owner of the bar, is a chronic alcoholic, or has a police record the application may be denied. Whenever a license is denied, the applicant is allowed to protest and to demonstrate the need for the license. Licenses that are received may be revoked or fines may be levied if the owner or an employee does not follow federal, state, or local laws and regulations.

INSURANCE

Insurance is essential when owning and operating a bar. Businesses may not be allowed to operate or even receive a license without the proper insurance coverage. There are insurance companies that specialize in covering bar operations. A business must have insurance to keep from going out of business in case of fire, theft, or damage.

Coverage is required on the property, building, equipment, and fixtures. This insurance is called either named peril or all risk coverage. The property can be insured for its full replacement or current cash value and allows for depreciation. In addition, liability insurance should be carried.

- **General comprehensive liability** will protect from losses due to claims of bodily injury and property damage as a result of an accident.
- **Contractual liability** interest insures against agreements the bar has on equipment leasing and other services that are performed by contractors.
- **Fire liability** protects against damages from fires that originated in the building and spread to other buildings.
- **Automobile liability** insures against damages that employees sustain while driving company owned cars.
- **Crime coverage** protects against loss of property, inventory, or money resulting from theft, robbery, or vandalism.
- **Business interruption or loss of income insurance** protects the business in the event that it must stop operating due to fire, large theft, or loss of important employees. This insurance reimburses expenses, revenues, and profits that are lost.
- **Employee health and life insurance packages** can cover medical, dental, optical, and death. Many owners will provide their "key employees" this type of coverage in an individual policy.
- **Product liability** provides protection if someone claims that the food, drinks, or other merchandise is defective.

Depending on the dram shop laws in the area, consider carrying liquor liability or third-party liability insurance for losses resulting from customers who become intoxicated and cause injury or damage to others and their property, either inside or outside the bar.

SAFE SERVICE

All bartenders and servers should be trained to serve alcohol responsibly. Alcohol awareness should be the number one concern of any bar owner or manager. Some states require that servers and bartenders be certified by the state and the owner may be responsible and fined for any servers that are not certified.

Creating rules on alcohol service can prevent headaches in the long run. Develop rules on when to cut off guests that have had too much to drink and how to find them transportation. The idea is to let guests have fun, but do so responsibly. It is inevitable that guests will get drunk; be prepared so that they do not injure anyone on their way home, as that responsibility may fall on the bar. Investigating local dram shop acts is important, as these laws go back to the root of the accident and not only will the drunk driver be punished, but the establishment, servers, and even the owner may be held responsible for injuries that happen to the drunk individual as well as anybody else who is injured or killed in an accident. These laws should not be taken lightly.

PROMOTIONS

Promotions are great ways to get people into the bar. If a grand opening is planned, consider inviting radio stations and giving away prizes. Sell drinks at a reduced rate for the first few hours of operation. Happy hours are also very popular for the after work crowd. When planning promotions, begin by having promotions on days that are slow. Offer a variety of different promotions on slow nights such as reduced prices, extended happy hours, karaoke, and contests. The majority of bars are busy on Thursday, Friday, and Saturday nights. Sundays can be difficult to promote as most people go to school or work on Mondays. Choose to build up business on either Mondays or Tuesdays. Once those two days are busy, move to Wednesdays.

STEPS TO DEVELOPING PROMOTIONS:

1. **Set a budget** that will enable the bar to sustain the promotion. A good promotion will produce at least three times its cost. A promotion will begin paying for itself after three weeks.
2. **Allow eight to 12 weeks** for a promotion to be established. Do not advertise an ending date for a promotion. This will allow the promotion to continue indefinitely.
3. **Involve as many people as possible** in any contest promotion.
4. **Do not stop music** during activities and contests; only lower it enough that people will be able to hear.
5. **Keep guests late.** Stage contests to occur around midnight.
6. **Each promotion should have different levels of participation.**
    a. Cheap drink prices
    b. Nightly prize giveaways
    c. Grand prizes later in the night
7. **Keep in touch with local and national trends** in the entertainment industry.
8. **Take an old and successful promotion and rework it** into something new.
9. **Each promotion should include something visual** such as prizes or giveaways.
10. **Create tie-ins** with other merchants.

Successful promotions may also involve other businesses. Offer to do trade-outs with various businesses for prizes such as movie coupons, discounts, and restaurant coupons. Holidays are also great times to have promotions. New Year's parties are always a hit, but do not overlook many of the holidays for great promotional ideas. Corporations and companies often like to rent out establishments for holiday parties, and this can be an excellent option for the bar. Offer a full staff and possibly even catering. Valentine's Day is another big holiday that people enjoy celebrating. Consider specialty drinks that are red and pink and put them on special for the evening.

CHAPTER 5:
1,500 DRINK RECIPES

A BAT AND A BALL

- **Whiskey**
- **Beer**

Directions: Fill shot glass with American whiskey. Serve with a draft or bottle of American beer.

A FURLONG TOO LATE

- **2 oz. Light Rum**
- **4 oz. Ginger Beer**
- **1 Lemon Twist**
- **Ice**

Directions: Pour the rum and ginger beer into a highball glass almost filled with ice cubes. Stir well. Garnish with the lemon twist.

A NIGHT IN OLD MANDALAY

- **1 oz. Light Rum**
- **1 oz. Anejo Rum**
- **1 oz. Orange Juice**
- **½ oz. Lemon Juice**
- **3 oz. Ginger Ale**
- **1 Lemon Twist**
- **Ice**

Directions: In a shaker half-filled with ice cubes, combine the light rum, anejo rum, orange juice, and lemon juice. Shake well. Strain into a highball glass almost filled with ice cubes. Top with the ginger ale. Garnish with the lemon twist.

A. J.

- **1 ½ oz. Applejack**
- **1 oz. Grapefruit Juice**
- **Ice**

Directions: Shake ice and ingredients, strain into a cocktail glass, and serve.

ABBY ROAD

- **1 oz. Amaretto**
- **1 oz. Black Raspberry Liqueur**
- **1 oz. Coffee Liqueur**
- **Ice**

Directions: Fill a short glass with ice. Pour in ingredients. Stir.

ABBY ROAD COFFEE

- 1 oz. Amaretto
- 1 oz. Black Raspberry Liqueur
- 1 oz. Coffee Liqueur
- Coffee
- Whipped Cream
- Chocolate Syrup

Directions: Fill a coffee mug with ingredients and hot, black coffee. Top with whipped cream and drizzle with chocolate syrup.

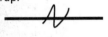

ABC

- ½ oz. Amaretto (bottom)
- ½ oz. Irish Cream
- ½ oz. Orange Liqueur or Cognac (top)

Directions: Build in order in a shot glass.

A-BOMB

- ½ oz. Vodka or Orange Vodka
- ½ oz. Coffee Liqueur
- ½ oz. Irish Cream
- ½ oz. Orange Liqueur
- Ice

Directions: Fill a mixing glass with ice. Pour in ingredients. Shake. Strain into a shot glass.

ABSCONDED FRENCH GIRLFRIEND

- 1 oz. Absinthe
- 1 oz. Black Raspberry Liqueur
- Sparkling Water
- Ice

Directions: Fill a tall Collins glass with ice. Pour in ingredients. Fill with sparkling water.

ABSINTHE COCKTAIL

- 1 ½ oz. Absinthe
- 1 ½ oz. Water
- Dash Bitters
- Dash Sugar Syrup
- Ice

Directions: Fill mixing glass with ice. Pour in ingredients. Shake. Strain into a chilled highball glass.

ABSINTHE DRIP COCKTAIL

- 1 or 2 oz. Absinthe
- Sugar Cube
- Water
- Ice

Directions: Fill a short glass with ice. Place a strainer on top of glass. Holding sugar cube over glass, drip cold water over sugar until it melts into drink.

ABSOLUTE IDIOT

- 1 oz. Vodka
- 1 oz. Jaegermeister
- Energy Drink
- Ice

Directions: Fill a highball glass with ice. Pour in ingredients and fill with energy drink.

ABSOLUTELY FABULOUS

- 2 oz. Vodka
- 1 oz. Cranberry Juice
- 1 oz. Champagne
- Ice

Directions: Fill mixing glass with ice and ingredients. Shake. Strain into chilled highball glass. Top with Champagne. Garnish with a twist.

ACAPULCO

- 1 ½ oz. Light Rum
- 1 ½ tsp. Triple Sec
- 1 tbs. Lime Juice
- 1 tsp. Sugar
- 1 Egg White
- 1 Mint Sprig
- Ice

Directions: Combine and shake all ingredients except mint with ice and strain into an old-fashioned glass over ice cubes. Add the mint sprig.

ACAPULCO GOLD

- 1 oz. Tequila
- 1 oz. Amber Rum
- 1 oz. Cream of Coconut
- 1 oz. Pineapple Juice
- 1 oz. Grapefruit Juice
- 1 Mint Sprig
- Ice

Directions: Fill a mixing glass with ice. Pour in ingredients. Shake. Pour into old-fashioned glass and garnish with sprig of mint.

ADAM

- 2 oz. Dark Rum
- 1 oz. Lemon Juice
- 1 tsp. Grenadine
- Ice

Directions: In a shaker half-filled with ice cubes, combine all of the ingredients. Shake well. Strain into a cocktail glass.

ADIOS MOTHER

- ½ oz. Vodka, Citrus Vodka, or Orange Vodka
- ½ oz. Rum
- ½ oz. Tequila
- ½ oz. Gin
- ½ oz. Blue Curacao
- Sweet and Sour Mix
- Ice

Directions: Fill tall glass with ice. Pour in ingredients and fill with sweet and sour mix. Shake. Pour into highball glass.

ADONIS COCKTAIL

- ¾ oz. Sweet Vermouth
- 1 ½ oz. Dry Sherry
- Dash Orange Bitters
- Ice

Directions: Stir all ingredients with ice, strain contents into a cocktail glass, and serve.

AFFAIR

- 2 oz. Strawberry Schnapps
- 2 oz. Orange Juice
- 2 oz. Cranberry Juice
- Club Soda
- Ice

Directions: Pour schnapps, orange juice, and cranberry juice over ice in a highball glass. Top with club soda and serve.

AFFINITY

- 1 ½ oz. Scotch
- 1 oz. Sweet Vermouth
- 1 oz. Dry Vermouth
- 2 dashes Orange Bitters
- Ice

Directions: In a mixing glass half-filled with ice, combine all ingredients. Stir well. Strain into a cocktail glass.

AFRICAN QUEEN

- ¾ oz. Amaretto
- ¾ oz. Triple Sec
- ¾ oz. Banana Liqueur
- Coffee
- Whipped Cream
- Shaved Chocolate

Directions: Fill a coffee cup with ingredients and fill with black coffee. Top with whipped cream. Sprinkle with shaved chocolate.

AFTER EIGHT

- ½ oz. Coffee Liqueur (bottom)
- ½ oz. White Crème de Menthe
- ½ oz. Irish Cream (top)

Directions: Float ingredients on top of each other in a shot glass.

AFTER FIVE

- ½ oz. Coffee Liqueur (bottom)
- ½ oz. Irish Cream
- ½ oz. Peppermint Schnapps (top)

Directions: Float ingredients on top of each other in a shot glass.

AFTER FIVE COFFEE

- ½ oz. Coffee Liqueur
- ½ oz. Irish Cream
- ½ oz. Peppermint Schnapps
- Coffee
- Whipped Cream
- Shaved Chocolate or Sprinkles

Directions: Pour ingredients in coffee cup. Fill with hot, black coffee. Top with whipped cream. Sprinkle with chocolate or sprinkles.

AFTER SEX

- 1 ½ oz. Vodka or Banana Vodka
- ½ oz. Banana Liqueur
- ¼ oz. Grenadine
- Orange Juice
- Ice

Directions: Fill a mixing glass with ice. Pour ingredients and fill with orange juice. Shake and pour into a highball glass. Top with grenadine.

AFTERBURNER

- 1 oz. Peppered Vodka
- 1 oz. Cinnamon Schnapps
- 1 oz. Coffee Liqueur
- Ice

Directions: Fill a mixing glass with ice. Pour in ingredients. Shake and strain into a rocks glass.

AFTERBURNER 2

- ½ oz. 151 Proof rum
- ½ oz. Jaegermeister
- ½ oz. Coffee Liqueur
- Ice

Directions: Fill a mixing glass with ice. Pour in ingredients. Stir and strain into a chilled rocks glass.

AFTERNOON

- 1 oz. Kahlua
- 1 oz Bailey's
- 1 ½ oz. Frangelico
- 4 oz. Hot Coffee
- Cream

Directions: Build into a coffee mug with no ice. Garnish with cream on top if wanted. Serve directly.

AGENT 99

- ¾ oz. Orange Liqueur (bottom)
- ¾ oz. Blue Curacao
- ¾ oz. Sambuca or Ouzo (top)

Directions: Float ingredients on top of each other in a shot glass.

AGENT 0

- ½ oz. Vodka or Orange Vodka
- ½ oz. Orange Liqueur
- 1 Orange Garnish
- Ice

Directions: Fill a mixing glass with ice. Pour in ingredients and shake. Pour into a rocks glass, and top with orange garnish.

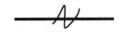

AGGRAVATION AKA TEACHER'S PET

- 1 oz. Scotch
- 1 oz. Coffee Liqueur
- Milk or Cream
- Ice

Directions: Fill serving glass with ice. Pour in ingredients and fill with milk or cream. Shake. Pour into a rocks glass.

AIR GUNNER

- 2 oz. Vodka or Citrus Vodka
- Dash Blue Curacao
- 1 oz. Sour Mix
- Ice

Directions: Fill mixing glass with ice and ingredients. Shake. Strain into chilled rocks glass.

ALABAMA RIOT

- 2 oz. Southern Comfort
- 1 oz. Peppermint Schnapps
- 1 oz. Vodka
- 8 oz. Fruit Punch
- 1 oz. Lime Juice
- Ice

Directions: Pour fruit punch and ice in highball glass; add Southern Comfort, schnapps, and vodka. Stir. Finish with lime juice.

ALABAMA SLAMMER

- 1 oz. Southern Comfort
- 1 oz. Amaretto
- ½ oz. Sloe Gin
- Dash Lemon Juice
- Ice

Directions: Except for lemon juice, pour ingredients over ice in highball glass. Stir. Add a dash of lemon juice.

ALASKA COCKTAIL

- 2 dashes Orange Bitters
- 1 ½ oz. Gin
- ¾ oz. Yellow Chartreuse
- Ice

Directions: Stir all ingredients with ice, strain contents into a cocktail glass, and serve.

ALEXANDER

- 1 oz. Gin
- 1 oz. White Crème de Cacao
- 1 oz. Light Cream
- Nutmeg
- Ice

Directions: Shake ingredients except nutmeg with ice. Strain into cocktail glass. Sprinkle nutmeg.

ALEXANDER THE GREAT

- 1 oz. Greek Brandy
- 1 oz. White Crème de Cacao
- 1 oz. Light Cream
- Nutmeg
- Ice

Directions: Shake ingredients except nutmeg with ice. Strain in cocktail glass. Sprinkle nutmeg.

ALEXANDER'S BIG BROTHER

- 2 oz. Gin
- ½ oz. Blue Curacao
- ½ oz. Heavy Cream
- Ice

Directions: In shaker half-filled with ice, combine ingredients. Shake well. Strain in cocktail glass.

ALEXANDER'S SISTER

- 1 ½ oz. Gin
- 1 oz. Green Crème de Menthe
- 1 oz. Heavy Cream
- ⅛ tsp. Grated Nutmeg
- Ice

Directions: In a shaker half-filled with ice, combine gin, crème de menthe, and heavy cream. Shake well. Strain into cocktail glass. Garnish with the nutmeg.

ALEXANDRA

- ¼ oz. Tia Maria
- ¼ oz. Cream
- ¼ oz. Rum
- ¼ oz. Cocoa Cream
- Ice

Directions: Mix in a shaker, add some ice, and shake very well. Strain into a cocktail glass.

ALFIE COCKTAIL

- 1 ½ oz. Lemon Vodka
- Dash Triple Sec
- 1 tbs. Pineapple Juice
- Ice

Directions: Combine and shake all ingredients with ice, strain into a cocktail glass, and serve.

ALGONQUIN

- 1 ½ oz. Blended Whiskey
- 1 oz. Dry Vermouth
- 1 oz. Pineapple Juice
- Ice

Directions: Combine and shake all ingredients with ice, strain contents into a cocktail glass, and serve.

ALICE IN WONDERLAND AKA DALLAS ALICE

- ¾ oz. Tequila
- ¾ oz. Orange Liqueur
- ¾ oz. Coffee Liqueur
- Ice

Directions: Fill mixing glass with ice and add ingredients. Shake and strain into a shot glass.

ALIEN LOVE JUICE

- 1 oz. Tequila
- 1 oz. Blue Curacao
- Orange Energy Drink
- Ice

Directions: Fill a rocks glass with ice and add ingredients. Fill with orange energy drink.

ALIEN ORGASM

- ¾ oz. Amaretto
- ¾ oz. Melon Liqueur
- ¾ oz. Peach Schnapps
- Orange Juice
- Pineapple Juice
- Ice

Directions: Pour ingredients into a mixing glass and fill with equal parts orange and pineapple juice. Shake and serve in a Collins glass.

ALIEN SECRETION

- ¾ oz. Coconut Rum
- ¾ oz. Melon Liqueur
- ¾ oz. Vodka
- Pineapple Juice
- 1 Cherry Garnish

Directions: Pour ingredients into a mixing glass and fill with pineapple juice. Shake and serve in a rocks glass. Garnish with a cherry.

ALIEN URINE SAMPLE

- ½ oz. Coconut Rum
- ½ oz. Banana Liqueur
- ½ oz. Peach Schnapps
- ½ oz. Melon Liqueur
- ½ oz. Blue Curacao
- Sour Mix
- Soda Water
- Ice

Directions: Fill a tall glass with ice. Add ingredients and fill with sour mix, leaving a half-inch at top. Shake. Splash with soda water. Top with blue curacao.

ALLEGHENY

- 1 oz. Dry Vermouth
- 1 oz. Bourbon
- 1 ½ tsp. Blackberry Brandy
- 1 ½ tsp. Lemon Juice
- Twist of Lemon Peel
- Ice

Directions: Shake all ingredients except lemon peel with ice and strain into a cocktail glass. Top with twist of lemon peel and serve.

ALLIES COCKTAIL

- 1 oz. Dry Vermouth
- 1 oz. Gin
- ½ tsp. Kummel
- Ice

Directions: Stir all ingredients with ice, strain contents into a cocktail glass, and serve.

ALMOND JOY

- ½ oz. Amaretto
- ½ oz. White Crème de Cacao
- 2 oz. Light Cream
- Ice

Directions: Shake all ingredients with ice, strain into a cocktail glass, and serve.

AMARETTO AND CREAM

- 1 ½ oz. Amaretto
- 1 ½ oz. Light Cream
- Ice

Directions: Shake well with cracked ice, strain contents into a cocktail glass, and serve.

AMARETTO MIST

- 1 ½ oz. Amaretto
- 1 Lime or Lemon Wedge
- Ice

Directions: Pour Amaretto into an old-fashioned glass over crushed ice. Add the lime wedge and serve. A lemon wedge may be substituted for lime, if preferred.

AMARETTO ROSE

- 1 ½ oz. Amaretto
- ½ oz. Lime Juice
- Club Soda
- Ice

Directions: Pour Amaretto and lime juice over ice in a Collins glass. Fill with club soda and serve.

AMARETTO STINGER

- 1 ½ oz. Amaretto
- ¾ oz. White Crème de Menthe
- Ice

Directions: Shake ingredients well with cracked ice, strain into a cocktail glass, and serve.

AMARETTO TEA

- 6 oz. Hot Tea
- 2 oz. Amaretto
- Chilled Whipped Cream

Directions: Pour hot tea into a pousse-café glass using a spoon to prevent cracking. Add Amaretto, but do not stir. Top with chilled whipped cream and serve.

AMBASSADOR REGGAE

- Vodka (Absolut Citron preferred)
- Pineapple-orange-banana fruit juice
- 4 tsp. Sugar
- Strawberries
- 1 Orange Slice
- Ice

Directions: Fill a blender half-full with ice. Fill one-fourth of the blender with vodka. Fill half-full with pine-orange-banana fruit juice. Fill the rest with fresh strawberries and sugar. Blend and pour into a pilsner. Serve with an orange slice.

AMER PICON COCKTAIL

- 1 tsp. Grenadine
- 1 ½ oz. Amer Picon
- Lime Juice
- Ice

Directions: Shake all ingredients with ice, strain into a cocktail glass.

AMERICAN BEAUTY

- 1 oz. Brandy
- ½ oz. Dry Vermouth
- ¼ tsp. White Crème de Menthe
- 1 oz. Orange Juice
- 1 tsp. Grenadine
- ½ oz. Tawny Port
- Ice

Directions: In shaker half-filled with ice, combine brandy, vermouth, crème de menthe, orange juice, and grenadine. Shake well. Strain into cocktail glass. Pouring slowly, float the Port on top.

AMY'S TATTOO

- ½ oz. Dark Rum
- ½ oz. Light Rum
- 2 oz. Pineapple Juice
- 2 oz. Orange Juice
- Splash Grenadine

Directions: Shake all in a tall glass.

ANDALUSIA

- ½ oz. Light Rum
- 1 ½ oz. Dry Sherry
- ½ oz. Brandy
- Ice

Directions: Stir all ingredients well with cracked ice, strain contents into a cocktail glass, and serve.

ANGEL FACE

- ½ oz. Apricot Brandy
- ½ oz. Apple Brandy
- 1 oz. Gin
- Ice

Directions: Stir all ingredients well with cracked ice, strain into a cocktail glass, and serve.

ANGEL'S KISS

- ¼ oz. White Crème de Cacao
- ¼ oz. Sloe Gin
- ¼ oz. Brandy
- ¼ oz. Light Cream

Directions: Pour ingredients carefully in the order given into a pousse-café glass so that they do not mix.

ANGEL'S WING

- ½ oz. White Crème de Cacao
- ½ oz. Brandy
- 1 tbs. Light Cream

Directions: Pour ingredients carefully in the order given into a pousse-café glass so that they do not mix. Serve without mixing.

ANGLER'S COCKTAIL

- 1 ½ oz. Gin
- Dash Grenadine
- 2 dashes Bitters
- 3 dashes Orange Bitters
- Ice

Directions: Shake all ingredients with cracked ice, pour contents into an old-fashioned glass over ice cubes, and serve.

ANTE

- 1 oz. Apple Brandy
- ½ oz. Triple Sec
- 1 oz. Dubonnet
- Ice

Directions: Stir all ingredients with ice, strain into cocktail glass, and serve.

APPLE BLOW FIZZ

- 2 oz. Apple Brandy
- Juice of ½ Lemon
- 1 tsp. Powdered Sugar
- 1 Egg White
- Carbonated Water
- Ice

Directions: Shake all ingredients except carbonated water with ice and strain into a highball glass over two ice cubes. Fill with carbonated water, stir, and serve.

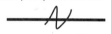

APPLE BRANDY HIGHBALL

- 2 oz. Apple Brandy
- Carbonated Water
- Twist of Lemon Peel
- Ice

Directions: Pour apple brandy over ice cubes in a highball glass. Fill with carbonated water and stir. Add a twist of lemon peel on top and serve. Ginger ale may be substituted for carbonated water, if preferred.

APPLE COLADA

- 2 oz. Apple Schnapps
- 1 oz. Cream of Coconut
- 1 oz. Half & Half
- 1 Apple Slice
- 1 Cherry
- Ice

Directions: Blend schnapps, cream of coconut, Half & Half, and two cups of crushed ice in an electric blender at a high speed. Pour contents into a Collins glass. Decorate with an apple slice and a cherry. Serve with a straw.

APPLE PIE

- 1 oz. Light Rum
- ½ oz. Sweet Vermouth
- 1 tsp. Applejack
- 1 tsp. Lemon Juice
- ½ tsp. Grenadine
- Ice

Directions: In a shaker half-filled with ice cubes, combine all of the ingredients. Shake well. Strain into a cocktail glass.

APPLE RUM RICKEY

- ¾ oz. Light Rum
- ¾ oz. Applejack
- ¼ Lime
- Carbonated Water
- Ice

Directions: Pour applejack and rum in highball glass over ice. Fill with carbonated water. Squeeze lime. Stir.

APPLECAR

- 1 oz. Applejack
- 1 oz. Triple Sec
- 1 oz. Lemon Juice
- Ice

Directions: Shake ingredients with ice, strain into cocktail glass.

APRICOT ANISE COLLINS

- ½ oz. Apricot Brandy
- 1 ½ oz. Gin
- 1 ½ tsp. Anisette
- 1 tbs. Lemon Juice
- Carbonated Water
- 1 Lemon Slice
- Ice

Directions: Shake gin, brandy, anisette, and lemon juice with ice. Strain into Collins glass over ice. Fill with carbonated water and stir. Decorate with lemon slice.

APRICOT COCKTAIL

- 1 tsp. Gin
- 1 ½ oz. Apricot Brandy
- Juice of ¼ Lemon
- Juice of ¼ Orange
- Ice

Directions: Shake all ingredients with ice, strain into a cocktail glass, and serve.

APRICOT LADY

- 1 ½ oz. Light Rum
- 1 oz. Apricot Brandy
- 1 tsp. Triple Sec
- ½ oz. Lemon Juice
- 1 Egg White
- 1 Orange Slice
- Ice

Directions: In a shaker half-filled with ice cubes, combine the rum, apricot brandy, Triple Sec, lemon juice, and egg white. Shake well. Strain into an old-fashioned glass almost filled with ice cubes. Garnish with the orange slice.

ARTHUR TOMPKINS

- 2 oz. Gin
- ½ oz. Grand Marnier
- 2 tsp. Lemon Juice
- 1 Lemon Twist
- Ice

Directions: In a shaker half-filled with ice cubes, combine the gin, Grand Marnier, and lemon juice. Shake well. Strain into a sour glass and garnish with the lemon twist.

ARTILLERY

- 1 ½ tsp. Sweet Vermouth
- 1 ½ oz. Gin
- 2 dashes Bitters
- Ice

Directions: Stir all ingredients with ice, strain into a cocktail glass, and serve.

ATOMIC LOKADE

- 5 oz. Lemonade
- 1 oz. Vodka
- ½ oz. Blue Curacao
- ½ oz. Triple Sec
- Sugar and Ice optional

Directions: In a shaker, place lemonade, vodka, blue curacao, and Triple Sec together. Shake with ice and strain into a glass. Add sugar to taste.

BACARDI COCKTAIL

- 1 ½ oz. Bacardi Light Rum
- 1 oz. Lime Juice
- 1 tsp. Grenadine
- Ice

Directions: In a shaker half-filled with ice cubes, combine all of the ingredients. Shake well. Strain into a cocktail glass.

BAHAMA MAMA

- ¼ oz. Coffee Liqueur
- ½ oz. Dark Rum
- ½ oz. Coconut Liqueur
- ¼ oz. 151 Proof Rum
- 4 oz. Pineapple Juice
- Juice of ½ Lemon
- Strawberry or Cherry Garnish
- Ice

Directions: Combine all ingredients and pour over cracked ice in a Collins glass. Decorate with strawberry or cherry and serve.

BAILEY'S BANANA COLADA

- Bailey's Irish cream
- 1 Banana
- Banana Liqueur
- Pina Colada Mix
- Rum (preferably dark)
- Ice

Directions: Put banana and banana liqueur into blender and blend until it is a thick paste. Add Bailey's to taste and Pina Colada mix and rum. Blend well, then add ice blend until smooth.

BALMORAL

- 1 ½ oz. Scotch
- ½ oz. Sweet Vermouth
- ½ oz. Dry Vermouth
- 2 dashes Bitters
- Ice

Directions: In a mixing glass half-filled with ice cubes, combine all of the ingredients. Stir well. Strain into a cocktail glass.

BALTIMORE BRACER

- 1 oz. Brandy
- 1 oz. Anisette
- 1 Egg White
- Ice

Directions: Shake all ingredients with ice, strain in cocktail glass.

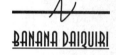

BALTIMORE EGGNOG

- 1 oz. Jamaica Rum
- 1 oz. Brandy
- 1 oz. Madeira
- 1 Whole Egg
- 1 tsp. Powdered Sugar
- ¾ cup Milk
- Nutmeg
- Ice

Directions: Shake all ingredients with ice. Strain in Collins glass. Sprinkle nutmeg on top.

BANANA COW

- 1 oz. Light Rum
- 1 oz. Crème de Bananas
- 1 ½ oz. Cream
- Dash Grenadine
- 1 Banana Slice
- Nutmeg
- Ice

Directions: Shake rum, crème de banana, cream, and grenadine with crushed ice. Strain into cocktail glass. Decorate with banana slice, sprinkle nutmeg on top.

BANANA CREAM PIE

- ½ cup of Ice
- 1 oz. Vodka
- ½ oz. Irish Cream
- ½ oz. Banana Liqueur
- ½ Peeled Ripe Banana
- Scoop of Vanilla Ice Cream

Directions: Place in blender and blend until smooth. Serve in a chilled daiquiri glass.

BANANA DAIQUIRI

- 1 ½ oz. Light Rum
- 1 tbs. Triple Sec
- 1 Banana
- 1 ½ oz. Lime Juice
- 1 tsp. Sugar
- 1 Cherry
- 1 Cup of Ice

Directions: Combine all ingredients except for the cherry with crushed ice in an electric blender. Blend at a low speed for five seconds, then blend at a high speed until firm. Pour contents into a Champagne flute, top with the cherry, and serve.

BARRIER BREAKER

- 1 ½ oz. Dark Rum
- ½ oz. Galliano
- 2 tsp. Dark Crème de Cacao
- 4 oz. Cold Coffee
- Crushed Ice

Directions: Pour all of the ingredients into an Irish coffee glass filled with crushed ice. Stir well.

BARTON SPECIAL

- ½ oz. Applejack
- ¼ oz. Gin
- ¼ oz. Scotch
- Ice

Directions: Shake all ingredients with ice, strain into an old-fashioned glass over ice cubes, and serve.

BATIDA MANGO

- 2 oz. Cachace
- 4 oz. Chopped Fresh Mango
- 2 tsp. Granulated Sugar
- 1 cup of Crushed Ice

Directions: Place all of the ingredients into a blender and blend well. Pour into a wine glass.

BATIDA MORANGO

- 2 oz. Cachaca
- 5 Ripe Strawberries
- ½ tsp. Granulated Sugar
- 1 cup of Crushed Ice

Dirctions: Place all of the ingredients into a blender and blend well. Pour into a wine glass.

BEAUTY SPOT COCKTAIL

- ½ oz. Sweet Vermouth
- ½ oz. Dry Vermouth
- 1 oz. Gin
- 1 tsp. Orange Juice
- Dash Grenadine
- Ice

Directions: Pour a dash of grenadine into a cocktail glass. Shake remaining ingredients with ice, strain into glass over grenadine, and serve.

BEE STINGER

- 1 ½ oz. Blackberry Brandy
- ½ oz. White Crème de Menthe
- Ice

Directions: Shake ingredients with ice, strain into a cocktail glass, and serve.

BENGAL

- 1 ½ oz. Brandy
- ½ oz. Maraschino Liqueur
- ½ oz. Triple Sec
- 1 oz. Pineapple Juice
- 2 dashes Bitters
- Ice

Directions: In a shaker half-filled with ice cubes, combine all of the ingredients. Shake well. Strain into a cocktail glass.

BENNETT COCKTAIL

- 1 ½ oz. Gin
- Juice of ½ Lime
- ½ tsp. Powdered Sugar
- 2 dashes Orange Bitters
- Ice

Directions: Shake all ingredients with ice, strain into a cocktail glass.

BENTLEY

- 1 ½ oz. Apple Brandy
- 1 oz. Dubonnet
- Twist of Lemon Peel
- Ice

Directions: Stir apple brandy and Dubonnet with cracked ice and strain into a cocktail glass. Add the twist of lemon peel and serve.

BERMUDA HIGHBALL

- ¾ oz. Brandy
- ¾ oz. Gin
- ¾ oz. Dry Vermouth
- Carbonated Water
- Twist of Lemon
- Ice

Directions: Pour brandy, gin, and dry vermouth into a highball glass over ice cubes. Fill with carbonated water and stir. Add the twist of lemon and serve. Ginger ale may be substituted for carbonated water, if preferred.

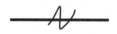

BERMUDA TRIANGLE

- 1 oz. Spiced Rum
- 1 oz. Peach Schnapps
- Orange Juice
- Ice

Directions: Fill a tall Collins glass with ice. Fill with orange juice. Shake.

BERMUDA TRIANGLE 2

- 3 ½ oz. Vodka or Citrus Vodka
- Dash Peach Schnapps
- Dash Amaretto
- Dash Orange Liqueur
- Dash Banana Liqueur
- Dash Pineapple Juice
- Dash Cranberry Juice
- Ice

Directions: Fill a mixing glass with ice. Shake. Strain into a chilled Collins glass.

BERRY DEADLY

- 2 pints Everclear
- 1 bottle Boones Strawberry Hill Wine
- ½ gallon Orange Juice
- 1 gallon Tropical Berry Kool-Aid
- A Variety of Fruit from Grapes to Pineapple

Directions: Add all ingredients into a large bowl. Stir gently. Serve chilled in a punch glass or plastic cup. The fruit will absorb the alcohol.

BERTA

- 2 oz. Tequila
- 2 oz. Honey
- 1 oz. Fresh Lime Juice
- Soda Water
- Ice

Directions: Stir until consistency is even. Fill with ice. Fill with soda water. Serve in a Collins glass.

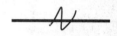

BETSY ROSS

- 1 oz. Brandy
- 1 oz. Port
- ½ oz. Triple Sec
- Dash Bitters
- Ice

Directions: Pour into a mixing glass with ice. Stir. Strain into a chilled cocktail glass.

BETWEEN THE SHEETS

- 1 oz. Rum
- 1 oz. Cognac or Brandy
- 1 oz. Triple Sec
- Ice

Directions: Fill a mixing glass with ice. Shake. Strain into a chilled cocktail glass.

BETWEEN THE SHEETS 2

- 1 oz. Brandy
- 1 oz. Light Rum
- 1 oz. Triple Sec
- 1 oz. Lemon Juice
- Ice

Directions: In a shaker half-filled with ice, combine all ingredients. Shake well. Strain into a cocktail glass.

BEVERLY HILLBILLY (FLOATER)

- 1 oz. 100 Proof Cinnamon
- Schnapps (bottom)
- 1 oz. Jaegermeister (top)

Directions: Layer in a shot glass.

BIBLE BELT

- 2 oz. Bourbon
- 1 oz. Triple Sec
- 2 oz. Lime Juice
- 2 oz. Sour Mix
- Powdered Sugar
- 1 Lemon Garnish
- Ice

Directions: Fill mixing glass with ice. Shake. Rim highball glass with powdered sugar. Garnish with a lemon.

BIFFY COCKTAIL

- 1 ½ oz. Gin
- 1 tbs. Swedish Punch
- Juice of ½ Lemon
- Ice

Directions: Shake all ingredients with ice, strain into a cocktail glass, and serve.

BIG DADDY

- ½ oz. Vodka
- ½ oz. Rum
- ½ oz. Tequila
- ½ oz. Whiskey
- Lemon-lime Soda
- 1 Lime Garnish
- Ice

Directions: Fill a tall glass with ice, vodka, rum, tequila, and whiskey. Fill with lemon-lime soda. Garnish with lime.

BIG KAHUNA

- 1 ½ oz. Gin
- ½ oz. Triple Sec
- ½ oz. Sweet Vermouth
- 2 oz. Pineapple Juice
- Ice

Directions: Pour into a tall glass with ice. Shake. Strain into a chilled glass.

BIKINI

- 1 oz. Vodka
- 1 oz. Rum
- 1 tsp. Sugar
- 1 oz. Sour Mix
- 1 oz. Milk or Cream

Directions: Shake all ingredients. Strain into a chilled glass.

BIKINI LINE

- ¾ oz. Vodka
- ¾ oz. Coffee Liqueur
- ¾ oz. Raspberry Liqueur
- Ice

Directions: Fill a rocks glass with ice. Pour in ingredients.

BILLIE HOLIDAY

- 2 oz. Vodka
- Dash Grenadine
- Ginger Ale
- 1 Cherry Garnish
- Ice

Directions: Fill a tall glass with ice. Fill with ginger ale. Garnish with cherry.

BIRD OF PARADISE

- Champagne
- Pineapple Juice
- Dash Grenadine
- Ice

Directions: Fill a wine glass three-fourths full with ice. Fill three-fourths full with Champagne. Fill with pineapple juice. Add a dash of grenadine.

BISCUIT NECK

- ½ oz. 101 Proof Bourbon
- ½ oz. Amaretto
- ½ oz. Irish Cream
- ½ oz. Hazlenut Liqueur
- Ice

Directions: Fill mixing glass with ice. Shake ingredients. Strain into a rocks glass.

BITCH FIGHT

- 1 oz. Peach Schnapps
- 1 oz. Orange Liqueur
- Cranberry Juice
- 1 Lime Garnish
- Ice

Directions: Fill a tall glass with ice, schnapps, orange liqueur, and cranberry juice. Shake. Garnish with lime.

BITCH-ON-WHEELS

- 2 oz. Gin
- ½ oz. Dry Vermouth
- ½ oz. White Crème de Menthe
- 1 tsp. Pernod
- Ice

Directions: In a mixing glass half-filled with ice, combine ingredients. Stir well. Strain into a cocktail glass.

BITTER SMILE

- 1 oz. Campari
- 2 oz. Grapefruit Juice
- Beer
- Ice

Directions: Fill a pint glass with ice. Add Campari and grapefruit juice. Fill with beer.

BLACK BALTIMORE

- 2 oz. Brandy
- 1 oz. Black Sambuca
- 1 Egg White
- Ice

Directions: In a shaker half-filled with ice, combine all of the ingredients. Shake well. Strain into a cocktail glass.

BLACK CAT

- 1 oz. Vodka
- 1 oz. Cherry Liqueur
- Cranberry Juice
- Cola
- Ice

Directions: Fill a tall glass with ice, vodka, and cherry liqueur. Add equal parts cranberry juice and cola.

BLACK COW

- 1 oz. Vodka
- Root Beer
- Scoop of Vanilla Ice Cream

Directions: Pour root beer over ice cream and vodka. Serve with a straw and spoon.

BLACK COW 2

- 1 oz. Vodka or Vandermint
- 1 oz. Dark Crème de Cacao
- Cream or Milk
- Ice

Directions: Fill a serving glass with ice, vodka, and dark crème de Cacao. Fill with cream or milk. Shake.

BLACK DEATH

- 1 oz. 12 year old Scotch
- Stout

Directions: Combine stout and Scotch in a pint glass.

BLACK DEVIL

- ½ oz. Dry Vermouth
- 2 oz. Light Rum
- 1 Black Olive
- Cracked Ice

Directions: Stir rum and vermouth with cracked ice and strain into a cocktail glass. Top with the black olive and serve.

BLACK DOG

- 2 oz. Bourbon
- 1 oz. Blackberry Brandy
- Ice

Directions: Fill a rocks glass with ice and pour ingredients. Stir.

BLACK EYE

- 1 ½ oz. Vodka
- ½ oz. Blackberry Brandy
- Ice

Directions: Fill a short glass with ice and add ingredients. Stir.

BLACK FORREST
(Floater)

- ½ oz. Coffee Liqueur
- ½ oz. Black Raspberry Liqueur
- ½ oz. Irish Cream
- ½ oz. Vodka (top)

Directions: Layer in a shot glass.

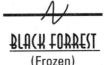

BLACK FORREST
(Frozen)

- ½ cup of Ice
- ¾ oz. Vodka
- ¾ oz. Coffee Liqueur
- ¾ oz. Black Raspberry Liqueur
- Scoop of Chocolate Ice Cream
- Shaved Chocolate or Sprinkles
- Milk (optional)

Directions: Blend ingredients until smooth. Garnish with shaved chocolate or sprinkles.

BLACK GOLD COFFEE

- 1 oz. Amaretto
- 1 oz. Orange Liqueur
- 1 oz. Irish Cream
- 1 oz. Hazelnut Liqueur
- ¼ oz. Cinnamon Schnapps
- Coffee
- Whipped Cream
- Chocolate Coins

Directions: Fill a glass with ingredients. Top with whipped cream. Garnish with chocolate coins.

BLACK HAWK

- 1 ¼ oz. Blended Whiskey
- 1 ¼ oz. Sloe Gin
- 1 Cherry
- Ice

Stir blended whiskey and sloe gin with ice and strain into a cocktail glass. Top with the cherry.

BLACK ICED TEA

- ¾ oz. Dark Rum
- ¾ oz. Brandy
- ¾ oz. Triple Sec
- 1 oz. Orange Juice
- Cola
- 1 Orange Garnish
- Ice

Directions: Fill a tall glass with ice, rum, brandy, and Triple Sec. Fill with cola. Garnish with orange.

BLACK JACK

- 1 ½ oz. Scotch
- 1 oz. Kahlua
- ½ oz. Triple Sec
- ½ oz. Lemon Juice
- Ice

Directions: In a shaker half-filled with ice, combine ingredients. Shake well. Strain into cocktail glass.

BLACK JAMAICAN

- 1 ½ oz. Jamaican Rum
- ½ oz. Coffee Liqueur
- Ice

Directions: Fill a short glass with ice and add ingredients. Stir.

BLACK LADY

- 2 oz. Orange Liqueur
- ½ oz. Coffee Liqueur
- ½ oz. Brandy
- Ice

Directions: Fill mixing glass with ice and ingredients. Shake. Strain into chilled glass.

BLACK MAGIC

- 1 ½ oz. Vodka
- 1 oz. Coffee Liqueur
- Dash Sour Mix
- 1 Lemon Twist

Directions: Stir ingredients in a glass. Garnish with lemon twist.

BLACK MAGIC 2

- ¾ oz. Amaretto
- ¾ oz. Irish Cream
- ¾ oz. Coffee Liqueur
- Hot Chocolate
- Whipped Cream
- Shaved Chocolate

Directions: Combine Amaretto, Irish cream, and coffee liqueur in a glass and fill with hot chocolate. Top with whipped cream and shaved chocolate.

BLACK MARIA

- 2 oz. Coffee Brandy
- 2 oz. Light Rum
- 4 oz. Strong Black Coffee
- 2 tsp. Powdered Sugar
- Cracked Ice

Directions: Combine and stir all ingredients in a brandy snifter. Add cracked ice and serve.

BLACK MARTINI

- 3 ½ oz. Gin, Vodka, or Rum
- ½ oz. Blackberry Brandy or Black Raspberry Liqueur
- 1 Lemon Twist
- Ice

Directions: Fill a mixing glass with ice ingredients. Stir and strain into a chilled glass. Garnish with lemon twist.

BLACK MONDAY

- 1 oz. Dark Rum
- ½ oz. Black Sambuca
- 1 tsp. Cherry Brandy
- ½ oz. Lemon Juice
- Ice

Directions: In a shaker half-filled with ice, combine all ingredients. Shake well. Strain into a cocktail glass.

BLACK PAGODA

- 1 ½ oz. Brandy
- ½ oz. Sweet Vermouth
- ½ oz. Dry Vermouth
- 2 tsp. Triple Sec
- Ice

Directions: In a mixing glass half-filled with ice cubes, combine all of the ingredients. Stir well. Strain into a cocktail glass.

BLACK PRINCE

- 1 oz. Blackberry Brandy
- Champagne
- Dash Lime Juice

Directions: Pour brandy into a wine glass. Fill with Champagne and add a dash of lime juice.

BLACK ROSE

- 2 oz. Rum
- 1 tsp. Sugar
- Coffee
- Ice

Directions: Fill a tall glass with ice, rum, and sugar. Fill with cold, black coffee. Shake.

BLACK RUSSIAN

- ¾ oz. Coffee Liqueur
- 1 ½ oz. Vodka
- Ice

Directions: Pour ingredients over ice cubes in an old-fashioned glass and serve.

BLACK SABBATH

- ¾ oz. Bourbon
- ¾ oz. Dark Rum
- ¾ oz. Jaegermeister

Directions: Shake all ingredients. Pour into a chilled glass.

BLACK SHEEP

- ½ oz. Blackberry Brandy
- ½ oz. Black Raspberry Liqueur
- ½ oz. Lime Juice
- 1 Lime Garnish

Directions: Stir all ingredients and strain into a chilled glass. Garnish with lime.

BLACK STRIPE COLD

- 2 oz. Dark Rum
- ½ oz. Molasses
- 1 tsp. Honey
- 1 oz. Boiling Water
- Crushed Ice

Directions: Pour ingredients in mixing glass; stir well to dissolve the honey and molasses. Pour in old-fashioned glass filled with crushed ice. Stir well.

BLACK VELVET

- 5 oz. Chilled Stout
- 5 oz. Chilled Champagne

Directions: Pour stout into a Champagne flute. Add Champagne carefully so it does not mix with the stout and serve.

BLACK-EYED SUSAN

- 2 oz. Bourbon
- Orange Juice
- Ice

Directions: Fill a serving glass with ice and add bourbon. Fill with orange juice.

BLACKJACK

- ½ oz. Brandy
- 1 oz. Kirschwasser
- 1 oz. Coffee
- Ice

Directions: Shake all ingredients with cracked ice, strain into an old-fashioned glass over ice cubes, and serve.

BLACKTHORN

- 1 oz. Sweet Vermouth
- 1 ½ oz. Sloe Gin
- Twist of Lemon

Directions: Stir sloe gin and vermouth with ice and strain into a cocktail glass. Add the twist of lemon peel and serve.

BLIMEY

- 2 oz. Scotch
- ½ oz. Lime Juice
- ½ tsp. Superfine Sugar
- Ice

Directions: In a shaker half-filled with ice, combine all of the ingredients. Shake. Strain into a cocktail glass.

BLOOD CLOT

- 1 shot Southern Comfort
- ½ lowball 7-Up
- ½ shot grenadine

Directions: Drop shot glass of Southern Comfort into lowball glass mixed with 7-Up and grenadine.

BLOODY BULL

- 1 oz. Vodka
- ½ glass Tomato Juice
- ½ glass Beef Bouillon
- 1 Lime Slice
- 1 Lemon Wedge
- Ice

Directions: Pour vodka, tomato juice, and beef bouillon over ice in a highball glass and stir. Add lime slice and the lemon wedge and serve.

BLOODY CAESAR

- 1 oz. Vodka
- Salt and Pepper
- Celery Salt
- Dash Worcestershire
- Dash Tabasco
- Clamato
- 1 Lime Garnish
- Celery Stick
- Ice

Directions: Rim a tall glass with celery salt, fill with ice, and ingredients. Garnish with a celery stick, straw, and lime.

BLOODY MARIA

- 1 oz. Tequila
- 2 oz. Tomato Juice
- Dash Lemon Juice
- Dash Tabasco Sauce
- Dash Celery Salt
- 1 Slice Lemon
- Ice

Directions: Shake all ingredients except lemon slice with cracked ice and strain into an old-fashioned glass over ice cubes. Add the lemon slice and serve.

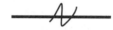

BLOODY MARY

- 1 ½ oz. Vodka
- 3 oz. Tomato Juice
- Dash Lemon Juice
- ½ tsp. Worcestershire Sauce
- 2 or 3 drops Tabasco Sauce
- 1 Lime Wedge
- Ice

Directions: Shake all ingredients except lime wedge with ice and strain into an old-fashioned glass over ice cubes. Add salt and pepper to taste. Add the lime wedge and serve.

BLOW JOB

- ½ oz. Cream (bottom)
- ½ oz. White Crème de Cacao
- ½ oz. Vodka (top)
- Whipped Cream

Directions: Layer all ingredients in a shot glass and top with whipped cream. Contents should mix slightly. To drink, place hands behind back and pick up with mouth.

BLUE BAYOU

- 1 cup of Ice
- 1 ½ oz. Vodka
- ½ oz. Blue Curacao
- ½ cup Fresh or Canned Pineapple
- 2 oz. Grapefruit Juice

Directions: Blend all ingredients until smooth. If too thick, add juice. If too thin, add ice. Serve in a hurricane glass and garnish with pineapple.

BLUE BIJOU

- 1 cup of Ice
- 1 ¼ oz. Rum or Orange Rum
- 1 oz. Blue Curacao
- 3 oz. Orange Juice
- 3 oz. Pineapple Juice
- 3 or 4 drops Lime Juice

Directions: Blend all ingredients on low for three to five seconds.

BLUE CANARY

- 1 ½ oz. Gin
- ½ oz. Blue Curacao
- Grapefruit Juice
- Ice

Directions: Fill a rocks glass with ice. Pour ingredients in and fill with grapefruit juice.

BLUE COWBOY

- Crushed Ice
- 1 ½ oz. Gin
- ½ oz. Blue Curacao

Directions: In a mixing glass half-filled with crushed ice, combine the ingredients. Stir well. Strain into a cocktail glass.

BLUE DAIQUIRI

- 1 cup of Ice
- 1 ½ oz. Rum
- ½ oz. Blue Curacao
- Dash Lime Juice
- Dash Sour Mix
- ½ tsp. Sugar

Directions: Blend all ingredients until smooth. If too thin, add sour mix. If too thick, add ice.

BLUE DEVIL COCKTAIL

- 1 oz. Gin
- Juice of ½ Lemon
- 1 tbs. Maraschino
- ½ tsp. Blue Curacao
- Ice

Directions: Shake all ingredients with ice, strain into a cocktail glass, and serve.

BLUE HAWAIIAN

- 1 oz. Light Rum
- 2 oz. Pineapple Juice
- 1 oz. Blue Curacao
- 1 oz. Cream of Coconut
- 1 Pineapple Slice
- 1 cup of Ice
- 1 Cherry

Directions: Blend light rum, blue curacao, pineapple juice, and cream of coconut with ice in an electric blender at high speed. Pour contents into a highball glass. Decorate with the slice of pineapple and a cherry.

BLUE KAMIKAZE

- 2 oz. Vodka or Lime Vodka
- ½ oz. Blue Curacao
- Dash Lime Juice
- 1 Lime Garnish
- Ice

Directions: Fill a mixing glass with ice. Pour in ingredients. Shake. Strain into a chilled rocks glass or cocktail glass. Garnish with lime.

BLUE MARGARITA

- 1 ½ oz. Tequila
- 1 oz. Blue Curacao
- 1 oz. Lime Juice
- Coarse Salt
- Ice

Directions: Rub the rim of a cocktail glass with lime juice. Dip rim in coarse salt. Shake tequila, blue curacao, and lime juice with ice, strain into the salt-rimmed glass, and serve.

BLUEBERRY CHEESECAKE

- 2 ½ oz. Vanilla Vodka
- Dash Coffee Liqueur (Jamaican)
- 1 tbs. Blueberry Syrup
- 1 oz. Cream
- Graham Crackers
- Ice

Directions: Fill a mixing glass with ice. Pour in ingredients. Shake and strain into a chilled rocks glass rimmed with crushed graham crackers.

BLUEBIRD

- 1 ½ oz. Gin
- ½ oz. Triple Sec
- ½ oz. Blue Curacao
- 2 dashes Bitters
- 1 Lemon Twist
- 1 Maraschino Cherry
- Crushed Ice

Directions: In a mixing glass half-filled with crushed ice, combine the gin, Triple Sec, curacao, and bitters. Stir well. Strain into a cocktail glass and garnish with the lemon twist and the cherry.

BOARDWALK BREEZER

- 1 ½ oz. Dark Rum
- ½ oz. Banana Liqueur
- ½ oz. Lime Juice
- Dash Grenadine
- Ice
- 1 Orange Garnish
- 1 Lime Garnish

Directions: Fill a tall Collins glass with ice. Pour ingredients in a mixing glass, shake. Strain into a Collins glass. Top with a dash of grenadine. Garnish with an orange and cherry.

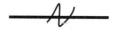

BOB MARLEY

- 1 oz. Dark Rum
- 1 oz. Tia Maria
- Dash Cream of Coconut
- Dash Milk or Cream
- Dash Pineapple Juice
- Ice

Directions: Fill a mixing glass with ice. Pour in ingredients and shake. Strain into a chilled rocks glass.

BOCA WEST FOREST CAKE

- 2 oz. Chocolate Chip Liqueur
- 1 oz. Vanilla Liqueur
- Splash Grenadine.
- Cream
- Whipped Cream
- 1 Cherry

Directions: Combine ingredients in a blender. Blend until smooth. Garnish with whipped cream and cherry.

BOCCI BALL

- 1 ½ oz. Vodka
- ½ oz. Amaretto
- Orange Juice
- Soda Water
- 1 Orange Garnish
- Ice

Directions: Fill a rocks glass with ice and pour in ingredients. Fill with orange juice. Splash with soda water. Garnish with an orange.

BOILERMAKER

- Whiskey
- Beer

Directions: Fill shot glass with whiskey. Fill chilled glass three-fourths full with beer. Either drink the shot and then chase it with beer or drop the shot glass into the beer.

BOMB

- ½ oz. Scotch
- ½ oz. Bourbon
- ½ oz. 151 Proof Rum
- ½ oz. Dark Rum
- Dash Grenadine
- Orange Juice
- Pineapple Juice
- Ice

Directions: Fill mixing glass with ice. Pour in ingredients and fill with equal parts orange and pineapple juice. Shake. Pour in rocks glass.

BOMB POP

- 2 oz. Raspberry Vodka
- ½ oz. Blue Curacao
- Lemonade
- Popsicle Stick
- Ice

Directions: Fill mixing glass with ice. Pour ingredients and fill with lemonade. Shake. Pour in rocks glass. Garnish with Popsicle stick.

BOMBAY COCKTAIL

- ½ oz. Dry Vermouth
- ½ oz. Sweet Vermouth
- 1 oz. Brandy
- ½ tsp. Triple Sec
- ¼ tsp. Anisette
- Ice

Directions: Stir ingredients with ice, strain into a cocktail glass.

BON BON

- ¾ oz. Irish Cream
- ¾ oz. Black Raspberry Liqueur
- ¾ oz. Truffles Liqueur
- Ice

Directions: Fill mixing glass with ice. Pour ingredients and shake. Strain into chilled rocks glass.

BOOMER

- 1 oz. Tequila
- 1 oz. Apricot Brandy
- Orange Juice
- Sour Mix
- Ice

Directions: Fill a mixing glass with ice. Pour in ingredients and fill glass with equal parts orange juice and sour mix. Shake. Pour into a rocks glass.

BOOTLEGGER

- ¾ oz. Bourbon
- ¾ oz. Tequila
- ¾ oz. Southern Comfort
- Ice

Directions: Fill a mixing glass with ice and all ingredients. Shake and strain into a chilled cocktail glass.

BORDER CROSSING

- 1 ½ oz. Tequila
- 2 tsp. Lime Juice
- 1 tsp. Lemon Juice
- 4 oz. Cola
- 1 Lime Wedge
- Ice

Directions: Pour the tequila, lime juice, lemon juice, and cola into a highball glass almost filled with ice cubes. Stir well and garnish with the lime wedge.

BOSOM CARESSER

- Crushed Ice
- 1 ½ oz. Brandy
- 1 oz. Madeira
- ½ oz. Triple Sec

In a mixing glass half-filled with crushed ice, combine all of the ingredients. Stir well. Strain into a cocktail glass.

BOSS

- ¾ oz. Bourbon
- ¾ oz. Amaretto
- Ice

Directions: Fill a short glass with ice and pour in ingredients. Stir.

BOSSA NOVA

- 1 oz. Galliano
- 1 oz. Amber Rum
- ¼ oz. Apricot Brandy
- Pineapple Juice
- Dash Sour Mix
- ½ Egg White
- 1 Cherry Garnish
- 1 Orange Garnish
- Ice

Directions: Fill a tall glass with ice, Galliano, rum, brandy, sour mix, and egg white. Fill with pineapple juice. Shake. Pour into a highball glass and garnish with a cherry and an orange.

BOSTON COCKTAIL

- ¾ oz. Gin
- ¾ oz. Apricot Brandy
- 1 ½ tsp. Grenadine
- Juice of ¼ Lemon
- Ice

Directions: Shake all ingredients with ice, strain into a cocktail glass, and serve.

BOSTON COOLER

- 2 oz. Rum or Citrus Rum
- 4 oz. Sour Mix
- Soda Water
- 1 Lemon Wedge
- Ice

Directions: Fill mixing glass with ice. Pour in ingredients. Shake and pour into a highball glass. Fill with soda water. Garnish with a lemon wedge.

BOSTON CREAM PIE

- 1 oz. Vanilla Vodka
- 1 oz. White Chocolate Liqueur
- 1 oz. Advokaat
- 1 oz. Light Cream
- Chocolate
- Ice

Directions: Fill mixing glass with ice. Pour in ingredients and shake. Strain into chilled cocktail glass with chocolate swirled inside.

BOSTON GOLD

- 1 ½ oz. Vodka
- ½ oz. Banana Liqueur
- Orange Juice
- Ice

Directions: Fill mixing glass with ice. Pour in ingredients and fill with orange juice. Shake. Strain into a cocktail glass.

BOSTON ICED TEA

- ½ oz. Vodka
- ½ oz. Gin
- ½ oz. Rum
- ½ oz. Coffee Liqueur
- ½ oz. Amaretto or Orange Liqueur
- 2 oz. Sour Mix
- Cola
- Ice
- 1 Lemon Garnish

Directions: Fill a Collins glass with ice and pour in ingredients. Fill with cola and garnish with a lemon.

BOSTON MASSACRE

- Dash Irish Cream
- Dash Orange Liqueur
- Dash Coffee Liqueur
- Dash Hazelnut Liqueur
- Dash Irish Whiskey
- Dash Amaretto
- Dash Dark Crème de Cacao
- Cream

Directions: Fill a tall glass with cream and add ingredients. Shake. Pour into a Collins glass.

BOSTON MASSACRE

(Frozen)

- ½ cup of Ice
- Dash Irish Cream
- Dash Orange Liqueur
- Dash Coffee Liqueur
- Dash Hazelnut Liqueur
- Dash Irish Whiskey
- Dash Amaretto
- Dash Dark Crème de Cacao
- Dash Grenadine
- Scoop of Vanilla Ice Cream
- Milk or Cream

Directions: Blend all ingredients until smooth. Pour into glass. Insert straw and dribble grenadine in straw. It should run down the inside of the glass and look like dripping blood.

BOSTON SIDECAR

- ¾ oz. Light Rum
- ¾ oz. Brandy
- ¾ oz. Triple Sec
- Juice of ½ Lime
- Ice

Directions: Shake all ingredients with ice, strain into a cocktail glass, and serve.

BOSTON SOUR

- 2 oz. Blended Whiskey
- Juice of ½ Lemon
- 1 tsp. Powdered Sugar
- 1 Egg White
- 1 Lemon Slice
- 1 Cherry
- Cracked Ice

Directions: Shake juice of lemon, powdered sugar, blended whiskey, and egg white with cracked ice and strain into a whiskey sour glass. Add the slice of lemon, top with the cherry, and serve.

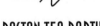

BOSTON TEA PARTY

- 1 oz. Vodka
- 1 oz. Amaretto
- 1 oz. Coffee Liqueur
- 1 oz. Orange Liqueur
- 2 oz. Sour Mix
- Cola
- Ice

Directions: Fill a mixing glass with ice and pour in ingredients. Shake. Pour into a Collins glass and fill with cola.

BOURBON COOLER

- 2 oz. Bourbon
- 4 oz. Lemon-lime Soda
- 1 Lemon Wedge
- Ice

Directions: Pour bourbon and soda into highball glass filled with ice. Stir well. Garnish with lemon wedge.

BOURBON COUNTY COWBOY

- 2 oz. Bourbon
- ½ oz. Light Cream
- Ice

Directions: In shaker half-filled with ice, combine bourbon and cream. Shake well. Strain into cocktail glass.

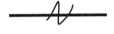

BOURBON DAISY

- 2 oz. Bourbon
- 1 oz. Lemon Juice
- ½ tsp. Grenadine
- ½ tsp. Superfine Sugar
- 1 Orange Slice
- 1 Maraschino Cherry
- Ice

Directions: In a shaker half-filled with ice, combine bourbon, lemon juice, grenadine, and sugar. Shake well. Pour into an old-fashioned glass. Garnish with the orange slice and the cherry.

BOURBON FIX

- 1 tsp. Superfine Sugar
- 1 oz. Lemon Juice
- 2 tsp. Water
- 2 oz. Bourbon
- 1 Maraschino Cherry
- 1 Lemon Slice
- Ice

Directions: In a shaker half-filled with ice cubes, combine the sugar, lemon juice, and water. Shake well. Strain into a highball glass almost filled with crushed ice. Add the bourbon. Stir well and garnish with the cherry and the lemon slice.

BOURBON FLIP

- 2 oz. Bourbon
- 1 Egg
- 1 tsp. Superfine Sugar
- ½ oz. Light Cream
- ⅛ tsp. Grated Nutmeg
- Ice

Directions: In a shaker half-filled with ice cubes, combine the bourbon, egg, sugar, and cream. Shake well. Strain into a sour glass and garnish with the nutmeg.

BOURBON HIGHBALL

- 2 oz. Bourbon
- Carbonated Water
- Twist of Lemon Peel
- Ice

Directions: Pour bourbon into a highball glass over ice cubes. Fill with carbonated water and stir. Add the twist of lemon peel and serve. Ginger ale may be substituted for carbonated water, if preferred.

BOURBON MANHATTAN

- 2 oz. Bourbon
- Dash Sweet Vermouth
- 1 Cherry Garnish
- Ice

Directions: Fill a mixing glass with ice, bourbon, and vermouth. Stir. Strain into a chilled cocktail glass and pour contents over ice into a short glass. Garnish with a cherry and serve.

Note: Sweet means extra sweet vermouth. Dry can mean to use either dry vermouth or use less sweet vermouth than usual, and garnish with a lemon twist or cherry.

BOURBON OLD-FASHIONED

- 3 dashes Bitters
- 1 tsp. Water
- 1 Sugar Cube
- 3 oz. Bourbon
- 1 Orange Slice
- 1 Maraschino Cherry
- Ice

Directions: In an old-fashioned glass, muddle the bitters and water into the sugar cube using the back of a teaspoon. Almost fill the glass with ice cubes and add the bourbon. Garnish with the orange slice and the cherry. Serve with a swizzle stick.

BOURBON SATIN

- 1 ½ oz. Bourbon
- 1 oz. White Crème de Cacao
- 2 oz. Milk or Cream
- Ice

Directions: Fill a mixing glass with ice. Pour in ingredients. Shake. Strain into a chilled cocktail glass.

BOURBON SLING

- 1 tsp. Superfine Sugar
- 2 tsp. Water
- 1 oz. Lemon Juice
- 2 oz. Bourbon
- 1 Lemon Twist
- Ice

Directions: In a shaker half-filled with ice cubes, combine the sugar, water, lemon juice, and bourbon. Shake well and strain into a highball glass. Garnish with the lemon twist.

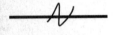

BOURBON SOUR

- 2 oz. Bourbon
- 1 oz. Lemon Juice
- ½ tsp. Superfine Sugar
- 1 Orange Slice
- 1 Maraschino Cherry
- Ice

Directions: In a shaker half-filled with ice cubes, combine the bourbon, lemon juice, and sugar. Shake well. Strain into a whiskey sour glass and garnish with the orange slice and cherry.

BOURBON STREET ICED TEA

- ½ oz. Jim Beam
- ½ oz. Jack Daniels
- ½ oz. Wild Turkey
- ½ oz. Yukon Jack
- ½ oz. Southern Comfort
- ½ oz. Triple Sec
- 1 oz. Sour Mix
- Cola
- 1 Lemon Garnish
- Ice

Directions: Fill a mixing glass with ice. Pour in ingredients and shake. Pour in Collins glass and top with cola. Garnish with lemon.

BOX CAR

- 1 ½ oz. Rum
- ½ oz. Triple Sec
- Sour Mix
- 1 Cherry Garnish
- 1 Orange Garnish
- Ice

Directions: Fill a rocks glass with ice. Pour in ingredients and fill with sour mix. Shake. Garnish with orange and cherry.

BRAHMA BULL

- 1 ½ oz. Gold Tequila
- ½ oz. Coffee Liqueur
- Ice

Directions: Fill rocks glass with ice and pour in ingredients. Stir.

BRAIN

- 1 oz. Strawberry Schnapps
- ¼ oz. Grenadine
- ½ oz. Irish Cream

Directions: Put in a shot glass drop by drop.

BRAIN (FLOATER)

- 1 oz. Coffee Liqueur (bottom)
- 1 oz. Peach Schnapps
- 1 oz. Irish Cream (top)
- Ice

Directions: Fill a glass with ice and layer ingredients into the glass.

BRAIN ERASER

- 1 oz. Vodka
- ½ oz. Coffee Liqueur
- ½ oz. Amaretto
- Club Soda
- Ice

Directions: Fill a Collins glass with ice. Pour in ingredients. Splash with club soda. This drink is supposed to be consumed in one shot through a straw.

RAINSTORM

- 2 oz. Scotch
- ½ oz. Benedictine
- 1 tsp. Sweet Vermouth
- Ice

Directions: In a mixing glass half-filled with ice cubes, combine all of the ingredients. Stir well. Strain into a cocktail glass.

BRANDIED MADEIRA

- 1 oz. Brandy
- ½ oz. Dry Vermouth
- 1 oz. Madeira
- Twist of Lemon Peel
- Ice

Directions: Stir all ingredients except lemon peel with cracked ice and strain into an old-fashioned glass over ice cubes. Add the twist of lemon peel and serve.

BRANDY AND SODA

- 2 oz. Brandy
- 5 oz. Club Soda
- Ice

Directions: Pour the brandy and club soda into a highball glass almost filled with ice cubes. Stir well.

BRANDY BLAZER

- 1 tsp. Granulated Sugar
- 2 oz. Brandy
- 1 Orange Slice
- 1 Lemon Twist

Directions: In an old-fashioned glass, dissolve the sugar in brandy. Add the orange slice. Tilt the glass and carefully ignite the drink with a match. Stir with a long spoon until the flame is extinguished. Strain into a punch cup and garnish with the lemon twist.

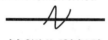

BRANDY COBBLER

- 1 tsp. Superfine Sugar
- 3 oz. Club Soda
- 1 Lemon Slice
- 2 oz. Brandy
- 1 Maraschino Cherry
- 1 Orange Slice
- Crushed Ice

Directions: In an old-fashioned glass, dissolve the sugar in the club soda. Add crushed ice until the glass is almost full. Add the brandy. Stir well. Garnish with the cherry and the orange and lemon slices.

BRANDY COCKTAIL

- 2 oz. Brandy
- ¼ tsp. Sugar Syrup
- 2 dashes Bitters
- Twist of Lemon Peel
- Ice

Directions: Stir all ingredients except lemon peel with ice and strain into a cocktail glass. Add the twist of lemon peel and serve.

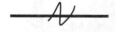

BRANDY COLLINS

- Juice of ½ Lemon
- 2 oz. Brandy
- 1 tsp. Powdered Sugar
- Carbonated Water
- 1 Orange Slice
- 1 Cherry
- Ice

Directions: Shake juice of lemon, brandy, and powdered sugar with cracked ice and strain into a Collins glass. Add ice cubes, fill with carbonated water, and stir. Garnish with a slice of orange and top with a cherry. Serve with a straw.

BRANDY COOLER

- 2 oz. Brandy
- 4 oz. Lemon-lime Soda
- 1 Lemon Wedge
- Ice

Directions: Pour the brandy and the soda into a highball glass almost filled with ice cubes. Stir well. Garnish with the lemon wedge.

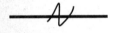

BRANDY DAISY

- 2 oz. Brandy
- 1 oz. Lemon Juice
- ½ tsp. Superfine Sugar
- ½ tsp. Grenadine
- 1 Maraschino Cherry
- 1 Orange Slice
- Ice

Directions: In a shaker half-filled with ice cubes, combine the brandy, lemon juice, sugar, and grenadine. Shake well. Pour into an old-fashioned glass and garnish with the cherry and the orange slice.

BRANDY FIX

- 2 ½ oz. Brandy
- Juice of ½ Lemon
- 1 tsp. Powdered Sugar
- 1 tsp. Water
- 1 Lemon Slice
- Shaved Ice

Directions: Combine juice of lemon, powdered sugar, and water in a highball glass. Stir, fill with shaved ice, and add brandy. Stir again, add the lemon slice, and serve with a straw.

BRANDY FIZZ

- 2 ½ oz. Brandy
- 1 oz. Lemon Juice
- 1 tsp. Superfine Sugar
- 4 oz. Club Soda
- Ice

Directions: In a shaker half-filled with ice cubes, combine the brandy, lemon juice, and sugar. Shake well. Strain into a Collins glass almost filled with ice cubes. Add the club soda. Stir well.

BRANDY FLIP

- 2 oz. Brandy
- 1 Whole Egg
- 1 tsp. Superfine Sugar
- ½ oz. Light Cream
- 1/8 tsp. Grated Nutmeg
- Ice

Directions: In a shaker half-filled with ice cubes, combine the brandy, egg, sugar, and cream. Shake well. Strain into a sour glass and garnish with the nutmeg.

BRANDY HIGHBALL

- 2 oz. Brandy
- Carbonated Water
- Twist of Lemon Peel
- Ice

Directions: Pour brandy into a highball glass over ice cubes. Fill with carbonated water, add the twist of lemon peel, stir gently, and serve. Ginger ale may be substituted for carbonated water, if preferred.

BRANDY SANGAREE

- 2 oz. Brandy
- ½ tsp. Powdered Sugar
- 1 tsp. Water
- Carbonated Water
- 1 tbs. Port
- Nutmeg
- Ice

Directions: Dissolve powdered sugar in water. Add brandy and pour into a highball glass over ice cubes. Fill with carbonated water and stir. Float Port on top, sprinkle lightly with nutmeg, and serve.

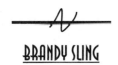

BRANDY SLING

- 1 tsp. Superfine Sugar
- 2 tsp. Water
- 1 oz. Lemon Juice
- 2 oz. Brandy
- 1 Lemon Twist
- Ice

Directions: In a shaker half-filled with ice cubes, combine the sugar, water, lemon juice, and brandy. Shake well. Strain into a highball glass. Garnish with the lemon twist.

BRANDY SMASH

- 4 Fresh Mint Sprigs
- 1 tsp. Superfine Sugar
- 1 oz. Club Soda
- 2 ½ oz. Brandy
- 1 Orange Slice
- 1 Maraschino Cherry
- Ice

Directions: In an old-fashioned glass, muddle the mint sprigs lightly with the sugar and club soda. Fill the glass with ice cubes. Add the brandy. Stir well and garnish with the orange slice and the cherry.

BRANDY SOUR

- 2 oz. Brandy
- Juice of ½ Lemon
- ½ tsp. Powdered Sugar
- ½ Lemon Slice
- 1 Cherry
- Ice

Directions: Shake brandy, lemon juice, and powdered sugar with ice and strain into a whiskey sour glass. Decorate with the lemon slice, top with the cherry, and serve.

BRANDY SWIZZLE

- 1 ½ oz. Lime Juice
- 1 tsp. Superfine Sugar
- 2 oz. Brandy
- 3 oz. Club Soda
- Dash Bitters
- Ice

Directions: In a shaker half-filled with ice cubes, combine the lime juice, sugar, brandy, and bitters. Shake well. Almost fill a Collins glass with crushed ice and stir until the glass is frosted. Strain the mixture into the glass and add the club soda.

BRANDY TODDY

- 2 oz. Brandy
- ½ tsp. Powdered Sugar
- 1 tsp. Water
- Twist of Lemon Peel
- Ice

Directions: Dissolve powdered sugar in water in an old-fashioned glass. Add brandy and one ice cube and stir. Add twist of lemon peel on top and serve.

BRANDY VERMOUTH COCKTAIL

- 1 ½ oz. Sweet Vermouth
- 2 oz. Brandy
- Dash Bitters
- Ice

Directions: Stir all ingredients with ice, strain into a cocktail glass, and serve.

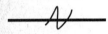

BRAVE BULL

- 1 ½ oz. Tequila
- 1 oz. Coffee Liqueur
- Twist of Lemon
- Ice

Directions: Pour tequila and coffee liqueur over ice cubes in an old-fashioned glass and stir. Add the twist of lemon and serve.

BRAZIL COCKTAIL

- 1 ½ oz. Dry Sherry
- 1 ½ oz. Dry Vermouth
- ¼ tsp. Anisette
- Dash Bitters
- Ice

Directions: Stir all ingredients with ice, strain into a cocktail glass, and serve.

BROKEN SPUR COCKTAIL

- ¾ oz. Sweet Vermouth
- 1 ½ oz. Port
- ¼ tsp. Triple Sec
- Ice

Directions: Stir all ingredients with ice, strain into a cocktail glass, and serve.

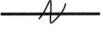

THE BRONX AINT SO SWEET

- 1 ½ oz. Gin
- 1 tsp. Dry Vermouth
- ½ oz. Orange Juice
- Ice

Directions: In a shaker half-filled with ice, combine all of the ingredients. Shake. Strain into cocktail glass.

BRONX COCKTAIL (DRY)

- 1 oz. Dry Vermouth
- 1 oz. Gin
- Juice of ¼ Orange
- 1 Orange Slice
- Ice

Directions: Shake all ingredients except orange slice with ice and strain into a cocktail glass. Add orange slice and serve.

BRONX GOLDEN COCKTAIL

- ½ oz. Dry Vermouth
- ½ oz. Sweet Vermouth
- 1 oz. Gin
- Juice of ¼ Orange
- 1 Orange Slice
- 1 Egg Yolk
- Ice

Directions: Shake all ingredients except orange slice with ice and strain into a whiskey sour glass. Add the orange slice and serve.

BRONX SILVER COCKTAIL

- ½ oz. Dry Vermouth
- 1 oz. Gin
- Juice of ½ Orange
- 1 Egg White
- Ice

Directions: Shake all ingredients with ice, strain into a whiskey sour glass, and serve.

BROWN COCKTAIL

- ¾ oz. Light Rum
- ¾ oz. Gin
- ¾ oz. Dry Vermouth
- Ice

Directions: Stir all ingredients with ice, strain into a cocktail glass, and serve.

BULLDOG COCKTAIL

- 1 ½ oz. Cherry Brandy
- ¾ oz. Gin
- Juice of ½ Lime
- Ice

Directions: Shake all ingredients with ice, strain into a cocktail glass, and serve.

BULLFROG

- 12 shots Vodka
- 1 qt. Lemonade
- 1 Lemon Slice
- Ice

Directions: Shake all ingredients well, preferably in a closed container. Stir, preferably with a spoon in an opened container. Serve in a punch bowl with glasses or out of a pitcher in rocks glasses with ice. Garnish with a slice of lemon.

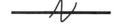

BULL'S EYE

- 1 oz. Brandy
- 2 oz. Hard Cider
- Ginger Ale
- Ice

Directions: Pour brandy and hard cider into a highball glass over ice cubes. Fill with ginger ale, stir, and serve.

BULL'S MILK

- 1 oz. Light Rum
- 1 ½ oz. Brandy
- 1 cup of Milk
- 1 tsp. Powdered Sugar
- Pinch Cinnamon
- Nutmeg
- Ice

Directions: Shake rum, brandy, milk, and powdered sugar with ice and strain into a Collins glass. Sprinkle nutmeg and cinnamon on top.

BUMBO

- 2 oz. Dark Rum
- 1 oz. Lemon Juice
- ½ tsp. Grenadine
- ¼ tsp. Grated Nutmeg
- Ice

Directions: In a shaker half-filled with ice cubes, combine all of the ingredients. Shake well. Strain into a cocktail glass.

BURNT EMBERS

- 1 ½ oz. Anejo Rum
- ½ oz. Apricot Brandy
- 1 oz. Pineapple Juice
- Ice

Directions: In a shaker half-filled with ice cubes, combine all of the ingredients. Shake well. Strain into a cocktail glass.

C & B

- 1 oz. Cognac
- 1 oz. Benedictine

Directions: Pour ingredients into a snifter and serve.

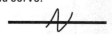

CABARET

- 1 oz. Gin
- ½ oz. Dry Vermouth
- ½ oz. Benedictine
- 2 dashes Bitters
- 1 Maraschino Cherry
- Ice

Directions: In a shaker half-filled with ice cubes, combine gin, vermouth, Benedictine, and bitters. Shake well. Strain into a cocktail glass and garnish with the cherry.

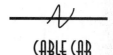

CABLE CAR

- 1 ½ oz. Gin
- ½ oz. Triple Sec
- ½ oz. Lime Juice
- Ice

Directions: Fill a mixing glass with ice. Pour ingredients in and shake. Strain into a chilled cocktail glass.

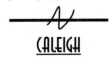

CABLEGRAM

- 2 oz. Blended Whiskey
- Juice of ½ Lemon
- 1 tsp. Powdered Sugar
- Ginger Ale
- Ice

Directions: Stir blended whiskey, lemon juice, and powdered sugar with ice cubes in a highball glass. Fill with ginger ale, stir, and serve.

CACTUS BITE

- 2 oz. Tequila
- 2 oz. Lemon Juice
- 2 tsp. Triple Sec
- 2 tsp. Drambuie
- ½ tsp. Superfine Sugar
- Dash Bitters
- Ice

Directions: In a shaker half-filled with ice cubes, combine all of the ingredients. Shake well. Strain into a cocktail glass.

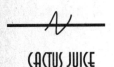

CACTUS JUICE

- 1 ½ oz. Tequila
- ½ oz. Amaretto
- Ice

Directions: Fill a mixing glass with ice. Pour in ingredients and shake. Pour into a rocks glass.

CADILLAC MARGARITA

- 1 ½ oz. Tequila
- ½ oz. Cointreau
- 3 oz. Sour Mix
- Dash Lime Juice
- Dash Grand Marnier
- Ice

Directions: Fill a mixing glass with ice. Pour in ingredients and shake. Serve in a Collins glass. Top with a dash of Grand Marnier.

CADIZ

- ¾ oz. Blackberry Brandy
- ¾ oz. Dry Sherry
- ½ oz. Triple Sec
- ¼ oz. Cream
- Ice

Directions: Fill a mixing glass with ice. Shake. Pour into a short glass and serve.

CAIPIRINHA

- 2 tbs. Granulated Sugar
- 2 Lime Wedges
- 2 ½ oz. Cachaca or Rum
- Ice

Directions: Muddle sugar into the lime wedges in rocks glass. Fill glass with ice. Fill with Cachaca or rum. Stir.

CAJUN MARTINI

- 3 ½ oz. Peppered Vodka
- ½ oz. Dry Vermouth
- Jalepeno Pepper
- Ice

Directions: Fill mixing glass with ice. Pour in ingredients and stir. Strain into a chilled cocktail glass. Garnish with a jalepeno pepper.

CALEIGH

- 1 ½ oz. Scotch
- ½ oz. Blue Curacao
- ½ oz. White Crème de Cacao
- Ice

Directions: In mixing glass half-filled with ice, combine ingredients. Stir well. Strain into a cocktail glass.

CALIFORNIA BREEZE

- 2 oz. Vodka
- Orange Juice
- Cranberry Juice
- 1 Orange or Lime Garnish
- Ice

Directions: Fill a highball glass with ice. Pour in vodka and fill with equal parts orange and cranberry juice. Stir. Garnish with orange or lime.

CALIFORNIA COOL AID

- 2 oz. Rum
- Orange Juice
- Milk
- Ice

Directions: Fill a glass with ice and add rum. Fill with equal parts orange juice and milk. Shake. Pour into a highball glass.

CALIFORNIA COOLER

- 2 oz. Vodka
- Orange Juice
- Grapefruit Juice
- Ice

Directions: Fill a highball glass with ice. Pour in vodka and fill with equal parts orange juice and grapefruit juice.

CALIFORNIA DREAM

- 2 oz. Tequila
- 1 oz. Sweet Vermouth
- ½ oz. Dry Vermouth
- 1 Maraschino Cherry
- Ice

Directions: In a mixing glass half-filled with ice cubes, combine the tequila, sweet vermouth, and dry vermouth. Stir well. Strain into a cocktail glass and garnish with the cherry.

CALIFORNIA ICED TEA

- ½ oz. Vodka
- ½ oz. Gin
- ½ oz. Rum
- ½ oz. Tequila
- ½ oz. Triple Sec
- 2 oz. Grapefruit Juice
- Cola
- Lemon Garnish
- Ice

Directions: Fill a Collins glass with ice and pour in ingredients. Top with cola and garnish with a lemon.

CALIFORNIA LEMONADE

- 2 oz. Blended Whiskey
- Juice of 1 Lemon
- Juice of 1 Lime
- 1 tbs. Powdered Sugar
- ¼ tsp. Grenadine
- Carbonated Water
- Orange Slices
- Lemon Slices
- 1 Cherry
- Ice

Directions: Shake all ingredients except carbonated water with ice and strain into Collins glass over shaved ice. Fill with carbonated water and stir. Decorate with slices of orange and lemon. Add the cherry

CALIFORNIA MOTHER

- 1 oz. Brandy
- 1 oz. Coffee Liqueur
- Milk or Cream
- Cola
- Ice

Directions: Fill rocks glass with ice. Pour in liquors. Fill the glass with equal parts milk or cream and cola.

CALIFORNIA ROOT BEER

- 1 oz. Coffee Liqueur
- ½ oz. Galliano
- Soda Water
- Dash Cola, Beer, or Milk (optional)
- Ice

Directions: Fill a Collins glass with ice and pour in coffee liqueur. Fill with soda water and top with Galliano. Dash of cola, beer, or milk optional.

CALYPSO COFFEE

- 1 oz. Tia Maria or Dark Crème de Cacao
- 1 oz. Rum
- Coffee
- Whipped Cream
- Shaved Chocolate

Directions: Warm a coffee cup. Pour in liquors and fill with hot, black coffee. Top with whipped cream and sprinkle with shaved chocolate.

CAMPARI AND SODA

- 2 oz. Campari
- Soda Water
- 1 Lemon or Lime Wedge
- Ice

Directions: Fill a rocks glass with ice and Campari. Fill with soda water. Garnish with a lemon or lime wedge.

CAMSHAFT

- ¾ oz. Irish Cream
- ¾ oz. Rootbeer Schnapps
- ¾ oz. Jaegermeister
- Ice

Directions: Fill mixing glass with ice and add liquors. Shake and strain into a shot glass.

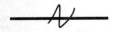

CANADIAN BLACKBERRY FIZZ

- 1 ½ oz. Canadian Whiskey
- ½ oz. Blackberry Brandy
- 2 oz. Sweet and Sour
- Soda Water
- Ice

Directions: Fill mixing glass with ice and add liquors. Shake and fill with soda water.

CANADIAN CIDER

- ½ cup of Ice
- 1 oz. Canadian Whiskey
- ½ oz. Cinnamon Schnapps
- 3 oz. Apple Cider
- ¼ Ripe Red Apple

Directions: Blend ingredients until smooth.

CANADIAN COCKTAIL

- 1 ½ oz. Canadian Whiskey
- ½ oz. Triple Sec
- 2 dashes Bitters
- 1 tsp. Powdered Sugar
- Ice

Directions: Shake all ingredients with ice, strain into a cocktail glass, and serve.

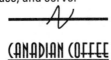

CANADIAN COFFEE

- 2 oz. Yukon Jack
- 5 - 6 drops Crème de Nouyax
- Coffee

Directions: Fill a glass with hot, black coffee and Yukon Jack. Dribble five or six drops of crème de nouyax on top.

CANADIAN PINEAPPLE

- 1 ½ oz. Canadian Whiskey
- 1 tsp. Pineapple Juice
- 1 tbs. Lemon Juice
- ½ tsp. Maraschino
- 1 Pineapple Stick
- Ice

Directions: Shake all ingredients except pineapple stick with ice. Strain into an old-fashioned glass over ice. Add the pineapple stick.

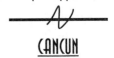

CANCUN

- ½ cup of Ice
- ¾ oz. Coffee Liqueur
- ¾ oz. Sambuca
- ¾ oz. Irish Cream
- 3 oz. Cold Espresso
- Scoop of Vanilla Ice Cream

Directions: Blend all ingredients until smooth.

CANDY APPLE

- 1 oz. Apple Brandy
- 1 oz. Cinnamon Schnapps
- Cranberry Juice
- Ice

Directions: Fill a rocks glass with ice, brandy, and schnapps. Fill with cranberry juice and stir.

CANDY APPLE MARTINI

- 3 ½ oz. Apple Vodka
- ½ oz. Cranberry Juice
- Dash Grenadine
- 1 Cherry
- Ice

Directions: Fill a mixing glass with ice. Pour in ingredients and shake. Strain into a chilled cocktail glass. Garnish with a cherry.

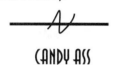

CANDY ASS

- ¾ oz. Black Raspberry Liquor
- ¾ oz. Crème de Cacao
- ¾ oz. Irish Cream
- Ice

Directions: Fill a rocks glass with ice and all ingredients. Shake and serve.

CANDY CANE

- 2 oz. Peppermint Schnapps
- ½ oz. Cherry Brandy
- Milk
- Ice

Directions: Fill a highball glass with ice. Pour in schnapps and fill with milk. Shake. Float cherry brandy on top.

CANDY CANE 2

- 1 ½ oz. Peppermint Schnapps (bottom)
- ½ oz. Crème de Nouyax (top)

Directions: Layer ingredients in a glass.

CANDY CANE MARTINI

- 2 oz. Vanilla Vodka
- 1 oz. White Chocolate Liqueur
- 1 oz. Peppermint Schnapps
- 1 tsp. Grenadine
- 1 Miniature Candy Cane
- Ice

Directions: Fill a mixing glass with ice. Pour in liquors and shake. Strain into a chilled glass. Top with grenadine. Garnish with a miniature candy cane.

CAPE CODDER

- 2 oz. Vodka
- Cranberry Juice
- 1 Lime Garnish
- Ice

Directions: Fill a rocks glass with ice and pour in vodka. Fill with cranberry juice and garnish with a lime.

CAPE OF GOOD WILL

- 1 ½ oz. Light Rum
- ½ oz. Apricot Brandy
- ½ oz. Lime Juice
- 1 oz. Orange Juice
- 2 dashes Orange Bitters
- Ice

Directions: In a shaker half-filled with ice, mix ingredients. Shake. Strain into cocktail glass.

CAPRI

- ¾ oz. White Crème de Cacao
- ¾ oz. Crème de Bananes
- ¾ oz. Light Cream
- Ice

Directions: Shake all ingredients with ice, strain into an old-fashioned glass over ice and serve.

CAPTAIN COOK

- 1 ½ oz. Gin
- ½ oz. Maraschino Liqueur
- 1 oz. Orange Juice
- Ice

Directions: In a shaker half-filled with ice, combine all of the ingredients. Shake. Strain into a cocktail glass.

CAPTAIN DO

- 1 ¾ oz. Captain Morgan Spiced Rum
- 20 oz. Mountain Dew

Directions: Combine ingredients.

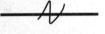

CAPTAIN'S TABLE

- 2 oz. Gin
- ½ oz. Campari
- 1 tsp. Grenadine
- 1 oz. Orange Juice
- 4 oz. Ginger Ale
- 1 Maraschino Cherry
- Ice

Directions: In a shaker half-filled with ice cubes, combine the gin, Campari, grenadine, and orange juice. Shake well. Pour into a Collins glass almost filled with ice cubes. Top with the ginger ale. Garnish with the cherry.

CARA SPOSA

- 1 oz. Coffee Liqueur
- 1 oz. Orange Liqueur
- Milk or Cream
- 1 Orange Garnish
- Ice

Directions: Fill a Collins glass with ice and pour in liquors. Fill with milk or cream. Shake. Garnish with orange.

CARAMEL APPLE MARTINI

- 3 ½ oz. Vodka
- Dash Apple Cider or Apple Juice
- Caramel
- Ice

Directions: Fill a mixing glass with ice. Pour in vodka and shake. Dip rim of a chilled glass in caramel or drizzle inside of glass. Strain into a chilled glass.

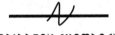

CARIBBEAN CHAMPAGNE

- 1 oz. Light Rum
- 1 oz. Banana Liqueur
- Champagne
- 1 Banana Garnish
- 1 Cherry Garnish

Directions: Combine liquors in champagne glass and stir. Fill with Champagne. Garnish with banana and cherry.

CARIBBEAN DREAM COFFEE

- ¾ oz. Dark Rum
- ¾ oz. Dark Crème de Cacao
- ¾ oz. Banana Liqueur
- Coffee
- 1 Banana Garnish

Directions: Warm coffee cup and pour in liquor. Fill with hot, black coffee. Garnish with banana.

CARIBBEAN MADRAS

- 2 oz. Dark Rum
- Cranberry Juice
- Orange Juice
- Ice

Directions: Fill rocks glass with ice and pour in rum. Fill with equal parts cranberry and orange juice.

CARIBBEAN PINEAPPLE

- 1 ½ oz. Malibu
- 3 oz. Pineapple juice
- 1 Cherry
- Ice

Directions: Mix ingredients in a lowball glass, garnish with a cherry, and serve over ice.

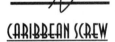

CARIBBEAN SCREW

- ¾ oz. Coconut Rum
- ¾ oz. Banana Liqueur
- ¾ oz. Peach Schnapps
- Milk
- Orange Juice
- Pineapple Juice
- Ice

Directions: Fill a mixing glass with ice and add liquor. Fill with equal parts milk, orange, and pineapple juice. Shake and serve in a Collins glass.

CARIBBEAN SCREW WITH A SUNBURN

- ¾ oz. Dark Rum
- ¾ oz. Coconut Rum
- ¾ oz. Light Rum
- Dash Grenadine
- Orange Juice
- Ice

Directions: Fill mixing glass with ice and add liquor. Fill with orange juice and shake. Pour into a Collins glass and add grenadine.

CARIBBEAN SURFER

- 1 ½ oz. Coconut Rum
- ½ oz. Banana Liqueur
- Pineapple Juice
- 1 Cherry
- Ice

Directions: Fill rocks glass with ice and add liquor. Fill with pineapple juice and shake. Garnish with a cherry.

CARIBOU SCREW

- 2 oz. Yukon Jack or Bourbon
- Orange Juice
- Ice

Directions: Fill rocks glass with ice and add liquor. Fill with orange juice.

CARIOUS

- 1 ½ oz. Gin
- 1 oz. Dry Vermouth
- 1 oz. Green Crème de Menthe
- Ice

Directions: In a mixing glass half-filled with ice, combine all ingredients. Stir well. Strain into a cocktail glass.

CARROL

- Crushed Ice
- 2 oz. Gin
- ½ oz. Apricot Brandy
- Dash Orange Bitters

Directions: In a mixing glass half-filled with crushed ice, combine all of the ingredients. Stir well. Strain into a cocktail glass.

CARROL COCKTAIL

- ¾ oz. Sweet Vermouth
- 1 ½ oz. Brandy
- 1 Cherry
- Ice

Directions: Stir vermouth and brandy with ice and strain into a cocktail glass. Top with the cherry and serve.

CARROT CAKE

- 1 oz. Irish Cream
- 1 oz. Coffee Liqueur
- 1 oz. Butterscotch Schnapps
- ½ oz. Cinnamon Schnapps
- Ice

Directions: Fill a mixing glass with ice and pour in liquor. Shake. Strain into a chilled cocktail glass.

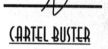

CARTEL BUSTER

- 1 oz. Coffee Liqueur (bottom)
- 1 oz. Orange Juice
- 1 oz. Gold Tequila (top)

Directions: Layer ingredients in a glass.

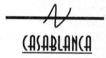

CASABLANCA

- 2 oz. Rum
- 1 ½ tsp. Triple Sec
- 1 ½ tsp. Cherry Liqueur or Cherry Rum
- 1 ½ oz. Lime Juice
- Ice

Directions: Fill a mixing glass with ice and add liquor. Shake and strain into a chilled cocktail glass.

CASINO COCKTAIL

- 2 oz. Gin
- ¼ tsp. Maraschino
- ¼ tsp. Lemon Juice
- 2 dashes Orange Bitters
- 1 Cherry
- Ice

Directions: Shake all ingredients except cherry with ice and strain into a cocktail glass. Add the cherry on top and serve.

CASINO ROYALE

- 2 oz. Gin
- ½ oz. Lemon Juice
- 1 tsp. Maraschino Liqueur
- Dash Orange Bitters
- 1 Egg Yolk
- Ice

Directions: In a shaker half-filled with ice cubes, combine all of the ingredients. Shake well. Strain into a sour glass.

CATALINA MARGARITA

- 1 ½ oz. Tequila
- 3 oz. Sweet & Sour
- Dash Blue Curacao
- Dash Peach Schnapps
- Dash Limejuice
- Ice

Directions: Fill a mixing glass with ice and add liquor. Shake. Serve or strain into a smaller glass.

CATFISH

- 1 ½ oz. Rum
- ½ oz. Triple Sec
- Cola
- 1 Lime Wedge
- Ice

Directions: Fill a rocks glass with ice and add liquor. Fill with cola. Garnish with a lime wedge.

CELTIC COMRADE

- ½ oz. Coffee Liqueur (bottom)
- ½ oz. Irish Cream
- ½ oz. Vodka
- ½ oz. Drambuie (top)

Directions: Layer ingredients in a glass.

CELTIC MIX COCKTAIL

- 1 ½ oz. Scotch
- 1 oz. Irish Whiskey
- ½ oz. Lemon Juice
- Dash Bitters
- Ice

Directions: In a shaker half-filled with ice cubes, combine all of the ingredients. Shake well. Strain into a cocktail glass.

CEMENT MIXER

- Irish Cream
- Dash Lime Juice

Directions: Fill shot glass with Irish Cream. Add dash of lime juice. Let sit for 30 seconds.

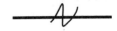

CEREBRAL HEMORRHAGE

- 1 oz. Coffee Liqueur (bottom)
- 1 oz. Peach Schnapps
- 1 oz. Irish Cream (top)
- Grenadine
- Ice

Directions: Fill rocks glass with ice and pour liquors in order. Add several drops of grenadine.

CHAIN LIGHTNING

- 3 oz. Gin
- ½ oz. Triple Sec
- 1 oz. Lime Juice
- 1 Lemon Garnish
- Ice

Directions: Fill mixing glass with ice and add liquor. Shake and serve or strain into chilled glass. Garnish with lemon.

CHAM CRAN CHAM

- Champagne
- Dash Black Raspberry Liqueur
- Cranberry Juice
- Ice

Directions: Fill wine glass three-fourths full with ice. Add Champagne. Add a dash of black raspberry liqueur. Fill with cranberry juice.

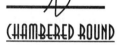

CHAMBERED ROUND

- 1 oz. Grain Alcohol or Vodka
- 1 oz. Tequila
- 1 Olive

Directions: Combine ingredients in a shot glass and garnish with an olive.

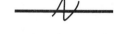

CHAMPAGNE COCKTAIL

- Chilled Champagne
- 1 Lump Sugar
- 2 dashes Bitters
- Twist of Lemon Peel

Directions: Place lump of sugar and bitters in a chilled Champagne flute. Fill with chilled Champagne. Add the twist of lemon peel and serve.

CHAMPAGNE JULEP

- 10 - 20 Fresh Mint Leaves
- 1 tsp. Sugar
- 2 tbs. Water
- ½ oz. Bourbon
- Champagne
- Crushed Ice
- 1 Mint Garnish

Directions: Muddle ten to 20 fresh mint leaves, sugar, and water. Fill glass with crushed ice, add bourbon, and fill with Champagne. Garnish with mint.

CHAMPAGNE PUNCH

- 1 tsp. Superfine Sugar
- 1 tsp. Lemon Juice
- ½ oz. Orange Liqueur
- ½ oz. Brandy
- ½ oz. Light Rum
- 2 oz. Pineapple Juice
- Dash Grenadine
- Champagne
- Ice

Directions: In serving glass, add ingredients until sugar dissolves. Add ice and fill with Champagne.

CHANNEL

- 2 oz. Blackberry Brandy
- Beer

Directions: Pour brandy in glass and fill with beer.

CHAOS

- ½ oz. 151 Proof Rum
- ½ oz. Gin
- ½ oz. Sloe Gin
- ½ oz. Orange Liqueur
- ½ oz. Lime Juice
- Ice

Directions: Fill mixing glass with ice. Add ingredients. Shake and strain into chilled cocktail glass.

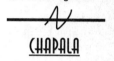

CHAPALA

- 1 ½ oz. Tequila
- Dash Triple Sec
- 2 tsp. Grenadine
- 1 tbs. Orange Juice
- 1 tbs. Lemon Juice
- 1 Orange Slice
- Ice

Directions: Shake all ingredients except orange slice with ice. Strain into old-fashioned glass over ice. Add orange slice.

CHARGER

- 1 ½ oz. Dark Rum
- ½ oz. Cherry Brandy
- ½ oz. Lemon Juice
- ½ tsp. Superfine Sugar
- Ice

Directions: In a shaker half-filled with ice cubes, combine all of the ingredients. Shake well. Strain into cocktail glass.

CHARLES COCKTAIL

- 1 ½ oz. Brandy
- 1 ½ oz. Sweet Vermouth
- Dash Bitters
- Ice

Directions: Stir all ingredients with ice, strain into a cocktail glass, and serve.

CHARLIE CHAPLIN

- 1 oz. Apricot Brandy
- 1 oz. Sloe Gin
- 1 oz. Lemon Juice
- Ice

Directions: Shake all ingredients with ice, strain into an old-fashioned glass over ice cubes, and serve.

CHARRO

- 1 oz. Tequila
- 1 oz. Coffee
- 1 oz. Milk
- Ice

Directions: Fill a mixing glass with ice and add ingredients. Stir and strain into a shot glass.

CHASTITY BELT

- ¾ oz. Coffee Liqueur (bottom)
- ¾ oz. Irish Cream
- ¾ oz. Hazelnut Liqueur
- ½ oz. Milk (top)

Directions: Combine liquor in glass and top with milk.

CHEAP SHADES

- 1 oz. Vodka
- ½ oz. Peach Schnapps
- ½ oz. Melon Liqueur
- Dash Sour Mix
- Dash Pineapple Juice
- Lemon-lime Soda
- 1 Pineapple Garnish
- Ice

Directions: Fill a Collins glass with ice and add ingredients. Fill with lemon-lime soda and garnish with pineapple.

CHEAP SUNGLASSES

- 2 oz. Vodka
- Cranberry Juice
- Lemon-lime Soda
- 1 Lime Garnish
- Ice

Directions: Fill a Collins glass with ice and fill with equal parts cranberry juice and lemon-lime soda. Garnish with a lime.

CHELADA

- Beer
- 1 tbs. Lemon Juice
- Salt
- Ice

Directions: Fill a pilsner with ice and add fresh lemon juice. Add a pinch of salt and beer.

CHELSEA SIDECAR

- 3 ½ oz. Gin
- ½ oz. Triple Sec
- 1 Orange Garnish
- 1 Cherry Garnish
- Ice

Directions: Fill a mixing glass with ice and pour in ingredients. Fill with sour mix and strain into a chilled cocktail glass. Garnish with an orange and cherry.

CHERIE

- ½ oz. Cherry Brandy
- 1 oz. Light Rum
- ½ oz. Triple Sec
- Juice of 1 Lime
- 1 Cherry
- Ice

Directions: Shake all ingredients except cherry with ice and strain into a cocktail glass. Top with the cherry and serve.

CHERRY BLOSSOM

- 1 ½ oz. Brandy
- ½ oz. Cherry Brandy
- 1 ½ tsp. Triple Sec
- 1 ½ tsp. Grenadine
- 2 tsp. Lemon Juice
- Powdered Sugar
- 1 Cherry
- Ice

Directions: Moisten rim of cocktail glass with cherry brandy. Rub rim in powdered sugar. Shake all ingredients except cherry with ice. Strain in sugar-rimmed glass. Top with cherry.

CHERRY COLA

- 1 ½ oz. Cherry Brandy
- Cola
- 1 Cherry
- Ice

Directions: Fill a Collins glass with ice and pour in brandy. Fill with cola and garnish with a cherry.

CHERRY COLA FROM HELL

- 1 oz. Grain Alcohol
- 1 oz. Cherry Brandy
- Cola

Directions: In a shot glass pour in grain alcohol and ignite. Drop the shot glass into a beer mug with cherry brandy and fill three-fourths full with cola.

CHERRY FIZZ

- 2 oz. Cherry Brandy
- Juice of ½ Lemon
- Carbonated Water
- 1 Cherry
- Ice

Directions: Shake lemon juice and cherry brandy with ice and strain into a highball glass over two ice cubes. Fill with carbonated water and stir. Top with the cherry.

CHERRY FLIP

- 1 ½ oz. Cherry Brandy
- 1 tsp. Powdered Sugar
- 2 tsp. Light Cream
- 1 Whole Egg
- Nutmeg
- Ice

Directions: Shake all ingredients except nutmeg with ice and strain into a whiskey sour glass. Sprinkle nutmeg on top and serve.

CHERRY HOOKER

- 2 oz. Cherry Brandy
- Orange Juice
- 1 Lime Garnish
- Ice

Directions: Fill a mixing glass with ice and add brandy. Fill with orange juice and shake. Garnish with lime.

CHERRY LIFE-SAVER

- 2 oz. Amaretto
- Cranberry Juice
- Ice

Directions: Fill a tall glass with ice and add Amaretto. Fill with cranberry juice.

CHERRY MARTINI

- 3 ½ oz. Cherry Vodka
- ½ oz. Cherry Brandy
- Dash Cherry Juice
- 1 Cherry
- Ice

Directions: Fill mixing glass with ice and add liquor. Shake. Strain into a chilled glass. Garnish with a cherry.

CHERRY PIE

- 1 oz. Vodka
- ½ oz. Brandy
- ½ oz. Cherry Vodka
- Ice

Directions: Fill mixing glass with ice and add ingredients. Stir. Strain into a chilled glass.

CHERRY SCREW

- 2 oz. Cherry Brandy
- Orange Juice
- 1 Orange Garnish
- 1 Lime Garnish
- Ice

Directions: Fill serving glass with ice and add ingredients. Fill with orange juice. Shake. Garnish with orange and lime.

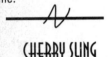

CHERRY SLING

- 2 oz. Cherry Brandy
- Juice of ½ Lemon
- Twist of Lemon Peel
- Ice

Directions: Pour brandy and lemon juice into an old-fashioned glass over ice cubes and stir. Add the twist of lemon peel and serve.

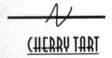

CHERRY TART

- 1 oz. Bourbon
- 1 oz. Cherry Brandy
- 1 oz. Lemon Juice
- 1 tsp. Sugar
- Ice

Directions: Fill mixing glass with ice and add ingredients. Shake. Strain into a chilled glass.

CHICAGO

- 1 ½ oz. Brandy
- Champagne
- Dash Curacao
- Dash Bitters
- Sugar
- Ice

Directions: Fill mixing glass with ice and add ingredients. Shake. Strain into a glass rimmed with sugar. Fill with Champagne.

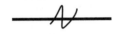

CHICAGO FIZZ

- 1 oz. Light Rum
- 1 oz. Port
- Juice of ½ Lemon
- 1 tsp. Powdered Sugar
- 1 Egg White
- Carbonated Water
- Ice

Directions: Shake all ingredients except carbonated water with ice and strain into a highball glass over two ice cubes. Fill with carbonated water, stir, and serve.

CHI-CHI

- 1 ½ oz. Vodka
- 4 oz. Pineapple Juice
- 1 oz. Cream of Coconut
- 1 Pineapple Slice
- 1 Cherry
- 1 cup of Ice

Directions: Blend vodka, pineapple juice, and cream of coconut with ice in an electric blender at a high speed. Pour into a red wine glass, decorate with the slice of pineapple and the cherry, and serve.

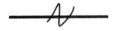

CHICKEN SHOT

- 1 oz. Vodka
- 1 oz. Chicken Bouillion
- Dash Worcestershire Sauce
- Dash Salt
- Dash Pepper

Directions: Combine ingredients in a shot glass.

CHILES FRITOS

- 2 oz. Tequila
- Dash Lime Juice
- Dash Celery Salt
- Dash Tabasco Sauce
- Dash Worcestershire Sauce
- Dash Pepper
- Dash Grenadine
- Dash Orange Juice
- 2 Chili Peppers
- Ice

Directions: Fill a tall glass with ice and ingredients. Shake. Garnish with chili peppers.

CHINA BEACH

- 1 oz. Vodka
- 1 oz. Ginger Liqueur
- Cranberry Juice
- Ice

Directions: Fill serving glass with ice and ingredients. Fill with cranberry juice. Stir.

CHINA BLUE MARTINI

- 3 ½ oz. Gin.
- Dash Ginger Liqueur
- Dash Blue Curacao
- Ginger Candy Garnish
- Ice

Directions: Fill a mixing glass with ice and add ingredients. Shake. Garnish with ginger candy.

CHINESE COCKTAIL

- 1 ½ oz. Dark Rum
- 1 tsp. Triple Sec
- 1 tsp. Cherry Liqueur
- 1 tsp. Grenadine
- Dash Bitters
- Ice

Directions: Fill a mixing glass with ice and add ingredients. Shake. Strain into a chilled glass.

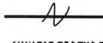

CHINESE TORTURE
(floater)

- 1 ½ oz. Ginger liqueur (bottom)
- ½ oz. 151 Proof Rum (top)

Directions: Layer ingredients in a glass and ignite.

CHIQUITA

- ½ oz. Banana Liqueur
- ½ oz. Orange Liqueur
- Orange Juice
- Milk
- Ice

Directions: Fill mixing glass with ice and add liquor. Fill with equal parts orange juice and milk. Shake.

CHOCOLATE BLACK RUSSIAN

- 1 oz. Kahlua
- ½ oz. Vodka
- 5 oz. Chocolate Ice Cream

Directions: Combine ingredients in electric blender and blend at a low speed for a short length of time. Pour into a chilled Champagne flute.

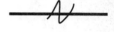

CHOCOLATE CAKE

- ¾ oz. Citrus Vodka
- ¾ oz. Hazlenut Liqueur
- Sugarcoated Lemon Garnish
- Ice

Directions: Fill a mixing glass with ice and ingredients. Strain into shot glass. Garnish with sugarcoated lemon.

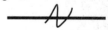

CHOCOLATE COCKTAIL

- 1 ½ tsp. Yellow Chartreuse
- 1 ½ oz. Port
- 1 tsp. Powdered Sugar
- 1 Egg White
- Ice

Directions: Shake all ingredients with ice, strain into rocks glass.

CHOCOLATE COVERED CHERRY

- ½ oz. Coffee Liqueur
- ½ oz. Amaretto
- ½ oz. White Crème de Cacao
- 1 drop Grenadine
- Ice

Directions: Fill a mixing glass with ice and add ingredients. Shake. Strain into a chilled glass. Add drop of grenadine.

CHOCOLATE KISS

- 1 ½ oz. Peppermint Schnapps
- ½ oz. Coffee Liqueur
- Hot Chocolate
- Whipped Cream
- Shaved Chocolate or Sprinkles

Directions: Fill a cup with hot chocolate and liquor. Top with whipped cream and shaved chocolate or sprinkles.

CHOCOLATE MALTED

- ½ cup of Ice
- 2 tbs. Malted Milk Powder
- 4 oz. Milk
- Scoop of Chocolate Ice Cream
- 2 tbs. Chocolate Syrup

Directions: Blend all ingredients until smooth.

CHOCOLATE MARTINI

- 2 oz. Vodka
- ½ oz. Crème de Cacao
- ½ oz. Godiva Dark Chocolate Liqueur
- Ice

Directions: Pour ingredients into a shaker filled with ice, then pour into a martini glass.

CHOCOLATE PARADISE

- 1 oz. Mint Schnapps
- 3 oz. Chocolate Milk
- Ice

Directions: Simply pour over ice into a Collins glass.

CHOCOLATE RATTLESNAKE

- 1 oz. Coffee Liqueur
- 1 oz. Irish Cream
- ½ oz. Crème de Cacao
- ½ oz. Peppermint Schnapps
- Ice

Directions: Fill a mixing glass with ice and add ingredients. Stir. Strain into a shot glass.

CHOCOLATE RUM

- 1 oz. Light Rum
- 1 tsp. 151 Proof Rum
- ½ oz. Brown Crème de Cacao
- ½ oz. White Crème de Menthe
- 1 tbs. Cream
- Ice

Directions: Shake all ingredients with ice, strain into an old-fashioned glass over ice.

CHOCOLATE SNOW BEAR

- 1 oz. Amaretto
- 1 oz. Crème de Cacao
- 5 oz. French Vanilla Ice Cream
- ¼ oz. Chocolate Syrup
- 2 dashes Vanilla Extract

Directions: Combine all ingredients in electric blender. Blend at a low speed for a short time. Pour into chilled Champagne flute.

CHOCOLATE SOLDIER

- 1 ½ oz. Gin
- ¾ oz. Dubonnet
- Juice of ½ Lime
- Ice

Directions: Shake all ingredients with ice, strain into a cocktail glass, and serve.

CHOCOLATE SQUIRREL

- ¾ oz. Amaretto
- ¾ oz. Hazelnut Liqueur
- ¾ oz. Dark Crème de Cacao
- Milk
- Ice

Directions: Fill mixing glass with ice and add ingredients. Fill with milk. Shake. Serve or strain into a chilled glass.

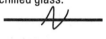

CHOCOLATE THUNDER

- 2 oz. Vodka
- Ovaltine

Directions: Pour vodka in glass. Fill with Ovaltine.

CHOCOLATIER

- 1 oz. Light Rum
- 1 oz. Crème de Cacao
- 5 oz. Chocolate Ice Cream
- 1 tbs. Sweet Chocolate Shavings

Directions: Combine ingredients except chocolate shavings in blender and blend on low speed for a short length of time. Pour in a chilled Champagne flute, garnish with chocolate shavings, and serve.

CHRISTIAN'S COFFEE

- 1 oz. Coffee Liqueur
- 1 oz. Irish Cream
- 1 oz. Amaretto
- Coffee
- Whipped Cream

Directions: Pour liquor into a cup, fill with coffee, and top with whipped cream.

CHRONIC ICED TEA

- 1 ½ oz. Cognac or Brandy
- ¼ oz. Honey Liqueur
- ½ oz. Limoncello
- Iced Tea
- 1 Lemon Garnish
- Ice

Directions: Fill mixing glass with ice and add ingredients. Fill with iced tea. Shake. Garnish with lemon.

CHUPACABRA

- 1 oz. Tequila
- 1 oz. Jaegermeister
- Ice

Directions: Fill mixing glass with ice and add ingredients. Shake. Strain into a shot glass.

CINCINNATI

- Beer
- Soda Water

Directions: Fill a tall glass with equal parts beer and soda water.

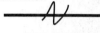

CLAM DIGGER

- 2 oz. Vodka or Gin
- Dash Tabasco Sauce
- Dash Worcestershire Sauce
- Dash Lime Juice
- Dash Salt
- Dash Pepper
- Dash Tomato Juice
- Ice

Directions: Fill glass with ice and ingredients. Shake.

CLAM SHOT

- 1 Small Raw Clam
- Vodka
- Bloody Mary Mix

Directions: Put clam into shot glass. Fill with equal parts vodka and bloody Mary mix.

CLAMATO COCKTAIL

- 1 ½ oz. Vodka
- 3 oz. Tomato Juice
- 1 oz. Clam Juice
- Ice

Directions: Shake all ingredients with ice, strain into old-fashioned glass over ice.

CLARIDGE COCKTAIL

- ¾ oz. Dry Vermouth
- ¾ oz. Gin
- 1 tbs. Apricot Brandy
- 1 tbs. Triple Sec
- Ice

Directions: Stir all ingredients with ice, strain into a cocktail glass, and serve.

CLEMENTINA

- 1 oz. Vodka
- 1 tsp. Lemon Juice
- Pinch Sugar
- 4 oz. Red Wine
- Sparkling Water
- Ice

Directions: Fill a tall glass with ice and add ingredients. Shake. Fill with sparkling water.

CLIMAX

- ½ oz. Amaretto
- ½ oz. White Crème de Cacao
- ½ oz. Triple Sec
- ½ oz. Vodka
- ½ oz. Crème de Bananes
- 1 oz. Light Cream
- Cracked Ice

Directions: Shake ingredients with ice, strain into a chilled cocktail glass, and serve.

CLOCKWORK ORANGE

- ½ cup of Ice
- 1 oz. Orange Vodka
- 1 oz. Orange Rum
- 1 oz. Orange Liqueur
- Scoop of Orange Sherbet
- 1 tbs. Marmalade

Directions: Blend ingredients until smooth.

CLOUDS OVER SCOTLAND

(floater)

- ½ oz. Green Crème de Menthe (bottom)
- ½ oz. Irish Cream

Directions: Layer ingredients in shot glass.

CLOVER CLUB COCKTAIL

- 1 ½ oz. Gin
- 2 tsp. Grenadine
- Juice of ½ Lemon
- 1 Egg White
- Ice

Directions: Shake all ingredients with ice, strain into a cocktail glass, and serve.

CLOVER LEAF COCKTAIL

- 1 ½ oz. Gin
- 2 tsp. Grenadine
- Juice of ½ Lemon
- 1 Egg White
- 1 Mint Sprig
- Ice

Directions: Shake all ingredients except mint with ice and strain into a cocktail glass. Add the mint sprig and serve.

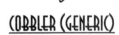

COBBLER (GENERIC)

- 2 oz. Desired Liquor
- Dash Fruit Syrup or Juice
- ½ tsp. Sugar
- Mint Garnish
- Fresh Fruit Garnish
- Ice

Directions: Fill a tall glass with ice and add ingredients. Stir. Garnish with mint and fresh fruit.

COBRA

- 2 oz. Coffee Liqueur
- Soda Water
- 1 Lime Garnish
- Ice

Directions: Fill a serving glass with ice and add liqueur. Fill with soda water. Garnish with lime.

COCA

- ¾ oz. Vodka
- ¾ oz. Southern Comfort
- ¾ oz. Black Raspberry Liqueur
- 1 oz. Orange Juice
- 1 oz. Cranberry Juice
- Ice

Directions: Fill mixing glass with ice and add ingredients. Shake. Strain into chilled glass.

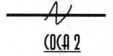

COCA 2

- 1 ½ oz. Vodka
- ½ oz. Black Raspberry Liqueur
- Dash Sour Mix
- Lemon-lime Soda
- Ice

Directions: Fill a tall glass with ice and add ingredients. Shake. Fill with lemon-lime soda.

COCA LADY

- ½ oz. Vodka
- ½ oz. Rum
- ½ oz. Coffee Liqueur
- ½ oz. Amaretto
- Milk or Cream
- Dash Cola
- Ice

Directions: Fill a tall glass with ice and add ingredients. Fill with milk or cream. Shake. Add a dash of cola.

COCOETTO

- 2 oz. Amaretto
- Hot Chocolate
- Whipped Cream
- Shaved Chocolate or Sprinkles

Directions: Combine hot chocolate and Amaretto. Stir. Top with whipped cream and shaved chocolate or sprinkles.

COCOPUFF

- 1 oz. Coffee Liqueur
- 1 oz. Irish Cream
- Hot Chocolate
- Whipped Cream
- Shaved Chocolate or Chocolate Syrup

Directions: Combine hot chocolate and liquor. Stir. Top with whipped cream and shaved chocolate or chocolate syrup.

CODE BLUE

- ½ oz. Vodka
- ½ oz. Gin
- ½ oz. Rum
- ½ oz. Tequila
- ½ oz. Blue Curacao
- Sour Mix
- Ice

Directions: Fill a tall glass with ice and add ingredients. Fill with sour mix. Shake.

COFFEE ALEXANDER

- 1 oz. Brandy
- 1 oz. Dark Crème de Cacao
- Coffee
- Whipped Cream
- Nutmeg

Directions: Combine brandy, crème de cacao, and hot, black coffee. Top with whipped cream and sprinkle with nutmeg.

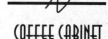

COFFEE CABINET

- ½ cup of Ice
- 2 oz. Coffee Syrup
- Scoop of Vanilla Ice Cream
- 2 oz. Milk

Directions: Blend ingredients until smooth. Add milk to thin.

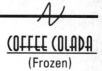

COFFEE COLADA
(Frozen)

- ½ cup of Ice
- 2 oz. Coffee Liqueur
- 1 oz. Rum
- 2 tbs. Cream of Coconut
- ½ cup Fresh Pineapple
- 1 tbs. Vanilla Ice Cream

Directions: Blend all ingredients until smooth. If too thick, add fruit or juice. If too thin, add ice or ice cream.

COFFEE FLIP

- 1 oz. Brandy
- 1 oz. Port
- 1 tsp. Powdered Sugar
- 1 Whole Egg
- 2 tsp. Light Cream
- Nutmeg
- Ice

Directions: Shake all ingredients except nutmeg with ice and strain into a whiskey sour glass. Sprinkle nutmeg on top and serve.

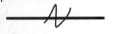

COFFEE GRASSHOPPER

- ¾ oz. Coffee Brandy
- ¾ oz. White Crème de Menthe
- ¾ oz. Light Cream
- Ice

Directions: Shake all ingredients with ice, strain into an old-fashioned glass over ice cubes, and serve.

COFFEE MILK

- 2 oz. Coffee Syrup
- Milk

Directions: Fill glass with syrup and milk. Shake.

COFFEE SOMBRERO

- 2 oz. Coffee Liqueur
- Milk or Cream
- Ice

Directions: Fill a serving glass with ice and add liqueur. Fill with milk or cream. Shake.

COFFEE SOUR

- 1 ½ oz. Coffee Brandy
- 1 oz. Lemon Juice
- 1 tsp. Powdered Sugar
- 1 Egg White
- Ice

Directions: Shake all ingredients with ice, strain into a whiskey sour glass, and serve.

COLLINS

- 2 oz. Desired Liquor
- Sour Mix
- Soda Water
- 1 Orange Garnish
- 1 Cherry Garnish
- Ice

Directions: Fill a tall glass with ice and add liquor. Fill with sour mix. Shake. Splash with soda water. Garnish with orange and cherry.

COLONIAL COCKTAIL

- 1 ½ oz. Gin
- ½ oz. Grapefruit Juice
- 1 tsp. Maraschino
- 1 Olive
- Ice

Directions: Shake all ingredients except olive with ice and strain into a cocktail glass. Add the olive and serve.

COLORADO BULLDOG

- 1 shot Vodka
- 1 shot Kahlua
- Milk
- Splash Coca-Cola

Directions: In a shaker, mix vodka, Kahlua, and milk. Pour into a rocks glass and add a splash of Coke.

COLORADO BULLDOG 2

- 1 oz. Coffee Liqueur
- 1 oz. Irish Cream
- Beer

Directions: Fill a short glass with ingredients. Fill chilled glass three-fourths full with beer. Drop the shot glass into the beer glass.

COLORADO MF

- ½ oz. 151 Proof Rum
- ½ oz. Vodka
- ½ oz. Dark Rum
- ½ oz. Coffee Liqueur
- ½ oz. Galliano
- Milk or Cream
- Dash Grenadine
- Ice

Directions: Fill a tall glass with ice and add ingredients. Fill with milk or cream. Shake. Top with a dash of grenadine.

COLORADO MOTHER

- ¾ oz. Vodka
- ¾ oz. Coffee Liqueur
- ¾ oz. Tequila
- Milk or Cream
- Dash Galliano
- Ice

Directions: Fill a tall glass with ice and add ingredients. Fill with milk or cream. Shake. Top with a dash of Galliano.

COLORADO MOTHER 2

- 1 oz. Tequila
- 1 oz. Coffee Liqueur
- Milk
- Dash Galliano
- Ice

Directions: Fill tall glass with ice. Add ingredients. Fill with milk. Shake. Top with a dash Galliano.

COMBUSTIBLE EDISON

- 1 oz. Campari
- 1 oz. Lemon Juice
- 2 oz. Brandy
- Ice

Directions: Fill mixing glass with ice and add Campari and lemon juice. Shake. Strain into a chilled glass. Heat brandy and ignite. Pour brandy into drink.

COMFORTABLE SCREW

- 1 oz. Southern Comfort
- 1 oz. Vodka
- Orange Juice
- Ice

Directions: Fill tall glass with ice; add ingredients. Fill with orange juice.

COMFORTING TIGER

- Crushed Ice
- 2 oz. Brandy
- ½ oz. Southern Comfort
- 1 tsp. Sweet Vermouth
- 1 Lemon Twist

Directions: In a mixing glass half-filled with crushed ice, combine brandy, Southern Comfort, and vermouth. Stir well. Strain into a cocktail glass and garnish with lemon twist.

COMMUNICATOR

- 1 ½ oz. Dark Rum
- ½ oz. Galliano
- 2 tsp. Dark Crème de Cacao
- Ice

Directions: Pour all of the ingredients into an old-fashioned glass almost filled with ice cubes. Stir well.

COMPADRE

- 1 ½ oz. Tequila
- ½ tsp. Maraschino Liqueur
- 1 tsp. Grenadine
- 2 dashes Orange Bitters
- Ice

Directions: In a mixing glass half-filled with ice cubes, combine all of the ingredients. Stir well. Strain into a cocktail glass.

CONCORD (FLOATER)

- ½ oz. Coffee Liqueur (bottom)
- ½ oz. Irish Cream
- ½ oz. 151 Proof Rum (top)

Directions: Layer ingredients in a glass.

CONCORDE

- 1 ½ oz. Cognac
- Dash Apple Juice or Pineapple Juice
- Champagne

Directions: Combine Cognac and juice in a wine glass. Fill with Champagne.

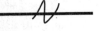

CONEY ISLAND

- 1 oz. Peppermint Schnapps
- 1 oz. Dark Crème de Cacao
- Soda Water
- Ice

Directions: Fill a serving glass with ice and add ingredients. Fill with soda water. Stir.

COOKIE MONSTER
(floater)

- ½ oz. Coffee Liqueur (bottom)
- ½ oz. Irish Cream
- ½ oz. 100 Proof Peppermint Schnapps (top)

Directions: Layer ingredients in a glass.

COOL AID

- ¾ oz. Vodka
- ¾ oz. Melon Liqueur
- ¾ oz. Amaretto
- Cranberry Juice
- Ice

Directions: Fill a tall glass with ice and add liquor. Fill with cranberry juice. Shake.

COOL AID 2

- 1 oz. Southern Comfort
- ½ oz. Amaretto
- ½ oz. Melon Liqueur
- Dash Orange Juice
- Dash Cranberry Juice
- Lemon-lime Soda
- Ice

Directions: Fill a tall glass with ice and add ingredients. Shake. Fill with lemon-lime soda.

COOL BREEZE

- 2 oz. Vodka
- Cranberry Juice
- Grapefruit Juice
- Ginger Ale
- 1 Lime Garnish
- Ice

Directions: Fill a tall glass with ice and ingredients. Fill with equal parts cranberry and grapefruit juice. Top with ginger ale. Garnish with lime.

COOL RUN

- ½ oz. Spiced Rum
- ½ oz. Coconut Rum
- ½ oz. Citrus Rum
- ½ oz. Orange Rum
- 1 oz. Cranberry Juice
- Pineapple Juice
- Dash Lime Juice
- Dash Grenadine
- Splash 151 Proof Rum

Directions: Fill tall glass with ice and ingredients. Add lime juice and grenadine. Fill with pineapple juice. Shake. Top with 151 Proof Rum.

COOPERSTOWN COCKTAIL

- ½ oz. Sweet Vermouth
- ½ oz. Dry Vermouth
- 1 oz. Gin
- 1 Mint Sprig
- Ice

Directions: Shake all ingredients except mint with ice. Strain in cocktail glass. Add mint sprig.

COPENHAGEN POUSSE-CAFÉ
(floater)

- ½ oz. Banana Liqueur (bottom)
- ½ oz. Cherry Brandy
- ½ oz. Cognac (top)

Directions: Layer ingredients in a glass.

COPPERHEAD

- 2 oz. Vodka
- Ginger Ale
- 1 Lime Garnish
- Ice

Directions: Fill a tall glass with ice and ingredients. Fill with ginger ale. Garnish with lime.

CORKSCREW

- 1 ½ oz. Light Rum
- ½ oz. Peach Schnapps
- ½ oz. Dry Vermouth
- 1 Lemon Twist
- Ice

Directions: In mixing glass half-filled with ice, combine the rum, peach schnapps, and vermouth. Stir well. Strain into a cocktail glass and garnish with the lemon twist.

CORNELL COCKTAIL

- 1 ½ oz. Gin
- ½ tsp. lemon juice
- 1 tsp. Maraschino
- 1 Egg White
- Ice

Directions: Shake all ingredients with ice, strain into a cocktail glass, and serve.

CORONATION COCKTAIL

- ¾ oz. Dry Vermouth
- ¾ oz. Gin
- ¾ oz. Dubonnet
- Ice

Directions: Stir all ingredients with ice, strain into a cocktail glass, and serve.

CORPSE REVIVER

- 1 ½ oz. Brandy
- ½ oz. Fernet Branca
- 1 oz. White Crème de Menthe
- Ice

Directions: In a mixing glass half-filled with ice cubes, combine all of the ingredients. Stir well. Strain into a cocktail glass.

COSMIC SCREW

- 1 ½ oz. Vodka
- ½ oz. Triple Sec
- Orange Juice
- Cranberry Juice
- 1 Lime Garnish

Directions: Fill a glass with orange juice, leaving the top half-inch empty. Top with cranberry juice. Garnish with lime.

COSMOPOLITAN

- 2 oz. Vodka
- ¾ oz. Cointreau
- Cranberry Juice
- 1 Lime Twist
- Ice

Directions: Fill mixing glass with ice. Pour in ingredients and fill with cranberry juice. Shake. Strain into a chilled martini glass. Garnish with lime.

COSMOS

- Crushed Ice
- 2 oz. Light Rum
- 1 oz. Lime Juice
- 1 tsp. Superfine Sugar

Directions: In a shaker half-filled with crushed ice, combine ingredients. Shake well. Strain in cocktail glass.

COTTON CANDY MARTINI

- 2 oz. Vanilla Vodka
- 2 oz. Coconut Rum
- Dash Amaretto
- Dash Blue Curacao
- Dash Grenadine
- Dash Cola
- ¼ cup of Cotton Candy
- Ice

Directions: Fill mixing glass with ice and add ingredients. Shake. Strain in chilled glass. Garnish with cotton candy.

COUGH DROP

- 1 oz. Mentholated Schnapps
- 1 oz. Blackberry Brandy
- Ice

Directions: Fill a mixing glass with ice and add ingredients. Stir.

COUNTRY CLUB COOLER

- 2 oz. Dry Vermouth
- Carbonated Water
- ½ tsp. Grenadine
- 1 Orange Spiral
- 1 Twist of Lemon Peel
- Ice

Directions: Pour grenadine and carbonated water into a Collins glass and stir. Add ice cubes and dry vermouth. Fill with carbonated water and stir again. Add the twist of lemon peel and the orange spiral so that the ends dangle over the rim of glass.

COWBOY

- 2 oz. Bourbon
- Milk
- Ice

Directions: Fill a mixing glass with ice and add ingredients. Fill with milk. Shake.

COWBOY SUCKER
(floater)

- 1 ½ oz. Butterscotch Schnapps (bottom)
- ½ oz. Irish Cream (top)

Directions: Layer ingredients in a glass.

CRAMP RELIEVER

- 1 oz. Blackberry Brandy

Directions: Simply enjoy.

CRANAPPLE COOLER

- 1 oz. Vodka or Rum
- 1 oz. Apple Brandy
- Cranberry Juice
- 1 Lime Garnish
- Crushed Ice

Directions: Fill a tall glass with crushed ice and add ingredients. Fill with cranberry juice. Stir. Garnish with lime

CRAN-APPLE MARTINI

- 3 ½ oz. Vodka
- ½ oz. Apple Vodka
- Dash Cranberry Juice
- Pinch Sugar
- Ice

Directions: Fill a mixing glass with ice and add ingredients. Shake. Strain into a chilled glass.

CRANBERRY KAMIKAZE

- 3 ½ oz. Cranberry Vodka
- ½ oz. Triple Sec
- Dash Lime Juice
- 1 Lime Garnish
- Ice

Directions: Fill a mixing glass with ice and add ingredients. Shake. Pour into a short glass or strain into a shot glass. Garnish with lime.

CRANES BEACH PUNCH

- 1 gallon Cherry Kool-Aid
- 1 liter Cheap Red Wine
- 1 500 ml bottle of Vodka
- Ice

Directions: Serve ingredients in a punch bowl with ice.

CRANIUM MELTDOWN

- ½ oz. 151 Proof Rum
- ½ oz. Coconut Rum
- ½ oz. Black Raspberry Liqueur
- ½ oz. Pineapple Juice
- Ice

Directions: Fill a mixing glass with ice and add ingredients. Shake. Strain into a chilled glass.

CRANKIN' WANKER

- ¾ oz. Vodka
- ¾ oz. Southern Comfort
- ¾ oz. Drambuie
- Orange Juice
- Pineapple Juice
- Ice

Directions: Fill a mixing glass with ice and add ingredients. Fill with equal parts orange and pineapple juice.

CRAZY BROAD

- 1 oz. Vodka
- 1 oz. Amaretto
- 1 oz. Southern Comfort
- Cranberry Juice
- Ginger Ale
- Ice

Directions: Fill mixing glass with ice and add ingredients. Fill with equal parts cranberry juice and ginger ale.

CRAZY RED HEAD

- 1 oz. Jaegermeister
- 1 oz. Peach Schnapps
- Cranberry Juice
- Ice

Directions: Fill a serving glass with ice and add ingredients. Fill with cranberry juice. Shake.

CREAM DREAM

- 1 ½ oz. Dark Crème de Cacao
- 1 oz. Hazlenut Liqueur
- Cream
- Ice

Directions: Fill a mixing glass with ice and add ingredients. Fill with cream. Shake.

CREAM SODA

- 2 oz. Vanilla Vodka
- Ginger Ale
- Dash Cola (optional)
- Ice

Directions: Fill a serving glass with ice and add ingredients. Fill with ginger ale. Add a dash of cola if desired.

CREAMSICLE

- 1 oz. Rum or Orange Rum
- ½ oz. Triple Sec
- ½ oz. Vanilla Liqueur
- Orange Juice
- Cream
- Ice

Directions: Fill a tall glass with ice. Fill with equal parts orange juice and cream. Shake.

CREAMSICLE (FROZEN)

- ½ cup of Ice
- 1 oz. Rum
- ½ oz. Triple Sec
- ½ oz. Vanilla Liqueur
- ½ scoop of Vanilla Ice Cream
- ½ scoop of Orange Sherbet
- Popsicle Stick

Directions: Blend all ingredients until smooth. If too, thick add milk. If too thin, add ice or ice cream. Garnish with Popsicle stick.

CREAMSICLE 2

- 1 oz. Banana Liqueur
- 1 oz. Triple Sec
- Orange Juice
- Milk
- Ice

Directions: Fill a tall glass with ice. Fill with equal parts orange juice and milk. Shake.

CREAMSICLE MARTINI

- 1 ¾ oz. Vanilla Vodka
- 1 ¾ oz. Orange Vodka
- Dash Triple Sec
- Dash Orange Juice
- Ice

Directions: Fill mixing glass with ice and add ingredients. Shake. Strain into a chilled glass.

CREAMY ORANGE

- ¾ oz. Brandy
- 1 oz. Cream Sherry
- 1 oz. Orange Juice
- 1 tbs. Light Cream
- Ice

Directions: Shake all ingredients with ice. Strain into a cocktail glass.

CREAMY SCREWDRIVER

- 2 oz. Vodka
- 6 oz. Orange Juice
- 1 tsp. Sugar
- 1 Egg Yolk
- ½ cup of Crushed Ice

Directions: Combine ingredients with crushed ice in an electric blender. Blend at a low speed for a short length of time. Pour into a Collins glass.

CREAMY SEX ON THE BEACH

- ¾ oz. Vodka
- ¾ oz. Coconut Rum
- ¾ oz. Peach Schnapps
- Dash Grenadine
- Pineapple Juice
- Whipped Cream
- 1 Cherry Garnish

Directions: Fill a tall glass with ice and ingredients. Fill with pineapple juice. Top with a dollop of whipped cream. Shake. Garnish with cherry.

CREATURE FROM THE BLACK LAGOON (FLOATER)

- 1 oz. Jaegermeister (bottom)
- 1 oz. Black Sambuca (top)

Directions: Layer ingredients in a glass.

CRÈME BRULEE MARTINI

- 3 ½ oz. Vanilla Vodka
- Dash Butterscotch Schnapps
- Dash Irish Cream
- Dash Black Raspberry Liqueur
- Dash Cream
- Ice

Directions: Fill a mixing glass with ice and add ingredients. Shake. Strain into a chilled glass.

CREOLE MARTINI

- 2 oz. Peppered Vodka
- ½ oz. Dry Vermouth
- Jalapeno Peppers
- Ice

Directions: Fill a mixing glass with ice and add ingredients. Stir and strain into a chilled glass. Serve with jalapeno peppers.

CRICKET

- 1 oz. Rum
- ¾ oz. White Crème de Menthe
- ¾ oz. Dark Crème de Cacao
- Milk or Cream
- Ice

Directions: Fill a mixing glass with ice and add ingredients. Fill with milk or cream. Shake. Serve or strain into a chilled glass.

CRIMSON SUNSET

- 2 oz. Gin
- 2 tsp. Lemon Juice
- ½ tsp. Grenadine
- ½ oz. Tawny Port
- Ice

Directions: In a shaker half-filled with ice cubes, combine the gin and lemon juice. Shake well. Strain into a cocktail glass. Drop the grenadine into the center of the drink and float the Port on the top.

CRIPPLER

- 1 oz. Grain Alcohol
- 1 oz. 151 Proof Rum
- Dash Triple Sec
- Ice

Directions: Fill mixing glass with ice and add ingredients. Shake. Strain into a shot glass.

CROCODILE COOLER

- 1 oz. Citrus Vodka or Citrus Rum
- 1 oz. Melon Liqueur
- Dash Sour Mix
- Lemon-lime Soda
- Ice

Directions: Fill a tall glass with ice and add ingredients. Fill with lemon-lime soda.

CRUISE CONTROL

- 1 oz. Rum
- ½ oz. Orange Liqueur or Triple Sec
- ½ oz. Sour Mix
- Soda Water
- 1 Orange Garnish
- 1 Lemon Garnish
- Ice

Directions: Fill a tall glass with ice and add ingredients. Shake. Fill with soda water. Garnish with lemon and orange.

CUBA LIBRE

- 2 oz. Light Rum
- Juice of ½ Lime
- Cola
- Ice

Directions: Pour lime juice into a highball glass over ice cubes. Add rum, fill with cola, stir, and serve.

CUBAN COCKTAIL NO. 1

- 2 oz. Light Rum
- Juice of ½ Lime
- ½ tsp. Powdered Sugar
- Ice

Directions: Shake all ingredients with ice, strain into a cocktail glass, and serve.

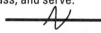

CUBAN PEACH

- 1 ½ oz. Light Rum
- 1 ½ oz. Peach Schnapps
- ½ oz. Lime Juice
- Dash Sugar Syrup
- 1 Mint Sprig
- Ice

Directions: Fill a mixing glass with ice and add ingredients. Shake. Strain into a chilled glass. Garnish with a mint sprig.

CUDDLER

- 1 oz. Irish Cream
- ¾ oz. Amaretto

Directions: Combine ingredients and heat in the microwave for seven to eight seconds.

CUPID'S POTION

- 1 ½ oz. Amaretto
- ½ oz. Triple Sec
- Dash Grenadine
- Orange Juice
- Sour Mix
- Ice

Directions: Fill a short glass with ice and add ingredients. Fill with equal parts orange juice and sour mix. Shake.

CURE-ALL

- 1 oz. Peppermint Schnapps
- ½ oz. Blackberry Brandy
- Ice

Directions: Fill a short glass with ice and add ingredients. Stir.

CURLEY'S DELIGHT COFFEE

- ¾ oz. Irish Cream
- ¾ oz. Irish Whiskey
- ¾ oz. Orange Liqueur
- Coffee
- Whipped Cream

Directions: Fill a glass with all ingredients. Top with whipped cream.

CURRENT AFFAIR

- 2 ½ oz. Currant Vodka
- ½ oz. Black Raspberry Liqueur
- 1 oz. Cranberry Juice
- Ice

Directions: Fill a mixing glass with ice and add ingredients. Stir. Strain into a hilled glass.

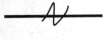

D.O.A.

- ¾ oz. Barenjager
- ¾ oz. Jaegermeister
- ¾ oz. 100 Proof Peppermint Schnapps
- Ice

Directions: Fill a mixing glass with ice and add ingredients. Shake. Strain into a shot glass.

DAIQUIRI

- 2 oz. Rum
- 2 oz. Lime Juice
- Dash Sour Mix
- ½ tsp. Sugar
- 1 Lime Garnish
- Ice

Directions: Fill a short glass with ice and add ingredients. Shake. Garnish with lime.

DAIQUIRI (FROZEN)

- 1 cup of Ice
- 2 oz. Rum
- 2 oz. Lime Juice
- Dash Sour Mix
- ½ tsp. Sugar
- 1 Lime Garnish

Directions: Blend all ingredients until smooth. Garnish with lime.

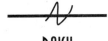

DAISY

- 2 oz. Desired Liqueur or Liquor
- ½ tsp. Powdered Sugar
- 1 tsp. Raspberry Syrup or Grenadine
- Ice

Directions: Fill mixing glass with ice and add ingredients. Shake. Strain into a chilled glass.

DAISY CUTTER 1

- ½ oz. Blue Curacao (bottom)
- 1 oz. Grain Alcohol (top)

Directions: Layer ingredients in a shot glass.

DAISY CUTTER 2

- ½ oz. Grenadine (bottom)
- Lemon-lime Soda

Directions: Fill pint glass three-fourths full with lemon-lime soda. Drop the shot of grenadine into the pint glass.

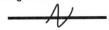

DALLAS ALICE

- ¾ oz. Tequila
- ¾ oz. Orange Liqueur
- ¾ oz. Coffee Liqueur
- Ice

Directions: Fill a mixing glass with ice and add ingredients. Shake. Strain into a chilled glass.

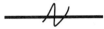

DAMN YOUR EYES

- 1 ½ oz. Anejo Rum
- ½ oz. Dubonnet Blonde
- 1 tsp. Dry Vermouth
- 1 Lemon Twist
- Ice

Directions: In a mixing glass half-filled with ice cubes, combine the rum, Dubonnet, and vermouth. Stir well. Strain into a cocktail glass and garnish with the lemon twist.

DAMN-THE-WEATHER COCKTAIL

- 1 tbs. Sweet Vermouth
- 1 oz. Gin
- 1 tbs. Orange Juice
- 1 tsp. Triple Sec
- Ice

Directions: Shake all ingredients with ice, strain into a cocktail glass, and serve.

DANCE MACHINE

- 2 oz. Tequila
- Sparkling Water
- Energy Drink
- 1 Lime Garnish
- Ice

Directions: Fill a tall glass with ice and add ingredients. Fill with equal parts sparkling water and energy drink. Garnish with lime.

DANGEROUS LIAISONS

- 2 oz. Orange Liqueur
- 2 oz. Coffee Liqueur
- 1 oz. Sour Mix
- Ice

Directions: Fill mixing glass with ice and add ingredients. Shake. Strain into a chilled glass.

DARB

- 1 oz. Gin
- 1 oz. Dry Vermouth
- 1 oz. Apricot Brandy
- ½ oz. Sour Mix
- 1 tsp. Sugar
- Ice

Directions: Fill mixing glass with ice and add ingredients. Shake. Strain into a chilled glass.

DARK AND STORMY

- 2 oz. Dark Rum
- Ginger Beer
- 1 Lime Garnish
- Ice

Directions: Fill a tall glass with ice and add ingredients. Fill with ginger beer. Garnish with lime.

DARK SECRET

- 1 ¼ oz. Black Sambuca
- Club Soda
- Ice

Directions: Fill a short glass with ice and add sambuca. Fill with club soda and stir.

DARK SIDE

- 1 ½ oz. Vodka
- 1 ½ oz. Brandy
- 1 oz. Coffee Liqueur
- ½ oz. White Crème de Menthe
- Ice

Directions: Fill a short glass with ice and add ingredients. Stir.

DARTH VADER

- ½ oz. Vodka
- ½ oz. Gin
- ½ oz. Rum
- ½ oz. Tequila
- ½ oz. Triple Sec
- 1 oz. Sour Mix
- ½ oz. Jaegermeister
- Darth Vader Action Figure (optional)

Directions: Fill a tall glass with ice and add ingredients. Top with Jaegermeister. Garnish with action figure.

DAY AT THE BEACH

- 1 oz. Amaretto
- 1 oz. Coconut Rum
- Dash Grenadine
- Orange Juice
- Ice

Directions: Fill a tall glass with ice and add ingredients. Fill with orange juice.

DC-3 (FLOATER)

- ½ oz. Sambuca (bottom)
- ½ oz. Irish Cream
- ½ oz. Crème de Cacao (top)

Directions: Layer ingredients in order in a shot glass.

DC-9 (FLOATER)

- ½ oz. Coffee Liqueur (bottom)
- ½ oz. Sambuca
- ½ oz. Rum Cream Liqueur (top)

Directions: Layer ingredients in order in a shot glass.

DE RIGUEUR

- 1 ½ oz. Whiskey
- ¾ oz. Grapefruit Juice
- 1 tsp. Honey
- Ice

Directions: Fill mixing glass with ice and add ingredients. Shake. Strain into a chilled glass.

DEAD NAZI

- 1 oz. Jaegermeister
- 1 oz. 100 Proof Peppermint Schnapps
- Ice

Directions: Fill a mixing glass with ice and add ingredients. Stir. Strain into a chilled glass.

DEAD RAT

- 1 ½ oz. Scotch
- ½ oz. Green Chartreuse
- Ice

Directions: Fill a mixing glass with ice and add ingredients. Shake. Strain into a shot glass.

DEATH CHAMBER

(floater)

- ½ oz. Coffee Liqueur (bottom)
- ½ oz. Irish Cream
- ½ oz. Amaretto (top)
- Beer

Directions: Combine liquor in a shot glass. Fill chilled glass with beer leaving an inch at the top. Drop the shot glass into the beer glass.

DEATH IN THE AFTERNOON

- 1 oz. Absinthe
- 2 - 3 dashes Bitters
- Champagne
- 1 Sugar Cube

Directions: Place sugar cube in a Champagne flute and drop two to three dashes of bitters on it. Add Absinthe and fill with Champagne.

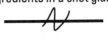

DEATH MINT

- 1 oz. Green Chartreuse
- 1 oz. 100 Proof Peppermint Schnapps

Directions: Combine ingredients in a shot glass.

DEATH ROW

- ½ oz. Vodka
- ½ oz. Citrus Vodka
- ½ oz. Orange Vodka
- ½ oz. Orange Liqueur
- ½ oz. Amaretto
- ½ oz. Sloe Gin
- Lemon-lime Soda
- Ice

Directions: Fill a tall glass with ice and add ingredients. Shake. Fill with lemon-lime soda.

DEATHWISH

- ½ oz. 151 Proof Rum
- ½ oz. 100 Proof Bourbon
- ½ oz. 100 Proof Peppermint Schnapps
- ½ oz. Grenadine
- Ice

Directions: Fill a mixing glass with ice and add ingredients. Shake. Strain into a chilled glass.

DEAUVILLE

- 1 ½ oz. Apple Brandy
- ½ oz. Triple Sec
- Dash Grenadine
- 2 oz. Sour Mix
- Ice

Directions: Fill a mixing glass with ice and add ingredients. Shake. Strain into a chilled glass.

DECEIVER

- 1 ½ oz. Tequila
- ½ oz. Galliano
- Ice

Directions: Fill a short glass with ice and add ingredients. Stir.

DEEP DARK SECRET

- 1 ½ oz. Dark Rum
- ½ oz. Anejo Rum
- ½ oz. Kahlua
- ½ oz. Heavy Cream
- Ice

Directions: In a shaker half-filled with ice cubes, combine all of the ingredients. Shake well. Strain into a cocktail glass.

DEEP SEA

- ½ oz. Gin
- ½ oz. Blue Curacao
- ½ oz. Pineapple Juice
- ½ oz. Lime Juice
- ½ oz. Sugar Syrup
- Ice

Directions: Fill a short glass with ice and add ingredients. Shake.

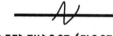

DEEP THROAT (FLOATER)

- 1 oz. Coffee Liqueur (bottom)
- 1 oz. Vodka (top)
- Whipped Cream

Directions: Layer ingredients in a shot glass. Top with whipped cream. To drink place hands behind back and pick up using only mouth.

DELMONICO

- 2 oz. Brandy
- ½ oz. Sweet Vermouth
- Dash Bitters
- 1 Cherry
- Ice

Directions: Fill mixing glass with ice and add ingredients. Stir. Strain into a chilled glass. Garnish with a cherry.

DELMONICO COCKTAIL

- 1 oz. Gin
- ½ oz. Brandy
- ½ oz. Sweet Vermouth
- ½ oz. Dry Vermouth
- Dash Bitters
- 1 Lemon Twist
- Ice

Directions: In a mixing glass half-filled with ice cubes, combine the gin, brandy, sweet vermouth, dry vermouth, and bitters. Stir well. Strain into a cocktail glass and garnish with the lemon twist.

DEPTH BOMB

- 1 ½ oz. Apple Brandy
- 1 ½ oz. Brandy
- ¼ tsp. Grenadine
- ¼ tsp. Sour Mix

Directions: Fill a mixing glass with ice and add ingredients. Shake. Strain into a chilled glass.

DEPTH CHARGE

- Whiskey, Peppermint Schnapps, or Drambuie
- Beer

Directions: Fill short glass with whiskey, schnapps, or Drambuie. Fill a chilled glass with beer, stopping an inch from the top. Drop the shot glass into the beer glass.

DERBY DAIQUIRI

- 1 ½ oz. Light Rum
- 1 oz. Orange Juice
- 1 tbs. Lime Juice
- 1 tsp. Sugar
- ½ cup of Shaved Ice

Directions: Blend all ingredients with shaved ice in an electric blender at a low speed. Pour into a Champagne flute and serve.

DESERT SUNRISE

- 2 oz. Tequila
- Dash Sour Mix
- ½ oz. Blue Curacao
- Orange Juice
- Ice

Directions: Fill tall glass with ice and add ingredients. Fill with orange juice. Top with blue curacao.

DESIGNER JEANS

- ½ oz. Dark Rum
- ½ oz. Irish Cream
- ½ oz. Raspberry Schnapps
- Ice

Directions: Fill a mixing glass with ice and add ingredients. Shake. Strain into a chilled glass.

DEVIL'S PUNCH

- 2 oz. Tequila
- 1 oz. Orange Liqueur
- 1 oz. Limoncello
- 1 oz. Sour Mix
- Dash Orange Juice
- Ice

Directions: Fill a short glass with ice and add ingredients. Shake.

DEVIL'S TRAIL (FROZEN)

- ½ cup of Ice
- 1 ½ oz. Rum
- 1 oz. Vodka
- ½ oz. Apricot Brandy
- 1 oz. Lime Juice
- ½ oz. Grenadine
- 1 Lime Garnish

Directions: Blend all ingredients for four to five seconds. Garnish with lime.

DIABLO

- 1 ½ oz. Brandy
- ½ oz. Triple Sec
- ½ oz. Dry Vermouth
- 2 dashes Bitters
- 1 Lemon Twist
- Ice

Directions: Fill a mixing glass with ice and add ingredients. Stir. Strain into a chilled glass. Garnish with a lemon twist.

DIAMOND FIZZ

- 2 oz. Gin
- Juice of ½ Lemon
- 1 tsp. Powdered Sugar
- Chilled Champagne
- Ice

Directions: Shake gin, lemon juice, and powdered sugar with ice and strain into highball glass over two ice cubes. Fill with chilled Champagne, stir.

DIAMOND HEAD

- 1 ½ oz. Gin
- ½ oz. Curacao
- 2 oz. Pineapple Juice
- 1 tsp. Sweet Vermouth
- 1 Pineapple Garnish
- Ice

Directions: Fill mixing glass with ice. Add ingredients. Shake. Strain into chilled glass. Garnish with pineapple.

DICKIE TOECHEESE
(floater)

- 1 oz. Blue Curacao (bottom)
- ½ oz. Vodka (top)
- Milk or Lemon-covered Bitters

Directions: Layer liquor in shot glass. Float milk on top or squeeze lemon-covered bitters in drink.

DIESEL

- ½ pint Lager
- ½ pint Cider
- Dash Blackcurrant Cordial

Directions: Pour the lager first then add the blackcurrant cordial. Top with cider. The color should be dark.

DIKI DIKI

- 1 ½ oz. Apple Brandy
- ¾ oz. Gin
- 1 oz. Grapefruit Juice
- Ice

Directions: Fill mixing glass with ice and add ingredients. Shake. Strain into a chilled glass.

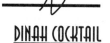

DINAH COCKTAIL

- 1 ½ oz. Blended Whiskey
- ½ tsp. Powdered Sugar
- Juice of ¼ Lemon
- 1 Mint Sprig
- Ice

Directions: Shake all ingredients except mint with ice. Strain into cocktail glass. Add the mint sprig.

DINGO

- ¾ oz. Rum
- ¾ oz. Amaretto
- ¾ oz. Southern Comfort
- Dash Grenadine
- Sour Mix
- Orange Juice
- Ice

Directions: Fill mixing glass with ice and add ingredients. Fill with equal parts sour mix and orange juice. Shake.

DIPLOMAT

- 1 ½ oz. Dry Vermouth
- ½ oz. Sweet Vermouth
- ½ tsp. Maraschino
- 2 dashes Bitters
- ½ Lemon Slice
- 1 Cherry
- Ice

Directions: Stir all ingredients except lemon and cherry with ice. Strain in cocktail glass. Add lemon slice. Top with cherry.

DIRE STRAITS

- 1 ½ oz. Brandy
- ½ oz. Coffee Liqueur
- ½ oz. Galliano
- ½ oz. Milk or Cream
- Ice

Directions: Fill a short glass with ice and add ingredients. Shake.

DIRTY BANANA

- 1 oz. Dark Crème de Cacao
- 1 oz. Banana Liqueur
- 1 oz. Cream or Milk
- Ice

Directions: Fill mixing glass with ice. Add ingredients. Shake. Strain into a chilled glass.

DIRTY BIRD

- 1 oz. Vodka or Tequila
- 1 oz. Coffee Liqueur
- Milk or Cream
- Ice

Directions: Fill a tall glass with ice and add ingredients. Fill with milk or cream. Shake.

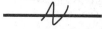

DIRTY DOG

- 2 oz. Vodka or Gin
- Grapefruit Juice
- 2 - 3 dashes Bitters
- Ice

Directions: Fill a tall glass with ice and add ingredients. Fill with grapefruit juice. Add two or three dashes of bitters.

DIRTY HARRY

- 1 oz. Orange Liqueur
- 1 oz. Coffee Liqueur
- Ice

Directions: Fill a mixing glass with ice and add ingredients. Shake. Strain into a shot glass.

DIRTY MARTINI

- 3 ½ oz. Gin or Vodka
- ½ oz. Olive Juice
- ½ oz. Dry Vermouth
- 1 Olive

Directions: Fill mixing glass with ice and add ingredients. Stir. Strain into a chilled glass. Garnish with an olive.

DIRTY MONKEY (FROZEN)

- ½ cup of Ice
- ¾ oz. Vodka
- ¾ oz. Coffee Liqueur
- ¾ oz. Banana Liqueur
- ½ scoop of Vanilla Ice Cream

Directions: Blend all ingredients until smooth.

DIRTY MOTHER

- 1 ½ oz. Brandy
- ½ oz. Kahlua
- Ice

Directions: Pour ingredients into an old-fashioned glass filled with ice cubes, stir well, and serve.

DIRTY WHITE MOTHER

- 1 ½ oz. Brandy
- ½ oz. Kahlua
- Light Cream
- Ice

Directions: Pour brandy and Kahlua into an old-fashioned glass filled with ice cubes and stir. Float cream on top and serve.

DIXIE COCKTAIL

- ½ oz. Dry Vermouth
- 1 oz. Gin
- 1 tbs. Anisette
- Juice of ¼ orange
- Ice

Directions: Shake all ingredients with ice, strain into a cocktail glass, and serve.

DIXIE DEW

- 1 ½ oz. Bourbon
- ½ tsp. White Crème de Menthe
- ½ tsp. Triple Sec
- Ice

Directions: In a mixing glass half-filled with ice cubes, combine all of the ingredients. Stir well. Strain into a cocktail glass.

DIXIE JULEP

- 2 ½ oz. Bourbon
- 1 tsp. Powdered Sugar
- 3 Mint Sprigs
- Ice

Directions: Combine bourbon and powdered sugar in a Collins glass. Fill with ice and stir gently until the glass is frosted. Add the three mint sprigs and serve with a straw.

DIXIE STINGER

- 3 oz. Bourbon
- ½ oz. White Crème de Menthe
- ½ tsp. Southern Comfort
- Ice

Directions: In a shaker half-filled with ice, combine all of the ingredients. Shake well. Strain into a cocktail glass.

DIXIE WHISKEY COCKTAIL

- 2 oz. Bourbon
- ½ tsp. White Crème de Menthe
- ¼ tsp. Triple Sec
- ½ tsp. Powdered Sugar
- Dash Bitters
- Ice

Directions: Shake all ingredients with ice, strain into a cocktail glass, and serve.

DOCTOR'S ELIXIR

- 1 oz. Mentholated Schnapps
- 1 oz. Black Raspberry Liqueur
- Ice

Directions: Fill mixing glass with ice and add ingredients. Stir.

DOG PISS

- 3 oz. vodka
- 12 oz. beer
- 4 oz. Southern Comfort

Directions: Put the ingredients into a container and stir.

DOG SLED

- 2 oz. Canadian Whiskey
- 1 tsp. Grenadine
- 1 tbs. Sour Mix
- Orange Juice
- Ice

Directions: Fill a tall glass with ice and add ingredients. Fill with orange juice. Shake.

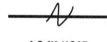

DOG'S NOSE

- 2 oz. Gin
- Beer

Directions: Pour gin into a glass and fill with beer.

DON JUAN

- 1 oz. Tequila
- 1 oz. Dark Rum
- 1 oz. Pineapple Juice
- 1 oz. Grapefruit Juice
- Ice

Directions: Fill mixing glass with ice and add ingredients. Shake. Strain into a chilled glass.

DORALTO

- 1 ½ oz. Tequila
- ½ oz. Lemon Juice
- ½ tsp. Superfine Sugar
- Dash Bitters
- 4 oz. Tonic Water
- 1 Lime Wedge
- Ice

Directions: In a shaker half-filled with ice, mix tequila, lemon juice, sugar, and bitters. Shake well. Strain into a highball glass almost filled with ice cubes. Top with tonic water and garnish with lime wedge.

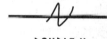

DOUBLE H

- 1 oz. Cognac
- 1 oz. Hypnotiq
- Ice

Directions: Fill short glass with ice. Add ingredients. Stir.

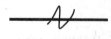

DOUBLE MINT BJ

- 1 oz. Coffee Liqueur
- 1 oz. Peppermint Schnapps
- Whipped Cream

Directions: Mix liquor in flute glass. Top with whipped cream. To drink, put hands behind back and pick up using mouth.

DOUBLE TROUBLE

- **4 oz. Prune Juice**
- **Beer**

Directions: Pour prune juice into a tall glass. Fill with beer.

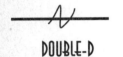

DOUBLE-D

- **¾ oz. Brandy**
- **¾ oz. Southern Comfort**
- **¾ oz. Cherry Brandy**
- **Dash Sour Mix**
- **Dash Cranberry Juice**
- **Ice**

Directions: Fill a mixing glass with ice and add ingredients. Shake. Strain into a chilled glass.

DOWNEASTER

- **2 oz. Vodka**
- **Cranberry Juice**
- **Pineapple Juice**
- **1 Lime Garnish**
- **Ice**

Directions: Fill a glass with ice and add ingredients. Fill with equal parts cranberry and pineapple juice. Garnish with a lime.

DR. FUNK

- **1 ½ oz. Dark Rum**
- **2 oz. Sour Mix**
- **2 oz. Pineapple Juice**
- **½ oz. Triple Sec**
- **Dash Grenadine**
- **Ice**

Directions: Fill a short glass with ice. Add ingredients. Shake. Top with Triple Sec.

DR. J

- **1 oz. Mentholated Schnapps**
- **1 oz. Jaegermeister**

Directions: Mix ingredients in shot glass.

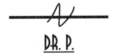

DR. P.

- **½ oz. Amaretto**
- **½ oz. Light Rum**
- **Beer**

Directions: Pour liquor into glass. Fill with beer.

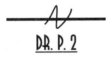

DR. P. 2

- **1 oz. Spiced Rum**
- **1 oz. Amaretto**
- **Cola**
- **Ice**

Directions: Fill tall glass with ice. Add ingredients. Fill with cola.

DR. P. FROM HELL

- **¾ oz. 151 Proof Rum**
- **¾ oz. Amaretto**
- **Beer**

Directions: Pour rum and Amaretto into a shot glass. Ignite. Drop into a glass of beer three-fourths full.

DRAGONFLY

- **1 ½ oz. Gin**
- **4 oz. Ginger Ale**
- **1 Lime Wedge**
- **Ice**

Directions: In a highball glass almost filled with ice cubes, combine the gin and ginger ale. Stir well. Garnish with the lime wedge.

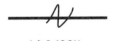

DRAGOON

- **½ oz. Coffee Liqueur**
- **½ oz. Irish Cream**
- **½ oz. Black Sambuca**
- **Ice**

Directions: Fill a short glass with ice and add ingredients. Stir.

DREAM COCKTAIL

- 1 ½ oz. Brandy
- ¾ oz. Triple Sec
- ¼ tsp. Anisette
- Ice

Directions: Shake all ingredients with ice, strain into a cocktail glass, and serve.

DREAMSICLE

- 1 ½ oz. Bailey's Irish Cream
- 3 ½ oz. Orange Juice

Directions: In a lowball glass, combine the ingredients and stir.

DRESSED UP LIKE A DOG'S DINNER

- 1 ½ oz. Brandy
- 1 oz. Applejack
- 1 oz. Sweet Vermouth
- Ice

Directions: In a mixing glass half-filled with ice cubes, combine all of the ingredients. Stir well. Strain into a cocktail glass.

DROOG'S DATE COCKTAIL

- 1 ½ oz. Light Rum
- 2 tsp. Cherry Brandy
- 2 tsp. Triple Sec
- ½ oz. Lime Juice
- Ice

Directions: In a shaker half-filled with ice, combine all ingredients. Shake well. Strain into a cocktail glass.

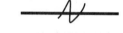

DROOLING PASSIONATE LADY

- 2 oz. Vodka or Citrus Vodka
- 1 oz. Triple Sec
- Pineapple Juice
- Ice

Directions: Fill tall glass with ice and add ingredients. Fill with pineapple juice. Shake.

DRUNKEN PALMER

- 1 oz. Citrus Vodka
- 1 oz. Southern Comfort
- Lemonade
- Iced Tea
- 1 Lemon Garnish
- Ice

Directions: Fill tall glass with ice. Add ingredients. Fill with equal parts lemonade and iced tea. Shake. Garnish with a lemon.

DRY ARROYO

- 1 oz. Black Raspberry Liqueur
- 1 oz. Coffee Liqueur
- 1 oz. Sour Mix
- 1 oz. Orange Juice
- Champagne
- 1 Orange Twist
- Ice

Directions: Fill mixing glass with ice and ingredients. Shake. Strain into a chilled glass. Fill with Champagne. Garnish with orange twist.

DRY MARTINI

- 3 ½ oz. Gin or Vodka
- ¼ oz. Dry Vermouth
- 1 Lemon Twist

Directions: Fill mixing glass with ice and ingredients. Strain in chilled glass. Garnish with a lemon twist.

DRY ROB ROY

- 2 ½ oz. Scotch
- 1 ½ tsp. Dry Vermouth
- 1 Lemon Twist
- Ice

Directions: In a mixing glass half-filled with ice, combine Scotch and vermouth. Stir well. Strain in cocktail glass. Garnish with lemon twist.

DU BARRY COCKTAIL

- 1 ½ oz. Gin
- ¾ oz. Dry Vermouth
- ½ tsp. Anisette
- Dash Bitters
- 1 Orange Slice
- Ice

Directions: Stir all ingredients except orange slice with ice and strain into a cocktail glass. Add the slice of orange.

DUBLIN COFFEE

- ¾ oz. Irish Whiskey
- ¾ oz. Irish Mist
- ¾ oz. Coffee Liqueur
- Crème de Menthe
- Coffee
- Whipped Cream

Directions: Combine liquor in a glass. Fill with hot, black coffee. Top with whipped cream and drizzle with crème de menthe.

DUBLIN MILKSHAKE

- 1 ½ oz. Irish Cream
- ½ oz. Irish Whiskey
- Chocolate Milk
- Ice

Directions: Fill mixing glass with ice and add ingredients. Fill with chocolate milk. Strain into a pint glass.

DUBONNET COCKTAIL

- 1 ½ oz. Dubonnet
- ¾ oz. Gin
- Dash Bitters
- 1 Twist Lemon Peel
- Ice

Directions: Stir all ingredients with ice except lemon peel. Strain into cocktail glass. Add lemon peel.

DUBONNET FIZZ

- 2 oz. Dubonnet
- 1 tsp. Cherry Brandy
- Carbonated Water
- Juice of ½ Orange
- Juice of ¼ Lemon
- Ice

Directions: Shake all ingredients except carbonated water with ice and strain into a highball glass over two ice cubes. Fill with carbonated water, stir, and serve.

DUBONNET MANHATTAN

- 1 ½ oz. Whiskey
- ¾ oz. Dubonnet Rouge
- 1 Cherry
- Ice

Directions: Fill mixing glass with ice and add ingredients. Shake. Strain into a chilled glass. Garnish with cherry.

DUCHESS

- 1 ½ oz. Anisette
- ½ oz. Sweet Vermouth
- ½ oz. Dry Vermouth
- Ice

Directions: Shake all ingredients with ice, strain into a cocktail glass, and serve.

DUCK FART (FLOATER)

- ½ oz. Coffee Liqueur (bottom)
- ½ oz. Irish Cream
- ½ oz. Blended Whiskey (top)

Directions: Layer ingredients in order in a shot glass.

DUDE

- 2 oz. Scotch
- ½ oz. Sherry
- Dash Grenadine
- Ice

Directions: Fill a short glass with ice and add ingredients. Stir. Float sherry on top.

DUNDEE

- 1 oz. Gin
- ½ oz. Drambuie
- ½ oz. Scotch
- ½ oz. Sour Mix
- 1 Lemon Twist
- Ice

Directions: Fill a short glass with ice and add ingredients. Shake. Garnish with lemon twist.

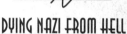

DUSTY ROAD (FROZEN)

- ½ cup of Ice
- 1 oz. Irish Cream
- 1 oz. Black Raspberry Liqueur
- ½ scoop of Vanilla Ice Cream
- Milk or Cream
- Ice

Directions: Blend ingredients until smooth. If too thick, add milk or cream. If too thin, add ice or ice cream.

DUSTY ROSE

- 1 oz. Irish Cream
- 1 oz. Black Raspberry Liqueur
- Ice

Directions: Fill a short glass with ice and add ingredients. Stir. Strain into a chilled glass.

DUTCH COFFEE

- 2 oz. Vandermint
- Coffee
- Whipped Cream
- Chocolate Shavings

Directions: Pour Vandermint into a glass and fill with hot, black coffee. Top with whipped cream and chocolate shavings.

DUTCH PIRATE

- 1 ½ oz. Vodka
- 1 oz. Vandermint
- ½ oz. Dark Rum
- 1 Orange Garnish
- Ice

Directions: Fill mixing glass with ice. Add ingredients. Shake and strain into a chilled glass. Garnish with orange.

DUTCH TREAT

- 2 oz. Brandy
- Hot Chocolate
- Whipped Cream
- Chocolate Shavings

Directions: Pour brandy into a glass and fill with hot chocolate. Top with whipped cream and chocolate shavings.

DUTCH VELVET

- ½ oz. Chocolate Mint Liqueur
- ½ oz. Banana Liqueur
- 2 oz. Light Cream
- 1 tsp. Shaved Chocolate
- Ice

Directions: Shake all ingredients with ice except chocolate and strain into a chilled cocktail glass. Garnish with shaved chocolate.

DYING NAZI FROM HELL

- 1 oz. Vodka
- 1 oz. Irish Cream
- 1 oz. Jaegermeister
- Ice

Directions: Fill a mixing glass with ice and add ingredients. Strain into a shot glass.

EARTHQUAKE

- ¾ oz. Amaretto
- ¾ oz. Anisette
- ¾ oz. Southern Comfort
- Ice

Directions: Fill mixing glass with ice and add ingredients. Stir. Strain into a shot glass.

EAST INDIA COCKTAIL NO. 1

- 1 ½ oz. Brandy
- 1 tsp. Jamaica Rum
- ½ tsp. Triple Sec
- ½ tsp. Pineapple Juice
- Dash Bitters
- 1 Cherry
- Ice

Directions: Shake all ingredients except cherry with ice and strain into a cocktail glass. Top with the cherry and serve.

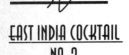

EAST INDIA COCKTAIL NO. 2

- 1 ½ oz. Dry Sherry
- 1 ½ oz. Dry Vermouth
- Dash Bitters
- Ice

Directions: Stir all ingredients with ice, strain into a cocktail glass.

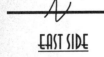

EAST SIDE

- ¾ oz. Rum
- ¾ oz. Amaretto
- ¾ oz. Coconut Rum
- Milk or Cream
- Ice

Directions: Fill a glass with ice and add ingredients. Fill with milk or cream. Shake.

EAT HOT DEATH

- 2 oz. 151 Proof Rum
- ½ oz. Lemon Juice

Directions: Stir ingredients and strain into a shot glass.

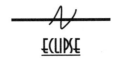

EAT THE CHERRY

- 1 tsp. Cherry Juice
- Vodka
- 1 Pitted, Stemless Cherry

Directions: Place pitted, stemless cherry in a shot glass with cherry juice. Fill with vodka.

ECLIPSE

- 2 oz. Black Sambuca
- Dash Cream
- Ice

Directions: Fill a glass with ice and ingredients. Stir. Strain into chilled glass.

ECSTASY

- 1 ½ oz. Vodka
- ½ oz. Black Raspberry Liqueur
- ½ oz. Pineapple Juice
- ½ oz. Cranberry Juice
- Ice

Directions: Combine ingredients in mixing glass and shake. Strain into chilled glass.

EDEN

- 2 oz. Vodka
- Apple Juice
- 1 Cherry
- Ice

Directions: Fill a serving glass with ice and add ingredients. Fill with apple juice. Garnish with a cherry.

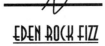

EDEN ROCK FIZZ

- 1 ½ oz. Whiskey
- Dash Pernod
- Dash Sugar Syrup
- Dash Sour Mix
- ½ Egg White
- Soda Water
- Ice

Directions: Fill a tall glass with ice and add ingredients. Shake. Fill with soda water.

EDITH DAY

- 2 oz. Gin
- 1 tsp. Sugar
- Grapefruit Juice
- Ice

Directions: Fill a tall glass with ice and add ingredients. Fill with grapefruit juice. Shake.

EGG CREAM

- 2/3 oz. Chocolate Syrup
- Milk
- Soda Water
- Ice

Directions: Fill a tall glass with ice and ingredients. Fill with equal parts milk and soda water. Stir.

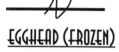

EGGHEAD (FROZEN)

- ½ cup of Ice
- 2 oz. Vodka
- 1 Egg
- Scoop of Orange Sherbet

Directions: Blend all ingredients until smooth.

EGGNOG

- 12 Eggs
- 2 cups Superfine Sugar
- 2 cups of Cognac
- 2 cups of Dark Rum
- 2 cups of Cream
- 6 cups of Milk
- Nutmeg

Directions: Separate eggs. Beat yolks and sugar until thick. Stir in Cognac, rum, cream, and milk. Refrigerate mixture. When chilled, beat egg whites until stiff. Fold them into the mixture. Garnish with nutmeg.

EGGNOG MARTINI

- 3 oz. Vanilla Vodka
- ½ oz. Amaretto
- Eggnog
- Ice

Directions: Fill mixing glass with ice. Add ingredients. Fill with eggnog. Shake. Strain into chilled glass.

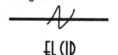

EL CID

- 1 ½ oz. Tequila
- ½ oz. Orgeat Syrup
- 1 oz. Lime Juice
- Tonic Water
- Dash Grenadine
- 1 Lime Garnish
- Ice

Directions: Fill tall glass with ice. Add ingredients. Shake. Fill with tonic water. Top with grenadine. Garnish with lime.

EL DIABLO

- 1 oz. Tequila
- ½ oz. Crème de Cassis
- Dash Lime Juice
- Ginger Ale
- Ice

Directions: Fill serving glass with ice. Add ingredients. Fill with ginger ale.

EL PRESIDENTE COCKTAIL NO. 1

- 1 ½ oz. Light Rum
- 1 tsp. Grenadine
- 1 tsp. Pineapple Juice
- Juice of 1 Lime
- Ice

Directions: Shake all ingredients with ice, strain into a cocktail glass, and serve.

EL SALVADOR

- 1 ½ oz. Rum
- ¾ oz. Hazelnut Liqueur
- Dash Grenadine
- ½ oz. Lime Juice
- Ice

Directions: Fill mixing glass with ice. Add ingredients. Shake. Strain into chilled glass.

ELMER FUDPUCKER

- 1 oz. Vodka
- 1 oz. Tequila
- Orange Juice
- Apricot Brandy
- 1 Orange Garnish
- Ice

Directions: Fill tall glass with ice. Add ingredients. Fill with orange juice. Top with apricot brandy. Garnish with orange.

ELVIRA

- 1 ½ oz. Vodka
- ½ oz. Blackberry Brandy
- Sour Mix
- Ice

Directions: Fill a serving glass with ice and add ingredients. Fill with sour mix. Shake.

ELYSEE PALACE

- 1 oz. Cognac
- ½ oz. Black Raspberry Liqueur
- Champagne
- Ice

Directions: Fill a serving glass with ice and add ingredients. Fill with Champagne. Float black raspberry liqueur on top.

EMBRYO (FLOATER)

- 1 oz. Coffee Liqueur (bottom)
- ¼ oz. Cream
- ½ oz. 100 Proof Vodka (top)

Directions: Layer ingredients in order in a shot glass.

EMERALD FOREST

- Crushed Ice
- 1 ½ oz. Gin
- 1 tsp. Green Crème de Menthe
- 1 tsp. White Crème de Menthe

Directions: In mixing glass half-filled with crushed ice, combine ingredients. Stir. Strain into a cocktail glass.

EMERALD ISLE COCKTAIL

- 2 oz. Gin
- 1 tsp. Green Crème de Menthe
- 3 dashes Bitters
- Ice

Directions: Stir all ingredients with ice, strain into a cocktail glass, and serve.

EMPIRE STATE SLAMMER

- 1 oz. Canadian Whiskey
- ½ oz. Sole Gin
- ½ oz. Banana Liqueur
- 2 oz. Orange Juice
- Ice

Directions: Fill mixing glass with ice and add ingredients. Shake. Strain into a chilled glass.

ENERGIZER (FLOATER)

- ¾ oz. Benedictine (bottom)
- ¾ oz. Irish Cream
- ¾ oz. Orange Liqueur (top)

Directions: Layer ingredients in order in a shot glass.

ENGAGEMENT MARTINI

- 3 ½ oz. Top Shelf Gin
- Dash Dry Vermouth
- 1 Engagement Ring
- Ice

Directions: Fill mixing glass with ice. Add ingredients. Stir. Strain into a chilled glass. Garnish with diamond engagement ring.

ENGLISH HIGHBALL

- ¾ oz. Brandy
- ¾ oz. Gin
- ¾ oz. Sweet Vermouth
- Carbonated Water
- Twist of Lemon Peel
- Ice

Directions: Pour brandy, gin, and vermouth into highball glass over ice. Fill with carbonated water. Add twist of lemon peel, stir, and serve.

ENGLISH ROSE COCKTAIL

- ¾ oz. Apricot Brandy
- 1 ½ oz. Gin
- ¾ oz. Dry Vermouth
- 1 tsp. Grenadine
- ¼ tsp. Lemon Juice
- Powdered Sugar
- 1 Cherry
- Ice

Directions: Rub rim of cocktail glass with lemon juice and dip in powdered sugar. Shake ingredients except cherry with ice and strain into glass. Top with cherry and serve.

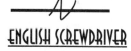

ENGLISH SCREWDRIVER

- 2 oz. Gin
- Orange Juice
- 1 Orange Garnish
- Ice

Directions: Fill tall glass with ice. Add ingredients. Fill with orange juice. Garnish with orange.

ERIE CANAL

- 1 ½ oz. Irish Whiskey
- ½ oz. Irish Mist
- ½ oz. Irish Cream
- Ice

Directions: Fill short glass with ice. Add ingredients. Stir.

EUROPEAN

- 1 oz. Gin
- ½ oz. Cream Sherry
- ½ oz. Dubonnet Rouge
- ½ oz. Dry Vermouth
- ½ tsp. Grand Marnier
- 1 Maraschino Cherry
- Ice

Directions: In an old-fashioned glass almost filled with ice cubes, combine the gin, sherry, Dubonnet, vermouth, and Grand Marnier. Stir well. Garnish with the cherry.

EVERGLADES SPECIAL

- ¾ oz. Rum
- ¾ oz. White Crème de Cacao
- ½ oz. Coffee Liqueur
- 1 oz. Cream or Milk
- Ice

Directions: Fill a shot glass with ice and add ingredients. Shake.

EVERYBODY'S IRISH COCKTAIL

- 2 oz. Irish Whiskey
- 1 tsp. Green Crème de Menthe
- 1 tsp. Green Chartreuse
- 1 Green Olive
- Ice

Directions: Stir all ingredients except green olive with ice and strain into a cocktail glass. Add the green olive and serve.

EWOK ATTACK

- ½ oz. Rum
- ½ oz. Tequila
- ½ oz. Apricot Brandy
- ½ oz. Melon Liqueur
- ½ oz. Galliano
- Orange Juice
- Cranberry Juice
- Pineapple Juice
- Ice

Directions: Fill a tall glass with ice and add ingredients. Fill with equal parts orange, cranberry and pineapple juice. Shake.

EXECUTIVE SUNRISE

- 1 ½ oz. Gold Tequila
- 4 oz. Fresh Orange Juice
- 2 tsp. Crème de Cassis
- Ice

Directions: Pour tequila and orange juice into Collins glass almost filled with ice. Stir well. Drop cassis into center of drink.

EXPRESS

- 1 ½ oz. Orange Liqueur
- ½ oz. Vodka
- 1 Orange Garnish
- Ice

Directions: Fill mixing glass with ice. Add ingredients. Shake. Strain into chilled glass. Garnish with orange.

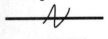

EYE-OPENER

- 1 ½ oz. Light Rum
- ½ oz. Triple Sec
- 2 tsp. Pernod
- 1 tsp. Crème de Cacao
- 1 Egg Yolk
- 1 tsp. Superfine Sugar
- Ice

Directions: In a shaker half-filled with ice, combine all of the ingredients. Shake well. Strain into a rocks glass.

F. U.

- 2 oz. Hazelnut Liqueur
- Lemon-lime Soda
- Ice

Directions: Fill serving glass with ice and add ingredients. Fill with lemon-lime soda.

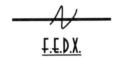

F.E.D.X.

- 1 ½ oz. Amaretto
- 1 oz. Black Raspberry Liqueur
- 2 oz. Sour Mix
- Champagne
- 1 Lemon Garnish
- Ice

Directions: Fill mixing glass with ice and add ingredients. Strain into a chilled champagne glass. Fill with Champagne. Garnish with lemon.

F-16 (FLOATER)

- ½ oz. Coffee Liqueur (bottom)
- ½ oz. Irish Cream
- ½ oz. Hazelnut Liqueur or Rum (top)

Directions: Layer all ingredients in order in a shot glass.

F-52 (FLOATER)

- ½ oz. Coffee Liqueur (bottom)
- ½ oz. Irish Cream
- ½ oz. Hazelnut Liqueur (top)

Directions: Layer all ingredients in order in a shot glass.

FACE ERASER

- 1 oz. Vodka
- 1 oz. Coffee Liqueur
- Lemon-lime Soda
- Ice

Directions: Fill a tall glass with ice and add ingredients. Fill with lemon-lime soda. Drink in one shot through a straw.

FACE ERASER 2

- 1 ½ oz. Vodka
- ½ oz. Coffee Liqueur
- ½ oz. Irish Cream
- Soda Water
- Ice

Directions: Fill a tall glass with ice and add ingredients. Fill with soda water. Drink in one shot through a straw.

FAHRENHEIT 5

- 1 oz. Peppered Vodka
- 1 oz. Cinnamon Schnapps
- Hot Sauce

Directions: Coat the inside of a shot glass with hot sauce. Pour ingredients into the glass.

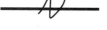

FAIR AND WARMER

- 1 ½ oz. Rum
- Dash Triple Sec
- ½ oz. Sweet Vermouth
- 1 Lemon Garnish
- Ice

Directions: Fill a mixing glass with ice and add ingredients. Shake. Serve or strain into a chilled glass. Garnish with lemon.

FAIRCHILD (FLOATER)

- 1 oz. Melon Liqueur (bottom)
- ½ oz. Orange Juice
- ½ oz. Irish Whiskey (top)

Directions: Layer ingredients in order in a shot glass.

FALLEN ANGEL

- 1 ½ oz. Gin
- ½ tsp. White Crème de Menthe
- Juice of ½ Lemon
- Dash Bitters
- 1 Cherry
- Ice

Directions: Shake ice and ingredients except cherry. Strain into a cocktail glass. Top with cherry.

FALLEN ANGEL MARTINI

- 1 oz. Vanilla Vodka
- 1 oz. Irish Cream
- 1 oz. Hazelnut Liqueur
- 1 oz. Chocolate Liqueur
- Dash Cream
- Ice

Directions: Fill a mixing glass with ice and add ingredients. Shake. Strain into a chilled glass.

FANCY BOURBON

- 2 oz. Bourbon
- ½ tsp. Triple Sec
- ¼ tsp. Superfine Sugar
- 2 dashes Bitters
- 1 Lemon Twist
- Ice

Directions: In a shaker half-filled with ice, combine bourbon, Triple Sec, sugar, and bitters. Shake well. Strain in cocktail glass. Garnish with lemon twist.

FANCY BRANDY

- 2 oz. Brandy
- ¼ tsp. Triple Sec
- ¼ tsp. Powdered Sugar
- Dash Bitters
- Twist of Lemon Peel
- Ice

Directions: Shake ice and ingredients except lemon peel. Strain into cocktail glass. Add lemon peel.

FANCY GIN

- 2 oz. Gin
- ¼ tsp. Triple Sec
- ¼ tsp. Powdered Sugar
- Dash Bitters
- Twist of Lemon Peel
- Ice

Directions: Shake all ingredients except lemon peel with ice. Strain into cocktail glass. Add the twist of lemon peel.

FANCY SCOTCH

- 2 oz. Scotch
- ½ tsp. Triple Sec
- ¼ tsp. Superfine Sugar
- 2 dashes Bitters
- 1 Lemon Twist
- Ice

Directions: In a shaker half-filled with ice, combine Scotch, Triple Sec, sugar, and bitters. Shake well. Strain into cocktail glass. Garnish with lemon twist.

FANCY WHISKEY

- 2 oz. Blended Whiskey
- ¼ tsp. Triple Sec
- ¼ tsp. Powdered Sugar
- Dash Bitters
- Twist of Lemon Peel
- Ice

Directions: Shake ingredients except lemon peel with ice. Strain into cocktail glass. Add lemon peel and serve.

FANTASIO COCKTAIL

- 1 oz. Brandy
- ¾ oz. Dry Vermouth
- 1 tsp. White Crème de Menthe
- 1 tsp. Maraschino
- Ice

Directions: Stir all ingredients with ice, strain into a cocktail glass, and serve.

FARE-THEE-WELL

- 1 ½ oz. Gin
- 1 oz. Dry Vermouth
- ½ oz. Triple Sec
- 2 dashes Sweet Vermouth
- Ice

Directions: Fill mixing glass with ice and add ingredients. Shake. Strain into chilled glass.

FASCINATION

- 1 ½ oz. Dark Rum
- ¾ oz. Orange Liqueur
- ½ tsp. Sugar
- ½ Egg White
- Sour Mix
- Ice

Directions: Fill a tall glass with ice and add ingredients. Fill with sour mix. Shake. Strain into a chilled glass.

FASTLAP

- 2 oz. Gin
- ½ oz. Pernod
- 1 oz. Orange Juice
- ½ tsp. Grenadine
- Ice

Directions: In a shaker half-filled with ice, mix ingredients. Shake well. Pour into an old-fashioned glass.

FAT CAT (FROZEN)

- ½ cup of Ice
- ¾ oz. Cognac
- ¾ oz. Galliano
- ¾ oz. White Crème de Cacao
- Scoop of Vanilla Ice Cream

Directions: Blend ingredients until smooth.

FAT FACE

- 1 ½ oz. Gin
- ½ oz. Apricot Brandy
- 1 tsp. Grenadine
- 1 Egg White
- Ice

Directions: In a shaker half-filled with ice cubes, combine all of the ingredients. Shake well. Strain into a rocks glass.

FATHER SHERMAN

- 1 ½ oz. Brandy
- ½ oz. Apricot Brandy
- 1 oz. Orange Juice
- Ice

Directions: Fill a mixing glass with ice and add ingredients. Shake. Strain into a chilled glass.

FAVORITE COCKTAIL

- ¾ oz. Apricot Brandy
- ¾ oz. Dry Vermouth
- ¾ oz. Gin
- ¼ tsp. Lemon Juice
- Ice

Directions: Shake all ingredients with ice, strain into a cocktail glass, and serve.

FEDORA

- ¾ oz. Dark Rum
- ¾ oz. Bourbon
- ¾ oz. Brandy
- Dash Triple Sec
- 1 oz. Sour Mix
- 1 Lemon Garnish
- Ice

Directions: Fill a mixing glass with ice and add ingredients. Shake and strain into a chilled glass. Garnish with lemon.

FERN GULLY

- 1 oz. Dark Rum
- 1 oz. Light Rum
- ½ oz. Crème de Nouyax or Amaretto
- 1 oz. Orange Juice
- ½ oz. Cream of Coconut
- ½ oz. Lime Juice
- 1 Lime Garnish
- 1 Orange Garnish
- Ice

Directions: Fill a short glass with ice and add ingredients. Shake and garnish with lime and orange.

FERRARI

- 1 oz. Amaretto
- 2 oz. Dry Vermouth
- 1 Lemon Twist
- Ice

Directions: Fill a short glass with ice and add ingredients. Stir. Garnish with a lemon twist.

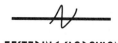

FESTERING SLOBOVIAN HUMMER

- ½ oz. 151 Proof Rum
- ½ oz. Galliano
- ½ oz. Peppermint Schnapps
- Ice

Directions: Fill mixing glass with ice and add ingredients. Shake. Strain into a shot glass.

FESTIVAL

- ¾ oz. Dark Crème de Cacao
- 1 oz. Apricot Brandy
- 1 tsp. Grenadine
- ¾ oz. Cream
- Ice

Directions: Fill a short glass with ice and add ingredients. Shake.

FIDEL'S MARTINI

- 3 ½ oz. Russian Vodka
- ½ oz. Banana Liqueur
- 1 Banana Garnish
- Ice

Directions: Fill a mixing glass with ice and add ingredients. Stir. Strain into a chilled glass. Garnish with banana.

FIERY KISS

- Honey
- Cinnamon Schnapps
- Dash Amaretto

Directions: Rim a shot glass with honey. Fill with cinnamon schnapps. Add a dash of Amaretto if desired.

FIERY REDHEAD

- 3 ½ oz. Peppered Vodka
- Dash Lime Juice
- Dash Grenadine
- 1 Cherry
- Ice

Directions: Fill mixing glass with ice and add ingredients. Shake. Strain into a chilled glass. Garnish with a cherry.

FIFTH AVENUE (FLOATER)

- ½ oz. Brown Crème de Cacao
- ½ oz. Apricot Brandy
- 1 tbs. Light Cream

Directions: Pour ingredients in parfait glass in order given so that each ingredient floats on preceding one. Serve without mixing.

FIFTY-FIFTY

- 1 ½ oz. Gin
- 1 ½ oz. Dry Vermouth
- 1 Cocktail Olive
- Ice

Directions: In a mixing glass half-filled with ice cubes, combine the gin and vermouth. Stir well. Strain into a cocktail glass and garnish with the olive.

FIG MARTINI

- 3 ½ oz. Vodka
- ½ oz. Fig Liqueur
- Dash Lemon Juice
- Dash Apple Juice
- Ice

Directions: Fill mixing glass with ice and add ingredients. Shake. Strain into chilled glass.

FINE AND DANDY

- 1 ½ oz. Gin
- ¾ oz. Orange Liqueur or Triple Sec
- ¾ oz. Sour Mix
- Dash Bitters
- 1 Cherry
- Ice

Directions: Fill a mixing glass with ice and add ingredients. Shake. Strain into a chilled glass. Garnish with a cherry.

FINO MARTINI

- 2 ½ oz. Gin or Vodka
- 1 ½ tsp. Fino Sherry
- 1 Lemon Twist
- Ice

Directions: In a mixing glass half-filled with ice, combine the gin or vodka and the sherry. Stir well. Strain into a cocktail glass. Garnish with the lemon twist.

FIRE AND ICE (FLOATER)

- 1 oz. Tequila (bottom)
- 1 oz. Peppermint Schnapps (top)

Directions: Layer ingredients in order in a shot glass.

FIREBALL

- Cinnamon Schnapps
- 4 - 5 drops Tabasco Sauce

Directions: Fill a shot glass with schnapps. Add four to five drops of tabasco sauce. Stir.

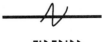

FIREBALL 2

- ½ oz. Vodka
- ½ oz. Cinnamon Schnapps
- ½ oz. Cherry Brandy
- 4 - 5 drops Tabasco Sauce
- Ice

Directions: Fill a mixing glass with ice and add ingredients. Stir. Strain into a chilled glass.

FIREBIRD

- 2 oz. Peppered Vodka
- Cranberry Juice
- Ice

Directions: Fill a tall glass with ice and add vodka. Fill with cranberry juice. Stir.

FIRECRACKER

- 2 oz. Spiced Rum
- ½ oz. Sloe Gin
- ½ oz. 151 Proof Rum
- Orange Juice
- 1 Orange Garnish
- Ice

Directions: Fill a tall glass with ice and add rum and gin. Fill with orange juice. Shake. Float 151 proof rum on top. Garnish with orange.

FIRECRACKER 2

- 1 ½ oz. Tequila
- ½ oz. Black Raspberry Liqueur
- Sour Mix
- Ice

Directions: Fill a tall glass with ice and add ingredients. Fill with sour mix. Shake.

FIREFLY

- 2 oz. Vodka
- Dash Grenadine
- Grapefruit Juice
- Ice

Directions: Fill a short glass with ice and add ingredients. Fill with grapefruit juice. Shake.

FIRE-IN-THE-HOLE

- Ouzo or Sambuca
- 3 - 5 dashes Tabasco Sauce

Directions: Fill a shot glass with ouzo or sambuca. Add three to five dashes of tabasco sauce. Stir.

FIREMAN'S SOUR

- 1 ½ oz. Light Rum
- 1 ½ oz. Lime Juice
- ½ oz. Grenadine
- 2 oz. Club Soda
- 1 Orange Slice
- 1 Maraschino Cherry
- Ice

Directions: In a shaker half-filled with ice cubes, combine rum, lime juice, and grenadine. Shake well. Strain into highball glass almost filled with ice. Top with club soda. Stir well. Garnish with the orange slice and the cherry.

FIRESTORM

- ¾ oz. Cinnamon Schnapps
- ¾ oz. Peppermint Schnapps
- ¾ oz. 151 Proof Rum
- Ice

Directions: Fill mixing glass with ice and add ingredients. Shake. Strain into a shot glass.

FIZZ

- 2 oz. Desired Liquor
- 1 oz. Lemon Juice
- 1 tsp. Powdered Sugar
- Soda Water
- Ice

Directions: Fill mixing glass with ice and add ingredients. Shake. Strain into a chilled glass. Fill with soda water.

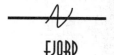

FJORD

- 1 oz. Brandy
- ½ oz. Aquavit
- 1 oz. Orange Juice
- ½ oz. Lime Juice
- 1 tsp. Grenadine
- Ice

Directions: Fill mixing glass with ice and add ingredients. Shake. Strain into chilled glass.

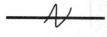

FLAMING BLUE J.

- 1 oz. Southern Comfort
- ½ oz. Blue Curacao
- ½ oz. Peppermint Schnapps
- ½ oz. 151 Proof Rum
- Ice

Directions: Fill a mixing glass with ice and add ingredients. Strain into a chilled glass. Float rum on top. Ignite.

FLAMING DR. PEPPER

- 1 oz. Amaretto
- 1 oz. Vodka
- 1 oz. Bacardi 151
- 1 oz. Dr. Pepper
- 1 oz. Beer

Directions: Add Amaretto, Bacardi, and vodka to a glass. Mix in the Dr. Pepper and beer.

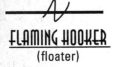

FLAMING HOOKER
(floater)

- 1 oz. Coffee Liqueur (bottom)
- 1 oz. Ouzo (top)

Directions: Layer ingredients in a shot glass. Ignite.

FLAMING HUSCROFT

- 1 oz. Blackened Voodoo Beer
- 2 oz. Southern Comfort
- ¼ oz. Bacardi 151
- ¼ oz. Everclear
- ½ oz. Captain Morgan
- 4 oz. Soda Water
- 1 oz. Mountain Dew
- 24 oz. Milwaukee's Best Ice

Directions: Throw all ingredients in a glass and light it. When the flame goes down, chug. Make sure there's a chaser or there could be trouble.

FLAMING NORWEGIAN
(floater)

- ½ oz. Strawberry Liqueur (bottom)
- ½ oz. Green Crème de Menthe
- ½ oz. Sugar Syrup
- ½ oz. 151 Proof Rum (top)

Directions: Layer ingredients in order in a shot glass. Ignite.

FLAMINGO

- 1 ½ oz. Gin
- ½ oz. Apricot Brandy
- ½ oz. Lime Juice
- Dash Grenadine
- Ice

Directions: Fill mixing glass with ice and add ingredients. Shake. Strain into chilled glass.

FLAMINGO COCKTAIL

- ½ oz. Apricot Brandy
- 1 ½ oz. Gin
- Juice of ½ Lime
- 1 tsp. Grenadine
- Ice

Directions: Shake all ingredients with ice, strain into a cocktail glass, and serve.

FLEET STREET

- 1 ½ oz. Gin
- ½ oz. Sweet Vermouth
- 1 tsp. Dry Vermouth
- 1 tsp. Triple Sec
- 1 tsp. Lemon Juice
- Ice

Directions: In a shaker half-filled with ice, combine all of the ingredients. Shake well. Strain into cocktail glass.

FLIM FLAM

- 1 ½ oz. Rum
- ¾ oz. Triple Sec
- ½ oz. Sour Mix
- ½ oz. Orange Juice
- Ice

Directions: Fill a mixing glass with ice and add ingredients. Shake. Strain into a chilled glass.

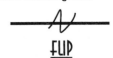

FLIP

- 2 oz. Desired Liquor
- 1 Raw Egg
- 1 tsp. Powdered Sugar
- Nutmeg
- Ice

Directions: Fill a mixing glass with ice and add ingredients. Shake. Strain into a chilled glass. Garnish with nutmeg.

FLIRTINI

- **3 oz. Vodka**
- **1 oz. Pineapple Juice**
- **Champagne**
- **Ice**

Directions: Fill mixing glass with ice. Add ingredients. Shake. Strain into chilled glass. Top with Champagne.

FLIRTINI 2

- **3 ½ oz. Raspberry Vodka**
- **½ oz. Orange Liqueur**
- **Dash Lime Juice**
- **Dash Pineapple Juice**
- **Dash Cranberry Juice**
- **2 or 3 Raspberries**
- **Champagne**
- **Ice**

Directions: Fill mixing glass with ice and add ingredients. Shake. In a chilled martini glass, muddle two or three raspberries. Strain into a chilled glass. Top with Champagne.

FLORIDA

- **½ oz. Gin**
- **1 ½ tsp. Kirschwasser**
- **1 ½ tsp. Triple Sec**
- **1 oz. Orange Juice**
- **1 tsp. Lemon Juice**
- **Ice**

Directions: Shake all ingredients with ice, strain into a cocktail glass, and serve.

FLORIDA ICED TEA

- **½ oz. Vodka**
- **½ oz. Gin**
- **½ oz. Rum**
- **½ oz. Tequila**
- **½ oz. Triple Sec**
- **2 oz. Orange Juice**
- **Cola**
- **1 Orange Garnish**

Directions: Fill tall glass with ice and add ingredients. Top with cola. Garnish with orange.

FLORIDA LOBSTER

- **1 ½ oz. Whiskey**
- **½ oz. Amaretto**
- **Cranberry Juice**
- **Ice**

Directions: Fill mixing glass with ice and add ingredients. Fill with cranberry juice.

FLORIDA PUNCH

- **1 ½ oz. Brandy**
- **½ oz. Dark Rum**
- **Orange Juice**
- **Grapefruit Juice**
- **Ice**

Directions: Fill mixing glass with ice and add ingredients. Fill glass with equal parts orange and grapefruit juice. Shake.

FLORIDA SUNRISE

- **2 oz. Rum**
- **Orange Juice**
- **½ oz. Grenadine**
- **1 Orange Garnish**
- **Ice**

Directions: Fill a tall glass with ice and add ingredients. Fill with orange juice. Pour grenadine down a spoon to the bottom of the glass. Garnish with orange.

FLUFFY DUCK

- **1 oz. Vodka**
- **1 oz. Advokaat**
- **Dash Cream**
- **Lemon-lime Soda**
- **Ice**

Directions: Fill mixing glass with ice and ingredients. Shake. Fill with lemon-lime soda. Shake.

FLUFFY DUCK 2

- 1 oz. Gin
- 1 oz. Advokaat
- Dash Orange Liqueur
- Dash Orange Juice
- Soda Water
- Ice

Directions: Fill a tall glass with ice and add ingredients. Shake. Top with soda water.

FLYING DUTCHMAN

- 2 oz. Gin
- ½ oz. Triple Sec
- Ice

Directions: In an old-fashioned glass almost filled with ice cubes, combine the gin and Triple Sec. Stir well.

FLYING GRASSHOPPER

- 1 oz. Vodka
- ¾ oz. Crème de Menthe
- ¾ oz. White Crème de Cacao
- Milk or Cream
- Ice

Directions: Fill a tall glass with ice and add ingredients. Fill with milk or cream. Shake. Strain into chilled glass.

FLYING KANGAROO
(frozen)

- ½ cup of Ice
- ¾ oz. Vodka
- ¾ oz. Rum
- ¾ oz. Galliano
- 2 tbs. Vanilla Ice Cream
- 1 Pineapple or Cherry

Directions: Blend all ingredients until smooth. Garnish with pineapple or cherry.

FLYING MADRAS

- 2 oz. Vodka
- 2 oz. Cranberry Juice
- 2 oz. Orange Juice
- Champagne
- 1 Orange Garnish
- Ice

Directions: Fill tall glass with ice. Add ingredients. Fill with Champagne. Garnish with orange.

FLYING SCOT

- 1 oz. Scotch
- 1 oz. Sweet Vermouth
- ¼ oz. Sugar Syrup
- 2 - 4 dashes Bitters
- Ice

Directions: Fill mixing glass with ice and add ingredients. Shake.

FLYING SCOTCHMAN

- 1 oz. Scotch
- 1 oz. Sweet Vermouth
- Dash Bitters
- ¼ tsp. Sugar Syrup
- Ice

Directions: Shake ingredients with ice, strain into cocktail glass, and serve.

FOG CUTTER

- 1 ½ oz. Light Rum
- ½ oz. Gin
- ½ oz. Brandy
- 1 oz. Orange Juice
- 3 tbs. Lemon Juice
- 1 ½ tsp. Orgeat Syrup
- 1 tsp. Sweet Sherry
- Ice

Directions: Shake ingredients and strain into a Collins glass over ice. Top with sherry and serve.

FOG HORN

- 2 oz. Gin
- Ginger Ale/Ginger Beer
- 1 Lemon Garnish
- Ice

Directions: Fill serving glass with ice and add ingredients. Fill with ginger ale or ginger beer. Garnish with lemon.

FORBIDDEN JUNGLE

- 1 ½ oz. Coconut Rum
- ½ oz. Peach Schnapps
- Dash Lime Juice
- Pineapple Juice
- Ice

Directions: Fill a tall glass with ice and add ingredients. Fill with pineapple juice. Shake.

FORESTER

- 1 ½ oz. Bourbon
- ¾ oz. Cherry Liqueur
- 1 tsp. Sour Mix
- Ice

Directions: Fill a short glass with ice and add ingredients. Shake.

FORT LAUDERDALE

- 1 ½ oz. Light Rum
- ½ oz. Sweet Vermouth
- Juice of ¼ Orange
- Juice of ¼ Lime
- 1 Orange Slice
- Ice

Directions: Shake all ingredients except orange slice with ice and strain into an old-fashioned glass over ice cubes. Add the orange slice and serve.

FOUR HORSEMEN

- ½ oz. Bourbon
- ½ oz. Sambuca
- ½ oz. Jaegermeister
- ½ oz. 100 Proof Peppermint Schnapps
- Ice

Directions: Fill mixing glass with ice and add ingredients. Shake. Strain into a shot glass.

FOUR HORSEMEN 2

- ½ oz. Tequila
- ½ oz. 151 Proof Peppermint Schnapps
- ½ oz. Jaegermeister
- Ice

Directions: Fill mixing glass with ice and add ingredients. Shake. Strain into a shot glass.

FOUR HORSEMEN 3

- ½ oz. Jim Bean
- ½ oz. Jack Daniels
- ½ oz. Johnnie Walker
- ½ oz. Jose Cuervo
- Ice

Directions: Fill a mixing glass with ice and add ingredients. Stir. Strain into a shot glass.

FOURTH OF JULY (FLOATER)

- ¾ oz. Grenadine (bottom)
- ¾ oz. Blue Curacao
- ¾ oz. Rum (top)

Directions: Layer ingredients in order in a shot glass.

FOX AND HOUNDS

- 1 ½ oz. Bourbon
- ½ oz. Pernod
- ½ oz. Lemon Juice
- ½ tsp. Superfine Sugar
- 1 Egg White
- Ice

Directions: In a shaker half-filled with ice cubes, combine all of the ingredients. Shake well. Strain into a cocktail glass.

FOX RIVER COCKTAIL

- 2 oz. Blended Whiskey
- 1 tbs. Brown Crème de Cacao
- 4 dashes Bitters
- Ice

Directions: Stir all ingredients with ice, strain into a cocktail glass, and serve.

FOX TROT

- 1 ½ oz. Rum
- ½ oz. Triple Sec
- 1 oz. Lime Juice
- Ice

Directions: Fill mixing glass with ice and add ingredients. Shake. Strain into chilled glass.

FOXY LADY

- ½ oz. Amaretto
- ½ oz. Brown Crème de Cacao
- 2 oz. Light Cream
- Ice

Directions: Shake ingredients with ice, strain into chilled cocktail glass, and serve.

FRANKENBERRY

- 1 oz. Currant Vodka
- 1 oz. Black Raspberry Liqueur
- Sour Mix
- Pineapple Juice
- Ice

Directions: Fill a tall glass with ice and add ingredients. Fill with equal parts sour mix and pineapple juice. Shake.

FRANKENJACK COCKTAIL

- 1 oz. Gin
- ¾ oz. Dry Vermouth
- ½ oz. Apricot Brandy
- 1 tsp. Triple Sec
- 1 Cherry
- Ice

Directions: Stir all ingredients with ice except cherry and strain into cocktail glass. Add the cherry and serve.

FRAPPE

- 2 oz. Desired Liquor or Liqueur
- Crushed Ice

Directions: Fill large stemmed glass with crushed ice. Add desired liquor or liqueur.

FREDDY FUDPUCKER

- 1 ½ oz. Tequila
- Orange Juice
- Galliano
- 1 Orange Garnish
- Ice

Directions: Fill a tall glass with ice and add ingredients. Fill with orange juice. Top with Galliano. Garnish with orange.

FREDDY KRUGER
(floater)

- 1 oz. Sambuca (bottom)
- 1 oz. Jaegermeister
- 1 oz. Vodka (top)

Directions: Layer ingredients in order in a shot glass.

FREE SILVER

- ½ oz. Dark Rum
- 1 ½ oz. Gin
- Juice of ¼ Lemon
- ½ tsp. Powdered Sugar
- 1 tbs. Milk
- Carbonated Water
- Ice

Directions: Shake all ingredients with ice except carbonated water and strain into a Collins glass over ice cubes. Fill with carbonated water, stir, and serve.

FREEDOM FIGHTER
(floater)

- 1 ½ oz. Irish Whiskey
- ½ oz. Irish Cream (top)

Directions: Layer ingredients in order in a shot glass.

FRENCH 125

- 2 oz. Sweet and Sour
- 1 oz. Brandy
- Chilled Champagne
- 1 Lemon Slice
- Ice

Directions: Pour brandy and sweet and sour into a Collins glass over ice cubes and stir well. Fill with chilled Champagne and stir lightly. Add the lemon slice and serve.

FRENCH 75

- 1 ½ oz. Gin
- 2 tsp. Superfine Sugar
- 1 ½ oz. Lemon Juice
- 4 oz. Chilled Champagne
- 1 Orange Slice
- 1 Maraschino Cherry
- Ice

Directions: In a shaker half-filled with ice cubes, combine the gin, sugar, and lemon juice. Shake well. Pour into a Collins glass. Top with the Champagne. Stir well and garnish with the orange slice and the cherry.

FRENCH 95

- 1 ½ oz. Bourbon
- 1 oz. Sour Mix
- 1 oz. Orange Juice
- 1 Cherry or Orange Garnish

Directions: Fill a tall glass with ice and add ingredients. Fill with Champagne. Float brandy on top. Garnish with orange or cherry.

FRENCH COFFEE

- 2 oz. Orange Liqueur
- Coffee
- Whipped Cream
- 1 Orange Garnish
- Cinnamon

Directions: Fill a glass with hot, black coffee and orange liqueur. Top with whipped cream. Garnish with orange and cinnamon.

FRENCH CONNECTION

- 1 ½ oz. Cognac
- ¾ oz. Amaretto
- Ice

Directions: Pour ingredients into an old-fashioned glass over ice, stir, and serve.

FRENCH CONNECTION COFFEE

- 1 ½ oz. Brandy
- ½ oz. Amaretto
- Coffee
- Whipped Cream
- Shaved Almonds

Directions: Fill a glass with hot, black coffee, brandy, and Amaretto. Top with whipped cream. Sprinkle with shaved almonds.

FRENCH DRAGON

- 1 oz. Brandy
- 1 oz. Green Chartreuse

Directions: Put ingredients in a snifter or short glass. Stir.

FRENCH DREAM

- 1 oz. Irish Cream
- 1 oz. Black Raspberry Liqueur
- 1 oz. Coffee Liqueur
- Ice

Directions: Fill a short glass with ice and add ingredients. Stir.

FRENCH HOOKER

- 1 ½ oz. Vodka
- 1 ½ oz. Black Raspberry Liqueur
- Dash Sour Mix
- Ice

Directions: Fill a mixing glass with ice and add ingredients. Shake. Strain into a chilled glass.

FRENCH KISS

- ¾ oz. Brandy
- ¾ oz. Benedictine
- ¾ oz. Orange Liqueur

Directions: Combine ingredients in a snifter and heat in microwave for five to seven seconds on high.

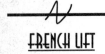

FRENCH LIFT

- Champagne
- Sparkling Water
- Dash Grenadine
- 3 – 4 Blueberries

Directions: Fill a flute glass half-full with Champagne. Add a dash of grenadine. Fill with sparkling water. Garnish with three to four blueberries.

FRENCH MARTINI

- 3 oz. Vodka
- ½ oz. Black Raspberry Liqueur
- ½ oz. Peach Schnapps
- 1 Cherry
- Ice

Directions: Fill mixing glass with ice and add ingredients. Shake. Strain into chilled glass. Garnish with a cherry.

FRENCH MARTINI 2

- 3 ½ oz. Vodka
- ¼ oz. Black Raspberry Liqueur
- Dash Pineapple Juice
- Ice

Directions: Fill mixing glass with ice and add ingredients. Shake. Strain into chilled glass.

FRENCH SUMMER

- 1 oz. Black Raspberry Liqueur
- Soda Water
- 1 Orange Garnish
- Ice

Directions: Fill a Champagne glass with ice and add ingredients. Fill with soda water. Garnish with orange.

FRENCH TICKLER

- 1 oz. Orange Liqueur
- 1 oz. 100 Proof Cinnamon Schnapps
- Ice

Directions: Fill mixing glass with ice and add ingredients. Stir. Strain into shot glass.

FRESCA

- ¾ oz. Raspberry Vodka
- ¾ oz. Orange Vodka
- ¾ oz. Orange Liqueur
- Lemon-lime Soda
- 1 Lemon Garnish
- 1 Lime Garnish
- Ice

Directions: Fill tall glass with ice and add ingredients. Fill with lemon-lime soda. Stir. Garnish with lemon and lime.

FRIAR TRUCK

- 2 oz. Hazelnut Liqueur
- 2 oz. Lemon Juice
- 2 dashes Grenadine
- 1 Orange Garnish
- 1 Cherry
- Ice

Directions: Fill short glass with ice and add ingredients. Shake. Garnish with orange and cherry.

FRISCO SOUR

- 2 oz. Blended Whiskey
- ½ oz. Benedictine
- Juice of ¼ Lemon
- Juice of ½ Lime
- 1 Lemon Slice
- 1 Lime Slice
- Ice

Directions: Shake all ingredients except slices of lemon and lime with ice and strain into a whiskey sour glass. Decorate with the slices of lemon and lime and serve.

FROG-IN-A-BLENDER
(frozen)

- 1 cup of Ice
- 2 oz. Vodka
- 4 oz. Cranberry Juice
- 2 Lime Wheels

Directions: Blend all ingredients for three to five seconds.

FROSTBITE

- 1 ½ oz. Tequila
- ½ oz. White Crème de Curacao
- ½ oz. Blue Curacao
- Cream
- Ice

Directions: Fill a tall glass with ice and add ingredients. Fill with cream. Shake.

FROSTBITE (FROZEN)

- 1 cup of Ice
- 1 ½ oz. Yukon Jack
- ¾ oz. Peppermint Schnapps
- 2 oz. Sour Mix

Directions: Blend all ingredients until smooth. If too thick, add ice. If too thin, add sour mix.

FROSTED ROMANCE
(frozen)

- ½ cup of Ice
- 1 oz. Black Raspberry Liqueur
- ½ oz. White Crème de Cacao
- Scoop of Vanilla Ice Cream
- Milk (optional)

Directions: Blend all ingredients until smooth. If too thick, add milk or liqueur. If too thin, add ice or ice cream.

FROZEN BIKINI

- 1 cup of Ice
- 2 oz. Vodka
- 1 oz. Peach Schnapps
- 3 oz. Peach Nectar
- 2 oz. Orange Juice
- Whole Peach (no pit, no skin)
- Champagne

Directions: Blend all ingredients until smooth. Pour into a large glass. Top with Champagne.

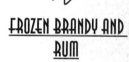

FROZEN BRANDY AND RUM

- 1 ½ oz. Brandy
- 1 oz. Light Rum
- 1 tbs. Lemon Juice
- tsp. Powdered Sugar
- 1 Egg White
- 1 cup of Crushed Ice

Directions: Combine all ingredients with ice in an electric blender and blend at a low speed for a short length of time. Pour into an old-fashioned glass and serve.

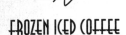

FROZEN DAIQUIRI

- 1 ½ oz. Light Rum
- 1 tbs. Triple Sec
- 1 ½ oz. Lime Juice
- 1 tsp. Sugar
- 1 Cherry
- 1 cup of Crushed Ice

Directions: Combine all ingredients except for the cherry in an electric blender and blend at a low speed for five seconds, and then blend at a high speed until firm. Pour contents into a Champagne flute, top with the cherry, and serve.

FROZEN ICED COFFEE

- ½ cup of Ice
- 2 - 3 oz. Desired Liquor
- 4 oz. Coffee or Espresso
- Scoop of Vanilla or Chocolate Ice Cream

Directions: Blend all ingredients until smooth.

FROZEN MARGARITA

- 2 tsp. Coarse Salt
- 1 Lime Wedge
- 3 oz. White Tequila
- 1 oz. Triple Sec
- 2 oz. Lime Juice
- 1 cup of Crushed Ice

Directions: Place salt in a saucer. Rub the rim of a Collins glass with a lime wedge and dip the glass into salt to coat the rim thoroughly. Pour tequila, Triple Sec, lime juice, and ice into a blender. Blend well at a high speed. Pour into a Collins glass.

FROZEN MATADOR

- 1 ½ oz. Tequila
- 2 oz. Pineapple Juice
- 1 tbs. Lime Juice
- 1 Pineapple Stick
- 1 cup of Crushed Ice

Directions: Blend all ingredients except pineapple stick with crushed ice in an electric blender at a low speed for a short length of time. Pour into an old-fashioned glass. Add the pineapple stick and serve.

FROZEN MINT DAIQUIRI

- 2 oz. Light Rum
- 1 tbs. Lime Juice
- 6 Mint Leaves
- 1 tsp. Sugar
- 1 cup of Crushed Ice

Directions: Combine all ingredients with crushed ice in an electric blender. Blend at a low speed for a short length of time. Pour into an old-fashioned glass.

FROZEN PINEAPPLE DAIQUIRI

- 1 ½ oz. Light Rum
- 4 Pineapple Chunks
- 1 tbs. Lime Juice
- ½ tsp. Sugar
- 1 cup of Crushed Ice

Directions: Pour crushed ice and ingredients in blender. Blend on low for a short time. Pour into Champagne flute. Serve.

FRU FRU

- 1 oz. Peach Schnapps
- 1 oz. Banana Liqueur
- Dash Lime Juice
- 1 oz. Pineapple Juice
- 1 Lime Garnish
- Ice

Directions: Fill mixing glass with ice and ingredients. Shake. Strain into chilled glass. Garnish with lime.

FRUITBAR

- 1 oz. Peach Schnapps
- 1 oz. Dark Crème de Cacao
- Ice

Directions: Fill a short glass with ice and add ingredients. Stir.

FRUTTI NUEB

- ½ oz. Vodka
- ½ oz. Coconut Rum
- ½ oz. Melon Liqueur
- ½ oz. Black Raspberry Liqueur
- Cranberry Juice
- Ice

Directions: Fill tall glass with ice and add ingredients. Fill with cranberry juice. Shake.

FU MANCHU

- 1 ½ oz. Dark Rum
- ½ oz. Triple Sec
- ½ oz. Crème de Menthe
- ½ oz. Lime Juice
- Dash Sugar Syrup
- Ice

Directions: Fill mixing glass with ice. Add ingredients. Shake. Strain into chilled glass.

FUBAR

- ½ oz. Vodka
- ½ oz. Gin
- ½ oz. Rum
- ½ oz. Tequila
- Hard Cider
- Ice

Directions: Fill mixing glass with ice and ingredients. Fill with hard cider

FUEL-INJECTION

- 1 ½ oz. Brandy
- ½ oz. Mentholated Schnapps
- Ice

Directions: Fill mixing glass with ice and add ingredients. Shake. Strain into chilled glass.

FULL MOON

- 1 oz. Orange Liqueur
- 1 oz. Amaretto
- Ice

Directions: Fill a short glass with ice and add ingredients. Stir.

FUZZY ASTRONAUT

- 1 ½ oz. Vodka
- ½ oz. Peach Schnapps
- Tang
- Ice

Directions: Fill a tall glass with ice and ingredients. Fill with Tang.

FUZZY BASTARD

- 1 oz. Dark Rum
- ½ oz. 151 Proof Rum
- ½ oz. Triple Sec
- Orange Juice
- Sour Mix
- ½ oz. Peach Schnapps
- Ice

Directions: Fill a tall glass with ice and add ingredients. Fill with equal parts orange juice and sour mix. Shake. Float schnapps on top.

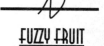

FUZZY FRUIT

- 2 oz. Peach Schnapps
- Grapefruit Juice
- Ice

Directions: Fill serving glass with ice and add ingredients. Fill with grapefruit juice. Stir.

FUZZY MONKEY

- 1 oz. Banana Liqueur
- 1 oz. Peach Schnapps
- Orange Juice
- 1 Orange or Banana
- Ice

Directions: Fill serving glass with ice. Add ingredients. Fill with orange juice. Stir. Garnish with orange or banana.

FUZZY MOTHER (FLOATER)

- 1 ½ oz. Gold Tequila (bottom)
- ¼ oz. 151 Proof Rum (top)

Directions: Layer ingredients in a shot glass. Ignite.

FUZZY NAVEL

- 1 oz. Vodka
- 1 oz. Peach Schnapps
- Orange Juice
- 1 Orange Garnish
- Ice

Directions: Fill a serving glass with ice and add ingredients. Fill with orange juice. Garnish with orange.

FUZZY NAVEL WITH LINT

- 1 oz. Vodka
- 1 oz. Peach Schnapps
- Orange Juice
- Irish Cream or Milk
- Ice

Directions: Fill serving glass with ice and add ingredients. Fill with orange juice. Top with Irish cream or milk.

GAELIC COFFEE

- ¾ oz. Irish Whiskey
- ¾ oz. Irish Cream
- ¾ oz. Crème de Cacao
- Coffee
- Green Crème de Menthe
- Whipped Cream

Directions: Fill glass with hot, black coffee, whiskey, cream, and cacao. Top with whipped cream. Drizzle green crème de menthe on top.

GALE FORCE

- 1 oz. Gin
- ½ oz. Gold Rum
- ¼ oz. 151 Proof Rum
- Dash Lime Juice
- Orange Juice
- Ice

Directions: Fill tall glass with ice and add ingredients. Fill with orange juice. Shake.

GALE WARNING

- 2 oz. Scotch
- Cranberry Juice
- Pineapple Juice
- Ice

Directions: Fill serving glass with ice and add ingredients. Fill with equal parts cranberry and pineapple juice.

GANDY DANCER

- 1 oz. Yukon Jack
- 1 oz. Amaretto
- 1 oz. Banana Liqueur
- 1 oz. Pineapple Juice
- Ice

Directions: Fill mixing glass with ice and add ingredients. Shake. Strain into a chilled glass.

GANG BANGER

- 1 oz. Vodka
- 1 oz. Tequila
- 1 oz. Bourbon
- Lemon-lime Soda
- Ice

Directions: Fill a tall glass with ice and add ingredients. Fill with lemon-lime soda

GANGRENE

- 1 oz. Light Rum
- ½ oz. Spiced Rum
- ½ oz. Melon Liqueur
- ½ oz. Blue Curacao
- Sour Mix
- Ice

Directions: Fill a tall glass with ice and add ingredients. Fill with sour mix. Shake.

GASOLINE (FLOATER)

- 1 oz. Southern Comfort (bottom)
- 1 oz. Tequila (top)

Directions: Layer ingredients in a shot glass.

GATES OF HELL

- 1 ½ oz. Tequila
- 2 tsp. Lemon Juice
- 2 tsp. Lime Juice
- 1 tsp. Cherry Brandy
- Ice

Directions: In a shaker half-filled with ice, combine tequila, lemon juice, and lime juice. Shake. Strain into old-fashioned glass almost filled with crushed ice. Drizzle the cherry brandy over the top.

GAUGIN

- 1 cup of Ice
- 2 oz. Rum
- 1 tsp. Passion Fruit Syrup
- 1 tsp. Lime Juice
- 1 tsp. Lemon Juice
- 1 Cherry
- 1 Lemon Twist

Directions: Blend ingredients until smooth. Garnish with cherry and lemon twist.

GEISS

- 2 oz. German Brandy
- Dark German Beer
- Cola

Directions: Fill a pint glass half full with dark, German beer. Add brandy and fill with cola.

GENOA

- 1 ½ oz. Vodka
- ¾ oz. Campari
- Orange Juice
- 1 Orange Garnish
- Ice

Directions: Fill a serving glass with ice and add ingredients. Fill with orange juice. Shake. Garnish with orange.

GENT OF THE JURY

- 2 oz. Gin
- 1 ½ tsp. Dry Vermouth
- 3 Cocktail Onions
- Ice

Directions: In a mixing glass half-filled with ice cubes, combine the gin and vermouth. Stir well. Strain into a cocktail glass. Garnish with the onions.

GENTLE BEN

- ¾ oz. Vodka
- ¾ oz. Gin
- ¾ oz. Rum
- Orange Juice
- 1 Orange Garnish
- Ice

Directions: Fill a serving glass with ice and add ingredients. Fill with orange juice. Shake. Garnish with orange.

GENTLE BULL

- 1 ½ oz. Tequila
- ¾ oz. Coffee Liqueur
- Cream or Milk
- Ice

Directions: Fill serving glass with ice and add ingredients. Fill with cream or milk. Shake.

GENTLEMAN'S CLUB

- 1 ½ oz. Gin
- 1 oz. Brandy
- 1 oz. Sweet Vermouth
- 1 oz. Club Soda
- Ice

Directions: In an old-fashioned glass almost filled with ice cubes, combine all of the ingredients. Stir well.

GEORGIA PEACH

- **2 oz. Peach Schnapps**
- **Cranberry Juice**
- **Ice**

Directions: Fill a serving glass with ice and add ingredients. Fill with cranberry juice. Stir.

GERMAN LEG SPREADER

- **¾ oz. Jaegermeister**
- **¾ oz. Chocolate Liqueur**
- **¾ oz. 100 Proof Peppermint Schnapps**
- **Ice**

Directions: Fill a mixing glass with ice and add ingredients. Shake. Strain into a shot glass.

GHETTO BLASTER
(floater)

- **½ oz. Coffee Liqueur (bottom)**
- **½ oz. Brandy**
- **½ oz. Tequila**
- **½ oz. Bourbon (top)**

Directions: Layer ingredients in order in a shot glass.

GHOSTBUSTER

- **1 oz. Peach Schnapps**
- **1 oz. Melon Liqueur**
- **3 – 5 drops Irish Cream**
- **Ice**

Directions: Fill mixing glass with ice and add ingredients. Shake. Strain into chilled glass. Add three to five drops of Irish cream into the center of the drink.

GILLIGAN

- **¾ oz. Light Rum**
- **¾ oz. Coconut Rum**
- **¾ oz. Banana Liqueur**
- **Pineapple Juice**
- **Orange Juice**
- **Ice**

Directions: Fill serving glass with ice and add ingredients. Fill with equal parts pineapple and orange juice. Shake.

GILLIGAN'S ISLE

- **2 oz. Rum**
- **Dash Amaretto**
- **Dash Maraschino Cherry Juice**
- **Dash Lime Juice**
- **Dash Grapefruit Juice**
- **Ice**

Directions: Fill mixing glass with ice and add ingredients. Stir. Strain into a chilled glass.

GILROY COCKTAIL

- **¾ oz. Cherry Brandy**
- **¾ oz. Gin**
- **1 tbs. Dry Vermouth**
- **Juice of ¼ Lemon**
- **Dash Orange Bitters**
- **Ice**

Directions: Shake all ingredients with ice, strain into a cocktail glass, and serve.

GIMLET

- **3 ½ oz. Gin**
- **1 oz. Lime Juice**
- **1 Lime Garnish**
- **Ice**

Directions: Fill mixing glass with ice and add ingredients. Stir. Strain into a chilled glass. Garnish with lime.

GIN AND BITTER LEMON

- **1 ½ oz. Gin**
- **½ oz. Lemon Juice**
- **½ tsp. Superfine Sugar**
- **4 oz. Tonic Water**
- **Ice**

Directions: In a shaker half-filled with ice, combine the gin, lemon juice, and sugar. Shake. Strain into a highball glass almost filled with ice cubes. Top with the tonic water.

GIN AND IT

- 2 oz. Gin
- 1 oz. Sweet Vermouth

Directions: Stir gin and vermouth in a cocktail glass.

GIN AND PINK

- 2 oz. Gin
- 5 oz. Tonic Water
- 2 dashes Bitters
- 1 Lemon Twist
- Ice

Directions: In a highball glass almost filled with ice cubes, combine the gin, tonic, and bitters. Stir well and garnish with the lemon twist.

GIN AND SIN

- 1 ½ oz. Gin
- 1 oz. Orange Juice
- 1 oz. Lemon Juice
- ½ tsp. Grenadine
- Ice

Directions: In a shaker half-filled with ice, combine all of the ingredients. Shake. Strain into a cocktail glass.

GIN AND TONIC

- 2 oz. Gin
- 5 oz. Tonic Water
- 1 Lime Wedge
- Ice

Directions: Pour gin and tonic water into highball glass almost filled with ice cubes. Stir well. Garnish with the lime wedge.

GIN BUCK

- 1 ½ oz. Gin
- Juice of ½ Lemon
- Ginger Ale
- Ice

Directions: Pour gin and juice of lemon into an old-fashioned glass over ice cubes. Fill with ginger ale, stir, and serve.

GIN-CASSIS FIZZ

- 2 ½ oz. Gin
- 1 ½ oz. Lemon Juice
- 1 oz. tsp. Superfine Sugar
- 4 oz. Club Soda
- ½ oz. Crème de Cassis
- Ice

Directions: In a shaker half-filled with ice, combine gin, lemon juice, and sugar. Shake. Strain into Collins glass almost filled with ice cubes. Add the club soda. Stir well. Drop the cassis into the center of the drink.

GIN COBBLER

- 1 tsp. Superfine Sugar
- 3 oz. Club Soda
- 2 oz. Gin
- 1 Maraschino Cherry
- 1 Orange Slice
- 1 Lemon Slice
- Ice

Directions: In an old-fashioned glass, dissolve the sugar in the club soda. Add crushed ice until the glass is almost full. Add the gin. Stir well. Garnish with the cherry and the orange and lemon slices.

GIN COCKTAIL

- 2 oz. Gin
- 2 dashes Bitters
- Twist of Lemon Peel
- Ice

Directions: Stir gin and bitters with ice and strain into a cocktail glass. Add the twist of lemon peel and serve.

GIN COOLER

- 2 oz. Gin
- Carbonated Water
- ½ tsp. Powdered Sugar
- 1 Orange Spiral
- 1 Twist of Lemon Peel
- Ice

Directions: Stir powdered sugar and two ounces of carbonated water in Collins glass. Fill glass with ice and add gin. Fill with carbonated water and stir. Add lemon peel and orange spiral. Dangle orange spiral over rim of glass.

GIN DAISY

- 2 oz. Gin
- 1 oz. Lemon Juice
- ½ tsp. Superfine Sugar
- ½ tsp. Grenadine
- 1 Maraschino Cherry
- 1 Orange Slice
- Ice

Directions: In a shaker half-filled with ice cubes, combine the gin, lemon juice, sugar, and grenadine. Shake well. Pour into an old-fashioned glass and garnish with the cherry and the orange slice.

GIN FIX

- 1 tsp. Superfine Sugar
- 1 oz. Lemon Juice
- 2 tsp. Water
- 2 oz. Gin
- 1 Maraschino Cherry
- 1 Lemon Slice
- Ice

Directions: In a shaker half-filled with ice cubes, combine the sugar, lemon juice, and water. Shake well. Strain into a highball glass almost filled with crushed ice. Add the gin. Stir well and garnish with the cherry and the lemon slice.

GIN HIGHBALL

- 2 oz. Gin
- Carbonated Water
- Twist of Lemon Peel
- Ice

Directions: Pour gin into highball glass over ice. Fill with carbonated water. Add lemon peel, stir, and serve.

GIN RICKEY

- 1 ½ oz. Gin
- Juice of ½ Lime
- Carbonated Water
- 1 Lime Wedge
- Ice

Directions: Pour lime juice and gin in highball glass over ice. Fill with carbonated water and stir. Add the lime wedge and serve.

GIN SANGAREE

- 2 oz. Gin
- Carbonated Water
- 1 tbs. Port
- ½ tsp. Powdered Sugar
- 1 tsp. Water
- Nutmeg
- Ice

Directions: Dissolve powdered sugar in water. Add gin. Pour in highball glass over ice. Fill with carbonated water and stir. Float Port on top, sprinkle lightly with nutmeg, and serve.

GIN SLING

- 2 oz. Gin
- Juice of ½ Lemon
- 1 tsp. Powdered Sugar
- 1 tsp. Water
- Twist of Orange Peel
- Ice

Directions: Dissolve powdered sugar in a mixture of water and lemon juice. Add gin. Pour into an old-fashioned glass over ice cubes and stir. Add the twist of orange peel and serve.

GIN SMASH

- 2 oz. Gin
- 1 oz. Carbonated Water
- 1 Sugar Cube
- 4 Mint Sprigs
- 1 Orange Slice
- 1 Cherry
- Ice

Directions: Muddle sugar with carbonated water and mint sprigs in an old-fashioned glass. Add gin and one ice cube. Stir, add the orange slice and the cherry, and serve.

GIN SOUR

- 2 oz. Gin
- 1 oz. Lemon Juice
- ½ tsp. Superfine Sugar
- 1 Orange Slice
- 1 Maraschino Cherry
- Ice

Directions: In a shaker half-filled with ice cubes, combine the gin, lemon juice, and sugar. Shake well. Strain into a sour glass and garnish with the orange slice and the cherry.

GIN SQUIRT

- 1 ½ oz. Gin
- 1 tsp. Grenadine
- 1 tbs. Powdered Sugar
- 3 Pineapple Chunks
- 2 Whole Strawberries
- Carbonated Water
- Ice

Directions: Stir gin, grenadine, and powdered sugar with ice and strain into a highball glass over ice cubes. Fill with carbonated water and stir. Decorate with the pineapple chunks and the strawberries and serve.

GIN SWIZZLE

- 1 ½ oz. Lime Juice
- 1 tsp. Superfine Sugar
- 2 oz. Gin
- Dash Bitters
- 3 oz. Club Soda
- Ice

Directions: In a shaker half-filled with ice, combine lime juice, sugar, gin, and bitters. Shake well. Fill a Collins glass with ice. Stir until glass is frosted. Strain mixture in shaker into glass. Add club soda.

GIN TODDY

- 2 oz. Gin
- 2 tsp. Water
- ½ tsp. Powdered Sugar
- Twist of Lemon Peel
- Ice

Directions: Mix sugar and water in old-fashioned glass. Add gin and ice cube. Stir, add lemon peel.

GINGER COSMOPOLITAN

- 3 ½ oz. Ginger Vodka
- ½ oz. Ginger Liqueur
- Dash Orange Juice
- Dash Lime Juice
- Dash Cranberry Juice
- Ice

Directions: Fill mixing glass with ice and add ingredients. Shake. Strain into chilled glass.

GINGER MARTINI

- 3 ½ oz. Vodka
- ½ oz. Ginger Liqueur
- 1 Lemon Twist
- Candled Ginger
- Ice

Directions: Fill mixing glass with ice. Add ingredients. Shake. Strain into chilled glass. Garnish with lemon twist and candled ginger.

GINGER SNAP

- 2 oz. Ginger Brandy
- Ginger Ale
- Ice

Directions: Fill a serving glass with ice and add ingredients. Fill with ginger ale.

GINGER SYLLABUB

- 2 tbs. Medium Dry Sherry
- 3 tbs. Brown Sugar
- Large pinch Nutmeg
- Large pinch Ground Ginger
- Juice of ½ Lemon
- ½ pint Heavy Whipping Cream
- 2 - 3 pieces Crystallized Stem Ginger, Minced

Directions: Put the sherry, sugar, spices, and lemon juice into a large mixing bowl. Stir until well-blended. Leave to soak for at least half an hour. Beat the cream until it is stiff. Fold in ginger. Chill thoroughly. Before serving, divide into four serving bowls and top with crumbs of crystallized ginger and a shake of nutmeg.

GINGERBREAD MAN

- 1 oz. Cinnamon Schnapps
- 1 oz. Irish Cream
- 1 oz. Butterscotch Schnapps
- Ice

Directions: Fill mixing glass with ice and add ingredients. Shake. Strain into chilled glass.

GINGERBREAD MAN 2
(floater)

- ¾ oz. Coffee Liqueur
- ¾ oz. Irish Cream
- ¾ oz. 100 Proof Cinnamon Schnapps (top)

Directions: Layer ingredients in order in shot glass.

GLAM TRASH

- 2 oz. Cinnamon Schnapps
- Dash Grenadine
- 1 oz. Beer
- Ice

Directions: Fill a mixing glass with ice and add ingredients. Stir. Strain into a shot glass.

GLASS TOWER

- 1 oz. Vodka
- 1 oz. Light Rum
- ½ oz. Triple Sec
- ½ oz. Peach Schnapps
- ½ oz. Sambuca
- Lemon-lime Soda
- 1 Lime Garnish
- Ice

Directions: Fill tall glass with ice and add ingredients. Fill with lemon-lime soda. Garnish with lime.

GLENDA

- ½ oz. Peach Schnapps
- ½ oz. Orange Liqueur
- Champagne

Directions: Pour schnapps and orange liqueur in Champagne flute. Fill with Champagne.

GLOOMLIFTER

- 1 ½ oz. Whiskey
- ½ oz. Brandy
- ½ oz. Raspberry Syrup
- 1 tsp. Sugar
- ½ oz. Lemon Juice
- ½ Egg White
- Ice

Directions: Fill serving glass with ice. Add ingredients. Shake.

GLUEWEIN

- 5 oz. Dry Red Wine
- 1 Cinnamon Stick (Broken Up)
- 2 Whole Cloves
- 1 tsp. Honey
- Pinch Ground Nutmeg
- 1 Lemon Twist
- 1 Orange Garnish

Directions: Heat ingredients in a saucepan without boiling. Pour into a mug. Garnish with lemon twist and orange.

GO GIRL

- 1 ¾ oz. Chambord
- 1 ¾ oz. Vodka
- ½ cup Club Soda
- 2 tbs. Sour Mix
- Ice

Directions: Mix ingredients together on ice in a rocks glass.

GODCHILD

- 1 ½ oz. Vodka
- ½ oz. Amaretto
- Milk or Cream
- Ice

Directions: Fill serving glass with ice and add ingredients. Fill with milk or cream. Shake.

GODCHILD 2

- 1 ½ oz. Brandy
- ½ oz. Amaretto
- Ice

Directions: Fill short glass with ice and add ingredients.

GODFATHER

- 1 ½ oz. Scotch
- ½ oz. Amaretto
- Ice

Directions: Fill short glass with ice and add ingredients. Stir.

GODMOTHER

- 1 ½ oz. Vodka
- ¾ oz. Amaretto
- Ice

Directions: Pour vodka and Amaretto in old-fashioned glass over ice.

GOGL-MOGL

- 1 Egg
- 1 ¾ oz. Whiskey
- 1 tbs. Honey
- Milk

Directions: This is essentially hot eggnog. Beat an egg, add honey and a jigger of whisky. Pour this into a glass and then fill the glass with warm milk and stir until well-mixed.

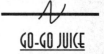

GO-GO JUICE

- ½ oz. Vodka
- ½ oz. Gin
- ½ oz. Rum
- ½ oz. Tequila
- ½ oz. Blue Curacao
- ½ oz. Orange Juice
- 1 oz. Sour Mix
- Soda Water
- Ice

Directions: Fill a tall glass with ice and add ingredients. Shake. Fill with soda water.

GOLDEN BRONX

- 2 oz. Gin
- 1 tsp. Dry Vermouth
- 1 tsp. Sweet Vermouth
- ½ oz. Orange Juice
- 1 Egg Yolk
- Ice

Directions: In a shaker half-filled with ice, mix ingredients. Shake. Strain into rocks glass.

GOLDEN BULL

- 1 oz. Southern Comfort
- 1 oz. Amaretto
- Orange Juice
- Lemon-lime Soda
- 1 Lemon Garnish
- Ice

Directions: Fill serving glass with ice and add ingredients. Fill with orange juice. Shake. Top with lemon-lime soda. Garnish with lemon.

GOLDEN CADILLAC

- 1 oz. Galliano
- 2 oz. Crème de Cacao
- 1 oz. Light Cream
- ½ cup of Crushed Ice

Directions: Combine ice with ingredients in blender. Blend on low for ten seconds. Strain into Champagne flute. Serve.

GOLDEN CAPPUCCINO

- 1 ½ oz. Galliano
- Espresso
- Steamed Milk
- 1 Lemon Twist

Directions: Fill glass with espresso and Galliano. Top with steamed milk. Garnish with lemon twist.

GOLDEN DAWN

- 1 oz. Gin
- 1 oz. Apricot Brandy
- 1 oz. Orange Juice
- Ice

Directions: Fill a mixing glass with ice and add ingredients. Shake. Strain into a chilled glass.

GOLDEN DAY

- 1 ½ oz. Vodka
- ½ oz. Galliano
- Ice

Directions: Fill a short glass with ice and add ingredients. Stir.

GOLDEN DAZE

- 1 ½ oz. Gin
- ½ oz. Peach Brandy
- 1 oz. Orange Juice
- Ice

Directions: Shake all ingredients with ice, strain into a cocktail glass, and serve.

GOLDEN DELICIOUS CIDER

- 2 oz. Goldschlager
- Hot Cider
- Whipped Cream

Directions: Fill glass with hot cider and Goldschlager. Top with whipped cream.

GOLDEN DELICIOUS MARTINI

- 2 oz. Vodka
- 1 oz. Apple Brandy
- Dash Goldschlager
- Ice

Directions: Fill a mixing glass with ice and add ingredients. Shake. Strain into a chilled glass.

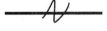

GOLDEN DRAGON

- 1 ½ oz. Yellow Chartreuse
- 1 ½ oz. Brandy
- 1 Lemon Twist
- Ice

Directions: Fill mixing glass with ice and add ingredients. Stir and strain into a chilled glass. Garnish with lemon twist.

GOLDEN DREAM

- 1 oz. Galliano
- ½ oz. Triple Sec
- Orange Juice
- Cream or Milk
- 1 Orange Garnish
- Ice

Directions: Fill mixing glass with ice and add ingredients. Fill with equal parts orange juice and cream or milk. Shake. Pour in short glass. Garnish with orange.

GOLDEN FIZZ

- 1 ½ oz. Gin
- Juice of ½ Lemon
- ½ tbs. Sugar
- 1 Egg Yolk
- Carbonated Water
- Ice

Directions: Shake all ingredients except the carbonated water with ice and strain into a highball glass. Fill with carbonated water and serve.

GOLDEN GATE

- 1 oz. Rum
- ½ oz. Gin
- ½ oz. White Crème de Cacao
- 1 tsp. 151 Proof Rum
- 1 tsp. Falernum
- 1 oz. Lemon Juice
- 1 Orange Garnish
- Ice

Directions: Fill short glass with ice, add ingredients and shake. Garnish with orange.

GOLDEN NAIL

- 2 oz. Drambuie
- Grapefruit Juice
- Ice

Directions: Fill serving glass with ice and add ingredients. Fill with grapefruit juice. Stir.

GOLDEN RUSSIAN

- 1 ½ oz. Vodka
- 1 oz. Galliano
- 1 Lime Garnish
- Ice

Directions: Fill short glass with ice and add ingredients. Stir. Garnish with lime.

GOLDEN SCREW

- 2 oz. Galliano
- Orange Juice
- Ice

Directions: Fill tall glass with ice and ingredients. Fill with orange juice. Shake.

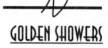

GOLDEN SHOWERS

- Champagne

Directions: Uncork Champagne bottle. Cover top with thumb and shake. Face the bottle in the direction of an unsuspecting friend. Remove thumb.

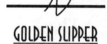

GOLDEN SLIPPER

- 2 oz. Apricot Brandy
- ¾ oz. Yellow Chartreuse
- 1 Unbroken Egg Yolk
- Ice

Directions: Stir brandy and chartreuse with ice and strain into a cocktail glass. Float unbroken egg yolk on top and serve.

GOLDEN TORPEDO

- 1 oz. Amaretto
- 1 oz. Galliano
- Cream or Milk
- Ice

Directions: Fill a tall glass with ice and add ingredients. Fill with cream or milk. Shake.

GOLDRUSH

- 1 oz. Gold Tequila
- 1 oz. Goldschlager
- Ice

Directions: Fill a short glass with ice and add ingredients.

GOLF

- 2 ½ oz. Gin
- ¾ oz. Dry Vermouth
- 2 dashes Bitters
- 1 Olive
- Ice

Directions: Fill mixing glass with ice and add ingredients. Stir. Strain into a chilled glass. Garnish with olive.

GOLF BALL

- 3 oz. Vodka
- 3 oz. Champagne
- Orange Juice
- Ice

Directions: Fill a tall glass with ice and add ingredients. Fill with orange juice. Stir gently.

GOLPEADO

- 1 oz. Tequila
- 1 oz. Ginger Ale

Directions: Combine ingredients in shot glass. Cover glass with napkin and slam on bar top. Drink while foaming.

GOOD AND PLENT-E

- 1 oz. Ouzo
- 1 oz. Coffee Liqueur

Directions: Combine ingredients in a shot glass.

GOOD FORTUNE

- 1 oz. Ginger Liqueur
- 1 oz. Irish Cream
- Ice

Directions: Fill a shot glass with ice and add ingredients. Stir.

GOOD GOLLY COFFEE

- 1 ½ oz. Dark Rum
- ½ oz. Galliano
- Dash Crème de Cacao
- Coffee
- Whipped Cream

Directions: Fill glass with hot, black coffee, rum, Galliano, and cacao. Top with whipped cream.

GOOD LIFE

- 3 ½ oz. Rum
- ½ oz. Triple Sec
- Dash Lime Juice
- Dash Grenadine
- Dash Orange Juice
- 1 Lime Garnish
- 1 Orange Garnish
- 1 Cherry
- Ice

Directions: Fill mixing glass with ice and add ingredients. Shake and strain into a chilled glass. Garnish with lime, orange, and cherry.

GOOMBAY SMASH

- ½ oz. Rum
- ½ oz. Banana Liqueur
- 1 tsp. Cream of Coconut
- Dash Orange Juice
- Pineapple Juice
- Dark Rum
- Ice

Directions: Fill a tall glass with ice and add ingredients. Fill with pineapple juice. Shake. Top with dark rum.

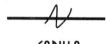

GORILLA

- 1 oz. Dark Crème de Cacao
- 1 oz. Banana Liqueur
- Orange Juice
- Ice

Directions: Fill serving glass with ice and add ingredients. Fill with orange juice.

GORILLA FART

- ¾ oz. 151 Proof Rum
- ¾ oz. Bourbon
- ¾ oz. Southern Comfort
- Ice

Directions: Fill mixing glass with ice and add ingredients. Stir. Strain into a chilled glass.

GORILLA SNOT

- $\frac{1}{5}$ Gill Port
- $\frac{1}{5}$ Bailey's Irish Cream

Directions: Measure Port into brandy glass. Pour the Bailey's in. As the Bailey's enters the Port it will solidify, forming a glob.

GRAND ALLIANCE

- 1 oz. Amaretto
- Champagne

Directions: In a Champagne glass, combine ingredients.

GRAND AM

- 1 oz. Orange Liqueur
- 1 oz. Amaretto
- Ice

Directions: Fill a short glass with ice and add ingredients. Stir.

GRAND APPLE

- 1 oz. Apple Brandy
- ½ oz. Cognac
- ½ oz. Orange Liqueur
- 1 Orange Garnish
- 1 Lemon Twist
- Ice

Directions: Fill mixing glass with ice and add ingredients. Stir. Strain into a chilled glass. Garnish with orange and lemon twist.

GRAND MASTER

- 2 oz. Scotch
- ½ oz. Peppermint Schnapps
- 3 oz. Club Soda
- 1 Lemon Twist
- Ice

Directions: Pour the Scotch, schnapps, and club soda into highball glass almost filled with ice cubes. Stir well. Garnish with the lemon twist.

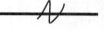

GRAPE APE

- 2 oz. Vodka
- Grape Juice
- Lemon-lime Soda
- Ice

Directions: Fill tall glass with ice and add ingredients. Fill glass with equal parts grape juice and lemon-lime soda.

GRAPE CRUSH

- 1 ½ oz. Vodka
- ½ oz. Black Raspberry Liqueur
- Dash Sour Mix
- Lemon-lime Soda
- Ice

Directions: Fill serving glass with ice and add ingredients. Shake. Fill with lemon-lime soda.

GRAPE MARTINI

- 2 oz. Vodka
- ½ oz. Dash Blue Curacao
- 1 ½ oz. Grape Juice
- Ice

Directions: Fill mixing glass with ice and add ingredients. Shake. Strain into chilled glass.

GRAPE MARTINI 2

- 3 ½ oz. Grape Vodka
- ½ oz. White Grape Juice
- 1 Frozen Grape
- Ice

Directions: Fill mixing glass with ice and add ingredients. Stir. Strain into chilled glass. Garnish with frozen grape.

GRAPE NEHI

- 1 ½ oz. Vodka
- ½ oz. Black Raspberry Liqueur
- 2 oz. Sour Mix
- Ice

Directions: Fill mixing glass with ice and add ingredients. Shake. Strain into a chilled glass.

GRAPE SOUR BALL

- 1 oz. Vodka
- 1 oz. Blue Curacao
- 2 oz. Sour Mix
- Cranberry Juice
- Ice

Directions: Fill tall glass with ice and add ingredients. Fill with cranberry juice. Shake. Strain in chilled glass.

GRAPEFRUIT COCKTAIL

- 1 oz. Gin
- 1 oz. Grapefruit Juice
- 1 tsp. Maraschino
- 1 Cherry
- Ice

Directions: Shake all ingredients except cherry with ice and strain into a cocktail glass. Add the cherry on top and serve.

GRAPEFRUIT MARTINI

- 3 ½ oz. Grapefruit Vodka
- ½ oz. Grapefruit Liqueur
- 2 oz. Grapefruit Juice
- Ice

Directions: Fill mixing glass with ice and add ingredients. Shake. Strain into chilled glass.

GRAPEFRUIT NOG

- 1 ½ oz. Brandy
- ½ cup of Grapefruit Juice
- 1 oz. Lemon Juice
- 1 tbs. Honey
- 1 Whole Egg
- Ice

Directions: Blend all ingredients with ice in an electric blender at a low speed for a short length of time. Pour into a Collins glass over ice cubes and serve.

GRASS SKIRT

- 1 ½ oz. Gin
- 1 oz. Triple Sec
- 1 oz. Pineapple Juice
- ½ tsp. Grenadine
- 1 Pineapple Slice
- Ice

Directions: In a shaker half-filled with ice cubes, combine the gin, Triple Sec, pineapple juice, and grenadine. Shake well. Pour into an old-fashioned glass and garnish with the pineapple slice.

GRASSHOPPER

- ¾ oz. Green Crème de Menthe
- ¾ oz. White Crème de Cacao
- ¾ oz. Light Cream

Directions: Shake all ingredients with ice, strain into a cocktail glass, and serve.

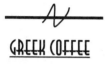

GREEK COFFEE

- 1 oz. Metaxa
- 1 oz. Ouzo
- Coffee
- Whipped Cream

Directions: Fill a glass with hot, black coffee and liquor. Top with whipped cream.

GREEN APPLE

- 1 oz. Apple Brandy
- 1 oz. Melon Liqueur
- 1 oz. Sour Mix

Directions: Fill a short glass with ice and add ingredients. Stir.

GREEN DEMON

- 1 oz. Vodka
- 1 oz. Rum
- 1 oz. Melon Liqueur
- Lemonade
- 1 Cherry
- Ice

Directions: Shake vodka, rum, and liqueur and pour over ice in a highball glass. Fill with lemonade, add the cherry on top, and serve.

GREEN DEVIL

- 1 ½ oz. Gin
- 1 ½ oz. Green Crème de Menthe
- 1 tbs. Lime Juice
- Mint Leaves
- Ice

Directions: Shake gin, crème de menthe, and lime juice with ice and strain into an old-fashioned glass over ice cubes. Decorate with mint leaves and serve.

GREEN DRAGON

- ½ oz. Kummel
- ½ oz. Green Crème de Menthe
- 1 ½ oz. Gin
- Juice of ½ Lemon
- 4 dashes Orange Bitters
- Ice

Directions: Shake all ingredients with ice, strain into a cocktail glass, and serve.

GREEN EYES

- 1 ½ oz. Vodka
- ½ oz. Blue Curacao
- Orange Juice
- Ice

Directions: Fill a short glass with ice and add ingredients. Fill with orange juice. Shake.

GREEN FAIRY COFFEE

- 1 oz. Absinthe
- Coffee
- Whipped Cream

Directions: Fill a glass with hot, black coffee. Top with whipped cream. Drizzle Absinthe over.

197

GREEN FIZZ

- 2 oz. Gin
- 1 tsp. Green Crème de Menthe
- Juice of ½ Lemon
- 1 tsp. Powdered Sugar
- 1 Egg White
- Carbonated Water
- Ice

Directions: Shake all ingredients except carbonated water with ice and strain into a highball glass over two ice cubes. Fill with carbonated water, stir, and serve.

GREEN GOBLIN

- 5 oz. Hard Cider
- 5 oz. Lager
- ½ oz. Blue Curacao

Directions: Combine cider and lager in a glass. Float blue curacao on top.

GREEN GODDESS

- 1 oz. Vodka
- ½ oz. Melon Liqueur
- ½ oz. Cream of Coconut
- Ice

Directions: Fill a short glass with ice and add ingredients. Shake.

GREEN HILL

- 8 oz. Green Kool-Aid
- 1 ¾ oz. Everclear
- Ice

Directions: Pour in Collins glass over ice.

GREEN HORNET

- 1 ½ oz. Brandy
- ½ oz. Green Crème de Menthe
- Ice

Directions: Fill short glass with ice and add ingredients. Stir. Serve or strain in chilled glass.

GREEN KAMIKAZE

- 2 oz. Vodka
- ½ oz. Melon Liqueur
- 1 oz. Lime Juice.
- Ice

Directions: Fill a short glass with ice and add ingredients. Shake.

GREEN LANTERN

- 1/3 oz. Midori
- 1/3 oz. Orange Juice
- 1/3 oz. 7-Up or Sprite

Directions: Mix ingredients together, shake once. Pour in glass.

GREEN LIZARD

- ½ oz. 151 Proof Rum
- 1 oz. Green Chartreuse
- Ice

Directions: Fill mixing glass with ice and add ingredients. Shake and strain in chilled glass.

GREEN MEANY

- 1 oz. Southern Comfort
- 1 oz. Melon Liqueur
- 1 oz. Pineapple Juice
- Ice

Directions: Fill mixing glass with ice and add ingredients. Stir. Strain into a shot glass.

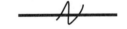

GREEN MOUNTAIN MELON

- 1 oz. Vodka
- ½ oz. Melon Liqueur
- 1 oz. Lime Juice
- Sour Mix
- 1 Lime Garnish
- Ice

Directions: Fill a tall glass with ice and add ingredients. Fill with sour mix. Shake. Garnish with lime.

GREEN OPAL

- ½ oz. Anisette
- ½ oz. Gin
- 1 oz. Anis
- Ice

Directions: Shake all ingredients with ice, strain into a cocktail glass.

GREEN RUSSIAN

- 1 ½ oz. Vodka
- ½ oz. Melon Liqueur
- Ice

Directions: Fill a short glass with ice and add ingredients. Stir.

GREEN RUSSIAN 2

- 1 ½ oz. Vodka
- ½ oz. Melon Liqueur
- Milk or Cream
- Ice

Directions: Fill tall glass with ice and add ingredients. Fill with milk or cream. Shake. Strain in chilled glass.

GREEN SPIDER

- 2 oz. Vodka
- 1 oz. Green Crème de Menthe
- Ice

Directions: Fill glass with ice and add ingredients. Stir. Strain into a chilled glass.

GREYHOUND

- 1 ½ oz. Gin or Vodka
- 5 oz. Grapefruit Juice
- Ice

Directions: Pour ingredients into a highball glass over ice cubes. Stir well and serve. Vodka may be substituted for gin, if preferred.

GRIZZLY BEAR

- 1 part Amaretto
- 1 part Jaegermeister
- 1 part Kahlua
- 2 ½ parts Milk

Directions: Combine all ingredients over ice in a highball glass and serve.

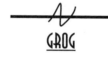

GROG

- 2 oz. Amber Rum
- 1 tsp. Sugar
- Water
- Dash Lemon Juice
- 3 Whole Cloves
- 1 Cinnamon Stick
- 1 Lemon Garnish

Directions: Boil water. Add ingredients to water. Stir. Garnish with lemon.

GROUND ZERO

- ¾ oz. Vodka
- ½ oz. Coffee Liqueur
- ¾ oz. Bourbon
- ¾ oz. Peppermint Schnapps
- Ice

Directions: Fill mixing glass with ice and add ingredients. Shake. Strain into a chilled glass.

GUMBY

- 1 oz. Vodka
- 1 oz. Melon Liqueur
- 1 oz. Sour Mix
- Lemon-lime Soda
- Ice

Directions: Fill a tall glass with ice and add ingredients. Shake. Fill with lemon-lime soda.

GUMDROP

- 1 oz. Amaretto
- 1 oz. Dark Crème de Cacao
- Ice

Directions: Fill mixing glass with ice and add ingredients. Strain into a chilled glass.

GUN RUNNER COFFEE

- 1 oz. Irish Whiskey
- ½ oz. Irish Cream
- ½ oz. Coffee Liqueur
- Coffee
- Whipped Cream
- Brown Sugar
- Ice

Directions: Fill tall glass with ice and add ingredients. Fill with hot, black coffee. Top with whipped cream. Sprinkle with sugar.

GUN RUNNER ICED COFFEE

- 1 oz. Irish Whiskey
- ½ oz. Irish Cream
- ½ oz. Coffee Liqueur
- Sugar
- Ice

Directions: Fill glass with ice and add ingredients. Add sugar to taste.

GYPSY

- 1 oz. Sweet Vermouth
- 1 Maraschino Cherry
- 1 ½ oz. Gin
- Ice

Directions: In a mixing glass half-filled with ice cubes, combine gin and vermouth. Stir well. Strain into a cocktail glass and garnish with the cherry.

GYPSY COCKTAIL

- 1 ½ oz. Sweet Vermouth
- 1 ½ oz. Gin
- 1 Cherry
- Ice

Directions: Stir gin and vermouth with ice and strain into a cocktail glass. Add the cherry on top and serve.

H. D. RIDER

- 1 oz. Bourbon
- 1 oz. Tequila

Directions: Combine ingredients in a glass.

H.P.W. COCKTAIL

- 1 ½ tsp. Dry Vermouth
- 1 ½ tsp. Sweet Vermouth
- 1 ½ oz. Gin
- Twist of Orange Peel
- Ice

Directions: Stir ingredients except orange peel with ice and strain in cocktail glass. Add orange peel.

HAIDIN-HAIDIN

- 2 oz. Light Rum
- ½ oz. Dry Vermouth
- Dash Bitters
- 1 Lemon Twist
- Ice

Directions: In a mixing glass half-filled with ice cubes, combine the rum, vermouth, and bitters. Stir well. Strain into a cocktail glass and garnish with the lemon twist.

HAIR RAISER

- 1 ½ oz. 100 Proof Vodka
- ½ oz. Rock and Rye
- 1 tbs. Lemon Juice
- Ice

Directions: Shake all ingredients with ice, strain into a cocktail glass, and serve.

HAIRY MARY

- 2 oz. Grain Alcohol
- Bloody Mary Mix
- Ice

Directions: Fill a tall glass with ice and add ingredients. Fill with Bloody Mary mix.

HAIRY NAVEL

- 1 oz. Vodka
- 1 oz. Peach Schnapps
- Orange Juice
- 1 Orange Garnish
- Ice

Directions: Fill serving glass with ice. Add ingredients. Fill glass with orange juice. Garnish with orange.

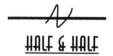

HALF & HALF

- Lager
- Stout

Directions: Fill tall glass half-full with lager and half-full with stout.

HALLEY'S COMFORT

- 1 ½ oz. Southern Comfort
- 1 ½ oz. Peach Schnapps
- Soda Water
- Ice

Directions: Fill tall glass with ice. Add ingredients. Fill glass with soda water.

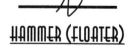

HAMMER (FLOATER)

- 1 ½ oz. Sambuca (bottom)
- ½ oz. Brandy (top)

Directions: Layer ingredients in shot glass.

HAMMER
AKA MEXICAN SCREW

- 2 oz. Tequila
- Orange Juice
- 1 Orange Garnish
- Ice

Directions: Fill a tall glass with ice and add ingredients. Fill with orange juice. Garnish with orange.

HAMMERHEAD

- 1 oz. Amber Rum
- 1 oz. Amaretto
- 1 oz. Curacao
- 1 - 2 dashes Southern Comfort
- Ice

Directions: Fill mixing glass with ice and add ingredients. Add one or two dashes of Southern Comfort. Strain into a chilled glass.

HAND JOB (FLOATER)

- 1 oz. Peach Schnapps (bottom)
- ½ oz. Soda Water
- ½ oz. 151 Proof Rum (top)

Directions: Layer ingredients in order in a shot glass. Ignite.

HAND RELEASE (FLOATER)

- ½ oz. Jaegermeister (bottom)
- ½ oz. Peppermint Schnapps
- ½ oz. 151 Proof Rum (top)

Directions: Layer ingredients in order in shot glass.

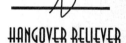

HANGOVER RELIEVER

- 1 B-Complex Vitamin
- 5 - 10 dashes Bitters
- Soda Water

Directions: Fill glass with soda water and add five to ten dashes of bitters.

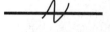

HANKY PANKY

- 3 oz. Lemon Vodka
- 1 oz. Limoncello
- Champagne
- 1 Lemon Twist
- Ice

Directions: Fill mixing glass with ice and add ingredients. Shake. Strain into a chilled glass. Top with Champagne. Garnish with lemon twist.

HAPPY FELLER

- 1 ½ oz. Vodka
- ½ oz. Black Raspberry Liqueur
- ½ oz. Orange Liqueur
- Dash Lime Juice
- Ice

Directions: Fill a mixing glass with ice and add ingredients. Strain into a chilled glass.

HAPPY JACK

- 1 oz. Bourbon
- 1 oz. Apple Brandy
- Ice

Directions: Fill mixing glass with ice and add ingredients. Stir. Strain into a chilled glass.

HAPPY SKIPPER

- 1 ½ oz. Captain Morgan's Spiced Rum
- Ginger Ale
- Lime (optional)
- Ice

Directions: Pour rum over ice. Fill glass to the top with ginger ale. Garnish with lime.

HAPPY SUMMER

- 1 ½ oz. Amber Rum
- 1 ½ oz. Melon Liqueur
- Orange Juice
- Ice

Directions: Fill a tall glass with ice and add ingredients. Fill with orange juice.

HARBOR LIGHTS
(floater)

- 1 oz. Galliano (bottom)
- 1 oz. Brandy (top)

Directions: Layer ingredients in a shot glass and ignite.

HARBOR LIGHTS 2
(floater)

- ¾ oz. Coffee Liqueur (bottom)
- ¾ oz. Tequila
- ¾ oz. 151 Proof Rum (top)

Directions: Layer ingredients in order in a shot glass and ignite.

HARD CANDY

- 1 oz. Melon Liqueur
- ½ oz. Crème de Menthe
- 2 oz. Sour Mix
- Ice

Directions: Fill mixing glass with ice and add ingredients. Shake. Strain into a chilled glass.

HARD NIPPLE (FLOATER)

- 1 oz. Irish Cream (bottom)
- 1 oz. Peppermint Schnapps (top)

Directions: Layer ingredients in a shot glass.

HARD ON (FLOATER)

- ¾ oz. Coffee Liqueur (bottom)
- ¾ oz. Amaretto
- ¾ oz. Milk (top)

Directions: Layer ingredients in order in a shot glass.

HARDCORE

- 1 oz. Grain Alcohol
- 1 oz. 151 Proof Rum
- ½ oz. Amaretto
- ½ oz. Triple Sec
- Cola
- Ice

Directions: Fill a tall glass with ice. Add ingredients. Fill with cola. Stir.

HARI KARI

- 1 ½ oz. Brandy
- ½ oz. Triple Sec
- 1 oz. Orange Juice
- Ice

Directions: Fill a mixing glass with ice and add ingredients. Shake. Strain into a chilled glass.

HARLEM COCKTAIL

- 1 ½ oz. Gin
- ¾ oz. Pineapple Juice
- ½ tsp. Maraschino
- 2 Pineapple Chunks
- Ice

Directions: Shake gin, pineapple juice, and maraschino with ice and strain into a cocktail glass. Decorate with pineapple chunks and serve.

HARMONY

- 1 ½ oz. Ginger Liqueur
- ½ oz. Peach Schnapps
- Orange Juice
- 1 Orange Garnish

Directions: Fill a mixing glass with ice and add ingredients. Fill with orange juice. Shake. Garnish with orange.

HARVARD

- 1 ½ oz. Brandy
- ¾ oz. Sweet Vermouth
- ¼ oz. Lemon Juice
- 1 tsp. Grenadine
- Dash Bitters
- Ice

Directions: Fill mixing glass with ice and add ingredients. Add a dash of bitters. Shake. Strain into a chilled glass.

HARVEY WALLBANGER

- 1 oz. Vodka
- ½ oz. Galliano
- 4 oz. Orange Juice
- Ice

Directions: Pour vodka and orange juice into a Collins glass over ice cubes and stir. Float Galliano on top and serve.

HASTY COCKTAIL

- 1 ½ oz. Gin
- ¾ oz. Dry Vermouth
- ¼ tsp. Anisette
- 1 tsp. Grenadine
- Ice

Directions: Stir all ingredients with ice, strain into a cocktail glass, and serve.

HAVANA

- 1 ½ oz. Amber Rum
- ½ oz. Sherry
- 1 ½ oz. Sour Mix
- 1 Orange Garnish
- Ice

Directions: Fill mixing glass with ice and add ingredients. Shake. Strain into a chilled glass. Garnish with orange.

HAVANA COCKTAIL

- 1 oz. Light Rum
- 1 oz. Pineapple Juice
- 1 tsp. Lemon Juice
- Ice

Directions: In a shaker half-filled with ice cubes, combine all of the ingredients. Shake well. Strain into a cocktail glass.

HAWAIIAN COCKTAIL

- 2 oz. Gin
- ½ oz. Triple Sec
- 1 tbs. Pineapple Juice
- Ice

Directions: Shake all ingredients with ice, strain into a cocktail glass, and serve.

H-BOMB

- 12 oz. Beer
- 6 oz. Water
- 1/8 oz. Vodka

Directions: Dump out six ounces of beer and add vodka. Fill up the rest of the beer can with water. Mix and let settle.

HEAD BANGER

- 1 oz. 151 Proof Rum
- 1 oz. Sambuca
- Dash Grenadine
- Ice

Directions: Fill a mixing glass with ice and add ingredients. Shake. Strain into a chilled glass.

HEAD ROOM (FLOATER)

- ½ oz. Banana Liqueur (bottom)
- ½ oz. Melon Liqueur
- ½ oz. Irish Cream (top)

Directions: Layer ingredients in order in a shot glass.

HEAD THROB

- 2 oz. Amaretto
- Orange Juice
- Cranberry Juice
- Ice

Directions: Fill serving glass with ice and add ingredients. Fill with equal parts orange juice and cranberry juice. Shake.

HEADLESS HORSEMAN

- 2 oz. Vodka
- 3 dashes Bitters
- Ginger Ale
- 1 Orange Slice

Directions: Put vodka and bitters into a Collins glass. Add several ice cubes, fill with ginger ale, and stir. Add the orange slice and serve.

HEARTBREAK

- 2 ½ oz. Blended Whiskey
- ½ oz. Brandy
- Cranberry Juice
- Ice

Directions: Fill serving glass with ice and add ingredients. Fill with cranberry juice. Top with brandy.

HEATHER COFFEE

- 1 oz. Scotch
- 1 oz. Drambuie
- Coffee
- Whipped Cream
- Cinnamon

Directions: Fill glass with hot, black coffee and liquor. Top with whipped cream. Sprinkle with cinnamon.

HEATWAVE

- 1 oz. Dark Rum
- ½ oz. Peach Schnapps
- Pineapple Juice
- Dash Grenadine
- 1 Cherry
- 1 Pineapple Garnish
- Ice

Directions: Fill tall glass with ice and add ingredients. Fill with pineapple juice. Add dash of grenadine. Stir. Garnish with a cherry and pineapple.

HEAVENLY SEX

- 1 oz. Spiced Rum
- 1 oz. Amaretto
- 1 oz. Chocolate Liqueur
- Dash Grenadine
- Ice

Directions: Fill mixing glass with ice and add ingredients. Shake. Strain into a chilled glass.

HEATH BAR (FROZEN)

- ½ cup of Ice
- 1 ½ oz. Vodka
- 1 oz. Dark Crème de Cacao
- 1 Toffee Bar
- ½ scoop of Vanilla Ice Cream
- Milk or Cream

Directions: Blend all ingredients until smooth.

HELLO NURSE

- 1 ½ oz. Vodka
- ½ oz. Amaretto
- 1 tbs. Cream of Coconut
- 1 oz. Milk or Cream
- Ice

Directions: Fill mixing glass with ice and add ingredients. Shake. Strain in chilled glass.

HENRY MORGAN'S GROG

- 1 ½ oz. Whiskey
- 1 oz. Pernod
- ½ oz. Dark Rum
- 1 oz. Cream
- Ground Nutmeg
- Ice

Directions: Fill a short glass with ice, add ingredients, and shake. Sprinkle ground nutmeg on top.

HIGH JAMAICAN WIND

- 1 ½ oz. Dark Rum
- ½ oz. Coffee Liqueur
- ½ oz. Milk or Cream
- Ice

Directions: Fill glass with ice and add ingredients.

HIGH ROLLER

- 1 ½ oz. Vodka
- ¾ oz. Orange Liqueur
- Dash Grenadine
- Orange Juice
- 1 Cherry
- 1 Orange Garnish
- Ice

Directions: Fill a glass with ice and add ingredients. Fill with orange juice. Shake. Garnish with orange and cherry.

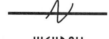

HIGHBALL

- 2 oz. Whiskey
- Water or Soda Water
- Ice

Directions: Fill a tall glass with ice and add ingredients. Fill with water or soda water.

HIGHLAND COFFEE

- 1 ½ oz. Scotch
- ½ oz. B&B
- Coffee
- Whipped Cream

Directions: Add ingredients to glass and fill with hot, black coffee. Top with whipped cream.

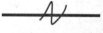

HIGHLAND FLING

- 1 ½ oz. Scotch
- ½ oz. Sweet Vermouth
- 2 - 3 dashes Bitters
- 1 Olive
- Ice

Directions: Fill mixing glass with ice and add ingredients. Shake. Strain into a chilled glass. Garnish with an olive.

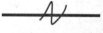

HIGHLAND FLING COCKTAIL

- 1 ½ oz. Scotch
- ¾ oz. Sweet Vermouth
- 2 dashes Orange Bitters
- 1 Olive
- Ice

Directions: Stir ingredients except olive with ice and strain in cocktail glass. Add olive.

HIGHLAND SLING

- 1 tsp. Superfine Sugar
- 2 tsp. Water
- 1 oz. Lemon Juice
- 2 oz. Scotch
- 1 Lemon Twist
- Ice

Directions: In shaker half-filled with ice, combine sugar, water, lemon juice, and Scotch. Shake well. Strain in highball glass. Garnish with lemon twist.

HILLARY WALLBANGER

- 4 oz. Dry White Wine
- ½ oz. Galliano
- Orange Juice
- Ice

Directions: Fill a wine glass with ice and add ingredients. Fill with orange juice. Top with Galliano.

HILLINATOR

- 3 oz. Captain Morgan
- 1 oz. Firewater
- 8 oz. Mountain Dew
- 4 tbs. sugar

Directions: Mix the Captain Morgan, Mountain Dew, and sugar in one glass. Pour the fire water into a shot glass. Take the shot, and then follow it with the mixed drink. Make sure to drink the mixed drink quickly.

HIT-IT

- 1 oz. Vodka
- ½ oz. Triple Sec
- ½ oz. Cherry Brandy
- 2 oz. Orange Juice
- 2 oz. Cranberry Juice
- Ice

Directions: Fill mixing glass with ice and add ingredients. Shake. Strain into a chilled glass.

HOG SNORT

- 1 oz. Coconut Rum
- 1 oz. Blue Curacao
- Dash Sour Mix
- Dash Pineapple Juice
- Ice

Directions: Fill mixing glass with ice and ingredients. Shake. Strain into shot glass.

HOGBACK GROWLER

- 1 oz. 151 Proof Rum
- 1 oz. Brandy

Directions: Combine ingredients in a shot glass.

HOKKAIDO COCKTAIL

- 1 ½ oz. Gin
- ½ oz. Triple Sec
- 1 oz. Sake
- Ice

Directions: Shake ice and ingredients, strain into cocktail glass, and serve.

HOLE IN ONE (FLOATER)

- 1 oz. Melon Liqueur (bottom)
- 1 oz. Apple Brandy (top)
- Cream

Directions: Layer liqueur and brandy in a shot glass. Add one drop of cream into the center of the drink.

HOLE-IN-ONE

- 1 ¾ oz. Scotch
- ¾ oz. Vermouth
- ¼ tsp. Lemon Juice
- Dash Orange Bitters
- Ice

Directions: Shake all ingredients with ice, strain into a cocktail glass, and serve.

HOLIDAY CHEER

- 1 bottle Champagne
- 1 can Frozen Cranberry Juice
- 1 Lime

Directions: Mix champagne and undiluted frozen cranberry juice. Slice lime and garnish each wine glass. Mix right before serving to retain the bubbles.

HOLLYWOOD

- 1 ½ oz. Vodka
- ½ oz. Black Raspberry Liqueur
- Pineapple Juice
- 1 Pineapple Garnish
- Ice

Directions: Fill a tall glass with ice and add ingredients. Fill with pineapple juice. Shake. Garnish with pineapple.

HOLLYWOOD 2

- 1 oz. Vodka
- ½ oz. Black Raspberry Liqueur
- ½ oz. Peach Schnapps
- Pineapple Juice
- Ice

Directions: Fill a tall glass with ice and add ingredients. Fill with pineapple juice. Shake.

HOMECOMING

- 1 oz. Amaretto
- 1 oz. Irish Cream
- Ice

Directions: Fill a mixing glass with ice and add ingredients. Shake. Strain into a chilled glass.

HONEY BEE

- 2 oz. Rum
- ½ oz. Honey
- ½ oz. Lemon Juice
- Ice

Directions: Fill a mixing glass with ice and add ingredients. Shake. Strain into a chilled glass.

HONEYDEW

- 1 ½ oz. Melon Liqueur
- 2 oz. Sour Mix
- ½ tsp. Sugar
- Champagne
- Ice

Directions: Fill a tall glass with ice and add ingredients. Shake. Fill with Champagne.

HONEYMOON COCKTAIL

- ¾ oz. Apple Brandy
- ¾ oz. Benedictine
- 1 tsp. Triple Sec
- Juice of ½ Lemon
- Ice

Directions: Shake all ingredients with ice, strain into a cocktail glass, and serve.

HONOLULU COCKTAIL NO. 2

- ¾ oz. Gin
- ¾ oz. Benedictine
- ¾ oz. Maraschino
- Ice

Directions: Stir all ingredients with ice, strain into a cocktail glass, and serve.

HOOPLA

- ¾ oz. Brandy
- ¾ oz. Orange Liqueur
- ¾ oz. Lillet
- ¾ oz. Lemon Juice
- 1 Lemon Twist
- Ice

Directions: Fill a mixing glass with ice and add ingredients. Shake. Strain into a chilled glass. Garnish with lemon twist.

HOOT MAN

- 1 ½ oz. Scotch
- ½ oz. Lillet
- ½ oz. Sweet Vermouth
- Ice

Directions: In a mixing glass half-filled with ice cubes, combine all of the ingredients. Stir well. Strain into a cocktail glass.

HOOTER

- 1 ½ oz. Vodka
- ½ oz. Amaretto
- Pineapple Juice
- Ice

Directions: Fill a short glass with ice and add ingredients. Fill with pineapple juice. Shake.

HOP TOAD

- ¾ oz. Apricot Brandy
- ¾ oz. Light Rum
- Juice of ½ Lime
- Ice

Directions: Pour ingredients into a mixing glass over ice and stir. Strain into a chilled glass.

HORNPIPE

- 1 ½ oz. Gin
- 2 tsp. Cherry Brandy
- 1 Egg White
- Ice

Directions: In a shaker half-filled with ice cubes, combine all of the ingredients. Shake well. Strain into a cocktail glass.

HORSE AND JOCKEY

- 1 oz. Anejo Rum
- 1 oz. Southern Comfort
- ½ oz. Sweet Vermouth
- 2 dashes Bitters
- Ice

Directions: In a mixing glass half-filled with ice cubes, combine all of the ingredients. Stir well. Strain into a cocktail glass.

HORSE'S NECK

- 1 Lemon Peel Spiral
- 2 oz. Brandy
- 5 oz. Ginger Ale
- 2 dashes Bitters
- Ice

Directions: Place the lemon peel spiral in a highball glass and drape one end of it over the rim. Fill the glass with ice cubes. Pour the brandy, ginger ale, and bitters into the glass. Stir well.

HORSLEY'S HONOR

- 1 ½ oz. Gin
- ½ oz. Dry Vermouth
- ½ oz. Applejack
- ½ oz. Triple Sec
- 1 Orange Slice
- Ice

Directions: In an old-fashioned glass almost filled with ice cubes, combine the gin, vermouth, applejack, and triple sec. Stir well and garnish with the orange slice.

HOT APPLE PIE

- 2 oz. Tuaca
- Apple Cider
- Whipped Cream
- 1 Cinnamon Stick

Directions: Pour liquor in a glass and fill with hot apple cider. Top with whipped cream. Garnish with a cinnamon stick.

HOT APPLE PIE 2

- 1 oz. Vodka
- 1 oz. Apple Brandy
- 2 oz. Apple Juice
- 1 oz. Lemon-lime Soda
- Ice

Directions: Fill a mixing glass with ice and add ingredients. Shake. Strain into a chilled glass. Add lemon-lime soda. Sprinkle with cinnamon.

HOT APPLE TODDY

- 2 oz. Whiskey
- 1 tsp. Honey or Sugar
- Apple Cider
- 1 Lemon Garnish
- 1 Cinnamon Stick
- 2 - 3 Whole Cloves

Directions: Fill a glass with hot apple cider, whiskey, and honey or sugar. Stir. Garnish with lemon, cinnamon stick, and cloves.

HOT BUTTERED RUM

- 1 tsp. Sugar
- ½ tsp. Butter
- 1 ¾ oz. Rum
- 4 Cloves
- Water

Directions: In a mug, combine sugar, butter, rum, and cloves. Fill with boiling water. Stir.

HOT DEVILISH DAIQUIRI

- 1 ½ cup of Hot Water
- ¼ cup of Sugar
- 2 Cinnamon Sticks
- 8 Whole Cloves
- 6 oz. Frozen Lemonade Concentrate
- 6 oz. Frozen Limeade Concentrate
- ½ cup Light Rum

Directions: In two quart microwave-safe casserole dish, combine hot water, sugar, spices, and concentrated juices. Stir, then cook on high for five to six minutes or until mixture boils. Heat rum in a microwave-safe container on high for 30 seconds. Ignite and pour over hot beverage. Ladle into punch cups for serving.

HOT DOG

- 2 oz. Peppered Vodka
- Grapefruit Juice
- Ice

Directions: Fill a tall glass with ice and add vodka. Fill with grapefruit juice.

HOT DOG 2

- Lime
- Kosher Salt
- Beer
- 5 - 7 drops Tabasco Sauce

Directions: Rub the rim of a beer glass with lime and dip one side of the glass in kosher salt. Fill the glass with beer and add five to seven drops of tabasco sauce.

HOT GOLD

- 3 oz. Amaretto
- 6 oz. Very Warm Orange Juice
- 1 Cinnamon Stick

Directions: Pour orange juice into a wine glass and add Amaretto. Garnish with the cinnamon stick as a stirrer and serve.

HOT LEMONADE

- Juice of Large Lemon
- 2 tsp. Maple Syrup
- Water
- ½ oz. Amber Rum

Directions: Fill a serving glass with lemon juice, hot water, and syrup. Stir or shake. Top with amber rum.

HOT MILK PUNCH

- 2 oz. Bourbon
- ½ oz. Sugar Syrup
- Milk
- Nutmeg

Directions: Fill a glass with hot milk, bourbon, and syrup. Stir. Sprinkle with nutmeg.

HOT NAIL

- 2 oz. Scotch
- 1 oz. Drambuie
- Dash Lemon Juice
- Water
- 1 Orange Garnish
- 1 Lemon Garnish
- 1 Cinnamon Stick

Directions: Fill a glass with boiling water and add ingredients. Garnish with orange, lemon, and cinnamon stick.

HOT PANTS

- 1 ½ oz. Tequila
- ½ oz. Peppermint Schnapps
- Dash Grenadine
- 1 oz. Grapefruit Juice
- Salt
- Ice

Directions: Fill a tall glass with ice and add ingredients. Shake and pour contents into a second glass rimmed with salt.

HOT RASPBERRY DREAM

- 1 oz. Black Raspberry Liqueur
- 1 oz. Dark Crème de Cacao
- 4 - 6 oz. Steamed Milk

Directions: Combine ingredients and stir.

HOT SCOTCH

- 1 oz. Scotch
- ¼ oz. Drambuie
- 1 oz. Lemon Juice
- ½ tsp. Sugar
- 2 oz. Hot Water
- 1 Lemon Garnish

Directions: Combine ingredients and stir. Garnish with lemon.

HOT SEX

- 1 oz. Coffee Liqueur
- 1 oz. Orange Liqueur

Directions: In a snifter, add ingredients. Microwave for 10 to 15 seconds.

HOT SHOT (FLOATER)

- 1 oz. Hot Coffee (bottom)
- 1 oz. Favorite Liqueur
- Cream or Whipped Cream

Directions: Add ingredients into a short glass. Top with cream or whipped cream.

HOT SPRINGS COCKTAIL

- 1 ½ oz. White Wine
- 1 tbs. Pineapple Juice
- ½ tsp. Maraschino
- Dash Orange Bitters
- Ice

Directions: Shake all ingredients with ice, strain into a cocktail glass, and serve.

HOT TAMALE

- 1 ½ oz. Cinnamon Schnapps
- ½ oz. Grenadine
- Hot Candy Garnish
- Ice

Directions: Fill tall glass with ice and add ingredients. Strain in shot glass. Garnish with hot candy.

HOT TODDY

- 2 oz. Whiskey
- 1 tsp. Honey
- Water
- 1 Lemon Garnish
- 1 Cinnamon Stick
- 2 - 3 Whole Cloves

Directions: Boil water and add to a glass with whiskey and honey. Stir. Garnish with lemon, cinnamon stick, and cloves.

HOTEL PLAZA COCKTAIL

- ¾ oz. Dry Vermouth
- ¾ oz. Sweet Vermouth
- ¾ oz. Gin
- 1 Crushed Pineapple Slice
- Ice

Directions: Stir all ingredients except pineapple with ice and strain into a cocktail glass. Decorate with the crushed slice of pineapple and serve.

HOUND DOG

- 2 oz. Rum
- Grapefruit Juice
- Ice

Directions: Fill a tall glass with ice and add ingredients. Fill with grapefruit juice. Stir.

HOUNDSTOOTH

- 2 oz. Vodka
- ½ oz. White Crème de Cacao
- ½ oz. Blackberry Brandy
- Ice

Directions: Fill a mixing glass with ice and add ingredients. Stir. Serve or strain into a chilled glass.

HOWELL SAYS SO

- 1 ½ oz. Dark Rum
- ½ oz. Triple Sec
- ½ oz. Amaretto
- ½ oz. Lemon Juice
- 2 dashes Orange Bitters
- Ice

Directions: In a shaker half-filled with ice cubes, combine all of the ingredients. Shake well. Strain into an old-fashioned glass almost filled with ice cubes.

HUDSON BAY

- ½ oz. Cherry Brandy
- 1 oz. Gin
- 1 ½ tsp. 151 Proof Rum
- 1 tbs. Orange Juice
- 1 ½ tsp. Lime Juice
- Ice

Directions: Shake all ingredients with ice, strain into a cocktail glass, and serve.

HUETCHEN

- 2 oz. Brandy
- Cola
- Ice

Directions: Fill a serving glass with ice and add brandy. Fill with cola.

THE HULK

- 1 oz. Cognac
- 1 oz. Hypnotiq
- Ice

Directions: Fill a short glass with ice and add ingredients. Stir.

HUMMER

- 1 oz. Coffee Liqueur
- 1 oz. Light Rum
- 2 Large scoops of Vanilla Ice Cream

Directions: Blend all ingredients in an electric blender at a low speed for a short length of time. Pour into a highball glass and serve.

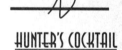

HUNTER'S COCKTAIL

- 1 oz. Bourbon
- 1 oz. Cherry Liqueur
- 1 oz. Cream or Milk
- Dash Triple Sec
- Ice

Directions: Fill a mixing glass with ice and add ingredients. Shake. Strain into a chilled glass.

HURRICANE

- 1 oz. Light Rum
- 1 oz. Dark Rum
- 1 tbs. Passion Fruit Syrup
- 2 tsp. Lime Juice

Directions: Shake all ingredients with ice, strain into a cocktail glass, and serve.

HUSSIE

- 1 oz. Amaretto
- 1 oz. Beer
- 1 oz. Sour Mix
- Ice

Directions: Fill a mixing glass with ice and add ingredients. Shake. Strain into a shot glass.

ICE BALL (FROZEN)

- 1 cup of Ice
- 1 oz. Gin
- 1 oz. Sambuca
- 1 oz. White Crème de Menthe
- 1 oz. Milk or Cream

Directions: Blend all ingredients until smooth.

ICE BOAT

- 1 ½ oz. Vodka
- 1 ½ oz. Peppermint Schnapps
- Ice

Directions: Fill a mixing glass with ice and add ingredients. Stir. Strain into a chilled glass.

ICE CREAM FLIP

- 1 oz. Triple Sec
- 1 oz. Maraschino
- Small scoop of Vanilla Ice Cream
- 1 Whole Egg
- Nutmeg
- Ice

Directions: Shake all ingredients except nutmeg with ice and strain into a whiskey sour glass. Sprinkle nutmeg on top and serve.

ICE CREAM FLOAT

- Scoop of Ice Cream
- Stout, Porter, Any Dark Beer, or Root Beer

Directions: Put ingredients in a pint glass or beer mug. Serve with straw and spoon.

ICE CREAM SODA

- 2 - 4 oz. Syrup
- ¼ scoop of Ice Cream
- Soda Water

Directions: In a pint glass, add ingredients. Fill with soda water.

ICE PALACE

- 1 oz. Light Rum
- ½ oz. Galliano
- ½ oz. Apricot Brandy
- 2 oz. Pineapple Juice
- ¼ oz. Lemon Juice
- 1 Orange Slice
- 1 Cherry (optional)
- Ice

Directions: Shake all ingredients except orange slice with ice and strain into a Collins glass over ice cubes. Garnish with the slice of orange and a cherry, if desired.

ICE PICK

- 2 oz. Vodka
- Lemon
- Sugar
- 1 Lemon Garnish
- Ice

Directions: Fill a tall glass with ice and add ingredients. Flavor with lemon and sugar as desired. Garnish with lemon.

ICEBERG

- 2 oz. Vodka
- 1 tsp. Pernod
- Ice

Directions: Fill a mixing glass with ice and add ingredients. Shake. Strain into a chilled glass.

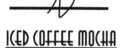

ICED COFFEE MOCHA

- 2 - 3 tbs. Chocolate Syrup
- Iced Coffee
- Ice

Directions: Fill a tall glass with ice and add ingredients. Fill with iced coffee. Shake.

ICHBIEN

- 2 oz. Apple Brandy
- ½ oz. Curacao
- 1 Egg Yolk
- 2 oz. Milk or Cream
- Nutmeg
- Ice

Directions: Fill a mixing glass with ice and add ingredients. Shake. Strain into a chilled glass. Garnish with nutmeg.

IDEAL

- 1 ½ oz. Gin
- ½ oz. Dry or Sweet Vermouth
- 1 tbs. Grapefruit Juice
- 1 tsp. Cherry Liqueur
- 1 Cherry
- Ice

Directions: Fill a mixing glass with ice and add ingredients. Shake. Strain into a chilled glass. Garnish with cherry.

IDEAL COCKTAIL

- 1 oz. Dry Vermouth
- 1 oz. Gin
- ¼ tsp. Maraschino
- ½ tsp. Grapefruit Juice
- 1 Cherry
- Ice

Directions: Shake all ingredients except cherry with ice and strain into a cocktail glass. Add the cherry on top and serve.

IGUANA

- ½ oz. Vodka
- ½ oz. Tequila
- ¼ oz. Coffee Liqueur
- 1 ½ oz. Sweet and Sour
- ½ Lime Slice
- Ice

Directions: Shake all ingredients except lime slice with ice and strain into a chilled cocktail glass. Add the lime slice and serve.

IL MAGNIFICO (FROZEN)

- 1 cup of Ice
- 1 oz. Tuaca
- 1 oz. Curacao
- 1 oz. Cream

Directions: Blend ingredients until smooth.

IMMACULATA

- 1 ½ oz. Light Rum
- ½ oz. Amaretto
- ½ oz. Lime Juice
- 1 tsp. Lemon Juice
- ½ tsp. Superfine Sugar
- Ice

Directions: In shaker half-filled with ice, combine ingredients. Shake well. Strain in cocktail glass.

IMPERIAL FIZZ

- ½ oz. Light Rum
- 1 ½ oz. Blended Whiskey
- Juice of ½ Lemon
- 1 tsp. Powdered Sugar
- Carbonated Water
- Ice

Directions: Shake all ingredients except carbonated water with ice and strain in highball glass over two ice cubes. Fill with carbonated water, stir, and serve.

INCIDER

- 2 oz. Whiskey
- Hard Cider
- Ice

Directions: Fill a tall glass with ice and add ingredients. Fill with hard cider. Stir.

THE INCREDIBLE HULK

- 2 oz. Captain Morgan's Spiced Rum
- 1 tbs. Sugar
- 2 liters Mountain Dew

Directions: Pour rum into a glass. Add sugar. Add Mountain Dew until the mix turns green.

INDIAN SUMMER

- 2 oz. Apple Brandy
- Pinch Sugar
- Pinch Cinnamon
- Apple Cider
- 1 Cinnamon Stick
- Ice

Directions: Fill a tall glass with ice and add ingredients. Fill with hot apple cider. Stir. Garnish with cinnamon stick.

INDIAN SUMMER 2

- 1 oz. Vodka
- 1 oz. Coffee Brandy
- 2 oz. Pineapple Juice
- Ice

Directions: Fill mixing glass with ice and add ingredients. Shake. Strain into a shot glass.

INDIAN SUMMER HUMMER

- 1 oz. Dark Rum
- ½ oz. Apricot Brandy
- ½ oz. Black Raspberry Liqueur
- Pineapple Juice
- Ice

Directions: Fill a tall glass with ice and add ingredients. Fill with pineapple juice. Shake.

INK STREET

- 2 oz. Whiskey
- Orange Juice
- Sour Mix
- 1 Orange Garnish
- Ice

Directions: Fill mixing glass with ice and add ingredients. Fill with equal parts orange juice and sour mix. Shake. Strain into a chilled glass. Garnish with orange.

INSTANT DEATH

- 3 oz. Bacardi 151
- 3 oz. Everclear
- 3 oz. Jaegermeister
- 5 oz. Water
- Dash Salt

Directions: Pour in all alcohol and then add water. Top with salt.

INTERNATIONAL STINGER

- 1 ½ oz. Metaxa
- ½ oz. Galliano
- Ice

Directions: Fill short glass with ice and add ingredients. Stir. Serve or strain in chilled glass.

INVERTED NAIL (FLOATER)

- 1 oz. Drambuie (bottom)
- 1 oz. Single Malt Scotch (top)

Directions: Layer ingredients in shot glass.

IRA COCKTAIL

- 1 ½ oz. Irish Whiskey
- 1 oz. Irish Cream

Directions: Combine ingredients and stir.

IRISH ANGEL

- 1 oz. Irish Whiskey
- ½ oz. Dark Crème de Cacao
- ½ oz. White Crème de Menthe
- Cream
- Ice

Directions: Fill tall glass with ice and add ingredients. Fill with cream. Shake.

IRISH COFFEE

- 8 oz. Coffee
- 2 oz. Bailey's Irish Cream
- 2 oz. Half & Half
- 1 tsp. Sugar

Directions: Mix coffee with chilled Irish cream and Half & Half. Add sugar and stir. Serve hot.

IRISH COW

- 4 oz. Irish Cream
- 4 oz. Milk
- Nutmeg

Directions: Combine cream and milk in a saucepan. Warm on low heat. Pour into a tempered glass. Garnish with nutmeg.

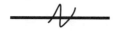

IRISH CREAM SODA

- 2 oz. Irish Cream
- Soda Water
- Ice

Directions: Fill a serving glass with ice and add cream. Fill with soda.

IRISH FLAG (FLOATER)

- ¾ oz. Green Crème de Menthe (bottom)
- ¾ oz. Irish Cream
- ¾ oz. Orange Liqueur (top)

Directions: Layer ingredients in order in a shot glass.

IRISH GENTLEMAN

- 1 oz. Irish Cream
- 1 oz. Irish Whiskey
- Coffee
- Whipped Cream
- Green Crème de Menthe

Directions: Fill glass with hot, black coffee, cream, and whiskey. Top with whipped cream. Drizzle green crème de menthe on top.

IRISH HEADLOCK

- ½ oz. Irish Whiskey
- ½ oz. Irish Cream
- ½ oz. Brandy
- ½ oz. Amaretto
- Ice

Directions: Fill mixing glass with ice and add ingredients. Shake. Strain in chilled glass.

IRISH ICED COFFEE

- 2 oz. Irish Whiskey
- Iced Coffee
- Cream or Milk
- Sugar
- Ice

Directions: Fill a tall glass with ice and add whiskey. Fill with iced coffee. Add cream or milk and sugar to taste.

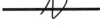

IRISH ICED TEA

- ½ oz. Vodka
- ½ oz. Gin
- ½ oz. Rum
- ½ oz. Triple Sec
- ½ oz. Melon Liqueur
- Lemon-lime Soda
- Ice

Directions: Fill a tall glass with ice and add ingredients. Fill with lemon-lime soda.

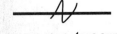

IRISH MARIA (FLOATER)

- 1 oz. Tia Maria (bottom)
- 1 oz. Irish Cream (top)

Directions: Layer ingredients in a shot glass.

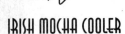

IRISH MOCHA COOLER

- 2 oz. Irish Whiskey
- 1 oz. Dark Crème de Cacao
- Iced Coffee
- Ice

Directions: Fill tall glass with ice and add ingredients. Fill with iced coffee.

IRISH MONEY COFFEE

- 1 oz. Irish Whiskey
- ½ oz. Dark Crème de Cacao
- Coffee
- Whipped Cream

Directions: Fill glass with whiskey, cacao, and hot, black coffee. Top with whipped cream.

IRISH MONK

- 1 oz. Irish Cream
- 1 oz. Hazelnut Liqueur
- Ice

Directions: Fill a short glass with ice and add ingredients. Stir.

IRISH MONK COFFEE

- 1 oz. Irish Whiskey
- 1 oz. Hazelnut Liqueur
- Coffee
- Whipped Cream

Directions: Fill glass with whiskey, liqueur, and hot, black coffee. Top with whipped cream.

IRISH RICKEY

- 1 ½ oz. Irish Whiskey
- Juice of ½ Lime
- 1 Lime Wedge
- Carbonated Water
- Ice

Directions: Pour Irish whiskey and lime juice into a highball glass over ice cubes. Fill with carbonated water and stir. Add the lime wedge and serve.

IRISH ROVER

- 1 oz. Irish Whiskey
- 1 oz. Irish Cream
- 1 oz. Coffee Liqueur
- Ice

Directions: Fill a short glass with ice and add ingredients. Shake.

IRISH RUSSIAN

- 1 oz. Vodka
- 1 oz. Coffee Liqueur
- Irish Stout
- Dash Cola

Directions: Put ingredients into a tall glass and add ingredients. Fill with Irish stout. Add a dash of cola.

IRISH SKIPPER COFFEE

- ¾ oz. Irish Mist
- ¾ oz. Irish Cream
- ¾ oz. White Crème de Cacao
- Coffee
- Whipped Cream

Directions: Fill a glass with mist, cream, cacao, and hot, black coffee. Top with whipped cream.

IRISH SPRING

- 1 oz. Irish Whiskey
- ½ oz. Peach Schnapps
- 1 oz. Orange Juice
- 1 oz. Sour Mix
- 1 Cherry
- 1 Orange Garnish
- Ice

Directions: Fill a short glass with ice, add ingredients, and shake. Garnish with range and cherry.

IRISH STINGER

- 1 ½ oz. Brandy
- ½ oz. Crème de Menthe
- Ice

Directions: Fill a short glass with ice and add ingredients. Stir. Serve or strain into a chilled glass.

IRON CROSS

- 1 oz. Apricot Brandy
- 1 oz. Peppermint Schnapps
- Ice

Directions: Fill a mixing glass with ice and add ingredients. Stir. Strain into a shot glass.

IS PARIS BURNING

- 2 oz. Cognac
- 1 oz. Chambord
- 1 Fresh Raspberry
- Ice

Directions: Combine ingredients and stir. Do not shake. Rocks are acceptable. Fresh raspberry optional.

ISRAELI COFFEE

- 2 oz. Sabra Liqueur
- Coffee
- Whipped Cream

Directions: Fill glass with liqueur and hot, black coffee. Top with whipped cream.

ITALIAN COFFEE

- 2 oz. Amaretto
- Coffee
- Whipped Cream
- Shaved Almonds

Directions: Fill a glass with Amaretto and hot, black coffee. Top with whipped cream. Sprinkle with shaved almonds.

ITALIAN COFFEE 2

- 2 oz. Galliano
- Coffee
- Whipped Cream
- Cinnamon

Directions: Fill glass with Galliano and hot, black coffee. Top with whipped cream. Sprinkle with cinnamon.

ITALIAN DELIGHT

- 1 oz. Amaretto
- ½ oz. Orange Juice
- 1 ½ oz. Cream
- 1 Cherry
- Ice

Directions: Shake all ingredients except cherry with ice and strain into a chilled cocktail glass. Add the cherry on top and serve.

ITALIAN HEATHER

- 1 ½ oz. Scotch
- 1 oz. Galliano
- Crushed Ice
- 1 Lime Wedge

Directions: Pour the Scotch and Galliano into an old-fashioned glass almost filled with crushed ice. Stir well. Garnish with the lime wedge.

ITALIAN SCREW

- 2 oz. Galliano
- Orange Juice
- Ice

Directions: Fill serving glass with ice and add ingredients. Fill with orange juice. Shake.

ITALIAN SOMBRERO

- 1 ½ oz. Amaretto
- 3 oz. Light Cream

Directions: Shake Amaretto and cream. Pour into a Champagne flute and serve.

ITALIAN STALLION

- 1 ½ oz. Scotch
- ½ oz. Galliano
- Ice

Directions: Fill a short glass with ice and add ingredients. Stir.

ITALIAN STINGER

- 1 ½ oz. Brandy
- ½ oz. Galliano
- Ice

Directions: Fill a short glass with ice and add ingredients. Stir. Serve or strain into a chilled glass.

ITALIAN SUNRISE

- 2 oz. Amaretto
- ½ oz. Crème de Cassis
- Orange Juice
- Ice

Directions: Fill serving glass with ice and add Amaretto. Fill with orange juice. Top with cassis.

ITALIAN SURFER

- 1 oz. Coconut Rum
- 1 oz. Amaretto
- Pineapple Juice
- Cranberry Juice
- Ice

Directions: Fill a tall glass with ice and add rum and Amaretto. Fill with pineapple juice. Shake. Top with a splash of cranberry juice.

IXTAPA

- 1 ½ oz. Coffee Liqueur
- ½ oz. Tequila
- Ice

Directions: Fill a mixing glass with ice and add ingredients. Stir. Strain into a chilled glass.

IZAYOI

- 1 oz. Lemon Liquor
- ²/₃ oz. Grapefruit juice
- ¹/₆ oz. Vodka
- ¹/ oz. Lemon juice
- ¹/ oz. Grenadine
- Ice

Directions: In a shaker half-filled with ice, combine ingredients. Shake well. Strain in cocktail glass.

J. R. 'S GODCHILD

- 2 oz. Bourbon
- ½ oz. Amaretto
- 1 oz. Milk
- Ice

Directions: In shaker half-filled with ice, combine the bourbon, Amaretto, and milk. Shake well. Pour in old-fashioned glass.

J. R. 'S REVENGE

- 3 oz. Bourbon
- ½ oz. Southern Comfort
- 2 dashes Bitters
- Ice

Directions: In mixing glass half-filled with ice, combine ingredients. Stir well. Strain in cocktail glass.

JACK & COKE

- 2 oz. Jack Daniels
- 10 oz. Coca-Cola
- Ice

Directions: Pour Jack Daniels into a large glass filled with ice. Pour Coke into the glass. Stir lightly.

JACK ROSE COCKTAIL

- 1 ½ oz. Apple Brandy
- 1 tsp. Grenadine
- Juice of ½ Lime
- Ice

Directions: Shake all ingredients with ice, strain into a cocktail glass, and serve.

JACK-IN-THE-BOX

- 1 oz. Apple Brandy
- 1 oz. Pineapple Juice
- Dash Bitters
- Ice

Directions: Shake all ingredients with ice, strain into a cocktail glass, and serve.

JADE

- 1 ½ oz. Light Rum
- ½ tsp. Green Crème de Menthe
- ½ tsp. Triple Sec
- 1 tbs. Lime Juice
- 1 tsp. Powdered Sugar
- 1 Lime Slice
- Ice

Directions: Shake all ingredients except lime slice with ice and strain in cocktail glass. Add lime slice and serve.

JAEGER BOMB

- 1 oz. Jaegermeister
- Red Energy Drink

Directions: Fill shot glass with Jaegermesiter. Drop shot glass into large glass filled with red energy drink.

JAEGER MONSTER

- 1 oz. Jaegermeister
- ½ oz. Amaretto
- Dash Grenadine
- 1 Orange Garnish
- Ice

Directions: Fill a tall glass with ice, add ingredients., and shake. Garnish with orange.

JAMAICA GLOW

- 1 oz. Gin
- 1 tsp. Jamaica Rum
- 1 tbs. Claret
- 1 tbs. Orange Juice
- Ice

Directions: Shake all ingredients with ice, strain into a cocktail glass, and serve.

JAMAICA HOP

- 1 oz. Coffee Brandy
- 1 oz. White Crème de Cacao
- 1 oz. Light Cream
- Ice

Directions: Shake all ingredients with ice, strain into a cocktail glass, and serve.

JAMAICA ME CRAZY

- ½ oz Amber Rum
- ½ oz. Tia Maria
- Pineapple juice
- Ice

Directions: Fill a tall glass with ice. Pour in rum and Tia Maria. Add pineapple juice.

JAMAICAN

- 1 oz. Dark Rum
- 1 oz. Coffee Liqueur
- 1 oz. Lime Juice
- Dash Bitters
- Lemon-lime Soda
- Ice

Directions: Fill a tall glass with ice and add ingredients. Add a dash of bitters and fill with lemon-lime soda.

JAMAICAN BANANA

- ½ oz. Light Rum
- ½ oz. White Crème de Cacao
- ½ oz. Crème de Bananes
- 2 scoops of Vanilla Ice Cream
- 1 oz. Half & Half
- 1 Sliced Banana
- 1 Strawberry
- Nutmeg

Directions: Blend all ingredients except sliced banana in an electric blender at a low speed for a short length of time. Pour into a large brandy snifter and add sliced banana. Sprinkle lightly with nutmeg, top with a whole strawberry, and serve.

JAMAICAN BOBSLED

- 1 ½ oz. Dark Rum
- ½ oz. Butterscotch Schnapps
- Root Beer
- Ice

Directions: Fill a tall glass with ice and add ingredients. Fill with root beer.

JAMAICAN DUST

- 1 oz. Dark Rum
- 1 oz. Tia Maria
- Pineapple Juice
- 1 Lime Garnish
- Ice

Directions: Fill a tall glass with ice and add ingredients. Fill with pineapple juice. Shake. Garnish with lime.

JAMAICAN KISS

- 1 oz. Amber Rum
- ½ oz. Tia Maria
- 2 oz. Milk
- ½ oz. Sugar Syrup
- Ice

Directions: Fill a short glass with ice and add ingredients. Shake.

JAMAICAN MULE

- 1 oz. Light Rum
- 1 oz. Dark Rum
- ½ oz. Amaretto
- Ginger Beer
- Ice

Directions: Fill a tall glass with ice and add ingredients. Fill with ginger beer. Stir.

JAMAICAN PINE

- 2 oz. Dark Rum
- Pineapple Juice
- 1 Lime Garnish
- Ice

Directions: Fill a serving glass with ice and add ingredients. Garnish with lime.

JAMAICAN WIND

- 1 ½ oz. Dark Rum
- ½ oz. Coffee Liqueur
- Ice

Directions: Fill a short glass with ice and add ingredients. Stir.

JAMES THE SECOND COMES FIRST

- 2 oz. Scotch
- ½ oz. Tawny Port
- ½ oz. Dry Vermouth
- Dash Bitters
- Ice

Directions: In a mixing glass half-filled with ice cubes, combine all of the ingredients. Stir well. Strain into a cocktail glass.

JAPANESE

- 2 oz. Brandy
- 1 ½ tsp. Orgeat Syrup
- 1 tbs. Lime Juice
- Dash Bitters
- Twist of Lime Peel
- Ice

Directions: Shake all ingredients except lime peel with ice and strain into a cocktail glass. Add the twist of lime peel.

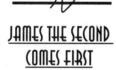

JAPANESE FIZZ

- 1 ½ oz. Blended Whiskey
- Juice of ½ Lemon
- 1 tsp. Powdered Sugar
- 1 tbs. Port
- 1 Egg White
- Carbonated Water
- Ice

Directions: Shake all ingredients except carbonated water with ice and strain into a highball glass over two ice cubes. Fill with carbonated water, stir, and serve.

JAWBREAKER

- Cinnamon Schnapps
- 4 - 5 drops Tabasco Sauce

Directions: Put schnapps in a short glass. Add four to five drops of tabasco sauce and stir.

JAY WALKER

- 1 oz. Rum
- ½ oz. Triple Sec
- Sour Mix
- Pineapple Juice
- 151 Proof Rum
- Ice

Directions: Fill a tall glass with ice and add ingredients. Fill with equal parts sour mix and pineapple juice. Shake. Top with 151 proof rum

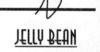

JELLY BEAN

- 1 oz. Anisette
- 1 oz. Blackberry Brandy
- Ice

Directions: Fill a short glass with ice and add ingredients. Stir.

JELLY BEAN (FLOATER)

- ½ oz. Blackberry Brandy (bottom)
- 1 oz. Anisette
- ½ oz. Southern Comfort (top)

Directions: Layer ingredients in order in a shot glass.

JELLY DOUGHNUT

- 1 ½ oz. Irish Cream
- ½ oz. Black Raspberry Liqueur
- Ice

Directions: Fill a short glass with ice and add ingredients. Stir.

JELLY FISH (FLOATER)

- 1 ½ oz. White Crème de Cacao (bottom)
- ½ oz. Irish Cream
- ½ oz. Amaretto (top)
- 2 - 3 drops Grenadine

Directions: Layer ingredients in order in a shot glass. Place two to three drops of grenadine in the center of the glass.

JENNY WALLBANGER

- 1 ½ oz. Vodka
- Orange Juice
- Milk or Cream
- ½ oz. Galliano
- Ice

Directions: Fill a tall glass with ice and add vodka. Fill with equal parts orange juice and milk or cream. Shake. Top with Galliano.

JERSEY LIGHTNING

- ½ oz. Sweet Vermouth
- 1 ½ oz. Apple Brandy
- Juice of 1 Lime
- Ice

Directions: Shake all ingredients with ice, strain into a cocktail glass, and serve.

JET BLACK

- 1 ½ oz. Gin
- 2 tsp. Sweet Vermouth
- 1 tsp. Black Sambuca
- Ice

Directions: In a mixing glass half-filled with ice cubes, combine all of the ingredients. Stir well. Strain into a cocktail glass.

JET FUEL

- ½ oz. Vodka
- ½ oz. Jaegermeister
- ½ oz. 100 Proof Cinnamon Schnapps
- Ice

Directions: Fill a mixing glass with ice and add ingredients. Strain into a shot glass.

JEWEL COCKTAIL

- ¾ oz. Sweet Vermouth
- ¾ oz. Green Chartreuse
- ¾ oz. Gin
- Dash Orange Bitters
- 1 Cherry
- Ice

Directions: Stir ingredients except cherry with ice and strain in cocktail glass. Top with cherry and serve.

JEWEL OF THE NILE

- 1 ½ oz. Gin
- ½ oz. Green Chartreuse
- ½ oz. Yellow Chartreuse
- Ice

Directions: In mixing glass half-filled with ice, combine ingredients. Stir well. Strain in cocktail glass.

JEYPLAK COCKTAIL

- 1 ½ oz. Gin
- ¾ oz. Sweet Vermouth
- ¼ tsp. Anisette
- 1 Cherry
- Ice

Directions: Stir all ingredients except cherry with ice and strain in cocktail glass. Top with cherry.

JEZEBEL (FLOATER)

- 1 ½ oz. Southern Comfort (bottom)
- ½ oz. Irish Cream (top)

Directions: Layer ingredients in a shot glass.

JILLIONAIRE

- 2 oz. Bourbon
- ½ oz. Triple Sec
- ½ tsp. Grenadine
- 1 Egg White
- Ice

Directions: In a shaker half-filled with ice cubes, combine all of the ingredients. Shake well and strain into a cocktail glass.

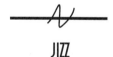

JIZZ

- 1 ½ oz. Cognac
- ½ oz. Irish Cream
- 1 oz. Cream
- Ice

Directions: Fill a mixing glass with ice and add ingredients. Shake. Strain into a shot glass.

JOCK COLLINS

- 2 oz. Scotch
- 1 oz. Lemon Juice
- 1 tsp. Superfine Sugar
- 3 oz. Club Soda
- 1 Maraschino Cherry
- 1 Orange Slice
- Ice

Directions: In a shaker half-filled with ice cubes, combine the Scotch, lemon juice, and sugar. Shake well. Strain into a Collins glass almost filled with ice cubes. Add the club soda. Stir and garnish with the cherry and the orange slice.

JOCK-IN-A-BOX

- 1 ½ oz. Scotch
- ½ oz. Sweet Vermouth
- ½ oz. Lemon Juice
- 1 Egg
- Ice

Directions: In a shaker half-filled with ice cubes, combine all of the ingredients. Shake well. Strain into an old-fashioned glass half-filled with ice cubes.

JOCOSE JULEP

- 2 ½ oz. Bourbon
- ½ oz. Green Crème de Menthe
- 1 oz. Lime Juice
- 1 tsp. Sugar
- 5 Chopped Mint Leaves
- Carbonated Water
- Ice

Directions: Blend all ingredients except carbonated water in an electric blender at a low speed for a short length of time. Pour into a Collins glass over ice cubes. Fill with carbonated water and serve.

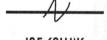

JOE COLLINS

- 1 oz. Scotch
- 2 oz. Sweet and Sour
- Cola
- 1 Cherry
- Ice

Directions: Pour Scotch and sweet and sour into a Collins glass over ice cubes and stir well. Fill with cola and stir lightly. Top with the cherry and serve.

JOHN COLLINS

- 2 oz. Bourbon
- 1 oz. Lemon Juice
- 1 tsp. Superfine Sugar
- 3 oz. Club Soda
- 1 Maraschino Cherry
- 1 Orange Slice
- Ice

Directions: In a shaker half-filled with ice cubes, combine the bourbon, lemon juice, and sugar. Shake well. Strain into a Collins glass almost filled with ice cubes. Add the club soda. Stir and garnish with the cherry and the orange slice.

JOHNNIE COCKTAIL

- ½ oz. Sloe Gin
- ¾ oz. Triple Sec
- 1 tsp. Anisette
- Ice

Directions: Shake all ingredients with ice, strain into a cocktail glass, and serve.

JOLLY RANCHER

- 1 ½ oz. Melon Liqueur
- ½ oz. Blueberry Schnapps
- Sweet and Sour
- ½ oz. Grenadine
- 1 Cherry
- Ice

Directions: Shake melon liqueur and schnapps with ice and strain into an old-fashioned glass over ice cubes. Fill with sweet and sour, add grenadine for color, and stir. Add cherry on top and serve.

JOLLY ROGER

- 1 oz. Rum
- 1 oz. Drambuie
- ½ oz. Lime Juice
- Dash Scotch
- Soda Water
- Ice

Directions: Fill a serving glass with ice and add ingredients. Shake. Fill with soda water.

JOLLY ROGER 2

- 1 oz. Dark Rum
- 1 oz. Banana Liqueur
- 2 oz. Lemon Juice
- Ice

Directions: Fill a short glass with ice and add ingredients. Shake.

JONESEY

- 2 oz. Dark Rum
- ½ oz. Dark Crème de Cacao
- Ice

Directions: In a mixing glass half-filled with ice cubes, combine the rum and crème de cacao. Stir well. Strain into a cocktail glass.

JOSÉ WALLBANGER

- 1 ½ oz. Tequila
- ½ oz. Galliano
- Orange Juice
- Ice

Directions: Fill a tall glass with ice and add ingredients. Fill with orange juice. Top with Galliano.

JOULOUVILLE

- 1 oz. Gin
- ½ oz. Apple Brandy
- 1 ½ tsp. Sweet Vermouth
- 1 tbs. Lemon Juice
- 2 dashes Grenadine
- Ice

Directions: Shake ingredients with ice, strain in cocktail glass.

JOURNALIST COCKTAIL

- 1 ½ tsp. Sweet Vermouth
- 1 ½ tsp. Dry Vermouth
- 1 ½ oz. Gin
- ½ tsp. Triple Sec
- ½ tsp. Lemon Juice
- Dash Bitters
- Ice

Directions: Shake ingredients with ice, strain in cocktail glass.

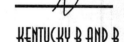

JOY-TO-THE-WORLD

- 1 ½ oz. Anejo Rum
- ½ oz. Bourbon
- ½ oz. Dark Crème de Cacao
- Ice

Directions: In a mixing glass half-filled with ice cubes, combine all of the ingredients. Stir well. Strain into cocktail glass.

JUDGETTE COCKTAIL

- ¾ oz. Dry Vermouth
- ¾ oz. Peach Brandy
- ¾ oz. Gin
- Juice of ¼ Lime
- 1 Cherry
- Ice

Directions: Shake ingredients except cherry with ice and strain in cocktail glass. Top with the cherry.

JUICY FRUIT

- 1 oz. Vodka
- ½ oz. Peach Schnapps
- ½ oz. Melon Liqueur
- Pineapple Juice
- Ice

Directions: Fill tall glass with ice and add ingredients. Fill with pineapple juice. Shake.

JUMP ME

- 2 oz. Dark Rum
- 3 dashes Bitters
- Pineapple Juice
- 2 Lime Wedges
- Ice

Directions: Fill tall glass with ice and add ingredients. Fill with pineapple juice. Squeeze two lime wedges over the drink. Stir.

KAMIKAZE

- 1 oz. Vodka
- 1 oz. Triple Sec
- 1 oz. Lime Juice
- Ice

Directions: Shake all ingredients with ice, strain into an old-fashioned glass over ice cubes, and serve.

KARSK

- 1 part coffee
- 2 parts 96 Percent Alcohol
- Copper Coin

Directions: Put the coin in a coffee-cup and fill up with coffee until the coin is no longer visible. Then add alcohol until the coin is visible again.

KENTUCKY B AND B

- 2 oz. Bourbon
- ½ oz. Benedictine

Directions: Pour the bourbon and Benedictine into a brandy snifter.

KENTUCKY COLONEL

- 3 oz. Bourbon
- ½ oz. Benedictine
- 1 Lemon Twist
- Ice

Directions: In a shaker half-filled with ice cubes, combine the bourbon and Benedictine. Shake and strain into a cocktail glass. Garnish with the lemon twist.

KEVIN'S SPECIAL BLEND

- **2 ounces Rye Whiskey**
- **1 ½ tsp. Iced Tea mix**
- **12 oz. Water**
- **Ice**

Directions: Put iced tea mix into a glass and fill about half-full with water. Add rye, then fill the remainder of the glass with cold water. Stir. Add ice cubes.

KGB

- **1 ½ oz. Gin**
- **½ oz. Kirsch**
- **2 tsp. Apricot Brandy**
- **½ oz. Lemon Juice**
- **½ tsp. Superfine Sugar**
- **1 Lemon Twist**
- **Ice**

Directions: In a shaker half-filled with ice cubes, combine the gin, Kirsch, apricot brandy, and lemon juice. Shake well. Strain into a highball glass almost filled with ice cubes. Garnish with the lemon twist.

KGB COCKTAIL

- **1 ½ oz. Gin**
- **½ oz. Kummel**
- **¼ tsp. Apricot Brandy**
- **¼ tsp. Lemon Juice**
- **Twist of Lemon Peel**
- **Ice**

Directions: Shake all ingredients except lemon peel with ice and strain into a cocktail glass. Add the twist of lemon peel.

KING COLE COCKTAIL

- **2 oz. Blended Whiskey**
- **1 Orange Slice**
- **1 Pineapple Slice**
- **½ tsp. Powdered Sugar**
- **Ice**

Directions: Muddle orange and pineapple slice and powdered sugar in old-fashioned glass. Add blended whiskey and two ice cubes. Stir well.

KISH WACKER

- **½ oz. Bailey's Irish Cream**
- **½ oz. Brown Crème de Cacao**
- **½ oz. Vodka**
- **¼ oz. Kahlua**
- **Ice**

Directions: Mix ingredients in blender with ice. Add Bailey's to taste.

KISS-IN-THE-DARK

- **¾ oz. Cherry Brandy**
- **¾ oz. Dry Vermouth**
- **¾ oz. Gin**
- **Ice**

Directions: Stir ingredients with ice, strain in cocktail glass.

KLONDIKE COOLER

- **2 oz. Blended Whiskey**
- **Carbonated Water**
- **½ tsp. Powdered Sugar**
- **Twist of Lemon Peel**
- **1 Orange Spiral**
- **Ice**

Directions: Mix powdered sugar and two ounces carbonated water in a Collins glass. Fill glass with ice and add blended whiskey. Fill with carbonated water and stir. Add twist of lemon peel and orange spiral so that the ends dangle over the rim of the glass.

KNICKERBOCKER COCKTAIL

- ¾ oz. Dry Vermouth
- ¼ tsp. Sweet Vermouth
- 1 ½ oz. Gin
- Twist of Lemon Peel
- Ice

Directions: Stir all ingredients except lemon peel with ice and strain into a cocktail glass. Add the twist of lemon peel and serve.

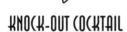

KNOCK-OUT COCKTAIL

- ¾ oz. Dry Vermouth
- ¾ oz. Gin
- ½ oz. Anisette
- 1 tsp. White Crème de Menthe
- 1 Cherry
- Ice

Directions: Stir all ingredients except cherry with ice and strain into a cocktail glass. Top with the cherry and serve.

KOOL-AID

- 1 ¾ oz. Vodka
- 1 ¾ oz. Amaretto
- 1 ¾ oz. Sloe Gin
- 1 ¾ oz. Triple Sec
- Cranberry Juice
- Ice

Directions: Put all ingredients in a Collins glass with ice and shake. Add cranberry juice to taste.

KRAZEE KEITH

- 1 ½ oz. Light Rum
- 2 tsp. Anisette
- ½ oz. Lemon Juice
- 4 oz. Cola
- 2 tsp. Cherry Brandy
- 1 Lemon Wedge
- Ice

Directions: In a shaker half-filled with ice cubes, combine the rum, anisette, cherry brandy, and lemon juice. Shake well. Strain into a highball glass almost filled with ice cubes. Add the cola and stir well. Garnish with the lemon wedge.

KRETCHMA COCKTAIL

- 1 oz. Vodka
- 1 oz. White Crème de Cacao
- Dash Grenadine
- 1 tbs. Lemon Juice
- Ice

Directions: Shake all ingredients with ice, strain into a cocktail glass, and serve.

LA JOLLA

- 2 oz. Brandy
- ½ oz. Crème de Bananes
- 1 tsp. Orange Juice
- ½ oz. Lemon Juice
- Ice

Directions: In shaker half-filled with ice, combine ingredients. Shake. Strain into cocktail glass.

LA STEPHANIQUE

- 1 ½ oz. Gin
- ½ oz. Triple Sec
- ½ oz. Sweet Vermouth
- Dash Bitters

Directions: In shaker half-filled with ice, combine ingredients. Shake. Strain into cocktail glass.

LADIES COCKTAIL

- 1 ¾ oz. Blended Whiskey
- ½ tsp. Anisette
- 2 dashes Bitters
- 1 Pineapple Stick
- Ice

Directions: Stir ingredients except pineapple stick with ice and strain into a cocktail glass. Add the pineapple stick on top.

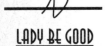

LADY BE GOOD

- 1 ½ oz. Brandy
- ½ oz. White Crème de Menthe
- ½ oz. Sweet Vermouth
- Ice

Directions: Shake ice and all ingredients. Strain into cocktail glass.

LADY LOVE FIZZ

- 2 oz. Gin
- 2 tsp. Light Cream
- 1 tsp. Powdered Sugar
- Juice of ½ Lemon
- 1 Egg White
- Carbonated Water
- Ice

Directions: Shake all ingredients except carbonated water with ice and strain in cocktail glass over two ice cubes. Fill with carbonated water, stir.

LADYFINGER

- 1 oz. Cherry Brandy
- 1 oz. Gin
- ½ oz. Kirschwasser
- Ice

Directions: Shake all ingredients with ice, strain in cocktail glass.

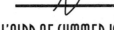

L'AIRD OF SUMMER ISLE

- 1 ½ oz. Scotch
- ½ oz. Pernod
- 3 oz. Pineapple Juice
- Ice

Directions: In a shaker half-filled with ice, combine all of the ingredients. Shake well. Strain in old-fashioned glass almost filled with ice.

LAMB BROTHERS

- 1 ½ oz. Dark Rum
- ½ oz. Crème de Cassis
- 2 oz. Pineapple Juice
- Ice

Directions: In shaker half-filled with ice, combine ingredients. Shake well. Strain into a cocktail glass.

LANDED GENTRY

- 1 ½ oz. Dark Rum
- ½ oz. Tia Maria
- 1 oz. Heavy Cream
- Ice

Directions: In a shaker half-filled with ice, combine all of the ingredients. Shake well. Strain into a cocktail glass.

LASKY COCKTAIL

- ¾ oz. Gin
- ¾ oz. Grape Juice
- ¾ oz. Swedish Punch
- Ice

Directions: Shake all ingredients with ice. Strain into a cocktail glass.

LAWHILL COCKTAIL

- 1 ½ oz. Blended Whiskey
- ¾ oz. Dry Vermouth
- ¼ tsp. Anisette
- ¼ tsp. Maraschino
- Dash Bitters
- Ice

Directions: Stir all ingredients with ice, strain into a cocktail glass, and serve.

LEANING TOWER

- Crushed Ice
- 2 oz. Gin
- 1 tsp. Dry Vermouth
- 2 dashes Orange Bitters

Directions: In a mixing glass half-filled with crushed ice, combine all of the ingredients. Stir well. Strain into a cocktail glass.

LEAP FROG HIGHBALL

- 2 oz. Gin
- Juice of ½ Lemon
- Ginger Ale
- Ice

Directions: Pour gin and lemon juice over ice cubes in a highball glass. Fill with ginger ale, stir, and serve.

LEAP YEAR COCKTAIL

- 1 ¼ oz. Gin
- ½ oz. Orange Gin
- ½ oz. Sweet Vermouth
- ¼ tsp. Lemon Juice
- Ice

Directions: Shake all ingredients with ice, strain into a cocktail glass, and serve.

LEAVE-IT-TO-ME COCKTAIL NO. 2

- 1 ½ oz. Gin
- 1 tsp. Raspberry Syrup
- 1 tsp. Lemon Juice
- ¼ tsp. Maraschino
- Ice

Directions: Stir all ingredients with ice, strain into a cocktail glass, and serve.

LIL NAUE

- 1 oz. Brandy
- ½ oz. Apricot Brandy
- ½ oz. Port
- 1 tsp. Powdered Sugar
- 1 Egg Yolk
- Cinnamon
- Ice

Directions: Shake ingredients except cinnamon with ice and strain in red wine glass. Sprinkle cinnamon on top.

LINSTEAD COCKTAIL

- 1 oz. Blended Whiskey
- 1 oz. Pineapple Juice
- ½ tsp. Sugar
- ¼ tsp. Anisette
- ¼ tsp. Lemon Juice
- Ice

Directions: Shake ice and ingredients. Strain into cocktail glass.

LITTLE PRINCESS COCKTAIL

- 1 ½ oz. Light Rum
- 1 oz. Sweet Vermouth
- Ice

Directions: In mixing glass half-filled with ice, combine ingredients. Stir well. Strain in cocktail glass.

LOCH LOMOND

- 2 oz. Scotch
- ½ oz. Drambuie
- ½ oz. Dry Vermouth
- 1 Lemon Twist
- Ice

Directions: In mixing glass half-filled with ice, combine liquors. Stir. Strain in cocktail glass. Garnish with lemon twist.

LONDON BUCK

- 2 oz. Gin
- ½ tsp. Maraschino
- 2 dashes Orange Bitters
- ½ tsp. Sugar Syrup
- Twist of Lemon Peel
- Ice

Directions: Stir ingredients except lemon peel with ice and strain in highball glass. Add twist of lemon peel.

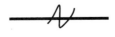

LONDON TOWN

- 1 ½ oz. Gin
- ½ oz. Maraschino Liqueur
- 2 dashes Orange Bitters
- Ice

Directions: In mixing glass half-filled with ice, combine ingredients. Stir well. Strain into cocktail glass.

LONE TREE COCKTAIL

- ¾ oz. Sweet Vermouth
- 1 ½ oz. Gin
- Ice

Directions: Stir ingredients with ice, strain into a cocktail glass.

LONE TREE COOLER

- Carbonated Water
- 2 oz. Gin
- 1 tbs. Dry Vermouth
- ½ tsp. Powdered Sugar
- 1 Orange Spiral
- 1 Twist of Lemon Peel
- Ice

Directions: Stir powdered sugar and two ounces of carbonated water in Collins glass. Fill glass with ice, gin, and vermouth. Stir. Fill with carbonated water and stir again. Add lemon peel and the orange spiral.

LONG ISLAND ICED TEA

- ½ oz. Vodka
- ½ oz. Light Rum
- ½ oz. Gin
- ½ oz. Tequila
- Juice of ½ Lemon
- Splash of Cola
- 1 Lemon Slice
- Ice

Directions: Combine all ingredients except cola and pour over ice in a highball glass. Add the splash of cola for color. Decorate with a lemon slice and serve.

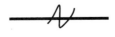

LONG ISLAND SUNSET

- 3 oz. Captain Morgan's Spiced Rum
- 3 oz. Peachtree Schnapps
- 3 oz. Sour Mix
- 3 oz. Cranberry Juice
- 1 Cherry
- 1 Orange Slice
- Ice

Directions: Pour all ingredients into a glass and shake. Add a cherry and an orange slice.

LONG VODKA

- 2 oz. Vodka
- ½ Lime
- 4 dashes Angostura Bitters
- Schweppes Tonic
- 4 Ice Cubes
- 1 Lime Slice

Directions: Shake tall glass with ice and Angostura to coat. Pour in vodka, add lime slice and squeeze juice out of the remainder. Mix with tonic and stir.

LORD AND LADY

- 1 ½ oz. Dark Rum
- ½ oz. Tia Maria
- Ice

Directions: Pour liquor in old-fashioned glass almost filled with ice cubes. Stir well.

LOS ANGELES COCKTAIL

- 1 ½ oz. Blended Whiskey
- ¼ oz. Sweet Vermouth
- Juice of ½ Lemon
- 1 tsp. Powdered Sugar
- 1 Whole Egg
- Ice

Directions: Shake ingredients with ice, strain in rocks glass.

LOVE FOR TOBY

- 1 ½ oz. Light Rum
- ½ oz. Brandy
- ½ oz. Cherry Brandy
- 1 tsp. Lime Juice
- Ice

Directions: In shaker half-filled with ice, mix ingredients. Shake. Strain into cocktail glass.

LOVE JUICE (U)

- 2 oz. Bacardi Light Rum
- 2 ½ oz. Orange Juice
- 2 oz. Apple Juice
- 6 ½ oz. Squirt (or any other citric soda)
- 1 Orange Slice
- Ice

Directions: Mix ingredients. Serve on the rocks in Collins glass with orange slice.

LUDWIG AND THE GANG

- 1 oz. Anejo Rum
- 1 oz. Vodka
- ½ oz. Amaretto
- ½ oz. Southern Comfort
- Dash Bitters
- Ice

Directions: In mixing glass half-filled with ice, Mix ingredients. Stir. Strain into old-fashioned glass filled with crushed ice.

LUGGER

- 1 oz. Apple Brandy
- 1 oz. Brandy
- Dash Apricot Brandy
- Ice

Directions: Stir ingredients with ice, strain into cocktail glass.

MA BONNIE WEE HEN

- 1 ½ oz. Scotch
- ½ oz. Cream Sherry
- ½ oz. Orange Juice
- ½ oz. Lemon Juice
- 1 tsp. Grenadine
- Ice

Directions: In shaker half-filled with ice, combine ingredients. Shake well. Strain in cocktail glass.

MACBETH'S DREAM

- 2 oz. Scotch
- 1 tsp. White Curacao
- 1 tsp. Amaretto
- 2 dashes Orange Bitters
- ½ oz. Lemon Juice
- ½ tsp. Superfine Sugar
- Ice

Directions: In a shaker half-filled with ice cubes, combine all of the ingredients. Shake well. Strain into a cocktail glass.

MADRAS

- 1 ½ oz. Vodka
- 4 oz. Cranberry Juice
- 1 oz. Orange Juice
- 1 Lime Wedge
- Ice

Directions: Pour ingredients except lime wedge in highball glass over ice. Add the lime wedge.

MAESTRO

- 1 ½ oz. Anejo Rum
- ½ oz. Cream Sherry
- ½ oz. Lime Juice
- 4 oz. Ginger Ale
- 1 Lemon Twist
- Ice

Directions: In a shaker half-filled with ice, combine rum, sherry, and lime juice. Shake well. Strain in Collins glass almost filled with crushed ice. Top with the ginger ale. Garnish with the lemon twist.

MAI TAI

- 1 oz. Light Rum
- ½ oz. Orgeat Syrup
- ½ oz. Triple Sec
- 1 ½ oz. Sweet and Sour
- 1 Cherry
- Ice

Directions: Shake all ingredients except cherry with ice and strain into a Collins glass over several ice cubes. Top with the cherry and serve.

MAIDEN-NO-MORE

- 1 ½ oz. Gin
- ½ oz. Triple Sec
- 1 tsp. Brandy
- 1 oz. Lemon Juice
- Ice

Directions: In a shaker half-filled with ice cubes, combine all of the ingredients. Shake well. Strain into a cocktail glass.

MAIDEN'S BLUSH

- 1 ½ oz. Gin
- ½ oz. Triple Sec
- 1 tsp. Cherry Brandy
- 1 oz. Lemon Juice
- 1 Maraschino Cherry
- Ice

Directions: In a shaker half-filled with ice, combine the gin, Triple Sec, cherry brandy, and lemon juice. Shake well. Strain into a cocktail glass. Garnish with the cherry.

MAIDEN'S PRAYER

- 1 ½ oz. Gin
- ½ oz. Triple Sec
- 1 oz. Lemon Juice
- Ice

Directions: Shake all ingredients with ice, strain into a cocktail glass, and serve.

MALIBU BAY BREEZE

- 1 ½ oz. Malibu Rum
- 2 oz. Cranberry Juice
- 2 oz. Pineapple Juice
- Ice

Directions: Mix ingredients and serve over ice in a highball glass.

MALIBU WAVE

- 1 oz. Tequila
- ½ oz. Triple Sec
- ⅛ oz. Blue Curacao
- 1 ½ oz. Sweet and Sour
- ½ Lime Slice
- Ice

Directions: Shake all ingredients except lime slice with ice and strain into a chilled cocktail glass. Add the lime slice and serve.

MALLELIEU

- 1 ½ oz. Light Rum
- ½ oz. Grand Marnier
- 2 oz. Orange Juice
- Ice

Directions: Pour the rum, Grand Marnier, and orange juice into an old-fashioned glass almost filled with ice cubes. Stir well.

MAMIE GILROY

- 2 oz. Scotch
- Juice of ½ Lime
- Ginger Ale
- Ice

Directions: Pour all ingredients into a Collins glass over ice cubes, stir, and serve.

MAN OF THE MOMENT

- 1 ½ oz. Scotch
- 1 oz. Grand Marnier
- 1 oz. Lemon Juice
- 1 tsp. Grenadine
- Ice

Directions: In a shaker half-filled with ice cubes, combine all of the ingredients. Shake well. Strain into a cocktail glass.

MANDEVILLE

- 1 oz. Light Rum
- 1 oz. Dark Rum
- 1 tsp. Anisette
- ½ oz. Lemon Juice
- ½ tsp. Grenadine
- 1 oz. Cola
- Ice

Directions: In a shaker half-filled with ice cubes, combine the light rum, dark rum, anisette, lemon juice, and grenadine. Shake well. Strain into an old-fashioned glass almost filled with ice cubes. Top with the cola. Stir well.

MANHASSET

- 1 ½ oz. Blended Whiskey
- 1 ½ tsp. Sweet Vermouth
- 1 ½ tsp. Dry Vermouth
- 1 tbs. Lemon Juice
- Ice

Directions: Shake all ingredients with ice, strain into a cocktail glass, and serve.

MANHATTAN (DRY)

- 1 ½ oz. Blended Whiskey
- ¾ oz. Dry Vermouth
- 1 Olive
- Ice

Directions: Stir ingredients with ice and strain in cocktail glass. Add olive and serve.

MANILA FIZZ

- 2 oz. Gin
- 2 oz. Root Beer
- Juice of ½ Lemon
- 1 Whole Egg
- 1 tsp. Powdered Sugar
- Ice

Directions: Shake all ingredients with ice, strain into a highball glass over two ice cubes, and serve.

MARDEE MINE

- 1 ½ oz. Dark Rum
- ½ oz. Sweet Vermouth
- 1 Lemon Twist
- Ice

Directions: In a mixing glass half-filled with ice, combine ingredients. Stir. Strain in cocktail glass. Garnish with lemon twist.

MARGARET IN THE MARKETPLACE

- 2 oz. Anejo Rum
- 2 tsp. Lime Juice
- 1 tsp. Grenadine
- ½ oz. Light Cream
- Ice

Directions: In a shaker half-filled with ice, mix ingredients. Shake. Strain in cocktail glass.

MARGARITA, ORIGINAL

- 1 ½ oz. Tequila
- ½ oz. Triple Sec
- 1 oz. Lime Juice
- Salt
- Ice

Directions: Rub rim of cocktail glass with lime juice and dip rim in salt. Shake ingredients with ice. Strain into glass.

MARIA'S DELIGHT

- 1 oz. Vodka
- 2 oz. Southern Comfort
- 1 oz. Safari
- ½ oz. Cointreau
- Ginger Ale
- Ice

Directions: Mix ingredients in mixer with ice. Pour in highball glass and fill with ginger ale

MARTINEZ COCKTAIL

- 1 oz. Gin
- 1 oz. Dry Vermouth
- ¼ tsp. Triple Sec
- Dash Orange Bitters
- 1 Cherry
- Ice

Directions: Stir all ingredients except cherry with ice and strain into a cocktail glass. Top with the cherry and serve.

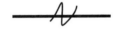

MARY GARDEN COCKTAIL

- 1 ½ oz. Dubonnet
- ¾ oz. Dry Vermouth
- Ice

Directions: Stir ingredients with ice, strain into a cocktail glass, and serve.

MARY PICKFORD COCKTAIL

- 1 ½ oz. Light Rum
- 1 oz. Pineapple Juice
- ½ tsp. Maraschino Liqueur
- ½ tsp. Grenadine
- 1 Maraschino Cherry
- Ice

Directions: In a shaker half-filled with ice cubes, combine the rum, pineapple juice, maraschino liqueur, and grenadine. Shake well. Strain into a cocktail glass. Garnish with the cherry.

MARY'S DREAM

- 2 oz. Light Rum
- ½ oz. Triple Sec
- 4 oz. Orange Juice
- 2 dashes Orange Bitters
- 1 Orange Slice
- Ice

Directions: Pour the rum, Triple Sec, orange juice, and orange bitters into a highball glass almost filled with ice cubes. Stir well and garnish with the orange slice.

MAX THE SILENT

- 1 oz. Anejo Rum
- ½ oz. Brandy
- ½ oz. Applejack
- 1 tsp. Anisette
- Ice

Directions: In mixing glass half-filled with ice, combine ingredients. Stir well. Strain in cocktail glass.

MAXIM

- 1 ½ oz. Gin
- 1 oz. Dry Vermouth
- Dash White Crème de Cacao
- Ice

Directions: Shake ingredients with ice, strain into cocktail glass.

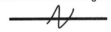

MAY BLOSSOM FIZZ

- 2 oz. Swedish Punch
- 1 tsp. Grenadine
- Juice of ½ Lemon
- Carbonated Water
- Ice

Directions: Shake ice with ingredients except carbonated water and strain in highball glass over two ice cubes. Fill with carbonated water, stir.

MCCLELLAND COCKTAIL

- 1 ½ oz. Sloe Gin
- ¾ oz. Triple Sec
- Dash Orange Bitters
- Ice

Directions: Shake ingredients with ice, strain in cocktail glass.

MCDUFF

- 1 ½ oz. Scotch
- ½ oz. Triple Sec
- 2 dashes Bitters
- 1 Orange Slice
- Ice

Directions: In a mixing glass half-filled with ice, combine Scotch, Triple Sec, and bitters. Stir well. Strain into a cocktail glass. Garnish with the orange slice.

MELON COCKTAIL

- 2 oz. Gin
- ¼ tsp. Lemon Juice
- ¼ tsp. Maraschino
- 1 Cherry
- Ice

Directions: Shake ice and ingredients except cherry. Strain into a cocktail glass. Add the cherry on top and serve.

MENAGE A TROIS

- 1 oz. Dark Rum
- 1 oz. Triple Sec
- 1 oz. Light Cream
- Ice

Directions: In a shaker half-filled with ice, combine ingredients. Shake well. Strain in cocktail glass.

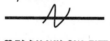

MERRY WIDOW COCKTAIL

- 1 ¼ oz. Cherry Brandy
- 1 ¼ oz. Maraschino
- 1 Cherry
- Ice

Directions: Stir ingredients with ice and strain in cocktail glass. Add the cherry. Serve.

MERRY WIDOW FIZZ

- 1 ½ oz. Sloe Gin
- Juice of ½ Orange
- Juice of ½ Lemon
- 1 Egg White
- 1 tsp. Powdered Sugar
- Carbonated Water
- Ice

Directions: Shake all ingredients except carbonated water with ice and strain in highball glass over two ice cubes. Fill with carbonated water, stir.

METROPOLITAN

- Crushed Ice
- 1 tsp. Superfine Sugar
- 2 oz. Brandy
- ½ oz. Sweet Vermouth
- Dash Bitters

Directions: In a shaker half-filled with crushed ice, mix ingredients. Shake well. Strain in cocktail glass.

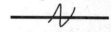

METROPOLITAN COCKTAIL

- 1 ¼ oz. Sweet Vermouth
- 1 ¼ oz. Brandy
- ½ tsp. Sugar Syrup
- Dash Bitters
- Ice

Directions: Stir all ingredients with ice, strain into a cocktail glass, and serve.

MEXICOLA

- 2 oz. Tequila
- Juice of ½ Lime
- Cola
- Ice

Directions: Pour tequila and lime juice over ice cubes in a Collins glass. Fill with cola, stir, and serve.

MIAMI BEACH COCKTAIL

- ¾ oz. Dry Vermouth
- ¾ oz. Scotch
- ¾ oz. Grapefruit Juice
- Ice

Directions: Stir ingredients with ice, strain in cocktail glass.

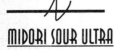

MIDNIGHT COWBOY

- 2 oz. Bourbon
- 1 oz. Dark Rum
- ½ oz. Heavy Cream
- Ice

Directions: In shaker half-filled with ice, mix ingredients. Shake. Strain in cocktail glass.

MIDORI SOUR ULTRA

- 2 oz. Midor Liqueur
- ¾ oz. Lemon Juice
- 1 tsp. Superfine Sugar
- 2 Maraschino Cherries
- 1 Lemon Wedge
- 1 tbs. Cherry Juice out
- Ice

Directions: Mix ingredients in shaker with cracked ice. Fill Champagne flute three-quarters full of ice. Pour cherry juice in glass before mixed ingredients. Garnish with cherries and lemon.

MIDORI SUNRISE

- 2 oz. Midori
- Orange Juice
- Splash Grenadine Syrup
- Ice

Directions: Pour Midori over ice and fill with orange juice in rocks glass. Add a splash of grenadine syrup.

MIKADO

- 1 ½ oz. Brandy
- ½ oz. Triple Sec
- 1 tsp. Crème de Noyaux
- 1 tsp. Grenadine
- Dash Bitters
- Ice

Directions: In old-fashioned glass almost filled with ice, combine ingredients. Stir well.

MIKADO COCKTAIL

- 1 oz. Brandy
- Dash Triple Sec
- Dash Grenadine
- Dash Crème de Noyaux
- Dash Bitters
- Ice

Directions: Pour ingredients over ice in old-fashioned glass, stir.

MILLION-DOLLAR COCKTAIL

- 1 ½ oz. Gin
- ¾ oz. Sweet Vermouth
- 2 tsp. Pineapple Juice
- 1 tsp. Grenadine
- 1 Egg White
- Ice

Directions: Shake all ingredients with ice, strain into a cocktail glass, and serve.

MIMOSA

- Chilled Champagne
- 2 oz. Orange Juice
- Ice

Directions: Pour orange juice in Collins glass over ice. Fill with chilled Champagne, stir very gently, and serve.

MIND ERASER

- 2 oz. Vodka
- 2 oz. Kahlua
- 2 oz. Tonic Water

Directions: In a small glass, pour vodka, then the Kahlua, and then the tonic water, varying the amount of alcohol to the size of the glass. Do not shake. Place glass on a table and drink from a straw.

MINT COLLINS

- 2 oz. Mint-Flavored Gin
- Juice of ½ Lemon
- Carbonated Water
- 1 Orange Slice Garnish
- 1 Lemon Slice Garnish
- 1 Cherry Garnish
- Ice

Directions: Shake gin and lemon juice with ice. Strain into Collins glass over ice. Fill with carbonated water. Stir. Add garnishes. Serve with a straw.

MINT GIN COCKTAIL

- 1 oz. Mint-Flavored Gin
- 1 oz. White Port
- 1 ½ tsp. Dry Vermouth

Directions: Stir all ingredients with ice, strain in cocktail glass.

MINT JULEP #1

- 4 Fresh Mint Leaves
- 2 ½ oz. Bourbon
- 1 tsp. Powdered Sugar
- 2 tsp. Water
- Ice

Directions: Muddle ingredients except bourbon in Collins glass. Fill glass with shaved ice and add bourbon. Top with more ice and garnish with mint sprig.

MINT JULEP #2

- 6 Fresh Mint Sprigs
- 1 tsp. Superfine Sugar
- Water
- Crushed Ice
- 3 oz. Bourbon

Directions: Lightly muddle four mint sprigs with sugar and a few drops of water in the bottom of the glass. Almost fill the glass with crushed ice. Add the bourbon and some short straws. Garnish with the remaining two mint sprigs.

MISS BELLE

- 1 ½ oz. Dark Rum
- ½ oz. Grand Marnier
- 2 tsp. Dark Crème de Cacao
- Ice

Directions: In a mixing glass half-filled with ice cubes, combine all of the ingredients. Stir well. Strain into a cocktail glass.

MISTER CHRISTIAN

- 1 ½ oz. Light Rum
- ½ oz. Brandy
- 1 oz. Orange Juice
- ½ oz. Lemon Juice
- ½ oz. Lime Juice
- 1 tsp. Grenadine
- Ice

Directions: In a shaker half-filled with ice, mix ingredients. Shake. Strain into cocktail glass.

MISTER WU

- 1 oz. Vodka
- 2 oz. Bourbon Whiskey
- 3 oz. Lemon-lime Soda
- Dash Orange juice
- Ice

Directions: Pour vodka and on ice into a regular glass. Add three ounces of lemon-lime soda and a dash of orange juice.

MITHERING BASTARD

- 1 ½ oz. Scotch
- ½ oz. Triple Sec
- 1 oz. Orange Juice
- Ice

Directions: In shaker half-filled with ice, combine ingredients. Shake. Strain in old-fashioned glass almost filled with ice cubes.

MOCHA MINT

- ¾ oz. Coffee Brandy
- ¾ oz. White Crème de Menthe
- ¾ oz. White Crème de Cacao
- Ice

Directions: Shake all ingredients with ice, strain into a cocktail glass, and serve.

MODERN COCKTAIL

- 1 ½ oz. Scotch
- 1 tsp. Dark Rum
- ½ tsp. Pernod
- ½ tsp. Lemon Juice
- 2 dashes Orange Bitters
- Ice

Directions: In a shaker half-filled with ice cubes, combine all of the ingredients. Shake well. Strain into cocktail glass.

MOGUL MASHER

- 1 pkg. Instant Hot Chocolate Mix
- 1 oz. Bacardi 151 Rum
- 1 oz. Rumpleminze
- 8 oz. Hot Water
- 1 dollop Whipped cream

Directions: Make hot chocolate according to instructions in a 12 ounce glass and add liquors. Top with whipped cream.

MONA LISA

- 2 oz. Absolut Vodka
- Lemon Soda

Directions: Stir ingredients and pour into a highball glass.

MONKEY GLAND COCKTAIL

- 2 oz. Gin
- 1 tsp. Benedictine
- ½ oz. Orange Juice
- 1 tsp. Grenadine
- Ice

Directions: In a shaker half-filled with ice cubes, combine all of the ingredients. Shake well. Strain into a cocktail glass.

MONKEY WRENCH

- 1 ½ oz. Light Rum
- 3 oz. Grapefruit Juice
- Dash Bitters
- Ice

Directions: Pour all of the ingredients into an old-fashioned glass almost filled with ice cubes. Stir well.

MONTANA

- 1 ½ oz. Brandy
- ½ oz. Dry Vermouth
- 1 oz. Port
- Ice

Directions: Stir all ingredients in an old-fashioned glass over ice cubes and serve.

MONTEZUMA

- 1 ½ oz. Tequila
- 1 oz. Madeira
- 1 Egg Yolk
- ½ cup of Crushed Ice

Directions: Blend all ingredients with ice in an electric blender at a low speed for a short length of time. Pour into a Champagne flute and serve.

MONTMARTRE COCKTAIL

- 1 ¼ oz. Dry Gin
- ½ oz. Sweet Vermouth
- ½ oz. Triple Sec
- 1 Cherry
- Ice

Directions: Stir all ingredients except cherry with ice and strain into a cocktail glass. Top with the cherry and serve.

MONTREAL CLUB BOUNCER

- 1 ½ oz. Gin
- ½ oz. Anisette
- Ice

Directions: Pour ingredients into an old-fashioned glass over ice cubes, stir, and serve.

MONTREAL GIN SOUR

- 1 oz. Gin
- 1 oz. Lemon Juice
- 1 tsp. Powdered Sugar
- ½ Egg White
- 1 Lemon Slice
- Ice

Directions: Shake all ingredients except lemon slice with ice and strain into a whiskey sour glass. Add the lemon slice and serve.

MOON QUAKE SHAKE

- 1 oz. Coffee Brandy
- 1 ½ oz. Dark Rum
- 1 tbs. Lemon Juice
- Ice

Directions: Shake all ingredients with ice, strain into a cocktail glass, and serve.

MOONLIGHT

- 2 oz. Apple Brandy
- Juice of 1 Lemon
- 1 tsp. Powdered Sugar
- Ice

Directions: Shake all ingredients with ice, strain into an old-fashioned glass over ice.

MORGAN'S MOUNTAIN

- 1 ½ oz. Light Rum
- ½ oz. White Crème de Cacao
- 1 oz. Heavy Cream
- 1 tsp. Kahlua
- Ice

Directions: In a shaker half-filled with ice, combine rum, crème de cacao, and cream. Shake well. Strain into cocktail glass. Drop Kahlua into center of drink.

MORNING GLORY FIZZ

- 2 oz. Scotch
- ½ tsp. Anisette
- Juice of 1 Lemon
- 1 tsp. Powdered Sugar
- 1 Egg White
- Carbonated Water
- Ice

Directions: Shake ice and ingredients except carbonated water and strain into highball glass over two ice cubes. Fill with carbonated water. Stir.

MORRO

- 1 oz. Gin
- ½ oz. Dark Rum
- 1 tbs. Pineapple Juice
- 1 tbs. Lime Juice
- ½ tsp. Powdered Sugar
- Ice

Directions: Rub rim of old-fashioned glass with lime juice. Dip rim in powdered sugar. Shake ingredients with ice, strain into the sugar-rimmed glass over ice.

MOSCOW MULE

- 2 oz. Vodka
- 2 oz. Lime Juice
- 8 oz. Ginger Beer
- Ice

Directions: Mix all ingredients in a Collins glass with ice.

MOSTLY MAL

- 1 ½ oz. Anejo Rum
- ½ oz. Dry Vermouth
- ½ oz. Triple Sec
- ½ tsp. Grenadine
- 1 Maraschino Cherry
- Ice

Directions: In a shaker half-filled with ice, combine rum, vermouth, Triple Sec, and grenadine. Shake well. Strain into cocktail glass. Garnish with cherry.

MOTOR OIL

- 1 oz. Jaegermeister
- ½ oz. Peppermint Schnapps
- ½ oz. Goldschlager
- ½ oz. Malibu Rum

Directions: Pour Jaegermeister into a triple shot glass. Add schnapps then Goldshlager. Top with Malibu rum.

MOUNTAIN COCKTAIL

- 1 ½ oz. Blended Whiskey
- ¼ tsp. Dry Vermouth
- ¼ tsp. Sweet Vermouth
- ¼ tsp. Lemon Juice
- 1 Egg White
- Ice

Directions: Shake all ingredients with ice, strain into a cocktail glass.

MOZART

- 1 ½ oz. Anejo Rum
- ½ oz. Sweet Vermouth
- 1 tsp. Triple Sec
- 2 dashes Orange Bitters
- 1 Lemon Twist
- Ice

Directions: In a mixing glass half-filled with ice, combine rum, vermouth, Triple Sec, and orange bitters. Stir well. Strain into cocktail glass and garnish with lemon twist.

MUDSLIDE

- 2 oz. Vodka
- 2 oz. Kahlua
- 2 oz. Bailey's Irish Cream
- Cracked Ice

Directions: Mix ingredients with ice in a shaker. Serve in a chilled cocktail glass.

MUMBO JUMBO

- 1 ½ oz. Dark Rum
- ½ oz. Applejack
- ½ oz. Lemon Juice
- ½ tsp. Superfine Sugar
- $\frac{1}{8}$ tsp. Ground Cinnamon
- $\frac{1}{8}$ tsp. Grated Nutmeg
- Ice

Directions: In a shaker half-filled with ice cubes, combine all of the ingredients. Shake well. Strain into an old-fashioned glass almost filled with ice.

MUMSICLE

- 1 ½ oz. Dark Rum
- ½ oz. Bourbon
- Dash Bitters
- 1 Maraschino Cherry
- Ice

Directions: In mixing glass half-filled with ice, combine ingredients. Stir well. Strain into cocktail glass. Garnish with cherry.

MUTINY

- 1 ½ oz. Dark Rum
- 2 dashes Bitters
- ½ oz. Dubonnet Rouge
- 1 Maraschino Cherry
- Ice

Directions: In a mixing glass half-filled with ice, combine ingredients. Stir well. Strain into a cocktail glass and garnish with cherry.

NAPOLEON

- 2 oz. Gin
- ½ tsp. Curacao
- ½ tsp. Dubonnet
- Ice

Directions: Stir all ingredients with ice, strain into a cocktail glass, and serve.

NARRAGANSETT

- 2 oz. Bourbon
- 1 oz. Sweet Vermouth
- ½ tsp. Anisette
- 1 Lemon Twist
- Ice

Directions: In an old-fashioned glass almost filled with ice, combine ingredients. Stir well and garnish with lemon twist.

NATIONAL AQUARIUM

- ½ oz. Rum
- ½ oz. Vodka
- ½ oz. Gin
- ½ oz. Blue Curacao
- 2 oz. Sour Mix
- Splash Lemon Lime Soda
- Ice

Directions: Pour ingredients in shaker of ice. Shake. Serve on the rocks.

NETHERLAND

- 1 oz. Triple Sec
- 1 oz. Brandy
- Dash Bitters
- Ice

Directions: Pour ingredients in old-fashioned glass over ice. Stir.

NEVADA COCKTAIL

- 1 ½ oz. Light Rum
- 1 ½ oz. Grapefruit Juice
- Dash Bitters
- 1 oz. Lime Juice
- 2 tsp. Superfine Sugar
- Ice

Directions: In a shaker half-filled with ice, combine ingredients. Shake well. Strain into a cocktail glass.

NEVINS

- 1 ½ oz. Bourbon
- 1 ½ tsp. Apricot Brandy
- 1 tbs. Grapefruit Juice
- 1 ½ tsp. Lemon Juice
- Dash Bitters
- Ice

Directions: Shake ingredients with ice, strain in cocktail glass.

NEW ORLEANS BUCK

- 1 ½ oz. Light Rum
- 1 oz. Orange Juice
- ½ oz. Lemon Juice
- Ginger Ale
- Ice

Directions: Shake all ingredients except ginger ale with ice and strain into a Collins glass over ice cubes. Fill with ginger ale. Stir.

NEW YORK LEMONADE

- 2 oz. Absolut Citron
- 1 oz. Grand Marnier
- 2 oz. Sweetened Lemon Juice
- 1 oz. Club Soda
- Sugar

Directions: Serve in a chilled cocktail glass. Lemon and sugar the rim. Stir and strain.

NEW YORK SOUR

- 2 oz. Blended Whiskey
- Juice of ½ Lemon
- 1 tsp. Sugar
- Claret
- ½ Lemon Slice
- 1 Cherry
- Ice

Directions: Shake blended whiskey, lemon juice, and powdered sugar with ice and strain into a whiskey sour glass. Float claret on top. Decorate with the half-slice of lemon and the cherry and serve.

NIGHTMARE

- 1 ½ oz. Gin
- ½ oz. Cherry Brandy
- ½ oz. Madeira
- 1 tsp. Orange Juice
- Ice

Directions: Shake all ingredients with ice, strain into a cocktail glass, and serve.

NORTH POLE COCKTAIL

- 1 oz. Gin
- ½ oz. Maraschino
- ½ oz. Lemon Juice
- 1 Egg White
- Whipped Cream
- Ice

Directions: Shake all ingredients except whipped cream with ice and strain into a cocktail glass. Top with whipped cream and serve.

NUTTY RUSSIAN

- 1 oz. Vodka
- 1 oz. Frangelico
- 1 oz. Coffee Liqueur
- Ice

Directions: Serve well-mixed over ice in a highball glass.

OATMEAL COOKIE

- 1 ¾ oz. Goldschlager
- 1 ¾ oz. Butterscotch Schnapps
- 1 ¾ oz. Bailey's
- Ice

Directions: Mix ice and ingredients. Shake. Serve in shot glass.

OAXACA JIM

- 2 oz. Gin
- 1 oz. Orange Juice
- 1 oz. Grapefruit Juice
- 2 dashes Bitters
- 1 Lemon Twist
- 1 Maraschino Cherry
- Ice

Directions: In a shaker half-filled with ice, mix ingredients. Shake. Strain in old-fashioned glass almost filled with ice cubes. Garnish with lemon twist and cherry.

OLD PAL COCKTAIL

- ½ oz. Sweet Vermouth
- 1 ¼ oz. Blended Whiskey
- ½ oz. Grenadine
- Ice

Directions: Stir all ingredients with ice, strain into a cocktail glass, and serve.

OLD-FASHIONED HOT BUTTERED RUM

- 1 cup of Sugar
- 1 cup of Firmly Packed Brown Sugar
- 1 cup of Butter
- 2 cups of Vanilla Ice Cream
- Rum
- Boiling water
- Nutmeg

Directions: In a two quart saucepan, combine sugar, brown sugar, and butter. Cook over low heat, stirring occasionally, until butter is melted, about six to eight minutes. In a large mixing bowl, combine the cooked mixture with ice cream. Beat at medium speed, scraping bowl often until smooth, about one to two minutes. Store refrigerated up to two weeks or in freezer up to one month. For each serving, fill mug with one-fourth cup mixture, one ounce rum and three-fourths cup boiling water. Sprinkle with nutmeg.

OLYMPIA

- 2 ½ oz. Dark Rum
- ½ oz. Cherry Brandy
- ½ oz. Lime Juice
- Ice

Directions: In a shaker half-filled with ice, combine ingredients. Shake well. Strain into a cocktail glass.

ONCE UPON A TIME

- Crushed Ice
- 1 ½ oz. Gin
- ½ oz. Apricot Brandy
- ½ oz. Lillet

Directions: In a mixing glass half-filled with crushed ice, combine all of the ingredients. Stir well. Strain into a cocktail glass.

OPAL COCKTAIL

- 1 ½ oz. Gin
- ½ oz. Triple Sec
- 1 oz. Orange Juice
- 2 dashes Orange Bitters
- Ice

Directions: In a shaker half-filled with ice cubes, combine all of the ingredients. Shake well. Strain into a cocktail glass.

OPENING COCKTAIL

- 1 ½ oz. Blended Whiskey
- ½ oz. Sweet Vermouth
- ½ oz. Grenadine
- Ice

Directions: Stir all ingredients with ice, strain into a cocktail glass, and serve.

OPERA COCKTAIL

- ½ oz. Dubonnet
- 1 ½ oz. Gin
- 1 tbs. Maraschino
- Ice

Directions: Stir all ingredients with ice, strain into a cocktail glass, and serve.

ORANGE BLOSSOM

- 2 oz. Gin
- 1 oz. Orange Juice
- 1 tsp. Superfine Sugar
- 1 Orange Slice
- Ice

Directions: In a shaker half-filled with ice, combine gin, orange juice, and sugar. Shake well. Strain in cocktail glass. Garnish with orange slice.

ORANGE BUCK

- 1 ½ oz. Gin
- 1 oz. Orange Juice
- 1 tbs. Lime Juice
- Ginger Ale
- Ice

Directions: Shake gin, orange juice, and lime juice with ice and strain into a highball glass over ice cubes. Fill with ginger ale, stir, and serve.

ORANGE OASIS

- ½ oz. Cherry Brandy
- 1 ½ oz. Gin
- 4 oz. Orange Juice
- Ginger Ale
- Ice

Directions: Shake brandy, gin, and orange juice with ice and strain into a highball glass over ice cubes. Fill with ginger ale, stir, and serve.

ORGASM

- ½ oz. Crème de Cacao
- ½ oz. Amaretto
- ½ oz. Triple Sec
- ½ oz. Vodka
- 1 oz. Light Cream
- Ice

Directions: Shake ice with ingredients, strain in chilled cocktail glass.

ORIENTAL COCKTAIL

- 1 oz. Blended Whiskey
- ½ oz. Sweet Vermouth
- ½ oz. Triple Sec
- Juice of ½ Lime
- Ice

Directions: Shake ingredients with ice, strain in cocktail glass.

ORIGINAL SINGAPORE SLING

- 1 oz. Gin
- 1 oz. Benedictine
- 1 oz. Cherry Brandy
- 4 oz. Club Soda
- Ice

Directions: In mixing glass half-filled with ice, combine ingredients except club soda. Stir. Strain in Collins glass filled with ice. Top with club soda and stir well.

ORIGINAL SINGAPORE SLING 2

- 2 oz. Gin
- 1 oz. Cherry Brandy
- 1 oz. Lime Juice
- ¼ tsp. Benedictine
- ¼ tsp. Brandy
- Ice

Directions: In shaker half-filled with ice, combine gin, cherry brandy, and lime juice. Shake well. Strain into a Collins glass almost filled with ice cubes. Drop the Benedictine and brandy into the center of the drink.

OUTRIGGER

- 1 oz. Peach Brandy
- 1 oz. Lime Vodka
- 1 oz. Pineapple Juice
- Ice

Directions: Shake all ingredients with ice, strain into an old-fashioned glass over.

OWEN MOORE

- 1 ½ oz. Light Rum
- ½ oz. White Crème de Cacao
- 1 oz. Heavy Cream
- 1 tsp. Blue Curacao
- Ice

Directions: In a shaker half-filled with ice cubes, combine the rum, crème de cacao, and heavy cream. Shake well. Strain into a cocktail glass. Drop the curacao into the center of the drink.

OWEN'S GRANDMOTHER'S REVENGE

- 12 oz. Whiskey
- 12 oz. Beer
- 12 oz. Frozen Lemonade Concentrate
- 1 cup of Crushed Ice

Directions: Add ingredients and mix in a blender.

P.T.O.

- 1 ½ oz. Dark Rum
- ½ oz. Vodka
- ½ oz. Triple Sec
- 2 oz. Orange Juice
- 1 Orange Slice
- Ice

Directions: Pour ingredients in highball glass filled with ice. Stir and garnish with orange slice.

PAISLEY MARTINI

- 2 oz. Gin
- 1 tsp. Scotch
- ½ oz. Dry Vermouth
- Twist of Lemon Peel
- Ice

Directions: Stir all ingredients except lemon peel over ice in an old-fashioned glass. Add the twist of lemon peel and serve.

PALM BEACH COCKTAIL

- 1 ½ oz. Gin
- 1 ½ tsp. Sweet Vermouth
- 1 ½ tsp. Grapefruit Juice
- Ice

Directions: Shake all ingredients with ice, strain into a cocktail glass, and serve.

PALMER COCKTAIL

- 2 oz. Blended Whiskey
- ½ tsp. Lemon Juice
- Dash Bitters
- Ice

Directions: Stir all ingredients with ice, strain into a cocktail glass, and serve.

PALMETTO COCKTAIL

- 1 ½ oz. Dry Vermouth
- 1 ½ oz. Light Rum
- 2 dashes Bitters
- Ice

Directions: Stir all ingredients with ice, strain into a cocktail glass, and serve.

PANTHER

- 1 ½ oz. Tequila
- ½ oz. Sweet and Sour
- Ice

Directions: Pour ingredients into an old-fashioned glass over several ice cubes. Stir well and serve.

PAPAYA SLING

- 1 ½ oz. Gin
- Juice of 1 Lime
- 1 tbs. Papaya Syrup
- Dash Bitters
- Carbonated Water
- 1 Pineapple Stick
- Ice

Directions: Shake ingredients except carbonated water and pineapple stick with ice and strain into a Collins glass over ice cubes. Fill with carbonated water and stir. Add pineapple stick and serve.

PARISIAN

- 1 oz. Dry Vermouth
- 1 oz. Gin
- ¼ oz. Crème de Cassis
- Ice

Directions: Shake ingredients with ice, strain into cocktail glass.

PARK AVENUE

- ¾ oz. Sweet Vermouth
- 1 ½ oz. Gin
- 1 tbs. Pineapple Juice
- Ice

Directions: Stir ingredients with ice, strain into cocktail glass.

PASSION DAIQUIRI

- 1 ½ oz. Light Rum
- 1 tbs. Passion Fruit Juice
- Juice of 1 Lime
- 1 tsp. Powdered Sugar
- Ice

Directions: Shake all ingredients with ice, strain into a cocktail glass, and serve.

PASSION MIMOSA

- 2 oz. Chilled Passion Fruit Juice
- Chilled Champagne
- 1 Strawberry

Directions: Pour passion fruit juice into a Champagne flute. Fill with chilled Champagne, decorate with the strawberry, and serve.

PAT MCPACKE

- 2 oz. Southern Comfort
- 2 oz. Vodka
- 2 oz. Kool-Aid
- Ice

Directions: Pour in a Collins glass over ice and serve.

PEACH BLOW FIZZ

- 2 oz. Gin
- 1 oz. Light Cream
- Juice of ½ Lemon
- ½ tsp. Powdered Sugar
- ¼ Peach
- Carbonated Water
- Ice

Directions: Shake all ingredients except carbonated water with ice and strain into a highball glass over ice cubes. Fill with carbonated water, stir, and serve.

PEACH BUNNY

- ¾ oz. Peach Brandy
- ¾ oz. White Crème de Cacao
- ¾ oz. Light Cream
- Ice

Directions: Shake all ingredients with ice, strain into a cocktail glass, and serve.

PEACH TREAT

- 1 oz. Peach Brandy
- 2 oz. Orange Juice
- 4 oz. Chilled Champagne
- 1 Peach Slice
- Ice

Directions: Shake brandy and orange juice with ice and strain into a Collins glass over several ice cubes. Top with chilled Champagne, add the peach slice, and serve.

PEGGY COCKTAIL

- 1 ½ oz. Gin
- ¾ oz. Dry Vermouth
- ¼ tsp. Anisette
- ¼ tsp. Dubonnet

Directions: Stir all ingredients with ice, strain into a cocktail glass, and serve.

PELTIKATTO

- 2 oz. Koskenkorva Vodka
- 2 oz. Lemon Juice
- Ice

Directions: Squeeze juice from a fresh lemon. Mix with Koskenkorva over ice in a rocks glass.

PENDENNIS

- ½ tsp. Superfine Sugar
- 2 oz. Bourbon
- 1 Lemon Slice
- Water
- Crushed Ice

Directions: In an old-fashioned glass, dissolve sugar in a few drops of water. Almost fill the glass with crushed ice. Add bourbon. Stir well. Garnish with the lemon slice.

PEPPERMINT STICK

- 1 oz. Peppermint Schnapps
- 1 ½ oz. White Crème de Cacao
- 1 oz. Light Cream
- Ice

Directions: Shake all ingredients with ice, strain into a Champagne flute.

PEREGRINE'S PERIL

- 1 oz. Dark Rum
- 1 tsp. Lime Juice
- ½ oz. Crème de Bananes
- ½ oz. Southern Comfort
- 1 tsp. Lemon Juice
- Ice

Directions: In a shaker half-filled with ice cubes, combine all of the ingredients. Shake well. Strain into cocktail glass.

PERFECT COCKTAIL

- 1 ½ tsp. Sweet Vermouth
- 1 ½ tsp. Dry Vermouth
- 1 ½ oz. Gin
- Dash Bitters
- Ice

Directions: Shake all ingredients with ice, strain into a cocktail glass, and serve.

PERFECT ROB ROY

- 2 ½ oz. Scotch
- 1 tsp. Sweet Vermouth
- 1 tsp. Dry Vermouth
- 1 Maraschino Cherry or Lemon Twist
- Ice

Directions: In a mixing glass half-filled with ice cubes, combine the Scotch, sweet vermouth, and dry vermouth. Stir well. Strain into a cocktail glass. Garnish with the cherry or a lemon twist.

PETER PAN COCKTAIL

- ¾ oz. Dry Vermouth
- ¾ oz. Gin
- ¾ oz. Orange Juice
- 2 dashes Bitters
- Ice

Directions: Shake all ingredients with ice, strain into a cocktail glass, and serve.

PETTICOAT LANE

- 2 oz. Gin
- ½ oz. Sweet Vermouth
- ½ oz. Campari
- 1 Lemon Twist
- Ice

Directions: In mixing glass half-filled with ice, combine ingredients. Stir well. Strain in cocktail glass and garnish with lemon.

PICCADILLY COCKTAIL

- 1 ½ oz. Gin
- ¾ oz. Dry Vermouth
- ¼ tsp. Anisette
- ¼ tsp. Grenadine
- Ice

Directions: Stir ice with ingredients, strain in cocktail glass. Serve.

PINA COLADA

- 3 oz. Light Rum
- 3 tbs. Coconut Milk
- 3 tbs. Crushed Pineapple
- 2 cups of Crushed Ice

Directions: Put ingredients in blender with crushed ice. Blend on high speed for a short time. Strain in Collins glass and serve with a straw.

PINEAPPLE COOLER

- 2 oz. White Wine
- 2 oz. Pineapple Juice
- Carbonated Water
- ½ tsp. Powdered Sugar
- 1 Orange Spiral
- Twist of Lemon Peel
- Ice

Directions: Put white wine, pineapple juice, powdered sugar, and two ounces of carbonated water in a Collins glass and stir. Add ice cubes, fill with carbonated water, and stir again. Add the lemon peel and the orange spiral so the ends dangle over the rim of the glass.

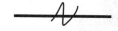

PING-PONG COCKTAIL

- 2 oz. Sloe Gin
- Juice of ¼ Lemon
- 1 Egg White
- Ice

Directions: Shake all ingredients with ice, strain into a cocktail glass, and serve.

PINK CREAM FIZZ

- 2 oz. Gin
- 1 oz. Lemon Juice
- 1 tsp. Superfine Sugar
- 1 oz. Light Cream
- 1 tsp. Grenadine
- 4 oz. Club Soda
- Ice

Directions: In a shaker half-filled with ice cubes, combine the gin, lemon juice, sugar, cream, and grenadine. Shake well. Strain into a Collins glass almost filled with ice. Add the club soda. Stir well.

PINK GIN

- 3 dashes Bitters
- 2 oz. Gin (Plymouth)

Directions: Pour the bitters into a wine glass. Swirl the glass to coat the inside with the bitters and shake out the excess. Pour the gin into the glass. Do not add ice.

PINK LADY

- 1 ½ oz. Gin
- 1 tsp. Grenadine
- 1 tsp. Light Cream
- 1 Egg White
- Ice

Directions: Shake all ingredients with ice, strain into a cocktail glass.

PINK PUSSYCAT

- 2 oz. Gin
- 4 oz. Pineapple Juice
- 1 tsp. Cherry Brandy
- Ice

Directions: In an old-fashioned glass almost filled with ice cubes, combine the gin and pineapple juice. Stir well. Drop the cherry brandy into the center of drink.

PINK SQUIRREL

- 1 oz. Crème de Noyaux
- 1 tbs. White Crème de Cacao
- 1 tbs. Light Cream
- Ice

Directions: Shake all ingredients with ice, strain into a cocktail glass, and serve.

PIPER AT ARMS

- 1 ½ oz. Scotch
- 1 oz. Dry Vermouth
- 1 Lemon Twist
- Ice

Directions: In a mixing glass half-filled with ice cubes, combine the Scotch and vermouth. Stir well. Strain into a cocktail glass. Garnish with the lemon twist.

PIPER AT THE GATES OF DAWN

- 1 ½ oz. Scotch
- 1 oz. Kahlua
- ½ oz. Maraschino Liqueur
- 1 oz. Heavy Cream
- Ice

Directions: In a mixing glass half-filled with ice cubes, combine the Scotch, Kahlua, and maraschino liqueur. Stir well. Strain into an old-fashioned glass almost filled with ice cubes. Pour the cream over the back of a teaspoon so that it floats on top of the drink.

PIRATE'S FLOAT

- ½ oz. Captain Morgan's Spiced Rum
- ½ oz. Rootbeer Schnapps
- Cola
- Ice

Directions: Mix all ingredients in a glass with ice. Serve on the rocks.

PISCO SOUR

- 3 parts Pisco
- 1 ½ parts Lemon Juice
- 1 - 2 tsp. Sugar
- Ice

Directions: Put all the ingredients in a mixer and shake well until ice is melted, then serve very cold in a cocktail glass.

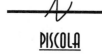

PISCOLA

- 1 ½ oz. Pisco
- 1 oz. Soda of Choice

Directions: Pour pisco over ice cubes in a highball glass. Fill with soda of choice and serve.

PISTACHIO CREAM

- 1 oz. Pistachio Liqueur
- 1 oz. Brandy
- 5 oz. Vanilla Ice Cream

Directions: Combine all ingredients in an electric blender and blend at a low speed for a short length of time. Pour into a chilled Champagne flute.

PLAZA COCKTAIL

- ¾ oz. Dry Vermouth
- ¾ oz. Sweet Vermouth
- ¾ oz. Gin
- 1 Pineapple Stick

Directions: Shake all ingredients except pineapple stick with ice and strain into a cocktail glass. Add the pineapple stick.

POLAR BEAR

- 1 part Vodka
- 1 part Lime
- 2 parts 7-Up or Sprite
- Ice

Directions: Pour vodka into a highball glass, then add lime. Add 7-Up or Sprite. Mix this together with a straw. Ice is recommended.

POLO COCKTAIL

- 1 oz. Gin
- 1 tbs. Lemon Juice
- 1 tbs. Orange Juice
- Ice

Directions: Shake all ingredients with ice, strain into a cocktail glass, and serve.

POLONAISE

- 1 ½ oz. Brandy
- 1 tbs. Blackberry Brandy
- ½ oz. Dry Sherry
- Dash Lemon Juice
- Ice

Directions: Shake ice with ingredients, strain in old-fashioned glass over ice, and serve.

POLYNESIAN COCKTAIL

- 1 ½ oz. Vodka
- ¾ oz. Cherry Brandy
- Juice of 1 Lime
- Powdered Sugar
- Ice

Directions: Rub rim of cocktail glass with lime and dip into powdered sugar. Shake vodka, cherry brandy, and lime juice with ice, strain into the sugar-rimmed glass, and serve.

PONCHE DE PINA

- 3 Pineapples
- 3 cups of Water
- 3 Cinnamon Sticks
- 2 tsp. Whole Cloves
- 2 tsp. Whole Allspice
- ¾ cup of Sugar
- 1 cup of Coconut milk
- 1 qt. Light Rum

Directions: Peel pineapples and chop or shred. Add water and let stand overnight. Put in a large saucepan with spices, sugar, and coconut milk. Boil for five minutes. Strain liquid into a large pitcher. Add rum and serve hot.

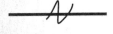

POOP DECK COCKTAIL

- 1 oz. Brandy
- 1 tbs. Blackberry Brandy
- 1 oz. Port
- Ice

Directions: Shake all ingredients with ice, strain into a cocktail glass, and serve.

POPPED CHERRY

- 2 oz. Vodka
- 2 oz. Cherry Liqueur
- 4 oz. Cranberry Juice
- 4 oz. Orange Juice
- 1 Cherry
- Ice

Directions: Pour ingredients over ice in a Collins glass and serve. Garnish with a cherry.

POPPY COCKTAIL

- 1 ½ oz. Gin
- ¾ oz. White Crème de Cacao
- Ice

Directions: Shake ingredients with ice, strain into a cocktail glass, and serve.

PORCH CRAWLERS

- 2 cans Frozen Pink Lemonade
- 10 bottles Beer
- 26 oz. Gin or Vodka

Directions: Combine ingredients in punch bowl.

PORT AND STARBOARD

- 1 tbs. Grenadine
- ½ oz. Green Crème de Menthe

Directions: Pour carefully into a pousse-café glass so that crème de menthe floats on top of the grenadine. Serve without mixing.

PORT WINE COCKTAIL

- 2 ½ oz. Port
- ½ tsp. Brandy
- Ice

Directions: Stir ingredients with ice, strain into a cocktail glass, and serve.

PORT WINE FLIP

- 1 ½ oz. Port
- 2 tsp. Light Cream
- 1 tsp. Powdered Sugar
- 1 Whole Egg
- Nutmeg
- Ice

Directions: Shake all ingredients except nutmeg with ice and strain into a whiskey sour glass. Sprinkle nutmeg on top and serve.

POWER SCREWDRIVER

- 2 oz. Vodka
- Orange Juice
- Coca-Cola
- Ice

Directions: Fill highball glass with ice. Pour in vodka and orange juice, leaving room for a splash of Coke.

PRAIRIE CHICKEN

- 1 oz. Gin
- 1 Whole Egg
- Salt and Pepper

Directions: Open egg without breaking yolk and put it into a red wine glass. Pour gin on top of egg, add salt and pepper to taste.

PREAKNESS COCKTAIL

- 1 ½ oz. Blended Whiskey
- ¾ oz. Sweet Vermouth
- ½ tsp. Benedictine
- Dash Bitters
- Twist of Lemon Peel
- Ice

Directions: Stir ice and ingredients except lemon peel and strain into a cocktail glass. Add lemon peel and serve.

PRESBYTERIAN

- 1 oz. Blended Whiskey
- Cola
- Ginger Ale
- 1 Lemon Slice
- Ice

Directions: Pour blended whiskey in highball glass filled with ice. Fill with equal parts cola and ginger ale. Stir well. Add the lemon slice and serve.

PRINCE'S SMILE

- ½ oz. Apple Brandy
- ½ oz. Apricot Brandy
- 1 oz. Gin
- ¼ tsp. Lemon Juice
- Ice

Directions: Shake all ingredients with ice, strain into a cocktail glass, and serve.

PRINCETON COCKTAIL

- 1 ½ oz. Gin
- 1 oz. Dry Vermouth
- 1 oz. Lime Juice
- Ice

Directions: In a shaker half-filled with ice, combine ingredients. Shake well. Strain into cocktail glass.

PUERTO APPLE

- 1 ½ oz. Applejack
- ¾ oz. Light Rum
- 1 oz. Orgeat Syrup
- 1 tbs. Lime Juice
- 1 Lime Slice
- Ice

Directions: Shake all ingredients except lime slice with ice and strain into an old-fashioned glass over ice cubes. Add the lime slice and serve.

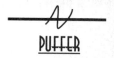

PUFFER

- 2 oz. Light Rum
- 2 oz. Orange Juice
- 2 oz. Grapefruit Juice
- 1 tsp. Grenadine
- Ice

Directions: Pour the rum, orange juice, and grapefruit juice into a highball glass almost filled with ice cubes. Stir well. Drop the grenadine into the center of the drink.

PURPLE MASK

- 1 oz. Vodka
- ½ oz. White Crème de Cacao
- 1 oz. Grape Juice
- Ice

Directions: Shake all ingredients with ice, strain into cocktail glass.

QUAKER'S COCKTAIL

- ¾ oz. Light Rum
- ¾ oz. Brandy
- Juice of ¼ Lemon
- 2 tsp. Raspberry Syrup
- Ice

Directions: Shake all ingredients with ice, strain into a cocktail glass, and serve.

QUARTER DECK COCKTAIL

- 1 ½ Light Rum
- $1/_3$ oz. Cream Sherry
- Juice of ½ Lime
- Ice

Directions: Stir all ingredients with ice, strain into a cocktail glass, and serve.

QUEEN BEE

- 1 oz. Coffee Brandy
- 1 ½ oz. Lime Vodka
- ½ oz. Cream Sherry
- Ice

Directions: Shake all ingredients with ice, strain into a cocktail glass, and serve.

QUEEN CHARLOTTE

- 2 oz. Red Wine
- 1 oz. Grenadine
- Lemon-lime Soda
- Ice

Directions: Pour red wine and grenadine into a Collins glass over ice cubes. Fill with lemon-lime soda, stir, and serve.

QUEEN ELIZABETH

- ½ oz. Dry Vermouth
- 1 ½ oz. Gin
- 1 ½ tsp. Benedictine
- Ice

Directions: Stir all ingredients with ice, strain into a cocktail glass, and serve.

QUENTIN

- 1 ½ oz. Dark Rum
- ½ oz. Kahlua
- 1 oz. Light Cream
- $1/_8$ tsp. Grated Nutmeg
- Ice

Directions: In a shaker half-filled with ice cubes, combine the rum, Kahlua, and cream. Shake well. Strain into a cocktail glass and garnish with the nutmeg.

RAGGED COMPANY

- 2 oz. Bourbon
- ½ oz. Sweet Vermouth
- 1 tsp. Benedictine
- 2 dashes Bitters
- 1 Lemon Twist
- Ice

Directions: In a mixing glass half-filled with ice cubes, combine the bourbon, vermouth, Benedictine, and bitters. Stir well. Strain into a cocktail glass and garnish with the lemon twist.

RASPBERRY CREAM

- 1 ½ oz. Vodka
- 1 ½ tbs. Raspberry Yogurt
- 1 ½ tbs. Raspberry Ice Cream
- 1 ½ oz. White Crème de Cacao
- 2 oz. Heavy Cream

Directions: Blend all ingredients in an electric blender at a low speed. Pour into a Champagne flute and serve.

RATTLESNAKE COCKTAIL

- 1 ½ oz. Blended Whiskey
- 1 tsp. Lemon Juice
- ¼ tsp. Anisette
- ½ tsp. Powdered Sugar
- 1 Egg White
- Ice

Directions: Shake all ingredients with ice, strain into a cocktail glass, and serve.

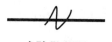

REBEL YELL

- 2 oz. Bourbon
- ½ oz. Triple Sec
- 1 oz. Lemon Juice
- 1 Egg White
- 1 Orange Slice
- Ice

Directions: In a shaker half-filled with ice cubes, combine the bourbon, Triple Sec, lemon juice, and egg white. Shake well. Pour into an old-fashioned glass and garnish with the orange slice.

RED APPLE

- 1 oz. 100 Proof Vodka
- 1 oz. Apple Juice
- 1 tbs. Lemon Juice
- 1 tsp. Grenadine
- Ice

Directions: Shake all ingredients with ice, strain into a cocktail glass, and serve.

RED CLOUD

- 1 ½ oz. Gin
- ½ oz. Apricot Brandy
- 1 tbs. Lemon Juice
- 1 tsp. Grenadine
- Ice

Directions: Shake all ingredients with ice, strain into a cocktail glass, and serve.

RED GIN

- Crushed Ice
- 2 oz. Gin
- 1 tsp. Cherry Heering
- 1 Maraschino Cherry

Directions: In mixing glass half-filled with crushed ice, combine gin and Cherry Heering. Stir well. Strain in cocktail glass. Garnish with cherry.

RED RAIDER

- ½ oz. Triple Sec
- 1 oz. Bourbon
- 1 oz. Lemon Juice
- Dash Grenadine
- Ice

Directions: Shake all ingredients with ice, strain in cocktail glass. Serve.

RED RUBY

- 1 ½ oz. Gin
- ½ oz. Cherry Brandy
- ½ oz. Dry Vermouth
- Ice

Directions: In mixing glass half-filled with ice, mix ingredients. Stir. Strain in cocktail glass.

REDCOAT

- 1 ½ oz. Light Rum
- ½ oz. Vodka
- ½ oz. Apricot Brandy
- ½ oz. Lime Juice
- 1 tsp. Grenadine
- Ice

Directions: In a shaker half-filled with ice cubes, combine all of the ingredients. Shake well. Strain into a cocktail glass.

REFORM COCKTAIL

- 1 ½ oz. Dry Sherry
- ¾ oz. Dry Vermouth
- Dash Orange Bitters
- 1 Cherry
- Ice

Directions: Stir all ingredients except cherry with ice and strain into a cocktail glass. Top with the cherry and serve.

REMSEN COOLER

- 2 oz. Gin
- Carbonated Water
- ½ tsp. Powdered Sugar
- 1 Orange Spiral
- Twist of Lemon Peel

Directions: Put powdered sugar and two ounces carbonated water in Collins glass and stir. Add ice and gin, fill with carbonated water, and stir again. Add lemon peel and orange, dangling ends over rim.

RESOLUTE COCKTAIL

- ½ oz. Apricot Brandy
- 1 oz. Gin
- Juice of ¼ Lemon
- Ice

Directions: Shake all ingredients with ice, strain into a cocktail glass,.

RILEY'S SPARROW

- 1 ½ oz. Dark Rum
- ½ oz. Southern Comfort
- 2 dashes Bitters
- Ice

Directions: In a mixing glass half-filled with ice, combine ingredients. Stir. Strain in cocktail glass.

RITZ FIZZ

- Chilled Champagne
- Dash Blue Curacao
- Dash Amaretto
- Dash Lemon Juice
- 1 Twist of Lemon

Directions: Fill a Champagne flute with chilled Champagne. Add blue curacao, Amaretto, and lemon juice. Stir, add the twist of lemon, and serve.

ROB ROY

- 1 ½ oz. Scotch
- ¾ oz. Sweet Vermouth
- Ice

Directions: Stir ingredients with ice, strain into a cocktail glass, and serve.

ROBIN'S NEST

- 1 oz. Vodka
- ½ oz. White Crème de Cacao
- 1 oz. Cranberry Juice
- Ice

Directions: Shake ingredients with ice, strain into a cocktail glass, and serve.

ROBSON COCKTAIL

- 1 oz. Jamaica Rum
- 1 ½ tsp. Grenadine
- 2 tsp. Lemon Juice
- 1 tbs. Orange Juice
- Ice

Directions: Shake all ingredients with ice, strain into a cocktail glass, and serve.

ROCK AND RYE COCKTAIL

- 1 oz. Rock and Rye
- 1 oz. White Port
- 1 ½ tsp. Dry Vermouth
- Ice

Directions: Stir all ingredients with ice, strain into a cocktail glass, and serve.

ROCOCO

- 1 oz. Cherry Vodka
- ½ oz. Triple Sec
- 1 oz. Orange Juice
- Ice

Directions: Shake all ingredients with ice, strain into a cocktail glass, and serve.

ROLLS ROYCE

- 1 ½ oz. Gin
- ½ oz. Sweet Vermouth
- ½ oz. Dry Vermouth
- 1 tsp. Benedictine
- Ice

Directions: In mixing glass half-filled with ice, mix ingredients. Stir. Strain in cocktail glass.

ROMULAN ALE

- 1 ½ oz. White Rum
- 1 oz. Blue Curacao
- Sprite or 7-Up
- 6 drops Tabasco Sauce
- Salt

Directions: Mix ingredients. Pour in tall, narrow glass. Add a grain of salt.

ROOT BEER FIZZ

- 2 oz. Gin
- 1 oz. Lemon Juice
- 1 tsp. Superfine Sugar
- 4 oz. Root Beer
- 1 Maraschino Cherry
- Ice

Directions: In a shaker half-filled with ice combine the gin, lemon juice, and sugar. Shake. Strain into Collins glass filled with ice. Add root beer. Stir. Garnish with cherry.

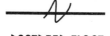

ROOTBEER FLOAT

- ½ oz. Vodka
- ½ oz. Galliano
- ½ oz. Light Cream
- Cola
- Whipped Cream
- Ice

Directions: Pour vodka, Galliano, and light cream in Collins glass filled with ice and stir. Fill with cola, stir lightly, top with whipped cream.

RORY O'MORE

- 1 ½ oz. Irish Whiskey
- ¾ oz. Sweet Vermouth
- Dash Orange Bitters
- Ice

Directions: Stir all ingredients with ice, strain into cocktail glass.

ROSE COCKTAIL (ENGLISH)

- ½ oz. Dry Vermouth
- 1 oz. Gin
- ½ oz. Apricot Brandy
- ½ tsp. Lemon Juice
- 1 tsp. Grenadine
- Powdered Sugar
- Ice

Directions: Rub cocktail glass rim with lemon juice. Dip in powdered sugar. Shake other ingredients with ice, strain in glass.

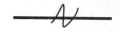

ROSE COCKTAIL (FRENCH)

- 1 ½ oz. Gin
- ½ oz. Dry Vermouth
- ½ oz. Cherry Brandy
- Ice

Directions: Stir all ingredients with ice, strain into a cocktail glass.

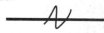

ROSELYN COCKTAIL

- 1 ½ oz. Gin
- ¾ oz. Dry Vermouth
- ½ tsp. Grenadine
- Twist of Lemon Peel
- Ice

Directions: Stir all ingredients except lemon peel with ice and strain into a cocktail glass. Add the twist of lemon peel.

ROUGE MARTINI

- 2 oz. Gin
- 1 tsp. Chambord
- Ice

Directions: In a mixing glass half-filled with ice cubes, combine the gin and Chambord. Stir well. Strain into a cocktail glass.

ROYAL CLOVER CLUB COCKTAIL

- 1 ½ oz. Gin
- Juice of ½ Lemon
- 1 tbs. Grenadine
- 1 Egg Yolk
- Ice

Directions: Shake all ingredients with ice, strain into a whiskey sour glass, and serve.

ROYAL COCKTAIL

- 1 ½ oz. Gin
- Juice of ½ Lemon
- ½ tsp. Powdered Sugar
- 1 Whole Egg
- Ice

Directions: Shake all ingredients with ice, strain into a whiskey sour glass, and serve.

ROYAL FIZZ

- 1 oz. Gin
- 2 oz. Sweet and Sour
- 1 Whole Egg
- Cola
- Ice

Directions: Shake all ingredients except cola with ice and strain into a chilled Collins glass. Fill with cola and serve.

ROYAL GIN FIZZ

- 2 oz. Gin
- Juice of ½ Lemon
- 1 tsp. Powdered Sugar
- 1 Whole Egg
- Carbonated Water
- Ice

Directions: Shake all ingredients except carbonated water with ice and strain into a highball glass over two ice cubes. Fill with carbonated water, stir, and serve.

ROYAL SMILE COCKTAIL

- 1 oz. Apple Brandy
- ½ oz. Gin
- Juice of ¼ Lemon
- 1 tsp. Grenadine
- Ice

Directions: Stir all ingredients with ice, strain into a cocktail glass, and serve.

ROYALTY FIZZ

- 2 oz. Gin
- 1 oz. Lemon Juice
- ½ tsp. Blue Curacao
- 1 tsp. Superfine Sugar
- 1 Whole Egg
- 3 oz. Club Soda
- Ice

Directions: In a shaker half-filled with ice cubes, combine the gin, lemon juice, curacao, sugar, and egg. Shake well. Strain into a Collins glass almost filled with ice cubes. Add the club soda. Stir well.

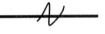

RUBY FIZZ

- 2 oz. Sloe Gin
- 1 tsp. Grenadine
- Juice of ½ Lemon
- 1 tsp. Powdered Sugar
- 1 Egg White
- Carbonated Water
- Ice

Directions: Shake all ingredients except carbonated water with ice and strain into a highball glass over two ice cubes. Fill with carbonated water, stir, and serve.

RUBY IN THE ROUGH

- 1 ½ oz. Gin
- ½ oz. Cherry Brandy
- 1 tsp. Sweet Vermouth
- Ice

Directions: In a mixing glass half-filled with ice cubes, combine all of the ingredients. Stir well. Strain into a cocktail glass.

RUM COBBLER

- 1 tsp. Superfine Sugar
- 3 oz. Club Soda
- 2 oz. Dark Rum
- 1 Lemon Slice
- 1 Maraschino Cherry
- 1 Orange Slice
- Crushed Ice

Directions: In an old-fashioned glass, dissolve the sugar in the club soda. Add crushed ice until the glass is almost full. Add the rum. Stir well. Garnish with the cherry and the orange and lemon slices.

RUM COLLINS

- 2 oz. Light Rum
- Juice of 1 Lime
- 1 tsp. Powdered Sugar
- Carbonated Water
- 1 Lemon Slice
- 1 Cherry
- Ice

Directions: Shake rum, lime juice, and powdered sugar with ice and strain into a Collins glass over ice cubes. Fill with carbonated water and stir. Add the lemon slice, top with the cherry, and serve.

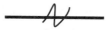

RUM COOLER

- 2 oz. Dark or Light Rum
- 4 oz. Lemon-lime Soda
- 1 Lemon Wedge
- Ice

Directions: Pour the rum and soda into a highball glass almost filled with ice cubes. Stir well and garnish with the lemon wedge.

RUM DAISY

- 2 oz. Dark Rum
- 1 oz. Lemon Juice
- ½ tsp. Superfine Sugar
- ½ tsp. Grenadine
- 1 Maraschino Cherry
- 1 Orange Slice
- Ice

Directions: In a shaker half-filled with ice, combine ingredients. Shake. Pour in old-fashioned glass and garnish with cherry and orange slice.

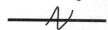

RUM DUBONNET

- 1 ½ tsp. Dubonnet
- 1 ½ oz. Light Rum
- 1 tsp. Lemon Juice
- Ice

Directions: Shake all ingredients with ice, strain in cocktail glass.

RUM EGGNOG

- 2 oz. Light or Dark Rum
- 6 oz. Milk
- 1 tsp. Powdered Sugar
- 1 Whole Egg
- Ice

Directions: Shake ice with ingredients. Strain in Collins glass.

RUM FIX

- 2 ½ oz. Light Rum
- Juice of 1 Lemon
- 1 tsp. Powdered Sugar
- 1 tsp. Water
- 1 Lemon Slice
- Ice

Directions: Stir lemon juice, powdered sugar, and water in a highball glass. Fill glass with ice, add rum. Stir. Add lemon slice and serve.

RUM GIMLET

- 2 oz. Light Rum
- ½ oz. Rose's Lime Juice
- 1 Lime Wedge
- Ice

Directions: Pour rum and lime juice in mixing glass half-filled with ice. Stir. Strain in cocktail glass. Garnish with lime wedge.

RUM HIGHBALL

- 2 oz. Light or Dark Rum
- Carbonated Water
- Twist of Lemon Peel
- Ice

Directions: Pour rum in highball glass over ice. Fill with carbonated water and stir. Add lemon peel.

RUM MARTINI

- 2 ½ oz. Light Rum
- 1 ½ tsp. Dry Vermouth
- 1 Lemon Twist or Olive
- Ice

Directions: In a mixing glass half-filled with ice cubes, combine the rum and vermouth. Stir well. Strain into a cocktail glass. Garnish with the lemon twist or an olive.

RUM OLD-FASHIONED

- 1 ½ oz. Light Rum
- 1 tsp. 151 Proof Rum
- ½ tsp. Powdered Sugar
- Dash Bitters
- 1 tsp. Water
- Twist of Lime Peel
- Ice

Directions: Stir powdered sugar, water, and bitters in an old-fashioned glass. When sugar has dissolved, add ice cubes and light rum. Add the twist of lime peel, float 151 proof rum on top.

RUM SCREWDRIVER

- 1 ½ oz. Light Rum
- 5 oz. Orange Juice
- Ice

Directions: Pour rum in highball glass over ice. Add orange juice, stir.

RUM SOUR

- 2 oz. Light Rum
- 1 oz. Lemon Juice
- ½ tsp. Superfine Sugar
- 1 Orange Slice
- 1 Maraschino Cherry
- Ice

Directions: In a shaker half-filled with ice, combine ingredients. Shake. Strain into sour glass. Garnish with orange and cherry.

RUM SWIZZLE

- 2 oz. Light or Dark Rum
- Carbonated Water
- Juice of 1 Lime
- 1 tsp. Powdered Sugar
- 2 dashes Bitters
- Ice

Directions: In Collins glass, dissolve powdered sugar in two ounces carbonated water and lime juice. Fill glass with ice and stir. Add bitters and rum. Fill with carbonated water. Stir.

RUM TODDY

- 2 oz. Light or Dark Rum
- 2 tsp. Powdered Sugar
- Twist of Lemon Peel
- 2 tsp. Water
- Ice

Directions: Dissolve sugar in water in an old-fashioned glass. Add rum and ice cube. Stir. Add lemon peel.

RUSSIAN COCKTAIL

- ¾ oz. Vodka
- ¾ oz. Gin
- ¾ oz. White Crème de Cacao
- Ice

Directions: Shake all ingredients with ice, strain into a cocktail glass, and serve.

RUSSIAN ROULETTE

- ½ oz. Kahlua
- ½ oz. Vodka
- 1 oz. Sambuca
- Orange Slices

Directions: Fill two or more one ounce shooter glasses with the Kahlua and vodka and place a slice of orange on the top of each glass. Put the sambuca in a wine glass and light. Pour the lit sambuca on the shooters and let burn for a short time. Blow out the fire. Drink the shooters first, and then chew the sambuca-soaked orange slice.

RUSTY NAIL

- 1 ½ oz. Scotch
- ½ oz. Drambuie
- 1 Lemon Twist
- Ice

Directions: Pour the Scotch and Drambuie into an old-fashioned glass almost filled with ice cubes. Stir well. Garnish with the lemon twist.

RYE WHISKEY COCKTAIL

- 2 oz. Rye Whiskey
- 1 tsp. Powdered Sugar
- Dash Bitters
- 1 Cherry
- Ice

Directions: Shake all ingredients except cherry with ice and strain into a cocktail glass. Top with the cherry and serve.

SAKETINI

- 2 ½ oz. Gin or Vodka
- 1 ½ tsp. Sake
- 1 Cocktail Olive
- Ice

Directions: In mixing glass half-filled with ice, combine gin or vodka with sake. Stir. Strain into a cocktail glass. Garnish with olive.

SALTY DOG

- 5 oz. Grapefruit Juice
- 1 ½ oz. Gin
- ¼ tsp. Salt
- Ice

Directions:: Pour ice and ingredients in highball glass. Stir well and serve.

SAN FRANCISCO COCKTAIL

- ¾ oz. Sweet Vermouth
- ¾ oz. Dry Vermouth
- ¾ oz. Sloe Gin
- Dash Orange Bitters
- Dash Bitters
- 1 Cherry
- Ice

Directions: Shake ingredients except cherry with ice and strain in cocktail glass. Add the cherry on top.

SAND-GROWN-UN

- 1 ½ oz. Dark Rum
- ½ oz. Sweet Vermouth
- ½ oz. Cherry Brandy
- ½ oz. Lemon Juice
- ½ tsp. Superfine Sugar
- Ice

Directions: In a shaker half-filled with ice, combine ingredients. Shake well. Strain into a cocktail glass.

SAND-MARTIN COCKTAIL

- 1 ½ oz. Sweet Vermouth
- 1 ½ oz. Gin
- 1 tsp. Green Chartreuse
- Ice

Directions: Stir all ingredients with ice, strain into a cocktail glass, and serve.

SANDRA BUYS A DOG

- 1 oz. Dark Rum
- 1 oz. Anejo Rum
- 3 oz. Cranberry Juice
- 1 oz. Orange Juice
- Dash Bitters
- Ice

Directions: Pour all of the ingredients into a highball glass almost filled with ice cubes. Stir well.

SANTIAGO COCKTAIL

- 1 ½ oz. Light Rum
- ¼ tsp. Grenadine
- Juice of 1 Lime
- ½ tsp. Powdered Sugar
- Ice

Directions: Shake all ingredients with ice, strain into a cocktail glass, and serve.

SARATOGA COCKTAIL

- 2 oz. Brandy
- 1 tsp. Pineapple Juice
- 1 tsp. Lemon Juice
- ½ tsp. Maraschino
- 2 dashes Bitters
- Ice

Directions: Shake all ingredients with ice, strain into a cocktail glass, and serve.

SAUCY SUE COCKTAIL

- 2 oz. Apple Brandy
- ½ tsp. Apricot Brandy
- ½ tsp. Pernod
- Ice

Directions: Stir all ingredients with ice, strain into a cocktail glass, and serve.

SAVANNAH

- 1 oz. Gin
- Dash White Crème de Cacao
- Juice of ½ Orange
- 1 Egg White
- Ice

Directions: Shake all ingredients with ice, strain into a cocktail glass, and serve.

SAXON COCKTAIL

- 1 ¾ oz. Light Rum
- ½ tsp. Grenadine
- Juice of ½ Lime
- Twist of Orange Peel
- Ice

Directions: Shake all ingredients except orange peel with ice and strain into a cocktail glass. Add the twist of orange peel and serve.

SAZERAC

- 1 tsp. Ricard
- ½ tsp. Superfine Sugar
- 2 dashes Peychaud Bitters
- 1 tsp. Water
- 2 oz. Bourbon
- 1 Lemon Twist
- Ice

Directions: Pour Ricard into a glass and swirl around to coat glass. Discard any excess. Place the sugar, Peychaud bitters, and water into the glass and muddle with the back of a teaspoon. Almost fill the glass with ice cubes. Pour the bourbon over the ice cubes. Garnish with the lemon twist.

SCOOTER

- 1 oz. Brandy
- 1 oz. Amaretto
- 1 oz. Light Cream
- Cracked Ice

Directions: Shake all ingredients well with cracked ice, strain into a cocktail glass, and serve.

SCOTCH AND WATER

- 2 oz. Scotch
- 5 oz. Water
- Ice

Directions: Pour the Scotch and the water into a highball glass almost filled with ice cubes. Stir well.

SCOTCH BIRD FLYER

- 1 ½ oz. Scotch
- ½ oz. Triple Sec
- 1 oz. Light Cream
- ½ tsp. Powdered Sugar
- 1 Egg Yolk
- Ice

Directions: Shake ingredients with ice, strain in Champagne flute, and serve.

SCOTCH BISHOP COCKTAIL

- 1 oz. Scotch
- ½ oz. Dry Vermouth
- ½ tsp. Triple Sec
- 1 tbs. Orange Juice
- ¼ tsp. Powdered Sugar
- Twist of Lemon Peel
- Ice

Directions: Shake all ingredients except lemon peel with ice and strain into a cocktail glass. Add the twist of lemon peel and serve.

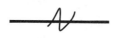

SCOTCH COBBLER

- 2 oz. Scotch
- 4 dashes Brandy
- 4 dashes Curacao
- 1 Orange Slice
- 1 Mint Sprig
- Ice

Directions: Pour Scotch, brandy, and curacao over ice in an old-fashioned glass. Add the orange slice, top with the mint sprig, and serve.

SCOTCH COOLER

- 2 oz. Scotch
- 3 dashes White Crème de Menthe
- Carbonated Water
- Ice

Directions: Pour Scotch and crème de menthe over ice cubes in a highball glass. Fill with carbonated water, stir, and serve.

SCOTCH DAISY

- 2 oz. Scotch
- 1 oz. Lemon Juice
- ½ tsp. Superfine Sugar
- ½ tsp. Grenadine
- 1 Maraschino Cherry
- 1 Orange Slice
- Ice

Directions: In a shaker half-filled with ice cubes, combine the Scotch, lemon juice, sugar, and grenadine. Shake well. Pour into an old-fashioned glass. Garnish with the cherry and the orange slice.

SCOTCH FIX

- 1 tsp. Superfine Sugar
- 1 oz. Lemon Juice
- 2 tsp. Water
- 2 oz. Scotch
- 1 Maraschino Cherry
- 1 Lemon Juice
- Crushed Ice

Directions: In a shaker half-filled with ice cubes, combine the sugar, lemon juice, and water. Shake well. Strain into a highball glass almost filled with crushed ice. Add the Scotch. Stir well and garnish with the cherry and the lemon slice.

SCOTCH FLIP

- 2 oz. Scotch
- 1 Egg
- 1 tsp. Superfine Sugar
- ½ oz. Light Cream
- ⅛ tsp. Grated Nutmeg
- Ice

Directions: In a shaker half-filled with ice, combine Scotch, egg, sugar, and cream. Shake. Strain into sour glass. Garnish with nutmeg.

SCOTCH HIGHBALL

- 2 oz. Scotch
- Carbonated Water
- Twist of Lemon Peel
- Ice

Directions: Pour scotch in highball glass over ice. Fill with carbonated water, stir, and serve.

SCOTCH HOLIDAY SOUR

- 1 ½ oz. Scotch
- 1 oz. Cherry Brandy
- ½ oz. Sweet Vermouth
- 1 oz. Lemon Juice
- 1 Lemon Slice
- Ice

Directions: Shake ice with ingredients except lemon. Strain in old-fashioned glass over ice. Add lemon and serve.

SCOTCH MIST

- 2 oz. Scotch
- Crushed Ice
- Twist of Lemon Peel

Directions: Fill an old-fashioned glass with crushed ice. Pour in Scotch. Add the twist of lemon peel and serve with a straw.

SCOTCH OLD-FASHIONED

- 3 dashes Bitters
- 3 oz. Scotch
- 1 tsp. Water
- 1 Sugar Cube
- 1 Orange Slice
- 1 Maraschino Cherry
- Ice

Directions: In an old-fashioned glass, muddle the bitters and water into the sugar cube, using the back of a teaspoon. Almost fill the glass with ice cubes and add the Scotch. Garnish with the orange slice and the cherry. Serve with a swizzle stick.

SCOTCH RICKEY

- 1 ½ oz. Scotch
- Juice of ½ Lime
- Carbonated Water
- 1 Lime Rind
- Ice

Directions: Pour Scotch and lime juice into a highball glass over ice cubes. Fill with carbonated water and stir. Add the lime rind and serve.

SCOTCH SOUR

- 1 ½ oz. Scotch
- Juice of ½ Lime
- ½ tsp. Powdered Sugar
- ½ Lemon Slice
- 1 Cherry
- Ice

Directions: Shake Scotch, lime juice, and powdered sugar with ice and strain into a whiskey sour glass. Decorate with lemon slice, top with the cherry, and serve.

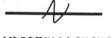

SCREAMING BANANA BANSHEE

- ½ oz. Banana Liqueur
- ½ oz. Vodka
- ½ oz. White Crème de Cacao
- 1 ½ oz. Cream
- 1 Cherry
- Ice

Directions: Shake all ingredients except cherry with ice and strain into a chilled cocktail glass. Add the cherry on top and serve.

SEABOARD

- 1 oz. Blended Whiskey
- 1 oz. Gin
- 1 tbs. Lemon Juice
- 1 tsp. Powdered Sugar
- 3 Mint Leaves
- Ice

Directions: Shake all ingredients except mint leaves with ice and strain into an old-fashioned glass over ice cubes. Decorate with mint leaves.

SECRET PLACE

- 1 ½ oz. Dark Rum
- ½ oz. Cherry Brandy
- 2 tsp. Dark Crème de Cacao
- 4 oz. Cold Coffee
- Crushed Ice

Directions: Pour ingredients in Irish coffee glass filled with crushed ice. Stir well.

SENSATION COCKTAIL

- 1 ½ oz. Gin
- Juice of ¼ Lemon
- 1 tsp. Maraschino
- 2 Mint Sprigs
- Ice

Directions: Shake all ingredients except mint sprigs with ice. Strain in cocktail glass. Add mint sprigs and serve.

SEPTEMBER MORNING

- 1 ½ oz. Light Rum
- 1 tsp. Cherry Brandy
- ½ oz. Lime Juice
- ½ tsp. Grenadine
- 1 Egg White
- Ice

Directions: In a shaker half-filled with ice, combine ingredients. Shake well. Strain into a cocktail glass.

SERPENTINE

- 1 oz. Light Rum
- ½ oz. Brandy
- ½ oz. Sweet Vermouth
- ½ oz. Lemon Juice
- ½ tsp. Superfine Sugar
- 1 Lemon Twist
- Ice

Directions: In a shaker half-filled with ice, combine ingredients. Shake. Strain in cocktail glass. Garnish with lemon twist.

SEVEN AND SEVEN

- 1 ¾ oz. Seagram's 7
- 6 oz. 7-Up
- Ice

Directions: Put a few cubes of ice inside glass. Pour a shot of Seagram's 7 in glass, add 7-Up. Shake or stir briskly.

SEVENTH HEAVEN COCKTAIL

- 1 ½ oz. Gin
- 2 tsp. Grapefruit Juice
- 1 tbs. Maraschino
- 1 Mint Sprig
- Ice

Directions: Shake all ingredients except mint sprig with ice and strain into a cocktail glass. Add the mint sprig and serve.

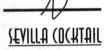

SEVILLA COCKTAIL

- 1 oz. Light Rum
- 1 oz. Port
- ½ tsp. Powdered Sugar
- 1 Whole Egg
- Ice

Directions: Shake all ingredients with ice, strain into a whiskey sour glass, and serve.

SEVILLA COCKTAIL #2

- 1 ½ oz. Light Rum
- 1 oz. Tawny Port
- 1 tsp. Superfine Sugar
- 1 Egg
- Ice

Directions: In a shaker half-filled with ice cubes, combine all of the ingredients. Shake well. Strain into a sour glass.

SEX ON THE BEACH

- 1 ½ oz. Vodka
- 1 ½ oz. Peach Schnapps
- 2 oz. Cranberry Juice
- 2 oz. Grapefruit Juice
- 2 oz. Pineapple Juice
- Ice

Directions: Combine ingredients in a shaker with ice. Shake and strain into a highball glass filled with ice.

SHADY LADY

- 1 oz. Melon Liqueur
- 1 oz. Tequila
- 4 oz. Grapefruit Juice
- 1 Lime Slice
- 1 Cherry
- Ice

Directions: Pour ice and ingredients into highball glass. Stir. Add lime slice. Top with cherry.

SHALOM

- 1 ½ oz. 100 Proof Vodka
- 1 oz. Madeira
- 1 tbs. Orange Juice
- 1 Orange Slice
- Ice

Directions: Shake ice and ingredients except orange slice . Strain in old-fashioned glass over ice. Add orange slice.

SHAMROCK

- 1 ½ oz. Irish Whiskey
- ½ oz. Dry Vermouth
- 1 tsp. Green Crème de Menthe
- 1 Olive
- Ice

Directions: Stir ice and ingredients except. Strain incocktail glass. Add olive and serve.

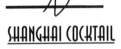

SHANGHAI COCKTAIL

- 1 oz. Jamaica Light Rum
- 1 tsp. Anisette
- ½ tsp. Grenadine
- Juice of ¼ Lemon
- Ice

Directions: Shake ice with ingredients. Strain into cocktail glass.

SHERRY EGGNOG

- 2 oz. Cream Sherry
- 1 tsp. Powdered Sugar
- 1 Whole Egg
- Milk
- Nutmeg
- Ice

Directions: Shake ice, sherry, powdered sugar, and egg. Strain in Collins glass. Fill with milk. Stir. Sprinkle nutmeg on top.

SHERRY FLIP

- 1 ½ oz. Cream Sherry
- 2 tsp. Light Cream
- 1 tsp. Powdered Sugar
- 1 Whole Egg
- Nutmeg
- Ice

Directions: Shake ice and ingredients except nutmeg. Strain in whiskey sour glass. Sprinkle nutmeg on top.

SHRINER COCKTAIL

- 1 ½ oz. Sloe Gin
- 1 ½ oz. Brandy
- ½ oz. Sugar Syrup
- 2 dashes Bitters
- Twist of Lemon Peel
- Ice

Directions: Stir all ingredients except lemon peel with ice and strain into a cocktail glass. Add the twist of lemon peel.

SIDECAR

- 2 oz. Brandy
- ½ oz. Triple Sec
- 1 oz. Lemon Juice
- Ice

Directions: In a shaker half-filled with ice cubes, combine all of the ingredients. Shake well. Strain into a cocktail glass.

SIDECAR COCKTAIL

- 1 oz. Brandy
- ½ oz. Triple Sec
- Juice of ½ Lemon
- Ice

Directions: Shake all ingredients with ice, strain into a cocktail glass, and serve.

SILENT BROADSIDER

- 1 ½ oz. Light Rum
- ½ oz. Anisette
- ½ oz. Lemon Juice
- ½ tsp. Grenadine
- Ice

Directions: In a shaker half-filled with ice, combine ingredients. Shake well. Strain into cocktail glass.

SILK STOCKINGS

- 1 ½ oz. Tequila
- 1 oz. Crème de Cacao
- Dash Grenadine
- 1 ½ oz. Light Cream
- Cinnamon
- Ice

Directions: Shake all ingredients except cinnamon with ice and strain into a cocktail glass. Sprinkle cinnamon on top and serve.

SILVER BRONX

- 2 oz. Gin
- 1 tsp. Orange Juice
- ½ oz. Dry Vermouth
- ½ oz. Sweet Vermouth
- 1 Egg White
- Ice

Directions: In a shaker half-filled with ice cubes, combine all of the ingredients. Shake well. Strain into a sour glass.

SILVER BULLET

- 2 ½ oz. Gin
- 1 ½ tsp. Scotch
- 1 Lemon Twist
- Ice

Directions: In a mixing glass half-filled with ice, combine gin and Scotch. Stir well. Strain into cocktail glass. Garnish with lemon twist.

SILVER COCKTAIL

- 1 oz. Gin
- 1 oz. Dry Vermouth
- ¼ tsp. Sugar Syrup
- ½ tsp. Maraschino
- 2 dashes Orange Bitters
- Twist of Lemon Peel
- Ice

Directions: Stir ice and ingredients except lemon peel. Strain in cocktail glass. Add twist of lemon peel.

SILVER KING COCKTAIL

- 1 ½ oz. Gin
- Juice of ¼ Lemon
- ½ tsp. Powdered Sugar
- 2 dashes Orange Bitters
- 1 Egg White
- Ice

Directions: Shake ice with ingredients. Strain in cocktail glass.

SILVER STALLION FIZZ

- Scoop of Vanilla Ice Cream
- 2 oz. Gin
- Carbonated Water
- Ice

Directions: Shake gin and ice cream with ice. Strain in highball glass. Fill with carbonated water. Stir.

SINGAPORE SLING

- ½ oz. Cherry Brandy
- ½ oz. Grenadine
- 1 oz. Gin
- 2 oz. Sweet and Sour
- Carbonated Water
- 1 Cherry
- Ice

Directions: Pour grenadine, gin, and sweet and sour into a Collins glass over ice cubes and stir well. Fill with carbonated water and top with cherry brandy. Add cherry on top.

SIR WALTER COCKTAIL

- ¾ oz. Brandy
- ¾ oz. Rum
- 1 tsp. Triple Sec
- 1 tsp. Grenadine
- 1 tsp. Lemon Juice
- Ice

Directions: Shake all ingredients with ice, strain into cocktail glass.

SISTER STARSEEKER

- 2 oz. Light Rum
- 1 oz. Lemon Juice
- 1 tsp. Grenadine
- 4 oz. Tonic Water
- 1 Lemon Wedge
- Ice

Directions: Pour the rum, lemon juice, grenadine, and tonic water into highball glass almost filled with ice. Stir well and garnish with lemon.

SITARSKI

- 1 ½ oz. Dark Rum
- ½ oz. Lime Juice
- 1 tsp. Lemon Juice
- 2 oz. Grapefruit Juice
- 1 tsp. Superfine Sugar
- Ice

Directions: In a shaker half-filled with ice, combine all of the ingredients. Shake well. Strain into an old-fashioned glass almost filled with ice.

SKIP AND GO NAKED

- 1 oz. Gin
- 2 oz. Sweet and Sour
- Chilled Beer
- Ice

Directions: Pour gin and sweet and sour into a Collins glass over ice cubes and stir well. Fill with chilled beer, stir lightly, and serve.

SLOE COMFORTABLE SCREW

- 1 oz. Sloe Gin
- ½ oz. Southern Comfort
- Orange Juice
- Ice

Directions: Pour sloe gin and Southern Comfort into a Collins glass filled with ice. Fill with orange juice, stir well, and serve.

SLOE GIN COCKTAIL

- 2 oz. Sloe Gin
- ¼ tsp. Dry Vermouth
- Dash Orange Bitters
- Ice

Directions: Stir all ingredients with ice, strain into a cocktail glass, and serve.

SLOE GIN COLLINS

- 2 oz. Sloe Gin
- Juice of ½ Lemon
- Carbonated Water
- 1 Lemon Slice
- 1 Orange Slice
- 1 Cherry
- Ice

Directions: Shake sloe gin and lemon juice with ice and strain into a Collins glass. Add several ice cubes, fill with carbonated water, and stir. Add slices of lemon and orange, top with the cherry, and serve with a straw.

SLOE GIN RICKEY

- 2 oz. Sloe Gin
- Juice of ½ Lime
- Carbonated Water
- 1 Lime Wedge
- Ice

Directions: Pour sloe gin and lime juice into a highball glass over ice cubes. Fill with carbonated water and stir. Drop the lime wedge in the glass and serve.

SLOE SCREW

- 1 oz. Sloe Gin
- Orange Juice
- Ice

Directions: Pour sloe gin into a highball glass filled with ice. Fill with orange juice, stir well, and serve.

SLOE VERMOUTH

- 1 oz. Dry Vermouth
- 1 oz. Sloe Gin
- 1 tbs. Lemon Juice
- Ice

Directions: Shake all ingredients with ice, strain into a cocktail glass.

SLOEBERRY COCKTAIL

- 2 oz. Sloe Gin
- Dash Bitters
- Ice

Directions: Stir ingredients with ice, strain into a cocktail glass, and serve.

SLOPPY JOE'S COCKTAIL NO. 1

- ¾ oz. Light Rum
- ¾ oz. Dry Vermouth
- ¼ tsp. Triple Sec
- ¼ tsp. Grenadine
- Juice of 1 Lime
- Ice

Directions: Shake ice and ingredients. Strain into cocktail glass, and serve.

SLOPPY JOE'S COCKTAIL NO. 2

- ¾ oz. Brandy
- ¼ tsp. Triple Sec
- ¾ oz. Port
- ¾ oz. Pineapple Juice
- ¼ tsp. Grenadine
- Ice

Directions: Shake ice with ingredients. Strain into cocktail glass.

SLY GOES TO HAVANA

- 1 ½ oz. Light Rum
- 1 tsp. Crème de Cacao
- 1 tsp. Green Chartreuse
- 1 oz. Pineapple Juice
- ½ oz. Lime Juice
- Ice

Directions: In a shaker half-filled with ice, combine ingredients. Shake well. Strain into old fashioned glass filled with crushed ice.

SMART CHRISTINE

- 2 oz. Gin
- ½ oz. Benedictine
- 2 oz. Orange Juice
- 1 Maraschino Cherry
- Ice

Directions: In a shaker half-filled with ice, combine gin, Benedictine, and orange juice. Shake well. Strain into old-fashioned glass filled with ice. Garnish with cherry.

267

SMILE COCKTAIL

- 1 oz. Gin
- 1 oz. Grenadine
- ½ tsp. Lemon Juice
- Ice

Directions: Shake all ingredients with ice, strain into a cocktail glass, and serve.

SMILER COCKTAIL

- ½ oz. Dry Vermouth
- ½ oz. Sweet Vermouth
- 1 oz. Gin
- ¼ tsp. Orange Juice
- Dash Bitters
- Ice

Directions: Shake all ingredients with ice, strain into a cocktail glass, and serve.

SMITH AND KEARNS

- 1 oz. Kahlua
- 1 oz. Light Cream
- Carbonated Water
- Ice

Directions: Pour Kahlua and light cream into a highball glass filled with ice and stir well. Fill with carbonated water, stir lightly, and serve.

SNAKE BITE

- 2 oz. Yukon Jack (Canadian Liqueur)
- Dash Lime Juice
- Ice

Directions: Pour Yukon Jack over ice. Add a dash of lime juice and serve.

SNYDER

- ½ oz. Dry Vermouth
- 1 ½ oz. Gin
- ½ oz. Triple Sec
- Twist of Lemon Peel
- Ice

Directions: Shake all ingredients except lemon peel with ice and strain into a cocktail glass. Add the twist of lemon peel.

SOL Y SOMBRA

- 1 ½ oz. Brandy
- 1 ½ oz. Anisette
- Ice

Directions: Shake ingredients with ice. Strain into brandy snifter.

SOMBRERO

- 1 ½ oz. Coffee Brandy
- 1 oz. Light Cream
- Ice

Directions: Pour brandy into an old-fashioned glass over ice cubes. Float cream on top and serve.

SON OF ADAM

- 1 ½ oz. Light Rum
- ½ oz. Apricot Brandy
- ½ oz. Lemon Juice
- ½ tsp. Superfine Sugar
- 1 tsp. Grenadine
- Ice

Directions: In a shaker half-filled with ice cubes, combine all of the ingredients. Shake well. Strain into a cocktail glass.

SONNY GETS KISSED

- 1 ½ oz. Light Rum
- ½ oz. Apricot Brandy
- 2 tsp. Lime Juice
- 2 tsp. Lemon Juice
- ½ tsp. Superfine Sugar
- Ice

Directions: In a shaker half-filled with ice cubes, combine all of the ingredients. Shake well. Strain into a cocktail glass.

SOOTHER COCKTAIL

- ½ oz. Apple Brandy
- ½ oz. Brandy
- ½ oz. Triple Sec
- Juice of ½ Lemon
- 1 tsp. Powdered Sugar
- Ice

Directions: Shake all ingredients with ice, strain into a cocktail glass, and serve.

SOUL KISS COCKTAIL

- ¾ oz. Dry Vermouth
- ¾ oz. Bourbon
- 1 ½ tsp. Dubonnet
- 1 ½ tsp. Orange Juice
- Ice

Directions: Shake all ingredients with ice, strain into a cocktail glass, and serve.

SOUTH OF THE BORDER

- 1 oz. Tequila
- ¾ oz. Coffee Brandy
- Juice of ½ Lime
- 1 Lime Slice
- Ice

Directions: Shake ice with ingredients except lime slice. Strain in whiskey sour glass. Add lime slice.

SOUTHAMPTON SLAM

- ½ oz. Green Crème de Menthe
- ½ oz. Anisette
- Club Soda

Directions: Serve in rocks glass without ice. Pour in liquor, fill with club soda, and roll once. Serve with a straw.

SOUTHERN BELLE

- ½ oz. Brandy
- ½ oz. White Crème de Cacao
- ½ oz. Benedictine

Directions: Pour the brandy in pousse-café glass. Tilt glass at 45 degree angle and slowly pour the crème de cacao down the side so that it floats on the brandy. Repeat with Benedictine.

SOUTHERN BRIDE

- 1 ½ oz. Gin
- 1 oz. Grapefruit Juice
- Dash Maraschino
- Ice

Directions: Shake all ingredients with ice, strain into a cocktail glass, and serve.

SOUTHERN GIN COCKTAIL

- 2 oz. Gin
- ½ tsp. Triple Sec
- 2 dashes Orange Bitters
- Twist of Lemon Peel
- Ice

Directions: Stir all ingredients except lemon peel with ice and strain into a cocktail glass. Add the twist of lemon peel and serve.

SOVIET

- 1 ½ oz. Vodka
- ½ oz. Amontillado Sherry
- ½ oz. Dry Vermouth
- Twist of Lemon Peel
- Ice

Directions: Shake ice with ingredients except lemon peel and strain in old-fashioned glass over ice. Add twist of lemon peel and serve.

SPARK IN THE NIGHT

- 1 ½ oz. Dark Rum
- ½ oz. Kahlua
- 2 tsp. Lime Juice
- Ice

Directions: In a shaker half-filled with ice, mix ingredients. Shake. Strain into cocktail glass.

SPECIAL ROUGH COCKTAIL

- 1 ½ oz. Brandy
- 1 ½ oz. Apple Brandy
- ½ tsp. Anisette
- Ice

Directions: Stir all ingredients with ice, strain into a cocktail glass, and serve.

SPENCER COCKTAIL

- ¾ oz. Apricot Brandy
- 1 ½ oz. Gin
- ¼ tsp. Orange Juice
- Dash Bitters
- Twist of Orange Peel
- 1 Cherry
- Ice

Directions: Shake brandy, gin, orange juice, and bitters with ice and strain into a cocktail glass. Add the twist of orange peel, top with the cherry.

SPHINX COCKTAIL

- 1 ½ tsp. Sweet Vermouth
- 1 ½ tsp. Dry Vermouth
- 1 ½ oz. Gin
- 1 Lemon Slice
- Ice

Directions: Stir all ingredients except lemon slice with ice and strain into a cocktail glass. Add the lemon slice and serve.

SPRING FEELING COCKTAIL

- 1 oz. Gin
- ½ oz. Green Chartreuse
- 1 tbs. Lemon Juice
- Ice

Directions: Shake all ingredients with ice, strain into a cocktail glass, and serve.

ST. PATRICK'S DAY

- ¾ oz. Green Crème de Menthe
- ¾ oz. Green Chartreuse
- ¾ oz. Irish Whiskey
- Dash Bitters
- Ice

Directions: Stir all ingredients with ice, strain into a cocktail glass, and serve.

STANLEY COCKTAIL

- ¼ oz. Light Rum
- ¾ oz. Gin
- Juice of ¼ Lemon
- 1 tsp. Grenadine
- Ice

Directions: Shake all ingredients with ice, strain into a cocktail glass, and serve.

STANLEY SENIOR

- 2 oz. Light Rum
- 1 oz. Grapefruit Juice
- ½ oz. Cranberry Liqueur
- Ice

Directions: In a shaker half-filled with ice cubes, combine all of the ingredients. Shake well. Strain into a cocktail glass.

STARSEEKER

- 2 oz. Light Rum
- 1 oz. Orange Juice
- 1 tsp. Grenadine
- 4 oz. Tonic Water
- 1 Lemon Wedge
- Ice

Directions: Pour ingredients in highball glass almost filled with ice. Stir. Garnish with lemon wedge.

STEVIE RAY VAUGHN

- 1 oz. Jack Daniels
- 1 oz. Southern Comfort
- 1 oz. Triple Sec
- 1 oz. Sweet and Sour Mix
- 5 oz. Orange Juice
- Ice

Directions: Shake ingredients over ice. Strain into shot glasses.

STILETTO

- 1 ½ tsp. Amaretto
- 1 ½ oz. Blended Whiskey
- Juice of ½ Lemon
- Ice

Directions: Pour all ingredients into an old-fashioned glass over ice cubes, stir, and serve. Bourbon may be substituted for blended whiskey, if preferred.

STIRRUP CUP

- 1 oz. Cherry Brandy
- 1 oz. Brandy
- Juice of ½ Lemon
- 1 tsp. Sugar
- Ice

Directions: Shake all ingredients with ice, strain into an old-fashioned glass over ice.

STOMACHACHE

- 1 oz. Nyquil
- 3 oz. Mountain Dew
- 3 oz. 7-Up
- 3 oz. Scotch
- 1 oz. Water

Directions: Pour Nyquil into a rocks glass. Add Mountain Dew, 7-Up, and Scotch. Pour water in last.

STONE COCKTAIL

- ½ oz. Sweet Vermouth
- 1 oz. Dry Sherry
- ½ oz. Light Rum
- Ice

Directions: Stir all ingredients with ice, strain into a cocktail glass, and serve.

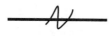

STONE FENCE

- 2 oz. Scotch
- Carbonated Water
- 2 dashes Bitters
- Ice

Directions: Fill a highball glass with ice cubes. Add Scotch and bitters and fill with carbonated water. Stir and serve.

STONE SOUR

- 1 oz. Apricot Brandy
- 1 oz. Orange Juice
- 1 oz. Sweet and Sour
- Ice

Directions: Shake all ingredients with ice, strain into a chilled whiskey sour glass, and serve.

STRAIGHT LAW COCKTAIL

- 1 ½ oz. Dry Sherry
- ¾ oz. Gin
- Ice

Directions: Stir ingredients with ice, strain into a cocktail glass, and serve.

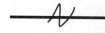

STRANGER-IN-TOWN

- 1 ½ oz. Light Rum
- ½ oz. Sweet Vermouth
- ½ oz. Calvados
- ½ oz. Cherry Brandy
- 1 Maraschino Cherry
- Ice

Directions: In a mixing glass half-filled with ice cubes, combine the rum, vermouth, Calvados, and cherry brandy. Stir well. Strain into a cocktail glass and garnish with the cherry.

271

STRAWBERRIES & CREAM

- **1 oz. Strawberry Schnapps**
- **2 oz. Half & Half**
- **1 ½ tbs. Sugar**
- **3 Whole Strawberries**
- **2 cups of Crushed Ice**

Directions: Place schnapps, Half & Half, sugar, and crushed ice in an electric blender and blend at a high speed. Add two of the strawberries and blend for ten seconds. Pour into a parfait glass, top with the other strawberry, and serve with a straw.

STRAWBERRY DAWN

- **1 oz. Gin**
- **1 oz. Cream of Coconut**
- **1/3 cup of Frozen Strawberries**
- **1 Mint Sprig**
- **1 cup of Crushed Ice**

Directions: Blend all ingredients except mint sprig with ice in an electric blender at a high speed. Pour into a cocktail glass, add the mint sprig, and serve.

STRAWBERRY FIELDS FOREVER

- **½ oz. Brandy**
- **2 oz. Strawberry Schnapps**
- **Carbonated Water**
- **1 Fresh Strawberry**
- **Ice**

Directions: Pour brandy and schnapps over ice in a highball glass. Fill with carbonated water and stir. Add the strawberry and serve.

STRAWBERRY MARGARITA

- **½ oz. Strawberry Schnapps**
- **1 oz. Tequila**
- **½ oz. Triple Sec**
- **1 oz. Lemon Juice**
- **1 oz. Strawberries**
- **Salt**
- **Ice**

Directions: Rub the rim of a cocktail glass with lemon juice and dip rim in salt. Shake schnapps, tequila, Triple Sec, lemon juice, and strawberries with ice, strain in salt-rimmed glass, and serve.

SUE RIDING HIGH

- **1 ½ oz. Dark Rum**
- **½ oz. Dark Crème de Cacao**
- **2 oz. Hot Chocolate**
- **1 tsp. Heavy Cream**
- **Ice**

Directions: Prepare the hot chocolate and let it cool to room temperature. In a shaker half-filled with ice, combine rum, crème de cacao, and hot chocolate. Shake. Strain into a cocktail glass. Drop the cream into the center of the drink.

SUFFRAGETTE CITY

- **1 ½ oz. Light Rum**
- **½ oz. Grand Marnier**
- **½ oz. Lime Juice**
- **½ tsp. Grenadine**
- **Ice**

Directions: In a shaker half-filled with ice cubes, combine all of the ingredients. Shake well. Strain into a cocktail glass.

SUGAR DADDY

- 2 oz. Gin
- 2 tsp. Maraschino Liqueur
- 1 oz. Pineapple Juice
- Dash Bitters
- Ice

Directions: In a shaker half-filled with ice cubes, combine all of the ingredients. Shake well. Strain into a cocktail glass.

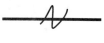

SUNSHINE COCKTAIL

- 1 ½ oz. Gin
- ¾ oz. Sweet Vermouth
- Dash Bitters
- Twist of Orange Peel
- Ice

Directions: Stir all ingredients except orange peel with ice and strain into a cocktail glass. Add the twist of orange peel and serve.

SURF RIDER

- 1 oz. Sweet Vermouth
- 3 oz. Vodka
- ½ cup of Orange Juice
- Juice of ½ Lemon
- ½ tsp. Grenadine
- 1 Orange Slice
- Ice

Directions: Shake all ingredients except orange slice with ice and strain into a cocktail glass. Add the orange slice, top with a cherry, and serve.

SUSAN LITTLER

- 1 oz. Dark Rum
- ½ oz. Bourbon
- 1 tsp. Galliano
- 2 oz. Orange Juice
- Ice

Directions: Pour all of the ingredients into a highball glass almost filled with ice cubes. Stir well.

SWEET MARIA

- ½ oz. Amaretto
- 1 oz. Vodka
- 1 tbs. Light Cream
- Cracked Ice

Directions: Shake all ingredients with cracked ice, strain into a cocktail glass, and serve.

SWEET PATOOTIE COCKTAIL

- ½ oz. Triple Sec
- 1 oz. Gin
- 1 tbs. Orange Juice
- Ice

Directions: Shake all ingredients with ice, strain into a cocktail glass, and serve.

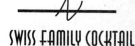

SWISS FAMILY COCKTAIL

- 1 ½ oz. Blended Whiskey
- ¾ oz. Dry Vermouth
- ½ tsp. Anisette
- 2 dashes Bitters
- Ice

Directions: Stir all ingredients with ice, strain into a cocktail glass, and serve.

T.N.T.

- 1 oz. Tequila
- Tonic Water
- Ice

Directions: Pour ingredients into an old-fashioned glass over ice cubes. Stir well and serve.

TAILSPIN COCKTAIL

- ¾ oz. Sweet Vermouth
- ¾ oz. Gin
- ¾ oz. Green Chartreuse
- Dash Orange Bitters
- Twist of Lemon Peel
- 1 Cherry
- Ice

Directions: Stir ice with ingredients except cherry. Strain in cocktail glass. Top with cherry.

TANGO COCKTAIL

- ½ oz. Sweet Vermouth
- ½ oz. Dry Vermouth
- 1 oz. Gin
- ½ tsp. Triple Sec
- 1 tbs. Orange Juice
- Ice

Directions: Shake ice with ingredients. Strain in cocktail glass.

TARANTULA

- 1 ½ oz. Scotch
- 1 oz. Sweet Vermouth
- ½ oz. Benedictine
- 1 Lemon Twist
- Ice

Directions: In mixing glass half-filled with ice,, mix ingredients. Stir. Strain in cocktail glass. Garnish with lemon twist.

TARTAN SWIZZLE

- 1 ½ oz. Lime Juice
- 1 tsp. Superfine Sugar
- 2 oz. Scotch
- Dash Bitters
- 3 oz. Club Soda
- Ice

Directions: In shaker half-filled with ice, combine ingredients except club soda. Shake. Fill Collins glass with crushed ice. Stir until frosted. Strain in glass. Add club soda.

TEMPTATION COCKTAIL

- 1 ½ oz. Blended Whiskey
- ½ tsp. Dubonnet
- ½ tsp. Triple Sec
- ½ tsp. Anisette
- Twist of Orange Peel
- Twist of Lemon Peel
- Ice

Directions: Shake ingredients with ice. Strain in cocktail glass. Add orange and lemon peel and serve.

TEMPTER COCKTAIL

- 1 oz. Apricot Brandy
- 1 oz. Port
- Ice

Directions: Stir ice with ingredients, strain in to cocktail glass.

TEN QUIDDER

- 1 ½ oz. Gin
- 1 oz. Triple Sec
- Dash Bitters
- 1 tsp. Blue Curacao
- Ice

Directions: In old-fashioned glass almost filled ice, mix gin, Triple Sec, and bitters. Stir. Pour curacao in center of drink.

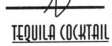

TEQUILA COCKTAIL

- 2 oz. Tequila
- Juice of ½ Lemon
- 4 dashes Grenadine
- $\frac{1}{3}$ Egg White
- 1 Lemon Slice
- Ice

Directions: Shake all ingredients except lemon slice with ice and strain into a cocktail glass. Add the lemon slice and serve.

TEQUILA FIZZ

- 2 oz. Tequila
- 1 tbs. Lemon Juice
- ¾ oz. Grenadine
- 1 Egg White
- Ginger Ale
- Ice

Directions: Shake all ingredients except ginger ale with ice and strain into a Collins glass over ice. Fill with ginger ale. Stir.

TEQUILA MANHATTAN

- 2 oz. Tequila
- 1 oz. Sweet Vermouth
- Dash Lime Juice
- 1 Orange Slice
- 1 Cherry
- Ice

Directions: Shake tequila, vermouth, and lime juice with ice and strain into an old-fashioned glass over ice cubes. Add the orange slice, top with the cherry, and serve.

TEQUILA MATADOR

- 1 ½ oz. Tequila
- 3 oz. Pineapple Juice
- Juice of ½ Lime
- Ice

Directions: Shake all ingredients with ice, strain into a Champagne flute, and serve.

TEQUILA MOCKINGBIRD

- 1 ½ oz. Tequila
- ½ oz. Triple Sec
- ½ oz. Blue Curacao
- 2 oz. Orange Juice
- 1 oz. Cranberry Juice
- 1 Lemon or Cherry Garnish (optional)
- Ice

Directions: Fill a tall rocks glass or tumbler with ice. Add tequila and Triple Sec, followed by the orange and cranberry juice. Add blue curacao. Do not mix. Garnish with lemon or cherry if desired.

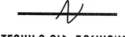

TEQUILA OLD-FASHIONED

- 1 ½ oz. Tequila
- 1 Splash Carbonated Water
- ½ tsp. Sugar
- 1 tsp. Water
- Dash Bitters
- 1 Pineapple Stick
- Ice

Directions: Mix sugar, bitters, and water in an old-fashioned glass. Add tequila, ice cubes, and carbonated water. Add the pineapple stick and serve.

TEQUILA SOUR

- 2 oz. Tequila
- Juice of ½ Lemon
- 1 tsp. Powdered Sugar
- ½ Lemon Slice
- 1 Cherry
- Ice

Directions: Shake tequila, lemon juice, and powdered sugar with ice and strain into a whiskey sour glass. Add the half-lemon slice, top with the cherry, and serve.

TEQUILA SUNSET

- 1 oz. Tequila
- Orange Juice
- ½ oz. Blackberry Brandy
- 1 Cherry
- Ice

Directions: Pour tequila into a Collins glass filled with ice cubes. Fill with orange juice and stir well. Top with blackberry brandy and stir lightly. Add the cherry on top and serve.

TEQUINI

- 1 ½ oz. Tequila
- ½ oz. Dry Vermouth
- Dash Bitters
- Twist of Lemon Peel
- 1 Olive
- Ice

Directions: Stir tequila, vermouth, and bitters with ice and strain into a cocktail glass. Add the twist of lemon peel, top with the olive, and serve.

THANKSGIVING SPECIAL

- ¾ oz. Apricot Brandy
- ¾ oz. Dry Vermouth
- ¾ oz. Gin
- ¼ tsp. Lemon Juice
- 1 Cherry
- Ice

Directions: Shake all ingredients except cherry with ice and strain into a cocktail glass. Top with the cherry and serve.

THE SHOOT

- 1 oz. Dry Sherry
- 1 oz. Scotch
- 1 tsp. Lemon Juice
- 1 tsp. Orange Juice
- ½ tsp. Powdered Sugar
- Ice

Directions: Shake all ingredients with ice. Strain into a cocktail glass.

THIRD RAIL COCKTAIL

- ¾ oz. Light Rum
- ¾ oz. Brandy
- ¾ oz. Apple Brandy
- ¼ tsp. Anisette
- Ice

Directions: Shake all ingredients with ice, strain into a cocktail glass, and serve.

THREE MILLER COCKTAIL

- 1 ½ oz. Light Rum
- ¾ oz. Brandy
- ¼ tsp. Lemon Juice
- 1 tsp. Grenadine
- Ice

Directions: Shake all ingredients with ice, strain into a cocktail glass, and serve.

THRILLER

- 1 ½ oz. Scotch
- 1 oz. Green Ginger Wine
- 1 oz. Orange Juice
- Ice

Directions: In a shaker half-filled with ice cubes, combine all of the ingredients. Shake well. Strain into a cocktail glass.

THUNDER

- 1 ½ oz. Brandy
- 1 tsp. Powdered Sugar
- Pinch Cayenne Pepper
- 1 Egg Yolk
- Ice

Directions: Shake all ingredients with ice, strain into a cocktail glass, and serve.

THUNDER AND LIGHTNING

- 1 ½ oz. Brandy
- 1 tsp. Powdered Sugar
- 1 Egg Yolk
- Ice

Directions: Shake all ingredients with ice, strain into a cocktail glass, and serve.

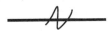

THUNDERCLAP

- ¾ oz. Blended Whiskey
- ¾ oz. Brandy
- ¾ oz. Gin
- Ice

Directions: Shake all ingredients with ice, strain into a cocktail glass, and serve.

TIDBIT

- 1 oz. Gin
- Scoop of Vanilla Ice Cream
- Dash Dry Sherry
- Ice

Directions: Blend all ingredients in an electric blender at a low speed for a short length of time. Pour into a highball glass.

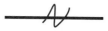

TIPPERARY COCKTAIL

- ¾ oz. Sweet Vermouth
- ¾ oz. Irish Whiskey
- ¾ oz. Green Chartreuse
- Ice

Directions: Stir all ingredients with ice, strain into a cocktail glass, and serve.

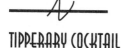

TO HELL WITH SWORDS AND GARTER

- 1 ½ oz. Scotch
- 1 oz. Dry Vermouth
- 1 ½ oz. Pineapple Juice
- Ice

Directions: In a shaker half-filled with ice cubes, combine all of the ingredients. Shake well. Strain into an old-fashioned glass almost filled with ice cubes.

TOM COLLINS

- 2 oz. Gin
- 1 oz. Lemon Juice
- 1 tsp. Superfine Sugar
- 3 oz. Club Soda
- 1 Maraschino Cherry
- 1 Orange Slice
- Ice

Directions: In a shaker half-filled with ice cubes, combine the gin, lemon juice, and sugar. Shake well. Strain into a Collins glass almost filled with ice cubes. Add the club soda. Stir and garnish with the cherry and the orange slice.

TOP BANANA

- 1 oz. Crème de Bananes
- 1 oz. Vodka
- Juice of ½ Orange
- Ice

Directions: Shake all ingredients with ice, strain into an old-fashioned glass over ice cubes, and serve.

TORRIDORA COCKTAIL

- 1 ½ oz. Light Rum
- 1 tsp. 151 Proof Rum
- ½ oz. Coffee Brandy
- 1 ½ tsp. Cream
- Ice

Directions: Shake light rum, brandy, and cream with ice and strain into a cocktail glass. Float 151 proof rum on top.

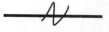

TOVARICH COCKTAIL

- 1 ½ oz. Vodka
- ¾ oz. Kummel
- Juice of ½ Lime
- Ice

Directions: Shake all ingredients with ice, strain into a cocktail glass, and serve.

TRIAD

- ½ oz. Anejo Rum
- ½ oz. Sweet Vermouth
- ½ oz. Amaretto
- 4 oz. Ginger Ale
- 1 Lemon Twist
- Ice

Directions: Pour the rum, vermouth, Amaretto, and ginger ale into a highball glass almost filled with ice cubes. Stir well and garnish with the lemon twist.

TRILBY COCKTAIL

- ¾ oz. Sweet Vermouth
- 1 ½ oz. Bourbon
- 2 dashes Orange Bitters
- Ice

Directions: Stir all ingredients with ice, strain into a cocktail glass, and serve.

TRINITY COCKTAIL

- ¾ oz. Dry Vermouth
- ¾ oz. Sweet Vermouth
- ¾ oz. Gin
- Ice

Directions: Stir all ingredients with ice. Strain into a cocktail glass.

TROPICAL COCKTAIL

- ¾ oz. Dry Vermouth
- ¾ oz. White Crème de Cacao
- ¾ oz. Maraschino
- Dash Bitters
- Ice

Directions: Stir ice with ingredients. Strain in cocktail glass.

TURF COCKTAIL

- 1 oz. Dry Vermouth
- 1 oz. Gin
- ¼ tsp. Anisette
- 2 dashes Bitters
- Twist of Orange Peel
- Ice

Directions: Stir ice and ingredients. Strain in cocktail glass. Add twist of orange peel.

TUXEDO COCKTAIL

- 1 ½ oz. Dry Vermouth
- 1 ½ oz. Gin
- ¼ tsp. Maraschino
- ¼ tsp. Anisette
- 2 dashes Orange Bitters
- 1 Cherry
- Ice

Directions: Stir ice and ingredients. Strain in cocktail glass. Top with cherry.

TWENTY THOUSAND LEAGUES

- Crushed Ice
- 1 ½ oz. Gin
- 1 oz. Dry Vermouth
- 1 tsp. Pernod
- 2 dashes Orange Bitters

Directions: In a mixing glass half-filled with crushed ice, combine ingredients. Stir well. Strain into cocktail glass.

TWIN HILLS

- 1 ½ oz. Blended Whiskey
- 1 ½ tsp. Lemon Juice
- 1 ½ tsp. Lime Juice
- 2 tsp. Benedictine
- 1 tsp. Sugar
- 1 Lemon Slice
- Ice

Directions: Shake all ingredients with ice and strain into a whiskey sour glass. Add the lemon slice.

TWISTER

- 2 oz. Vodka
- Lemon-lime Soda
- Juice of 1/3 Lime
- Ice

Directions: Pour vodka and lime juice into a Collins glass over ice. Fill with lemon-lime soda.

TYPHOON

- Chilled Champagne
- 1 oz. Gin
- ½ oz. Anisette
- 1 oz. Lime Juice
- Ice

Directions: Shake all ingredients except Champagne with ice and strain into a Collins glass over ice cubes. Fill glass with chilled Champagne, stir lightly, and serve.

ULANDA COCKTAIL

- 1 ½ oz. Gin
- ¼ tsp. Anisette
- ¾ oz. Triple Sec
- Ice

Directions: Stir all ingredients with ice, strain into a cocktail glass, and serve.

UNION JACK COCKTAIL

- 1 ½ oz. Gin
- ¾ oz. Sloe Gin
- ½ tsp. Grenadine
- Ice

Directions: Shake all ingredients with ice, strain into a cocktail glass, and serve.

VALENCIA COCKTAIL

- 1 ½ oz. Apricot Brandy
- 1 tbs. Orange Juice
- 2 dashes Orange Bitters
- Ice

Directions: Shake all ingredients with ice, strain into a cocktail glass, and serve.

VAN VLEET

- 3 oz. Light Rum
- 1 oz. Maple Syrup
- 1 oz. Lemon Juice
- Ice

Directions: Shake all ingredients with ice, strain into an old-fashioned glass over ice cubes, and serve.

VELVET HAMMER

- 1 tbs. Crème de Cacao
- 1 ½ oz. Vodka
- 1 tbs. Cream
- Ice

Directions: Shake all ingredients with ice, strain into a cocktail glass, and serve.

VERBOTEN

- 1 ½ oz. Gin
- 1 tbs. Forbidden Fruit
- 1 tbs. Lemon Juice
- 1 tbs. Orange Juice
- 1 Cherry
- Ice

Directions: Shake all ingredients except cherry with ice and strain into a cocktail glass. Top with the cherry and serve.

VERMOUTH CASSIS

- 1 ½ oz. Dry Vermouth
- ¾ oz. Crème de Cassis
- Carbonated Water
- Ice

Directions: Stir vermouth and crème de cassis in a highball glass with ice cubes. Fill with carbonated water, stir again, and serve.

VESUVIO

- 1 oz. Light Rum
- ½ oz. Sweet Vermouth
- Juice of ½ Lemon
- 1 tsp. Powdered Sugar
- 1 Egg White
- Ice

Directions: Shake all ingredients with ice, strain into an old-fashioned glass over ice cubes, and serve.

VETERAN

- 2 oz. Dark Rum
- ½ oz. Cherry Brandy
- Ice

Directions: Pour rum and brandy in old-fashioned glass almost filled with ice. Stir well.

VICIOUS SID

- 1 ½ oz. Light Rum
- ½ oz. Southern Comfort
- ½ oz. Triple Sec
- 1 oz. Lemon Juice
- Dash Bitters
- Ice

Directions: In a shaker half-filled with ice cubes, combine all of the ingredients. Shake well. Strain into an old-fashioned glass almost filled with ice cubes.

VICTOR

- 1 ½ oz. Gin
- ½ oz. Sweet Vermouth
- ½ oz. Brandy
- Ice

Directions: Shake ice with ingredients. Strain in cocktail glass.

VICTORY COLLINS

- 1 ½ oz. Vodka
- 3 oz. Lemon Juice
- 3 oz. Unsweetened Grape Juice
- 1 tsp. Powdered Sugar
- 1 Orange Slice
- Ice

Directions: Shake ice and ingredients. Strain in Collins glass over ice. Add orange slice.

VIVA VILLA

- 1 ½ oz. Tequila
- Juice of 1 Lime
- 1 tsp. Sugar
- Ice

Directions: Rub the rim of an old-fashioned glass with lemon juice and dip it in salt. Shake all ingredients with ice, strain into the salt-rimmed glass over ice.

VODKA 7

- 2 oz. Vodka
- Juice of ½ Lime
- Lemon-lime Soda
- 1 Lime Wedge
- Ice

Directions: Pour vodka and lime juice into a Collins glass over several ice cubes. Drop the lime wedge in the glass and fill with lemon-lime soda. Stir well and serve.

VODKA AND APPLE JUICE

- 2 oz. Vodka
- Apple Juice
- Ice

Directions: Pour vodka into a highball glass over two or three ice cubes. Fill with apple juice, stir, and serve.

VODKA AND TONIC

- 2 oz. Vodka
- Tonic Water
- Ice

Directions: Pour vodka in highball glass over ice. Fill with tonic water. Stir.

VODKA COLLINS

- 2 oz. Vodka
- Juice of ½ Lemon
- 1 tsp. Powdered Sugar
- Carbonated Water
- 1 Cherry
- 1 Orange Slice
- 1 Lemon Slice
- Ice

Directions: Shake vodka, lemon juice, and powdered sugar with ice and strain into a Collins glass. Add several ice cubes, fill with carbonated water, and stir. Decorate with orange and lemon slices and top with the cherry.

VODKA GIMLET

- 1 oz. Lime Juice
- 1 ½ oz. Vodka
- 1 tsp. Powdered Sugar
- Ice

Directions: Stir all ingredients with ice. Strain into a cocktail glass.

VODKA GRASSHOPPER

- ¾ oz. Green Crème de Menthe
- ¾ oz. White Crème de Cacao
- ¾ oz. Vodka
- Ice

Directions: Shake ice and ingredients. Strain in cocktail glass.

VODKA SALTY DOG

- 5 oz. Grapefruit Juice
- 1 ½ oz. Vodka
- ¼ tsp. Salt
- Ice

Directions: Pour ingredients in highball glass over ice. Stir.

VODKA SLING

- 2 oz. Vodka
- Juice of ½ Lemon
- 1 tsp. Powdered Sugar
- 1 tsp. Water
- Twist of Orange Peel
- Ice

Directions: Dissolve powdered sugar in a mixture of water and lemon juice. Add vodka. Pour into an old-fashioned glass over ice and stir. Add twist of orange peel and serve.

VODKA STINGER

- 1 oz. White Crème de Menthe
- 1 oz. Vodka
- Ice

Directions: Shake ingredients with ice. Strain into a cocktail glass.

WAHOO

- 1 ¾ oz. 151 Rum
- 1 ¾ oz. Amaretto
- Pineapple Juice
- Ice

Directions: Over ice, add rum and Amaretto. Top off with pineapple juice. Serve in a rocks glass.

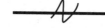

WAIKIKI BEACHCOMBER

- ¾ oz. Triple Sec
- ¾ oz. Gin
- 1 tbs. Pineapple Juice
- Ice

Directions: Shake all ingredients with ice. Strain into a cocktail glass.

WALLICK COCKTAIL

- 1 ½ oz. Gin
- 1 ½ oz. Dry Vermouth
- 1 tsp. Triple Sec
- Ice

Directions: Stir ice with ingredients. Strain into cocktail glass.

WARD EIGHT

- 2 oz. Blended Whiskey
- Juice of ½ Lemon
- 1 tsp. Grenadine
- 1 tsp. Powdered Sugar
- 1 Orange Slice
- 1 Cherry
- Ice

Directions: Shake ice with ingredients. Strain in red wine glass filled with cracked ice. Add orange slice, top with cherry, and serve with a straw.

WARSAW COCKTAIL

- 1 ½ oz. Vodka
- ½ oz. Dry Vermouth
- ½ oz. Blackberry Brandy
- 1 tsp. Lemon Juice
- Ice

Directions: Shake ice with ingredients. Strain in cocktail glass.

WASHINGTON COCKTAIL

- 1 ½ oz. Dry Vermouth
- ¾ oz. Brandy
- ½ tsp. Sugar Syrup
- 2 dashes Bitters
- Ice

Directions: Stir all ingredients with ice, strain into a cocktail glass, and serve.

WATERMELON

- 1 oz. Strawberry Liqueur
- 1 oz. Vodka
- 1 oz. Sweet and Sour
- 1 oz. Orange Juice
- Ice

Directions: Shake all ingredients with ice, strain into a Collins glass over ice.

WEBSTER COCKTAIL

- 1 ½ tsp. Apricot Brandy
- ½ oz. Dry Vermouth
- 1 oz. Gin
- Juice of ½ Lime
- Ice

Directions: Shake all ingredients with ice, strain into a cocktail glass, and serve.

WEDDING BELLE COCKTAIL

- ¾ oz. Dubonnet
- ¾ oz. Gin
- 1 ½ tsp. Cherry Brandy
- 1 ½ tsp. Orange Juice
- Ice

Directions: Shake all ingredients with ice, strain into a cocktail glass, and serve.

WEEP NO MORE COCKTAIL

- ¾ oz. Dubonnet
- ¾ oz. Brandy
- ¼ tsp. Maraschino
- Juice of ½ Lime
- Ice

Directions: Shake all ingredients with ice, strain into a cocktail glass, and serve.

WEMBLY COCKTAIL

- 1 ½ oz. Gin
- ¾ oz. Dry Vermouth
- ¼ tsp. Apricot Brandy
- ½ tsp. Apple Brandy
- Ice

Directions: Stir all ingredients with ice, strain into a cocktail glass, and serve.

WESTERN ROSE

- ½ oz. Apricot Brandy
- ½ oz. Dry Vermouth
- 1 oz. Gin
- ¼ tsp. Lemon Juice
- Ice

Directions: Shake all ingredients with ice, strain into a cocktail glass, and serve.

WHAT THE HELL

- 1 oz. Dry Vermouth
- 1 oz. Gin
- 1 oz. Apricot Brandy
- Dash Lemon Juice
- Ice

Directions: Stir all ingredients with ice cubes in an old-fashioned glass and serve.

WHIP COCKTAIL

- ½ oz. Sweet Vermouth
- ½ oz. Dry Vermouth
- 1 ½ oz. Brandy
- 1 tsp. Triple Sec
- ¼ tsp. Anisette
- Ice

Directions: Stir all ingredients with ice, strain into a cocktail glass, and serve.

WHISKEY COCKTAIL

- 2 oz. Blended Whiskey
- 1 tsp. Sugar Syrup
- Dash Bitters
- 1 Cherry
- Ice

Directions: Stir all ingredients except cherry with ice and strain into a cocktail glass. Top with the cherry and serve.

WHISKEY COLLINS

- 2 oz. Blended Whiskey
- 1 tsp. Powdered Sugar
- Juice of ½ Lemon
- Carbonated Water
- 1 Cherry
- 1 Orange Slice
- 1 Lemon Slice
- Ice

Directions: Shake blended whiskey, lemon juice, and powdered sugar with ice and strain into a Collins glass. Add several ice cubes, fill with carbonated water, and stir. Decorate with slices of orange and lemon, and top with the cherry. Serve with a straw.

WHISKEY EGGNOG

- 2 oz. Blended Whiskey
- 1 tsp. Powdered Sugar
- 1 Whole Egg
- 5 oz. Milk
- Nutmeg
- Ice

Directions: Shake all ingredients except nutmeg with ice and strain into a Collins glass. Sprinkle nutmeg on top and serve.

WHISKEY FIX

- 2 ½ oz. Blended Whiskey
- Juice of ½ Lemon
- 1 tsp. Powdered Sugar
- 1 Lemon Slice
- Ice

Directions: Shake the juice of lime and powdered sugar with ice and strain into a highball glass over ice cubes. Add blended whiskey and stir. Add the lemon slice and serve with a straw.

WHISKEY FLIP

- 1 ½ oz. Blended Whiskey
- 2 tsp. Light Cream
- 1 tsp. Powdered Sugar
- 1 Whole Egg
- Nutmeg
- Ice

Directions: Shake all ingredients except nutmeg with ice and strain into a whiskey sour glass. Sprinkle nutmeg on top and serve.

WHISKEY HIGHBALL

- 2 oz. Blended Whiskey
- Carbonated Water
- Twist of Lemon
- Ice

Directions: Pour blended whiskey into a highball glass over ice cubes. Fill with carbonated water and stir. Add the twist of lemon peel and serve.

WHISKEY RICKEY

- 1 ½ oz. Blended Whiskey
- Juice of ½ Lime
- Carbonated Water
- 1 Lime Wedge
- Ice

Directions: Pour blended whiskey and lime juice into a highball glass over ice cubes. Fill with carbonated water and stir. Drop the lime wedge in the glass and serve.

WHISKEY SOUR

- 2 oz. Blended Whiskey
- Juice of ½ Lemon
- ½ tsp. Powdered Sugar
- 1 Cherry
- ½ Lemon Slice
- Ice

Directions: Shake blended whiskey, lemon juice, and powdered sugar with ice and strain into a whiskey sour glass. Decorate with the half-slice of lemon, top with the cherry, and serve.

WHISKY MAC

- 1 ½ oz. Scotch
- 1 oz. Green Ginger Wine

Directions: Pour both of the ingredients into a wine goblet with no ice.

WHITE HEART

- ½ oz. Sambuca
- ½ oz. White Crème de Cacao
- 2 oz. Cream
- Ice

Directions: Shake all ingredients with ice, strain into a cocktail glass, and serve.

WHITE LADY

- 2 oz. Gin
- 1 Egg White
- 1 oz. Light Cream
- 1 tsp. Superfine Sugar
- Ice

Directions: In a shaker half-filled with ice cubes, combine all of the ingredients. Shake well. Strain into a cocktail glass.

WHITE LILY COCKTAIL

- ¾ oz. Light Rum
- ¾ oz. Gin
- ¾ oz. Triple Sec
- ¼ tsp. Anisette
- Ice

Directions: Shake all ingredients with ice, strain into a cocktail glass, and serve.

WHITE LION COCKTAIL

- 1 ½ oz. Light Rum
- Juice of ½ Lemon
- ½ tsp. Grenadine
- 1 tsp. Powdered Sugar
- 2 dashes Bitters
- Ice

Directions: Shake all ingredients with ice, strain into a cocktail glass, and serve.

WHITE RUSSIAN

- 2 oz. Vodka
- 1 oz. Coffee Liqueur
- Light Cream or Milk
- 1 Cherry
- Ice

Directions: Pour vodka and coffee liqueur over ice cubes in an old-fashioned cocktail glass. Fill with light cream and serve. Garnish with a cherry.

WHITE WAY COCKTAIL

- 1 ½ oz. Gin
- ¾ oz. White Crème de Menthe
- Ice

Directions: Shake ingredients with ice, strain into a cocktail glass, and serve.

WHY NOT

- 1 oz. Apricot Brandy
- 1 oz. Gin
- ½ oz. Dry Vermouth
- Dash Lemon Juice
- Ice

Directions: Shake all ingredients with ice, strain into a cocktail glass, and serve.

WIDOW WOODS' NIGHTCAP

- 2 oz. Scotch
- ½ oz. Dark Crème de Cacao
- 4 oz. Milk
- Ice

Directions: In a shaker half-filled with ice cubes, combine all of the ingredients. Shake well. Strain into a cocktail glass.

WIDOW'S KISS

- 1 oz. Brandy
- ½ oz. Yellow Chartreuse
- ½ oz. Benedictine
- Dash Bitters
- Ice

Directions: Shake all ingredients with ice, strain into a cocktail glass, and serve.

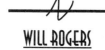

WILL ROGERS

- 1 ½ oz. Gin
- ½ oz. Dry Vermouth
- Dash Triple Sec
- 1 tbs. Orange Juice
- Ice

Directions: Shake all ingredients with ice, strain into a cocktail glass, and serve.

WINE COOLER

- 2 oz. Wine, With or Without Alcohol
- 5 oz. Lemon-lime Soda
- Ice

Directions: Mix wine and soft drink. Pour into a wine goblet or a highball glass. Add ice.

WOO WOO

- 1 ½ oz. Peach Schnapps
- 1 ½ oz. Vodka
- 3 ½ oz. Cranberry Juice
- Ice

Directions: Pour all ingredients into a highball glass over ice cubes. Stir.

WOODWARD COCKTAIL

- ½ oz. Dry Vermouth
- 1 ½ oz. Scotch
- 1 tbs. Grapefruit Juice
- Ice

Directions: Shake all ingredients with ice, strain into cocktail glass.

XANTHIA COCKTAIL

- ¾ oz. Cherry Brandy
- ¾ oz. Gin
- ¾ oz. Yellow Chartreuse
- Ice

Directions: Stir all ingredients with ice, strain into cocktail glass.

XERES COCKTAIL

- 2 oz. Dry Sherry
- Dash Orange Bitters
- Ice

Directions: Stir ingredients with ice, strain into a cocktail glass, and serve.

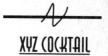

XYZ COCKTAIL

- 1 oz. Light Rum
- ½ oz. Triple Sec
- 1 tbs. Lemon Juice
- Ice

Directions: Shake all ingredients with ice, strain into a cocktail glass, and serve.

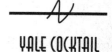

YALE COCKTAIL

- ½ oz. Dry Vermouth
- 1 ½ oz. Gin
- 1 tsp. Blue Curacao
- Dash Bitters
- Ice

Directions: Stir all ingredients with ice, strain into a cocktail glass, and serve.

YELLOW BIRD

- 1 cup of Ice
- 1 oz. Rum or Pineapple Vodka
- ½ oz. Coffee Liqueur
- ½ oz. Banana Liqueur
- 2 tbs. Cream of Coconut
- ½ cup of Fresh or Canned Pineapple

Directions: Blend ingredients until smooth. Serve in chilled hurricane glass.

YELLOW FEVER

- 2 oz. Vodka or Citrus Vodka
- Lemonade
- 1 Lemon Wedge
- Ice

Directions: Fill Collins glass with ice. Pour in ingredients. Garnish with lemon wedge.

YELLOW JACKET AKA KENTUCKY SCREWDRIVER, BLACK-EYED SUSAN

- 2 oz. Bourbon
- Orange Juice
- Ice

Directions: Fill Collins glass with ice. Pour in bourbon. Fill with orange juice.

YELLOW PARROT

- 1 oz. Apricot Brandy
- 1 oz. Pernod
- 1 oz. Yellow Chartreuse
- Ice

Directions: Fill a mixing glass with ice, pour in ingredients and shake. Strain into a chilled rocks glass.

YELLOW RATTLER

- 1 oz. Gin
- ½ oz. Sweet Vermouth
- ½ oz. Dry Vermouth
- 1 tbs. Orange Juice
- 1 Cocktail Onion
- Ice

Directions: Shake all ingredients except cocktail onion with ice and strain into a cocktail glass. Add the cocktail onion and serve.

YELLOW RUSSIAN

- 1 oz. Vodka or Banana Vodka
- 1 oz. Banana Liqueur
- Ice

Directions: Fill a Collins glass with ice. Pour in liquor and fill with milk or cream.

YELLOW STRAWBERRY

- 1 oz. Light Rum
- ½ oz. Crème de Bananes
- 4 oz. Thawed Strawberries
- 1 oz. Sweet and Sour
- 1 Banana Slice

Directions: Shake ice and ingredients except banana. Strain in chilled whiskey sour glass. Garnish with banana.

YELLOW SUBMARINE

- 2 oz. Vodka or Pineapple Vodka
- Pineapple Juice
- Milk
- Ice

Directions: Fill mixing glass with ice and pour in vodka. Fill with equal parts pineapple juice and milk. Shake. Serve in highball glass.

YO MAMA COCKTAIL

- 1 ½ oz. Stoli Orange Vodka
- Soda
- Splash Orange Juice
- Ice

Directions: Pour vodka in highball glass over ice. Add soda. Top with a splash of orange juice.

YODEL

- 2 oz. Fernet Branca
- 2 oz. Orange Juice
- Soda Water
- 1 Orange Wedge
- Ice

Directions: Fill Collins glass with ice. Pour ingredients and stir. Fill with soda water. Garnish with orange wedge.

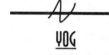

YOG

- 2 oz. Yukon Jack
- Orange Juice
- Grapefruit Juice
- Ice

Directions: Pour Yukon Jack in ice filled glass. Fill with equal parts of both juices. Shake. Pour in Collins glass.

YOKOHAMA MAMA

- 1 ½ oz. Brandy
- ½ oz. Melon Liqueur
- Dash Amaretto
- Dash Grenadine
- Orange Juice
- Pineapple Juice
- Ice

Directions: Fill mixing glass with ice. Pour ingredients. Fill with equal parts of both juices. Shake. Pour in Collins glass.

YOLANDA

- ½ oz. Gin
- ½ oz. Brandy
- 1 oz. Sweet Vermouth
- ½ oz. Anisette
- Dash Grenadine
- 1 Twist of Orange Peel
- Ice

Directions: Shake ice with ingredients. Strain in cocktail glass. Add twist of orange peel.

YORSH

- 2 oz. Vodka
- Beer

Directions: Pour vodka in a beer mug and fill with beer.

YOUR TONGUE, MY PANTIES

- ½ oz. Rum
- ½ oz. Coconut Rum
- ½ oz. Peach Schnapps
- ½ oz. Southern Comfort
- Cranberry Juice
- Orange Juice
- Lemon-lime Soda
- Ice

Directions: Fill Collins glass with ice. Pour ingredients and fill with equal parts of both juices. Top with lemon-lime soda.

ZAMBOANGA HUMMER

- ½ oz. Amber Rum
- ½ oz. Gin
- ½ oz. Brandy
- ½ oz. Curacao or Triple Sec
- 2 oz. Orange Juice
- 2 oz. Pineapple Juice
- ½ oz. Lemon Juice
- 1 tsp. Brown Sugar.
- Ice

Directions: Fill a mixing glass with ice and add ingredients. Shake. Pour into a Collins glass.

ZAZA

- 1 ½ oz. Gin or Orange Gin
- 1 ½ oz. Dubonnet
- ½ oz. Triple Sec
- 2 oz. Orange Juice
- Ice

Directions: Fill a mixing glass with ice. Add ingredients and shake. Strain into a chilled highball glass.

ZAZARAC

- 1 oz. Whiskey
- ¼ oz. Rum
- ¼ oz. Anisette
- ¼ oz. Sugar Syrup
- 3 dashes Bitters
- 1 oz. Water
- 1 Lemon Garnish
- Ice

Directions: Fill a highball glass with ice and pour in ingredients. Stir and garnish with lemon.

ZHIVAGO STANDARD

- 1 ½ oz. Vodka or Lime Vodka
- ½ oz. Kummel
- ½ oz. Lime Juice
- 1 Olive
- Ice

Directions: Fill a mixing glass with ice. Pour in ingredients and shake. Strain into a chilled cocktail glass and garnish with an olive.

ZIPPER

- 1 oz. Tequila
- 1 oz. Orange Liqueur
- ½ oz. Milk or Cream
- Ice

Directions: In mixing glass with ice, add ingredients. Shake and strain in shot glass.

ZIPPER HEAD

- 1 ½ oz. Vodka
- ½ oz. Black Raspberry Liqueur
- Soda Water
- Ice

Directions: Fill highball glass with ice, add ingredients. Fill with soda water. Drink in one shot through straw.

ZOMBIE

- 1 oz. Light Rum
- ½ oz. Crème de Almond
- 1 ½ oz. Sweet and Sour
- ½ oz. Triple Sec
- 1 ½ oz. Orange Juice
- ½ oz. 151 Proof Rum
- 1 Cherry (optional)
- Ice

Directions: Shake ice with ingredients except 151 proof rum. Strain in Collins glass over ice. Float 151 proof rum on top. Add cherry.

ZONKER

- 1 oz. Vodka or Citrus Vodka
- 1 oz. Triple Sec
- 1 oz. Amaretto
- 1 oz. Cranberry Juice
- Ice

Directions: Fill a mixing glass with ice. Pour in ingredients and shake. Strain into a chilled glass.

ZOO

- ½ oz. Gin
- ½ oz. Rum
- ½ oz. Tequila
- ½ oz. Bourbon
- Dash Grenadine
- Orange Juice
- Pineapple Juice
- Ice

Directions: Fill mixing glass with ice. Add ingredients. Fill with equal parts orange and pineapple juice. Shake. Serve in a Collins glass.

ZOOM

- 1 ½ oz. Brandy
- ¼ oz. Honey
- ½ oz. Cream
- Ice

Directions: Fill mixing glass with ice. Add ingredients. Shake. Strain into chilled cocktail glass.

ZUMA BUMA

- 1 ½ oz. Citrus Vodka
- ½ oz. Black Raspberry Liqueur
- Orange Juice
- Splash Cranberry Juice
- Ice

Directions: Fill a highball glass with ice and add ingredients. Fill with orange juice and a splash of cranberry juice.

009

- 4 oz. Apple Juice
- 1 oz. Tequila
- Ice

Directions: Mix ingredients in a Collins glass and add ice.

OH OH

- 1 oz. Blue Curacao
- 3 oz. Limeade
- 3 oz. Orange Juice
- 3 oz. Rum
- ½ oz. Guava Nectar
- Ice

Directions: Vigorously mix all ingredients with ice, either blended or on the rocks. Serve in a Collins glass.

1 RANDINI

- 2 parts Cranberry Juice Cocktail
- 2 oz. Bombay Sapphire Gin
- 1 Lime Wedge
- ½ oz. Triple Sec
- ½ oz. Stolichnaya Vodka
- Ice

Directions: Mix ingredients in a shaker with ice and strain into large martini glass. Garnish with a small lime wedge.

10 LB SLEDGEHAMMER

- 1 ¾ oz. Jose Cuervo Tequila
- 1 ¾ oz. Jack Daniel's

Directions: Pour ingredients into a shot glass.

100% ECSTASY

- 1 oz. Vodka
- 1 oz. Bailey's Irish Cream
- Ice

Directions: Pour ingredients over ice and serve in a rocks glass.

1001 NIGHTS

- 1 ¾ oz. Bols Crème de Cacao Brown
- 1 ¾ oz. Bols Triple Sec Curacao
- 1 ¾ oz. Bols Dry Orange Curacao
- Fruit Pieces
- Ice

Directions: Mix ingredients in a shaker filled with ice. Strain into a chilled cocktail glass. Garnish with little pieces of fruit.

101 DEGREES IN THE SHADE

- 1 Part Beer
- 1 Part Absolut Peppar
- Tabasco Sauce
- Tomato Juice

Directions: Mix beer, tomato juice, and vodka and pour into a Collins glass. Add tabasco sauce to taste.

1234...GO!

- 4 oz. Mineral Water
- 3 oz. Light Rum
- 1 oz. Sugar Syrup
- ½ oz. Bols Lychee
- 3 dashes Angostura
- 1 Cherry
- 1 Lemon Slice
- 1 Mint Sprig

Directions: Put all ingredients except angostura in a mixer with a half scoop of crushed ice. Shake and pour into a highball glass. Drop angostura on top. Garnish with cherry, lemon slice, and mint sprig.

151 FLORIDA BUSHWHACKER

- ½ oz. Coconut Rum
- ½ oz. Bacardi Light Rum
- ½ oz. Bacardi 151
- 1 oz. Crème de Cacao (Dark)
- 1 oz. Cointreau
- 3 oz. Milk
- 1 oz. Coconut Liqueur
- 1 cup of Vanilla Ice Cream
- Chocolate Shavings

Directions: Combine ingredients in blender. Blend until smooth. Pour in beer mug and garnish with chocolate shaving.

1800 BITE THE BERRY

- 1 ¼ oz. Jose Cuervo 1800 Tequila
- ½ oz. Triple Sec
- ¼ oz. Chambord Raspberry Liqueur
- 2 ½ oz. Sweet and Sour mix
- 2 oz. Cranberry Juice Cocktail
- 1 Orange Slice
- Ice

Directions: Pour over ice in a Collins. Garnish with orange slice.

1800 LEMON DROP

- 1 ¼ oz. Tequila
- ½ oz. Triple Sec
- 1 oz. Sweet and Sour Mix
- 1 oz. Lemon Lime Soda
- Lemon Juice
- 1 Lemon

Directions: Pour ingredients into a rocks glass. Float lemon juice on top. Garnish with fresh lemon.

1800 PINK CAD

- 1 oz. Tequila
- ½ oz. Triple Sec
- 2 oz. Sweet and Sour Mix
- ½ oz. Lime Juice
- Splash Cranberry Juice Cocktail
- 1 Lime Garnish
- Ice

Directions: Pour in a highball glass over ice and garnish with lime.

19 DUKE DRIVE

- 1/3 oz. Chocolate Mint Liqueur
- 1/3 oz. Cherry Brandy
- 1/3 oz. Crème de Banana

Directions: Layer ingredients in order in a shot glass.

1-900-FU*-ME-UP

- ½ oz. Absolut Kurant
- ¼ oz. Grand Marnier
- ¼ oz. Chambord Raspberry Liqueur
- ¼ oz. Midori
- ¼ oz. Coconut Rum
- ¼ oz. Amaretto
- ½ oz. Cranberry Juice Cocktail
- ¼ oz. Pineapple Juice
- Ice

Directions: Mix all the ingredients with ice then pour into shot glasses.

2001

- 2 oz. Pineapple Juice
- 1 oz. Rum
- ½ oz. Apricot Brandy
- ½ oz. Bols Crème de Cassis
- 1 Orange Garnish
- 1 Cherry
- Ice

Directions: Pour ingredients over ice into a rocks glass. Garnish with orange and cherry.

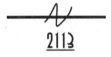

2113

- Ginger Ale
- Splash Lemon Juice
- 1 oz. Melon liqueur
- 1 oz. Vodka

Directions: Add all ingredients, stir, and serve in a Collins glass.

22 PARK LANE

- 1 ½ oz. Gin
- ¼ oz. Sweet Vermouth
- ¼ oz. Bols Dry Orange Curacao
- 1 Orange Wedge

Directions: Shake and strain into a cocktail glass. Garnish with an orange wedge.

24K NIGHTMARE

- ½ oz. Goldschlager
- ½ oz. Jaegermeister
- ½ oz. Rumplemintz
- ½ oz. Bacardi 151
- Ice

Directions: Mix ice and ingredients. Shake. Strain in shot glass.

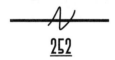

252

- ½ oz. Bacardi 151
- ½ oz. Wild Turkey 101

Directions: Add ingredients to shot glass.

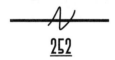

3 A.M. ON A SCHOOL NIGHT

- 1 ¾ oz. Wild Turkey
- Kool-Aid Fruit Punch

Directions: Mix Kool-Aid and the Wild Turkey together in Collins glass.

3 DISTANT ISLANDS

- 1 oz. Pisang Ambon
- 1 oz. Bols Coconut
- Ice

Directions: Combine ingredients in shaker half-filled with ice. Strain in chilled cocktail glass.

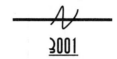

3001

- 1 oz. Blue Curacao
- 1 oz. Vodka
- ½ oz. Tonic Water
- Splash Lime Juice
- 2 Ice Cubes
- 1 Pineapple Slice
- Sprite

Directions: Combine blue curacao, vodka, tonic water, and a splash of lime juice in a Collins glass. Stir. Fill with Sprite. Stir. Add pineapple slice and ice cubes.

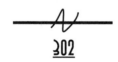

302

- 2 oz. 151 Proof Rum
- 5 oz. Strawberry Juice

Directions: Blend ingredients in a blender. Pour into a pint glass and serve with a straw.

333

- 1 oz. Bols Triple Sec Curacao
- 1 oz. Grapefruit Juice
- 1 Cherry
- Ice

Directions: Mix over ice and strain into a cocktail glass. Garnish with a cherry.

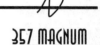

357 MAGNUM

- 1 oz. Smirnoff Vodka
- 1 oz. Captain Morgan's Spiced Rum
- 1 ½ oz. Amaretto
- 7-Up
- Ice

Directions: Pour vodka and rum over ice in a Collins glass. Add 7-Up and stir. Add Amaretto without stirring and serve.

3-MILE LONG ISLAND ICED TEA

- ½ oz. Gin
- ½ oz. Light Rum
- ½ oz. Tequila
- ½ oz. Triple Sec
- ½ oz. Vodka
- Cola
- Sweet and Sour
- Dash Bitters
- 1 Lemon Wedge
- Ice

Directions: Fill a Collins glass with ice and alcohol. Fill glass two-thirds full with cola and add sweet and sour. Top with a dash of bitters and a lemon wedge.

3RD STREET PROMENADE

- 1 ½ oz. Stolichnaya Vanilla
- 1/3 oz. Gin
- 1/3 oz. Triple Sec
- 1/3 oz. Tequila
- ½ oz. Cinnamon Schnapps
- 6 oz. Orange Juice
- Ice

Directions: In a blender, combine ice, orange juice, vodka, cinnamon schnapps, gin, tequila, and Triple Sec. Blend well and pour into a tall chilled glass. Sip through a straw.

4 HORSEMEN

- ¼ oz. Goldschlager
- ¼ oz. Jaegermeister
- ¼ oz. Rumplemintz
- ¼ oz. Bacardi 151

Directions: Layer in a shot glass in the given order.

401

- ¼ oz. Kahlua
- ¼ oz. Crème de Banana
- ¼ oz. Bailey's Irish Cream
- ¼ oz. Yukon Jack

Directions: Layer ingredients in a shot glass.

420 KICKER

- 2 oz. Absolut Peppar
- 1 oz. Sweet and Sour Mix
- 1 oz. Peppermint Extract
- 1 Cherry
- Ice

Directions: Pour ingredients in a rocks glass over ice. Garnish with a cherry.

43 AMIGOS

- 3 oz. Jose Cuervo Tequila
- ½ oz. Liquor 43
- ½ oz. Triple Sec
- ½ oz. Lime Juice
- 1 Lime Wedge

Directions: Shake all ingredients. Strain into a chilled martini glass. Garnish with a lime wedge.

43 DREAMSICLE

- 4 oz. Orange Juice
- 2 oz. Licor 43
- 1 Orange Wedge
- Ice

Directions: Serve in a rocks glass over ice. Garnish with an orange wedge.

43 DUMMIES

- 1 oz. Bols Triple Sec Curacao
- 1 oz. Licor 43
- 1 Cherry
- Ice

Directions: Stir ingredients given in a mixing glass with ice. Strain into a chilled cocktail glass with crushed ice. Garnish with a cherry.

43 OLE

- 2 oz. Orange Juice
- 1 oz. Brandy
- 1 oz. Licor 43
- 1 Cherry
- Ice

Directions: Serve over ice in a rocks glass and garnish with a cherry.

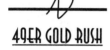

49ER GOLD RUSH

- ½ oz. Cinnamon Schnapps
- ½ oz. Jose Cuervo Tequila

Directions: Combine tequila and schnapps in a shot glass.

4TH OF JULY

- 1 ½ oz. Vodka
- ½ oz. Triple Sec
- ½ oz. Sweet and Sour Mix
- ½ oz. Blue Curacao
- Dash Grenadine

Directions: Mix all ingredients except grenadine in a shaker and chill. Add a dash of grenadine. Serve in a martini glass.

501 BLUES

- 2 oz. Lemon-lime soda
- 2 oz. Blue Curacao
- 1 oz. Club Soda
- 2 oz. Blueberry Schnapps
- Ice

Directions: Mix ingredients well. Serve over ice in a Collins glass.

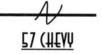

57 CHEVY

- 1 ¾ oz. Southern Comfort
- 1 ¾ oz. Gin
- 1 ¾ oz. Vodka
- Orange Juice
- Pineapple Juice
- Grenadine

Directions: Put Southern Comfort, gin, and vodka in a glass. Fill with orange juice and pineapple juice, and then top with grenadine. Serve in a highball glass.

'57 CHEVY (IN OHIO)

- ¾ oz. Amaretto
- ¾ oz. Sloe Gin
- ¾ oz. Southern Comfort
- Dash Grapefruit Juice
- Cranberry juice
- 1 Cherry
- Ice

Directions: Shake all ingredients and serve over ice in a hurricane glass. Garnish with a cherry.

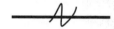

'57 CHEVY WITH A WHITE LICENSE PLATE

- 1 oz. White Crème de Cacao
- 1 oz. Vodka
- Ice

Directions: Fill a rock glass with ice. Add white crème de cacao and vodka. Stir

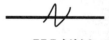

57 T-BIRDS

- ½ oz. Vodka
- ½ oz. Bols Amaretto
- ½ oz. Orange Juice
- 1 Orange Slice
- Ice

Directions: Serve over ice in a rocks glass. Garnish with an orange slice.

607 SPECIAL

- 2 oz. Rum
- 8 oz. Chocolate Milk

Directions: Stir ingredients and serve in a Collins glass.

8 IRON

- 1/3 oz. Blue Curacao
- 1/3 oz. Ouzo
- 1/3 oz. Banana Liqueur

Directions: Pour equal parts of each ingredient in a shot glass.

8 SECONDS

- 1 oz. Jaegermeister
- 1 oz. Goldschlager
- 1 oz. Hot Damn Cinnamon Schnapps
- 1 oz. Rumplemintz
- Ice

Directions: Mix all ingredients with ice and strain into a rocks glass.

8TH BIRTHDAY

- ¾ oz. Chambord Raspberry Liqueur
- ¼ oz. Dark Crème de Cacao
- 1 oz. Vodka
- 1 oz. Milk
- Ice

Directions: Fill a shaker glass with ice. Add all ingredients. Shake. Pour into a martini glass.

8TH WONDER

- 2 oz. White Wine
- 1 oz. Brandy
- 1 oz. Bols Dry Orange Curacao
- 1 oz. Bols Maraschino
- 1 oz. Sweet and Sour Mix
- 1 Cherry

Directions: Pour ingredients into a wine glass and garnish with a cherry.

9 ½ WEEKS

- 2 oz. Absolut Citron
- ½ oz. Orange Curacao
- Splash Strawberry Liqueur
- 1 oz. Orange Juice
- 1 Sliced Strawberry

Directions: Combine all ingredients in a mixer. Chill and strain into a cocktail glass. Garnish with a sliced strawberry.

911 SHOT

- ½ oz. Cinnamon Schnapps
- ½ oz. Peppermint Schnapps
- Dash Tabasco Sauce

Directions: Mix all ingredients and pour into a shot glass.

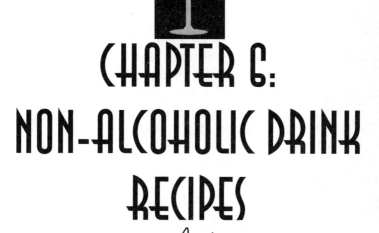

CHAPTER 6:
NON-ALCOHOLIC DRINK
RECIPES

ARNOLD PALMER

- **Iced Tea**
- **Lemonade**
- **Ice**

Directions: Fill a tall glass with ice. Fill glass half-full with iced tea and half-full with lemonade.

AFFOGATO

- **Espresso**
- **Vanilla or Chocolate Gelato or Ice Cream**

Directions: Pour espresso over vanilla or chocolate gelato or ice cream.

BEACH BLANKET BINGO

- **3 oz. Grapefruit Juice**
- **3 oz. Cranberry Juice**
- **Soda Water**
- **1 Lime Garnish**
- **Ice**

Directions: Fill a tall glass with ice. Add grapefruit juice and cranberry juice. Fill with soda water. Garnish with a lime.

BROWN COW

- **Root Beer or Cola**
- **1 - 2 scoops of Vanilla Ice Cream**
- **Whipped Cream**
- **Chocolate Candies**

Directions: Fill a large mouthed wide glass half-full with root beer or cola. Add one or two scoops of vanilla ice cream. Top with root beer. Add long spoon and straw and top with whipped cream and chocolate candies.

CAFÉ AU LAIT

- **Coffee**
- **Steamed Milk**
- **Chocolate Shavings**
- **Cinnamon or Nutmeg**

Directions: Heat a coffee cup, mug, or specialty glass. Pour equal parts of dark roasted coffee and scalding steamed milk in simultaneously. Leave a layer of froth on top of the mix. Sprinkle with chocolate shavings or cinnamon and/or nutmeg.

CAFÉ LATTE

- **Milk**
- **Espresso**
- **Cocoa Powder**

Directions: Heat a coffee cup, mug, or specialty glass. Pour milk to the top of the handle. Pour an espresso shot over the back of a spoon on the inside edge of the glass. Garnish with a layer of foam and cocoa powder.

CAPPUCCINO

- **Water**
- **Espresso**
- **Steamed Milk**
- **Chocolate Shavings**
- **Cinnamon or Nutmeg**

Directions: Heat a coffee cup, mug, or specialty glass by filling it with hot water and allowing it to sit while preparing the espresso and milk. Fill glass with one shot of espresso, one-third full with steamed milk, and one-third full with foam. Sprinkle with chocolate shavings or cinnamon and/or nutmeg.

CHOCOLATE MALTED

- **½ cup of Ice**
- **2 - 3 tbs. Malted Milk Powder**
- **4 oz. Milk**
- **Scoop of Chocolate Ice Cream**
- **2 tbs. Chocolate Syrup**

Directions: Blend all ingredients until smooth.

COFFEE MILK

- **2 oz. Coffee Syrup**
- **Milk**

Directions: Fill a glass with coffee syrup and milk. Shake. Serve in a pint glass.

DOUBLE CAPPUCCINO

- **Espresso**
- **Steamed Milk**
- **Chocolate Shavings**
- **Cinnamon or Nutmeg**

Directions: Heat a coffee cup, mug, or specialty glass. Fill two-thirds full with espresso and fill with liquid steamed milk. Top with foamed steam milk. Sprinkle with chocolate shavings or cinnamon and/or nutmeg.

DOUBLE ESPRESSO

- **2 shots Espresso**

Directions: Heat a coffee cup, mug, or specialty glass. Fill with espresso.

EGG CREAM

- 2 - 3 oz. Chocolate Syrup
- Milk
- Soda Water

Directions: In a tall glass, add chocolate syrup. Fill half-full with milk and add soda water. Stir.

ESPRESSO CON PANNO

- Shot Espresso
- Whipped Cream
- Shaved Chocolate or Powdered Chocolate

Directions: Pour one shot of espresso into a glass. Top with whipped cream and garnish with shaved or powdered chocolate.

FRAPPE

- ½ cup of Ice
- ½ cup of Milk
- Scoop of Desired Flavor of Ice Cream
- 3 tbs. Desired Flavor Syrup
- ½ cup of Fresh or Frozen Berries or Fruit
- 1 tbs. Sugar

Directions: Blend all ingredients until smooth. Serve in a daiquiri glass.

FROZEN CAPPUCCINO

- ½ cup of Ice
- 2 Cappuccinos or 2 Espressos
- ½ cup of Milk
- Scoop of Vanilla Ice Cream

Directions: Blend all ingredients until smooth.

HAMMERHEAD

- 2 shots Espresso
- Coffee

Directions: In a large coffee cup, add espresso and fill with hot, black coffee.

ICE CREAM COFFEE

- Coffee
- Scoop of Desired Flavor of Ice Cream
- Whipped Cream
- Shaved Chocolate
- Chocolate Syrup
- Shaved Coconut
- Crushed Candy

Directions: Fill a large coffee cup three-fourths full with hot, black coffee and gently place a small scoop of desired ice cream on top. Garnish with whipped cream, shaved chocolate, chocolate syrup, shaved coconut or crushed candy if desired. Serve with a spoon.

ICE CREAM FLOAT

- Scoop of Ice Cream
- Root Beer or Cola

Directions: In a pint glass or beer mug, add one scoop of ice cream and fill with root beer or cola. Serve with a spoon and straw.

ICE CREAM SODA

- 2 - 4 oz. Strawberry, Chocolate, or Raspberry Syrup
- 1 - 4 Scoops Ice Cream
- Soda Water

Directions: In a pint glass or beer mug, add strawberry, chocolate, or raspberry syrup, add ice cream, and fill gently with soda water.

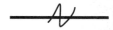

ICED COFFEE MOCHA

- 2 - 3 tbs. Chocolate Syrup
- Iced Coffee
- Ice

Directions: Fill a tall glass with ice and add chocolate syrup. Fill with iced coffee. Shake.

JULIUS

- ½ cup of Ice
- 1 cup of Fresh or Frozen Fruit
- 4 oz. Juice Concentrate
- 2 oz. Milk
- 1 tsp. Vanilla Extract
- Scoop of Vanilla Ice Cream

Directions: Blend all ingredients until smooth. If too thick, add juice or water. If too thin, add ice or ice cream.

KICKSTART

- 2 shots Espresso
- Coffee

Directions: In a large coffee cup, add espresso, and fill with hot, black coffee.

LATTE

- Milk
- Shot Espresso
- Cocoa Powder

Directions: Heat a coffee cup, mug, or specialty glass. Pour milk to the top of the handle. Pour an espresso shot over the back of a spoon on the inside edge of the glass. This will produce a layered effect between the coffee and the milk. Garnish with a layer of foam and cocoa powder.

LEMONADE

- 2 tsp. Sugar
- 2 oz. Lemon Juice
- Ice
- Water
- 1 Lemon Wedge

Directions: In a mixing glass, add sugar and lemon juice. Fill with ice and water. Garnish with a lemon wedge. Shake and serve in a Collins glass.

LIME RICKEY

- 1 oz. Lime Juice
- 1 tsp. Sugar
- Soda Water
- Ice

Directions: Fill a tall glass with ice and add lime juice and sugar. Fill with soda water. Stir.

MILKSHAKE

- ½ cup of Ice
- ½ cup of Milk
- Scoop of Desired Flavor of Ice Cream
- 3 tbs. Desired Flavor of Syrup
- ½ cup of Fresh or Frozen Berries or Fruit
- 1 tbs. Sugar

Directions: Blend all ingredients until smooth. Serve in a daiquiri glass.

MOCK PINK CHAMPAGNE #1

- ½ cup of Sugar
- 1 ½ cup of Water
- ½ cup of Orange Juice
- 2 cups of Cranberry Juice
- 1 cup of Pineapple Juice
- 2 bottles Lemon-lime Carbonated Beverage

Directions: Boil sugar and water until sugar dissolves. Cool. Stir in cranberry, pineapple, and orange juices. Chill. Just before serving, add carbonated beverage.

MOCK PINK CHAMPAGNE #2

- 3 quarts Ginger Ale
- 1 gallon Hawaiian Fruit Punch
- 1 quart Lemon Juice
- 2 lb. Sugar
- 1 quart Pineapple Juice
- Ice

Directions: Combine everything but the ginger ale and the ice. Chill. Add ginger ale and ice before serving.

MONSTER SLIME JUICE

- 6 oz. Pre-sweetened Berry Blue Kool-Aid
- 12 oz. Orange Juice Concentrate
- 1 gallon Water

Directions: Mix juice and Kool-Aid, add water, and stir.

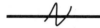

RASPBERRY LIME RICKEY

- ¼ cup of Fresh Berries
- 1 tsp. Sugar
- 2 oz. Syrup or 1 tbs. Concentrate or Jam
- Juice of 1 Lime
- Soda Water or Seltzer

Directions: In a pint glass, add fresh berries, sugar, syrup or concentrate or jam. Add lime juice and muddle or mix together. Add soda water or seltzer slowly. Stir gently and taste. Add sugar if needed.

RED EYE

- 2 shot Espresso
- Coffee

Directions: In a large coffee cup, add espresso and fill with hot, black coffee.

ROY ROGERS

- Cola
- Dash Grenadine
- 1 Cherry
- Ice

Directions: Fill a tall glass with ice and cola. Add a dash of grenadine and garnish with a cherry.

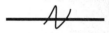

SHIRLEY TEMPLE

- Ginger Ale or Lemon-lime Soda
- Dash Grenadine
- 1 Cherry
- Ice

Directions: Fill a tall glass with ice, ginger ale or lemon-lime soda, and a dash of grenadine. Garnish with a cherry.

UPTOWN

- Iced Tea
- Lemonade
- Ice

Directions: Fill a tall glass with ice. Fill glass half-full with iced tea and half-full with lemonade.

VIRGIN BANANA-ORANGE FROSTY

- 1 cup of Ice
- 2 oz. Milk or Cream
- Dash Grenadine
- ½ Peeled Banana
- ½ Peeled Orange

Directions: Blend all ingredients until smooth.

VIRGIN MARY

- 1 tsp. Horseradish
- 3 dashes Tabasco Sauce
- 3 dashes Worcestershire Sauce
- Dash Lime Juice
- 3 dashes Celery Salt
- 3 dashes Pepper
- 1 oz. Clam juice (optional)
- Tomato Juice
- 1 Lemon or Lime Garnish
- 1 Celery or Cucumber
- 1 Shrimp Cocktail

Directions: Fill a mixing glass with ice, horseradish, Tabasco sauce, Worcestershire sauce, lime juice, celery salt, pepper, and clam juice. Fill with tomato juice and pour from one glass to another until mixed. Garnish with a lemon and/or lime, celery and/or cucumber and/or shrimp cocktail.

VIRGIN PINA COLADA

- 1 cup of Ice
- 2 tbs. Cream of Coconut
- 1 cup of Fresh or Canned Pineapple
- 1 tsp. Vanilla Ice Cream (optional)
- 1 Pineapple Garnish
- 1 Cherry

Directions: Blend ingredients until smooth. If too thick, add fruit or juice. If too thin, add ice. Garnish with a pineapple and a cherry.

VIRGIN STRAWBERRY DAIQUIRI

- 1 cup of Ice
- Dash Lime Juice
- 1 cup of Fresh or Frozen Strawberries
- 1 Strawberry or Lime Garnish

Directions: Blend all ingredients until smooth. If too thick, add berries or juice. If too thin, add ice. Garnish with strawberry and/or lime.

CHAPTER 7:
BAR ADD-ONS

FOOD AND SNACKS

Snacks and food service are great for attracting business to a bar, especially during the daytime hours. Even a small and simple menu will keep people coming in, whether for lunch or for a quick snack and a drink. Many bars also offer buffets on the weekends before they get really busy with the night crowd. This is a great way to get the profits flowing a little earlier in the night, and many patrons may choose to stay. Food can be offered for a fee or for free, but since people are at a bar, they are sure to have drinks as well.

Happy hour is a great time to offer food. This will keep people drinking without lowering drink prices. Simply offer free snacks. Food counteracts the effects of alcohol and guests will drink more when food is available. Many tavern-style bars will serve food all day and evening, then close the grill around midnight. These bars typically give a last call for food. Food service should be consistent and go with the theme of the bar. For example, tiki bars might consider serving exotic flavors along with a few staples.

If food service is offered, let customers know and give them a menu when they arrive. If the bar is less formal, consider a dry-erase board or a blackboard above the bar with food offerings. Perhaps place small menus at the tables. Have the DJ announce food and drink specials or have prerecorded commercials. Appetizer sales have been shown to increase as much as 25-40 percent when employing these tactics. Hold contests with the staff so that they will be motivated to sell appetizers and food items. Make sure prizes have some real value to the staff and food sales will skyrocket.

Many bars have had success offering combinations of food and drinks. Guests can have the option of buying a combo at a reduced price. Beer and sour drinks go well with spicy foods, pizzas, fried cheese, vegetables, and pastas. Wines go well with fruits, cheese, pastas, and desserts. Sweet drinks go well with fruit, salads, and sandwiches. Servers should also know what drinks go best with the different types of foods served.

To begin getting customers accustomed to the idea of buying appetizers, try offering appetizers free with the first round of drinks or allow guests to sample new menu items. Even if they don't initially want the food, they are bound to want it later in the night. Make sure menus are unique and catch the eye of the customer. Give menu items names that go with the bar's theme and style.

Snacks are the cheapest and simplest food item to serve. As long as they are fresh, they will keep customers munching and drinking all night long. Peanuts and pretzels are classics and bowls of them should be prominently displayed on the bar top. Bowls of peanuts and pretzels can also be offered for free at individual tables whenever a guest sits down.

Snacks can also be offered to the guests in packages to ensure freshness. Packaged snacks are easy to deal with and servers do not have to handle the food with bare hands. These can also be stored easily and bought in bulk from restaurant and small business suppliers. Peanuts and pretzels are notoriously salty and go great with beer.

Finger foods are also very popular and are great if for weekend buffets. Fresh popcorn popped in an old-fashioned popcorn popper will attract a lot of attention. Other foods that are great are little hot dogs, chicken wings, sausages, mini pizzas, large slices of pizza, meatballs, egg rolls, hot wings, and burritos. Many of these can be heated in microwaves, convection ovens, or small counter-top ovens. Those establishments that hold buffets on a regular basis might consider investing in a small buffet line to keep foods hot. This also allows a wider variety of foods to be served. Designated staff should be responsible for the upkeep of the buffet while it is being offered.

Catering is another option to consider. Local restaurants, delis, and pizza restaurants may be interested in catering for a trade out of some sort. For example, a local restaurant may be interested in having a holiday party at the bar and will provide free food in exchange. This does not necessarily mean that they should be given free drinks, but perhaps open the bar an hour or two earlier so they can have their party without other customers there. Many bars will also allow local pizza restaurants to send delivery drivers over with a few simple pizzas such as cheese and pepperoni. This is great because it can help sober your patrons up a bit.

OTHER NECESSITIES

There are several other necessities that should not be forgotten when offering food and drinks. First of all, napkins, straws, and coasters will always be of utmost importance. This is a great branding opportunity for a bar. Cocktail napkins and coasters are great places to show off the bar's logo. If food is offered, provide to-go boxes and bags for those customers who do not finish their food.

Straws should be included with every mixed drink, soda, and even water. Bartenders will also want to make these items easy accessible for customers. The traditional straw and napkin holder will suffice. These are often available from vendors with their name and logo on it.

CHAPTER 8:
GAMES, TRICKS, & TOASTS

Games, tricks, and toasts provide a feel of camaraderie and fun in a bar. The bartender is often responsible for this and he or she should always have a few good tricks to keep things interesting at the bar top. Keeping the guests entertained helps to sell drinks and fill up tip jars.

DRINKING GAMES

CLASSIC QUARTERS

Quarters is a classic game and there are a few varieties of it as well. This game is for two or more players. A shot glass and a quarter are needed to play. It is useful to have a hard surface on which to play. The shot glass should be in the center of the table or moved to where everybody can reach it.

To Play: Players have one chance to bounce a quarter off of the table and into the shot glass. When the player misses, they pass the quarter on to the next player. If they get the quarter into the glass, then they can assign another player to drink and then they get another chance. If the player is successful three times in a row, then the player can make a rule. Such as, players cannot say any word that starts with the letter "a." If they do, then they have to drink. The rule must apply to all players and can be anything that governs how the game is played by the group.

Bouncing the quarter properly takes some practice. It is best if the quarter is held between the thumb and forefinger. Hold the quarter about six inches above the table and horizontally. Use a quick, jerking action when to bounce the quarter. The quarter should bounce about two inches above the shot glass.

A variation on the rules is for a player to cancel an existing rule that they do not care for.

CHANDELIERS

Chandeliers is a variation on Quarters. This game requires two or more players. To set up the game, place a large glass in the center of the table with shot glasses around it. The shot glasses should touch each other and the center glass. All glasses should be empty.

To play: As in Quarters, players will take turns trying to bounce quarters into any of the glasses. When a shot glass is made, that player assigns another player to drink. If the center glass is made, that player can pour some of his drink in that glass. If a player makes any glass, then they get another turn. If a shot glass is made three times in a row, then the player assigns someone to drink the center glass' contents. A replacement drink can be used.

SPEED QUARTERS

This is a variation on Quarters in which two players shoot at two shot glasses simultaneously. This game is for four or more players.

To Play: Both players will start at the same time and will try to make as many shots as possible. When a player is successful, the shot glass is passed on to the next person. A shot glass cannot be passed until the player has made a shot. A starting player will pass his shot glass to the right if it takes more than one bounce to land a quarter. If they are successful on their first attempt, they will pass the glass to their right. If the next player hits the shot on the first attempt, then they will pass the glass back to the person who passed to them. If both players take more than one attempt, then the glasses and quarters are passed in the same direction.

DAREDEVIL

This game is for two or more players and requires five shot glasses lined up in a row and touching each other.

To Play: Players will take turns bouncing the quarter into the shot glasses. The shot glasses should be in a straight row in front of the players. The player that makes the quarter in the first glass can assign one drink, the second glass assigns two drinks, and so on. If the player makes the fifth glass, he or she can assign five drinks and make a rule. Assigned drinks may be split among different players or given to one person.

ROYALTY

This game requires a deck of cards and two to six players. Cards with the values of two through seven are removed and the remaining cards are spread out on the table. Cards must be placed face down.

Card Rankings: A, K, Q, J, 10, 9, 8. Pairs are rank higher than non-pairs. Sequences and royalty card combinations do not have higher rankings than the non-specialty ranking cards.

To Play: Each player will take two cards from the pile and place them face down in front of them. The player who won the lead from the previous round will be the first to turn over his or her cards. In the first round, the player on the left of the dealer will turn over his or her cards first.

- If a player receives a pair, which is two cards of the same rank, then that player makes a rule. The rule can be anything that governs how the game is played and anyone who violates the rule has to drink.
- If a player receives two cards that are sequential in ranking, then he or she can assign two drinks to a player.
- If a Q and J are received, the player can assign any number of drinks to any other player, but also has to drink the same amount of drinks.
- If a K and J are received, the player chooses another card. That card is the number of drinks that the person must take. If an ace is drawn, the person does not have to drink. That player can then instruct another player to draw and to drink as many drinks as the card shows. If that player turns over an ace, then he or she tells the original player how many drinks to drink.
- If a K and Q are turned over, then all players take three drinks.
- If none of these combinations are drawn, then that player does not have to drink.

The next player will flip cards over and the game continues as described. After all cards have been turned over, the player with the highest-ranking cards becomes the leader for the next round. If there is a tie, then the player who went first wins the tie and is the leader for the next round.

FOOTBALL MADNESS

This game is for two or more players and must be played during a football game. The game is more fun if there are individuals rooting for different teams. Before the game begins, each person must announce which team they are supporting.

To Play: Players take the corresponding number of drinks when the team they are not supporting gets a:

- First down: 1 drink
- Touchdown: 3 drinks
- Field goal: 1 drink
- Two-point conversion: 2 drinks
- Interception: Finish drink

When the team you are rooting for receives one of the following, the player must take the corresponding number of drinks:

- Fumble: 3 drinks
- Safety: 3 drinks

I NEVER

This game is best played with two or more players. The more the merrier.

To Play: Players take turns announcing actions that they have never done, such as "I have never smoked a cigarette." After the player makes their statement, all of those players who have done this action must take a drink. If a player makes a statement and nobody else has done it either, that player must take a drink.

If a player makes a statement and is accused of lying, the accuser must have proof that the individual is lying and must provide an accurate description or circumstance in which the person did that action. If the player is caught lying, then the player must take five drinks.

TRICKS

MAKE ANY DRINK A SHOT

The key to making any drink a shot is to resize the drink. For example, if the drink is served on the rocks, simply pour the ingredients over ice and strain into a shot glass. This will chill the liquors and produce a shot. If a drink calls for two ounces of vodka, pour one and a half ounces and add a dash of sour mix or other mixer. If the drink calls for numerous liquors, resize the pour according to the size of the shot glass.

MULTI-MIXING

At most bars, shots are ordered in rounds for groups of people. To make two to four shots, quadruple the recipe to save mixing time. Line up the shot glasses and pour down the line.

MYSTERY SHOT

Many people will sit down at the bar and just ask for a shot, or a group of friends will sit down and ask for a round of shots. They do not care what they are as long as they are good and strong. In this case, memorize a few recipes of some strong drinks. Make the recipe as normal and strain into shot glasses. Serve them up and the guests will keep ordering.

FLOATERS

Floaters always amaze people, especially if they are done correctly. All liquids have a specific gravity. Notice that in the recipes the liquid to be poured first is indicated. Pour the first liquor and then pour the next liquor over the back of a bar spoon and allow it to pour down the side of the glass. The spoon allows the liquor to pour slowly so as not to disturb the layers below it. Clean the spoon between each layer.

If specific layered drinks will be sold, try pouring them and then putting them in the refrigerator. The liquors will separate into layers, but it works better on some drinks than others.

KNOW WHAT IS HAPPENING

Bartenders gain a lot of respect when they keep up with what is going on around town. Be sure to check out the entertainment section of the newspaper and get up to date on current events, parties, bars, movies, and concerts. Many out-of-towners will come to a bartender for information on the city and directions. Be prepared for these situations.

OLIVE IN A BRANDY SNIFTER – NO HANDS!

This is a bar trick that takes a little practice to get down. The idea is to put the olive in the brandy snifter with no hands, mouth, etc. The olive cannot be scooped or rolled off the bar. With the olive on the bar top, place the brandy snifter over the olive so that the olive is surrounded by the glass. Slowly rotate the brandy snifter around the olive. The olive will roll around and come up into the glass. When the olive is spinning around the walls, flip the glass quickly and place on the bar. The olive has a tendency to fly out, but with practice this is a great trick.

FLAIR

The movie *Cocktail* with Tom Cruise made bartending flair very popular. Flipping bottles, shakers, etc. became really cool and many bartenders began practicing these tricks. One of the best places to see these types of tricks is to watch the bartenders in Las Vegas. When they are bored they will flip and juggle bottles of liquor.

One way to get the attention of customers while working is to use working flair. Working flair consists of doing little things that are not going to make liquor costs jump when a bottle hits the floor. Try flipping the shaker tins before scooping ice into them and then pouring two liquors at once. Add flair to shaking, stirring, and pouring. Make garnishes look great and stand out.

The key to flair bartending is to start small and slowly build as confidence is gained. Many bartenders learn how to flip bottles by taking an empty bottle and wrapping it in tape. This will keep it from shattering all over the floor if you drop it.

TOASTS

Toasting is a great way to honor someone whether it be a birthday, retirement, anniversary, or wedding. Toasts are often difficult to come up with, but one rule of thumb is to keep it short. At small parties, it is fine to remain seated if others are seated. At large parties, stand so that everyone can see and hear the toast. Before beginning the toast, be sure that everyone has a full drink whether it be alcoholic, water, or otherwise. It is not couth to have a toast when not everyone has a drink. When toasting, hold the glass out at shoulder length and give the toast; then take a drink. Other may clink glasses and drink as well or simply hold their glass up and take a drink after the toast is finished. The one being celebrated does not usually take part in the toast, but thanks the person that gave the toast.

Here are a few toasts that to keep in mind should the situation arise. Or, being a bartender, someone might ask for toasting ideas and suggestions.

May all your troubles be little ones.

May we always be happy and our enemies know it.

Here's to God's first thought: Man
Here's to God's second thought: Woman
And since second thoughts are always the best, here's to women!

To a full moon on a dark night and a smooth
road all the days of your life.

May the most you wish for be the least you get.

Here's lookin' at you kid.
-Humphrey Bogart (Casablanca)

May you live all the days of your life.
-Jonathan Swift

Candy is dandy, but liquor is quicker.
-Ogden Nash

May the road rise to meet you,
May the wind be always at your back,
The sun shine warm on your face,
The rain fall soft upon your fields,
And until we meet again,
May God hold you in the hollow of his hand.
-Traditional Irish Toast

Here's to kissing those we please and pleasing those we kiss.

To your birthday – no matter how old you are, you don't look it!

To long lives and short wars.
-Colonel Potter (M*A*S*H)

Here's to good friends, who know you well and like you anyway.

Here's to you, as good as you are,
And here's to me, as bad as I am;
And as bad as I am, and as good as you are,
I'm as good as you are, as bad as I am.

Here's hoping that you live forever and mine is the last voice you hear.
-Willard Scott

You're not as young as you used to be, but then you're not as
old as you're going to be.
-George Ade

Here's to cold nights, fine wine, and good friends to share them with.

To wine – God's next best gift to man.
-Ambrose Bierce

To men: *(Women) You can't live with 'em, and you can't shoot 'em.*

Wine improves with age – the older I get the more I like it.

May you live as long as you want,
And never want as long as you live.

Let us toast the fools – but for them, the rest of us could not succeed.
-Mark Twain

If you're not the lead dog, the view never changes – here's to success.

Old friends are scarce,
New friends are few,
I'm glad to find both in you.

Here's to Cupid, the little squirt,
He's lost his pants; he's lost his shirt,
He lost it all except his aim,
Which proves that love's a losing game.

I've know many and liked a few,
But loved just one, so here's to you!

Here's to the girls that call you "honey,"
They drink your wine and spend your money,
They put you to bed and hug you tight,
And cross their legs and say "good night!"
-George Ade

CHAPTER 9:
CASE STUDIES

CASE STUDY: TERRIL CONRAD

What is your favorite drink to make a customer?

"Vodka and Seven, because it is easy. Just kidding. I like to make Kryptonite. They are pretty strong, and if you make them just right, they are the prettiest color of green."

What is your least favorite drink to make a customer? Why?

"I do not enjoy making layered shots. They are time consuming and if you make the smallest mistake, the drink is ruined."

What is your favorite bar tool?

"My favorite bar tools are the fun bottle openers. I like the ones with sayings on them and ones in the shape of different people and things. My favorite bottle opener is shaped and colored like Betty Boop."

What is a bartending pet peeve of yours?

"Customers that stand in front of the service area and customers that do not tip."

CASE STUDY: TERRIL CONRAD

What drink do you prefer for yourself?

"I enjoy drinking Red Headed Slut shots."

What made you decide to become a bartender?

"I thought it would be fun. I knew that I was going to be out in the bar scene anyway, and that it would be nice to actually get paid for it at the same time."

What was your most unusual drink request?

"I have had several crazy requests. Some of them have been for odd drinks with liquors that I had never heard of, while others were pretty obscene and had to do with me performing sexual acts in front of the customers. I once had a customer try to order a shot of one of my bodily fluids."

What is the best thing about being a bartender?

"Getting to smoke on the job, and also getting paid to look good and flirt with customers."

What is the worst thing about being a bartender?

"The hours can be pretty rough. I missed out on a lot of fun things with my friends because I had to work until 3 a.m. on Friday and Saturday nights when everyone else got to go out."

CASE STUDY: GORDON McGRAW

What is your favorite drink to make a customer?

"Margarita on the Rocks. They are a classic drink and people really appreciate a well made margarita."

What is your least favorite drink to make a customer? Why?

"Under Tow."

What is your favorite bar tool?

"A wall mounted corkscrew makes life so much easier when you serve a large amount of wine."

What is a bartending pet peeve of yours?

"Bartenders who do more harm than good behind the bar."

CASE STUDY: GORDON McGRAW

What drink do you prefer for yourself?

"Slutty Martini."

What made you decide to become a bartender?

"Different styles of bars. I go to many different bars and there are different types of bartenders at them all. I enjoy seeing the way things are done at different bars. I also enjoy the atmosphere at bars with different styles and themes."

What was your most unusual drink request?

"Margarita made with whiskey and tomato juice instead of sweet and sour."

What is the best thing about being a bartender?

"Regulars are great and if you remember what they like then they reward you for it."

What is the worst thing about being a bartender?

"Ten people who drink diet soda."

CASE STUDY: AUTUMN WARD

What is your favorite drink to make a customer?

"Vodka Martini. I do not know why. They are just fun to make and people appreciate a good martini."

What is your least favorite drink to make a customer? Why?

"Pina Colada. Frozen drinks are so time consuming and I am usually so busy that I do not have time for them."

What is your favorite bar tool?

"Soda guns are awesome. I cannot imagine working without them."

What is a bartending pet peeve of yours?

"People snapping their fingers at you."

What drink do you prefer for yourself?

"Beer and Vodka Martini."

CASE STUDY: AUTUMN WARD

What made you decide to become a bartender?

"Bartending is better than waiting tables. There is less running around and better money."

What was your most unusual drink request?

"Hennessy and Dr. Pepper and Corona with grenadine."

What is the best thing about being a bartender?

"The money can be great. You can make more in a weekend than you would in a week at a regular job."

What is the worst thing about being a bartender?

"The hours are rough."

CASE STUDY: LACEY WALLENDORF

What is your favorite drink to make a customer?

"Long Island Iced Tea, made with lots of liquor. Customers cannot drink just one."

What is your least favorite drink to make a customer? Why?

"Virgin Margarita. Do people know they are drinking straight sweet and sour?"

What is your favorite bar tool?

"Bottle openers."

What is a bartending pet peeve of yours?

"Other than not getting tipped – people who ask for a taster of every wine on the list."

What drink do you prefer for yourself?

"Pina Colada."

What made you decide to become a bartender?

"I was a waitress and the management asked me if I would like to bartend."

What was your most unusual drink request?

CASE STUDY: LACEY WALLENDORF

"Virgin Cosmo – straight cranberry juice."

What is the best thing about being a bartender?

"There is more business and more money."

What is the worst thing about being a bartender?

"More responsibilities (cleaning, etc.) and dealing with drunk people."

CASE STUDY: TERRY WATSON

What is your favorite drink to make a customer?

"Bloody Mary."

What is your least favorite drink to make a customer? Why?

"Just a beer. It is not any fun."

What is your favorite bar tool?

"My forearm to open bottles."

What is a bartending pet peeve of yours?

"Not putting your drink on a coaster."

What drink do you prefer for yourself?

"Crown and Coke."

What made you decide to become a bartender?

"The atmosphere."

What was your most unusual drink request?

"Strip and go naked."

What is the best thing about being a bartender?

"Conversing with new people all the time."

What is the worst thing about being a bartender?

"Conversing with the same people all the time."

CASE STUDY: JOSEPH ANGUILANO

What is your favorite drink to make a customer?

"It always depends on the customer. If it is a girl, I like to make something sweet like a Sex on the Beach or something similar to that. If it is a dude, then I usually offer beer. If they want liquor that is not in shot form, I offer Crown and Coke or some other whiskey."

What is your least favorite drink to make a customer? Why?

"Anything involving a blender. Pina Coladas and daiquiris are definitely two of my least favorite drinks to make. Oh yeah, and anything virgin."

What is your favorite bar tool?

"Just the basic metal bar tool works for me, but the ones with the rubber cover are nice."

What is a bartending pet peeve of yours?

"When people snap at me to get my attention."

What drink do you prefer for yourself?

"BEER. I also like tequila when I am taking shots. If I am having a mixed drink, I like SoCo and Coke."

What made you decide to become a bartender?

"The glamour that comes with the title. Everyone that works in the restaurant bizz wants the coveted 'bartender' gig."

What was your most unusual drink request?

"I never really had anything that unusual requested. Sorry, I know that is a crappy answer."

What is the best thing about being a bartender?

"Being able to socialize with all types of people. You never know whom you will run into."

What is the worst thing about being a bartender?

"Dealing with the angry drunks that want to fight you when you cut them off."

CASE STUDY: CRYSTAL TERCERO

What is your favorite drink to make a customer?

"I like to make martinis, especially specialty martinis like Apples or Cosmos. People really like them and they really like a well made one."

What is your least favorite drink to make a customer? Why?

"Anything involving the blender. I don't know of a bartender who likes to take the time to make frozen drinks."

What is your favorite bar tool?

"My wine tool. It has a handy little knife and after opening a few hundred bottles of wine you get pretty handy with it."

What is a bartending pet peeve of yours?

"When people do not tell me everything they need and I keep having to walk back and forth from the bar to the table and vice versa. I am just too busy for all that."

What drink do you prefer for yourself?

"Screwdrivers. It is the only time I like orange juice."

What made you decide to become a bartender?

"The money and the respect. Usually only the best servers are promoted and you feel good about yourself."

What was your most unusual drink request?

"A virgin margarita on the rocks. Just as bad as a frozen one. I do not have any strange stories for requests."

What is the best thing about being a bartender?

"Having your own little world behind the bar. You set it up the way you want it and nobody else can come behind your bar without permission. You also don't have to deal with the insanity of the rest of the restaurant."

CASE STUDY: CRYSTAL TERCERO

What is the worst thing about being a bartender?

"Dealing with people who know you are busy but they choose to be rude and impatient anyways."

CASE STUDY: TROY MELLEMA

What is your favorite drink to make a customer?

"Hurricanes, it is a lot of alcohol but they do not taste like it."

What is your least favorite drink to make a customer? Why?

"I hate frozen drinks. They are way too time consuming."

What is your favorite bar tool?

"My bar tool. Could not live without it."

What is a bartending pet peeve of yours?

"When people sit down and get a drink and then they get buzzed for a table and they do not pay me. Then I have to go hunt them down in the restaurant."

What drink do you prefer for yourself?

"Jack and Coke. It is an American favorite."

What made you decide to become a bartender?

"The money. The hours are not great, but you can get stuff done during the day which is nice."

What was your most unusual drink request?

"A margarita made with Jack Daniels instead of tequila. Yuck."

What is the best thing about being a bartender?

"The money, and you do not have to deal with the rest of the restaurant. Plus you can watch sports on the TVs in your down time."

What is the worst thing about being a bartender?

"Working every weekend."

CASE STUDY: STEPHANIE LUJAN

What is your favorite drink to make a customer?

"I like to make mixed drinks. They are just fun and it does not matter what is. The more alcohol that are in them the more attention you get when you are making them."

What is your least favorite drink to make a customer? Why?

What is your favorite bar tool?

"I cannot live without my bar tool."

What is a bartending pet peeve of yours?

"When people will not let me take care of other tables and they act like they are the only guests I have."

What drink do you prefer for yourself?

"I like margaritas and daiquiris."

What made you decide to become a bartender?

"The money. You can work less and make more."

What was your most unusual drink request?

"A martini with whiskey. Not a Manhattan, but a regular martini."

What is the best thing about being a bartender?

"Making good money and meeting new people."

What is the worst thing about being a bartender?

"When people talk to me by yelling across the room."

CASE STUDY: KELI WATSON

What is your favorite drink to make a customer?

"Bloody Bitch. It is a great twist on a Bloody Mary."

CASE STUDY: KELI WATSON

What is your least favorite drink to make a customer? Why?

"Margarita. They are just too main stream these days."

What is your favorite bar tool?

"Bottle opener. You cannot be a bartender without one."

What is a bartending pet peeve of yours?

"Having to clean up after drunks."

What drink do you prefer for yourself?

"Dark beer. Shiner is my fave."

What made you decide to become a bartender?

"The money."

What was your most unusual drink request?

"Bud Light. They are not real beer drinkers if they order Bud Light."

What is the best thing about being a bartender?

"The money and the atmosphere of the bar are great."

What is the worst thing about being a bartender?

"Getting home late and cleaning the bar after everyone is gone."

GLOSSARY

Ale: A variety of beers made from straining the yeast that ferments on top of the vat. There are several styles of ales that exist including amber ales, barley wines, bitter ales, cream ales, India pale ales, porters, lambics, Scotch ales, stouts, trappist ales, and wheat beers.

Aperitif: A beverage drunk before dinner as an appetite stimulant, usually of the alcoholic variety.

Armagnac: A French grape-based brandy that is aged and made in Gascony.

Aromatized Wines: Wines that are flavored by herbs, spices, or other botanical ingredients. Vermouth, Dubonnet, and Lillet are examples.

Bar spoon: A long-handled spoon with a twisted shaft that is used for stirring among other things.

Bitters: An alcoholic-based infusion of a base-spirit and a number of herbs, spices, botanicals, and other flavorings.

Boston Shaker: A cocktail-shaker that consists of a metal cone and a 16 to 20 ounce shaking glass.

Botanicals: A term describing the fresh and dried herbs, spices, fruits, and other ingredients used to flavor some liquors, beers, and wines.

Buck: A highball made of a base spirit, juice of a squeezed lemon, and ginger ale.

Calvados: An aged brandy made in a specific geographical area in Normandy, France from fermented mashed apples.

Church key: A tool that has a rounded bottle opener at one end and a V-shaped piercing can opener on the other.

Cobbler: Cocktail made from a base spirit or wine and simple syrup, which is poured into a wine goblet with crushed ice and stirred together.

Cocktail: A combination of ingredients that have been shaken or stirred with ice and strained into a chilled or ice filled glass.

Collins: A mixed drink made from a base liquor, lemon juice, simple syrup, and club soda served over ice in a Collins glass with a fresh fruit garnish.

Cooler: A drink made from a base spirit, wine, or liqueur topped with a sweet, carbonated beverage that is served in a Collins glass with a lemon twist.

Cordial: Also known as liqueur. Bottled beverage made from liquor, one or more sweeteners, and other flavorings.

Crusta: A mixed drink made from a base liquor with lemon juice, maraschino liqueur, and strained into a sugar-rimmed sour glass with a lemon twist.

Daisy: A mixed drink made from a base liquor with lemon juice and grenadine and served over ice in a highball glass with a lemon twist.

Digestif: A single drink or combination of ingredients drunk after dinner to stimulate digestion.

Eaux-de-vie: The French name for the colorless brandies that are distilled from fruit juices.

Fix: A drink made from a base liquor, lemon juice, and pineapple juice. Served over ice in a highball glass with fresh fruit for garnish.

Fizz: A drink made from a base liquor with lime or lemon juice, simple syrup, and club soda that is served straight in a wine glass with a fresh fruit garnish.

Flip: A drink made from a base

wine, beer or spirit with a whole egg, and simple syrup that is served straight in a wine goblet or beer glass with grated nutmeg as a garnish.

Frappe: A drink composed of a base liquor or spirit that is served over ice in a saucer, Champagne glass, or sour glass.

Highball: The simplest form of a mixed drink that is composed of two ingredients, such as Scotch and soda or vodka and tonic. Served in a highball glass.

Julep Strainer: A perforated bar tool that is used to strain ingredients that have been stirred together in a mixing glass.

Lager: A variety of beer made with bottom-fermenting yeast.

Madeira: A wine fortified with brandy and produced on the island of Madeira.

Mixed Drink: A combination of two or more ingredients, at least one of them containing alcohol.

Mixing Glass: A 16 to 20-ounce glass designed for stirring ingredients for cocktails.

Muddling: The process in which a wooden pestle is used to crush together ingredients such as fruit wedges, sugar cubes, and bitters.

Neat: Liquors served straight from the bottle without being chilled or mixed.

Perfect: A term describing a cocktail that contains equal parts sweet and dry vermouths.

Proof: In the United States, the alcohol content of a liquor by degree and based on 200 degrees equaling 100 percent.

Rickey: A cocktail made from a base liquor with fresh lime juice and club soda. Served over ice in a highball glass with a lime wedge to garnish.

Sangaree: A cocktail made from a base wine, spirit, or beer plus a sweetener and garnished with grated nutmeg.

Shooter: A cocktail meant to be taken in a single gulp.

Sling: A mixed drink made from a base liquor, citrus juice, simple syrup, or liqueur and club soda that is served over ice in a Collins glass.

Smash: A drink made from a base liquor, simple syrup, and crushed mint leaves served over ice in a rocks glass and garnished with mint.

Sour: A mixed drink composed of base liquor, lemon juice, simple syrup, and served in a sour glass or over ice in a rocks glass.

Splash: An inexact measure that should equal about a teaspoon.

Straight Up: A drink served without ice.

Swizzle: A cocktail made in Tennessee that is distilled from a fermented mash of grains that is filtered through sugar-maple charcoal before aging.

Toddy: A drink made from a base liquor, hot water, and various spices and served in a footed mug.

Zest: The colorful outer layer of citrus fruit peels where the essential oils are located.

REFERENCES

Cunningham, Stephen Kittredge. *The Bartender's Black Book*. The Bartender's Black Book Co. Brockton, MS. 2006.

Herbst, Ron and Sharon Tyler. *The Ultimate A-Z Bar Guide*. Broadway Books. New York, New York. 1998.

Feller, Robyn M. *The Complete Bartender*. Berkley Books. New York. 1990.

Pellham, Brian L. *A Partier's Guide to 51 Drinking Games*. Kheper Publishing. Seattle, WA. 1995.

Fier, Bruce. *Start and Run a Money-Making Bar*. TAB Books. New York, New York. 1993.

Foley, Ray. *Bartending for Dummies*. Wiley Publishing, Inc. Indianapolis, IN. 2003.

Regan, Gary. *The Bartender's Bible*. Harper Paperbacks. New York, New York. 1991.

Regan, Mardee Haidin. *The Bartender's Best Friend*. Wiley & Sons. Hoboken, NJ. 2003.

Sora, Joseph. W. Edited by. *International Bartender's Guide*. Gramercy Books. New York, New York. 2002.

ABOUT THE AUTHOR

Dedicated to Troy Mellema, my loving husband and fearless recipe typer, and my many bartending friends in Amarillo.

Valerie Mellema

Great customer service and bartending is not something that is foreign to Valerie. She has served many a happy customer from behind the bar in a restaurant bar for many years. She has also had the opportunity to work with many great bartenders on busy Friday and Saturday nights where the bar top was the place to be. She especially enjoyed training new bartenders and chatting with her many regulars. Valerie resides with her husband, Troy, in Amarillo, Texas where together they operate her freelance writing business, Words You Want, from their home.

INDEX

228, 234, 236, 267, 284, 286, 287, 288, 290, 292, 298, 304, 307, 308

Prices 48, 66, 73, 91, 92, 299

Promotions 80, 91, 92, 93

Proof 14, 15, 20, 57, 89, 171, 219, 256, 275, 286, 307

Q

Quality 25

Quarter 84, 303, 304, 305

R

Recipe 58, 308

Red wine 25, 27, 43, 44, 136, 227, 249, 250, 279

Restaurant 26, 30, 72, 73, 93, 301, 318, 319, 320

Rum 14, 15, 16, 43, 44, 57, 95, 98, 103, 104, 105, 108, 110, 112, 114, 117, 125, 126, 127, 130, 145, 149, 150, 158, 163, 171, 192, 193, 195, 198, 200, 207, 212, 216, 218, 219, 222, 225, 229, 230–232, 237, 238, 240, 242, 248, 249, 250, 255, 256, 264, 269, 270, 275, 277, 279, 286, 289

S

Sake 23, 36, 204, 257

Selection 24, 67

Service 82, 91

Sherry 28, 29, 37, 53, 97, 102, 124, 126, 148, 160, 162, 165, 170, 174, 188, 201, 229, 247, 250, 252, 262, 263, 267, 269, 274, 275, 283

Shot 52, 54, 87, 95, 96, 97, 98, 100, 108, 110, 113, 115, 120, 128, 132–140, 142, 146, 148, 150, 152–154, 156, 158, 160–162, 164, 165, 166, 167, 169, 170–172, 175, 176, 178, 182–184, 188, 192, 196, 199, 200, 202, 204, 208, 210, 212, 213–215, 217, 219–221, 238, 240, 261, 268, 286, 287–289, 290–292, 294–297, 303–305, 307, 308, 314, 318

Sports 67, 73, 75, 320

Stock 22, 33, 41, 42, 44, 64, 83

Storage 10, 12, 14, 16–22, 24, 32

Stout 23, 36, 110, 112, 199, 210, 214

T

Taps 36, 41

Taste 29

Taxes 62, 63, 64, 76, 80, 84

Temperature 10, 12, 23, 24, 25, 31, 39, 40, 270